CAMERA HISTORICA

EUROPEAN PERSPECTIVES

EUROPEAN PERSPECTIVES

A Series in Social Thought and Cultural Criticism

Lawrence D. Kritzman, *Editor*

For a complete list of books in the series, see pages 399–400.

CAMERA HISTORICA ▶
THE CENTURY IN CINEMA

ANTOINE de BAECQUE

TRANSLATED BY *Ninon Vinsonneau* AND *Jonathan Magidoff*

COLUMBIA UNIVERSITY PRESS   NEW YORK

COLUMBIA UNIVERSITY PRESS
Publishers Since 1893
New York   Chichester, West Sussex

L'Histoire-Caméra © Editions Gallimard, Paris, 2008
English Translation © 2012 Columbia University Press
All rights reserved

This work, published as part of a program providing publication assistance, received financial support from the French Ministry of Foreign Affairs, the Cultural Services of the French Embassy in the United States and FACE (French American Cultural Exchange).

Ouvrage publié avec le concours du Ministère français chargé de la culture—Centre national du livre.
This book is published with support from the French Ministry of Culture/National Book Center.

Library of Congress Cataloging-in-Publication Data

Baecque, Antoine de.
 [Histoire-caméra. English]
 Camera historica : the century in cinema / Antoine de Baecque ;
 translated by Ninon Vinsonneau and Jonathan Magidoff.
     p. cm. — (European perspectives: a series in social thought and cultural criticism)
 Includes bibliographical references and indexes.
 ISBN 978-0-231-15650-9 (cloth) — ISBN 978-0-231-15651-6 (pbk.)
 1. Motion pictures and history.   I. Title.

PN1995.2.B3313   2012
791.4309—DC23

2011035568

BOOK DESIGN BY VIN DANG

À Emmanuelle

All true thought retains a taste of dust in the mouth—
a trace of the soil, scar from a fall, a remainder of
the handful of earth from which we come.

Valère Novarina, *Lumières du corps*

CONTENTS

PRELUDE ▶ The Tree of History *xi*

INTRODUCTION ▶ The Cinematographic Forms of History *1*
Disciplinary Uncertainties *5*
Cinema as Historian *12*
Cinema and History: An Analogy of the "Half-Cooked State" *18*
Cinema Pursues the Path of History to Reveal What Is Hidden
   Even from Memory *20*
The Sensible Fabric of the World *28*

FORECLOSED FORMS ▶ How Images of Mass Death Reemerged in
   Modern Cinema *31*
The Look-to-Camera: A Modern Form of History *32*
The Gaze of Death in Action *37*
How History Reemerges Through Cinema *44*
Alain Resnais and the Editing of Time *47*
Monsieur Verdoux, or How Chaplin Puts to Death His Inner Wandering Jew *52*
"Faces with Black, Rat-Like Eyes" *56*
Hitchcock and the Indelible Corpse *61*
Man Alone in the Face of the Machine of Death *65*
Mass Death: Neither Reconstruction nor Mise-en-scène *69*

FROM VERSAILLES TO THE SILVER SCREEN ▶ Sacha Guitry, Historian of
   France *77*
"Doing Versailles": Controversial Project and Historical Polemic *79*
Guitry and the Revenge of History *88*
A Certain Vision of History *90*
The Spectacle of Court Society *96*

"ME? UH, NOTHING!" ▶ The French New Wave, Politics, and History *103*
Hussar Thought *105*
A Cinema "That Has Nothing to Say" *114*
Heroes of the New Wave and Militants of Disarray *118*
Politicization via Malraux *128*
An Intrinsically Political Cinema: Filming Life with Style *132*
The Algerian War: The Intimate Drama of the New Wave *140*
Torture: The Limit Experience of the New Wave *149*
A Political Janus-Face *151*

4 — PETER WATKINS, LIVE FROM HISTORY ▶ The Films, Style, and Method of Cinema's Special Correspondent *159*

Making War Through Making Films *162*
The Time of Filmed Reportage *171*
The Trials and Tribulations of an Exiled Filmmaker *176*
The Deathblow as a Stylistic Form *183*
Edvard Munch, or How to Resist the Passage of Time *189*
The Watkins Way: History in Common *192*
The Besieged Citadel and the Martyr Figure *201*
The Alter-Filmmaker *203*

5 — THE THEORY OF SPARKS ▶ A History in Images, According to Jean-Luc Godard *207*

Taking Art Out of the Museum and Projecting It into History *212*
From Langlois to Godard: A Historical Passage Through Images *222*
From *The Voices of Silence* to *Histoire(s) du cinéma,* or, The Fraternity of Metaphors *228*
The Historiographical Virtue of *Histoire(s) du cinéma* *235*
Can *Histoire(s)* Redeem History? *241*

6 — DEMODERN AESTHETICS ▶ Filming the End of Communism *247*

A Demodern Collapse *248*
Andrei Tarkovsky's *Stalker*: Communism Put to the Test of the Zone *254*
Alexei Guerman's *Khrustalyov, My Car!* Communism at the Bottom of History's Closet *268*
Aleksandr Sokurov's *Russian Ark*: Communism Sapped by Nostalgia *276*
Emir Kusturica's *Underground*: Into the Bowels of Communism *287*
A Few Images for "Those Who Are Lost" *299*

7 — AMERICA UNRAVELED ▶ Master Fictions in Contemporary Hollywood Cinema *305*

Revealing Resurgences: Under the Whip of Catwoman *306*
End-of-the-World Films *312*
"Very Bad Films": Inside the Laboratory of Bad-Taste Films *322*
Tim Burton, America's Primitive *332*
American Cinema Put to the Test of 9/11 *345*

CONCLUSION ▶ All Histories Are Possible *355*

NOTES *363*   ACKNOWLEDGMENTS *383*   INDEX *385*

Preface ▶ *The Tree of History*

AN ENORMOUS TREE, somewhere in Africa. A kapok tree, in Angola, placed at the start of a film. The tree fills the opening shot of Manoel de Oliveira's masterpiece, *No, or the Vain Glory of Command*, surely one of the most beautiful films on history, which tells the story of Portugal through its defeats.

The majestic tree stands like an enigma, its lush foliage shimmering in the sun, its trunk thick and gnarled. The shot that presents it is, itself, majestic: in a single measured movement the camera introduces the tree—centered in the frame, its foliage almost palpable—approaching it tentatively, coming up alongside it, and then circling around its massive trunk. The progression from one movement to the next is almost imperceptible, so that the spectator feels, all at once and in a single cinematic motion, that he or she is facing the tree, moving alongside it, and circling around it.

What is it doing here, on the threshold of a film? Through it, Manoel de Oliveira appears to be inviting us into a game of deciphering. It is a *hermeneutic* tree: it materializes the triple gaze that the filmmaker casts toward history. The kapok tree, a solitary old man, both wise and strong under the scorching heat, seems to embody history—an allegorical figure of time. Like Saint Louis who administered justice under an oak, Oliveira films history in the shade of a tree. It is indeed at the foot of the tree that, a little while later in the film, a second lieutenant played by Luís Miguel Cintra, a history professor in civilian life, who is leading a small brigade of Portuguese forces in Angola in the spring of 1974, continues his history lecture to his men, recounting several episodes of the Lusitanian chronicle.

But in this first shot the various ways the tree is seen—variations that serve, in effect, to multiply it—contribute to its allegorical role. Just as the tree is visually fragmented—presented in full length, in detail, and then encircled—in a single shot, Oliveira recounts the story of his country through three ways of producing history: at once poetic and legendary chronicle, historical narrative, and mythical vision, *No, or the Vain Glory of Command* combines three representations of historical time.

No is, first of all, a chronicle inspired by *O Lusíadas*, an epic poem composed by Luís de Camões in 1572, of which several scenes are literal adaptations: the discovery of Love Island by Vasco de Gama, the funerals of the crown prince, the prophecy of King Sebastian's misfortunes. The film also offers a historical narrative, both linear and precise, of the four major Lusitanian defeats: the assassination of Viriathus, in 139 BC; the death of Prince Afonso, in 1490; the defeat of Alcazarquivir at the hands of the Arabs, in 1578; and the recent decolonization of Portuguese Africa. The narrative is recounted by the lieutenant, a historian and participant in the final episode, who gives meaning to history through his narrative. He thus appears to implicate his spectators, through recurring and insistent glances at the camera. Finally, in its third mode of historical writing and temporality, the film seeks to embody the melancholy soul of a country, the Portugal of *saudade*, and to illustrate the mythical cycle and eternal return of glory and decline in a history that is opened by discoverers yet always resistant to their conquests, a history of blessed origins struck down by disaster before they can be fully realized.

Oliveira, thus, brings together three modes of historical interpretation: the figuring of history, following in the footsteps of a poet chronicler, through wide-angle static shots that, at regular intervals, provide recitatives of complete chapters of Camões's account; the narrating of history, through the group of soldiers helping the second lieutenant recall Portuguese defeats, supported by the vision (a dolly shot) of a truck moving through the countryside—itself the cinematographic sign of a linear historical narrative that links together four defeats spanning more than two thousand years; and finally, the circling of history, like Manoel de Oliveira around his tree, to capture the myth that cyclically drives each epoch, that of "Sebastianism," the Portuguese dream of unattainable grandeur.

The Angolan tree is what I will call throughout this book a *cinematographic form of history*: the mise-en-scène developed by a filmmaker to give form to his vision of history. In this film by Manoel de Oliveira, who was born in 1908 (the last active director to have been born in the silent era), this particular form appears to be not only meticulously composed but also at the very center of the project.

This is sumptuously illustrated, two thirds of the way into the film, by the mise-en-scène of the battle of Alcazarquivir, which the spectator sees, here again, from three different angles. Like the initial tree, the 1578 battle is filmed according to the three modes of representation of history. First, from the narrative angle: the film follows the destiny of a limping officer who leads his reluctant troops into combat. For the war film this is the Fordian angle par excellence, "at human level," not unlike the one Stendhal opted for in *The Charterhouse of Parma* to follow Fabrice's wanderings at Waterloo. Yet the battle is also considered from the perspective of a visionary chronicle: distancing itself, the film is punctuated by sweeping movements that enable it to capture the various maneuvers deployed to surround, divide, and isolate the troops and to represent the final outcome of the engagement. Finally, Manoel de Oliveira's mise-en-scène offers a mythical reinterpretation of the event: the Catholic soldiers, abandoned by God, confront the infidels and are ineluctably defeated, even if their sacrifice transforms them into martyrs and heroes. This mystical vision of the combat begins with the prayer that precedes the clash and culminates with the appearance of the shadows of the dead, who, their black armor drenched in blood, provide commentary on their fall before rising to heaven.

The blood that flows along the cursed sword of the battle of Alcazarquivir is the same as that which, at the end of the film, drips from the dying second lieutenant's IV and then pours out of the mouth of this historian-narrator as he expires—the same suffering bodies, the same melancholy soul. *Portugality* is the link that turns the country into a single wounded body through the centuries, a single sad soul, and Oliveira's film into a single block of interwoven time and narrative in the agony of defeat (fig. 1).

This form, in Manoel de Oliveira, is the sign of the composition of a monumental film on history. It may be compared to that which governs a no less monumental book of history, Fernand Braudel's *The Mediterranean*, which also rests, following a similar harmony, on a subtle terracing of time and historical narrative, which interlaces a civilizational vision—the opposition between Spaniards and Turks—a historical vision—Braudel's *longue durée*, with which Manoel de Oliveira's long memory resonates—and the chronicle of an event—with the death of Philip II in Braudel finding echo in the Portuguese defeats, taken one by one.

In *No, or the Vain Glory of Command*, this form can only lead to one shot, the film's finale: a doctor's hand inscribes in a register the date of death of the

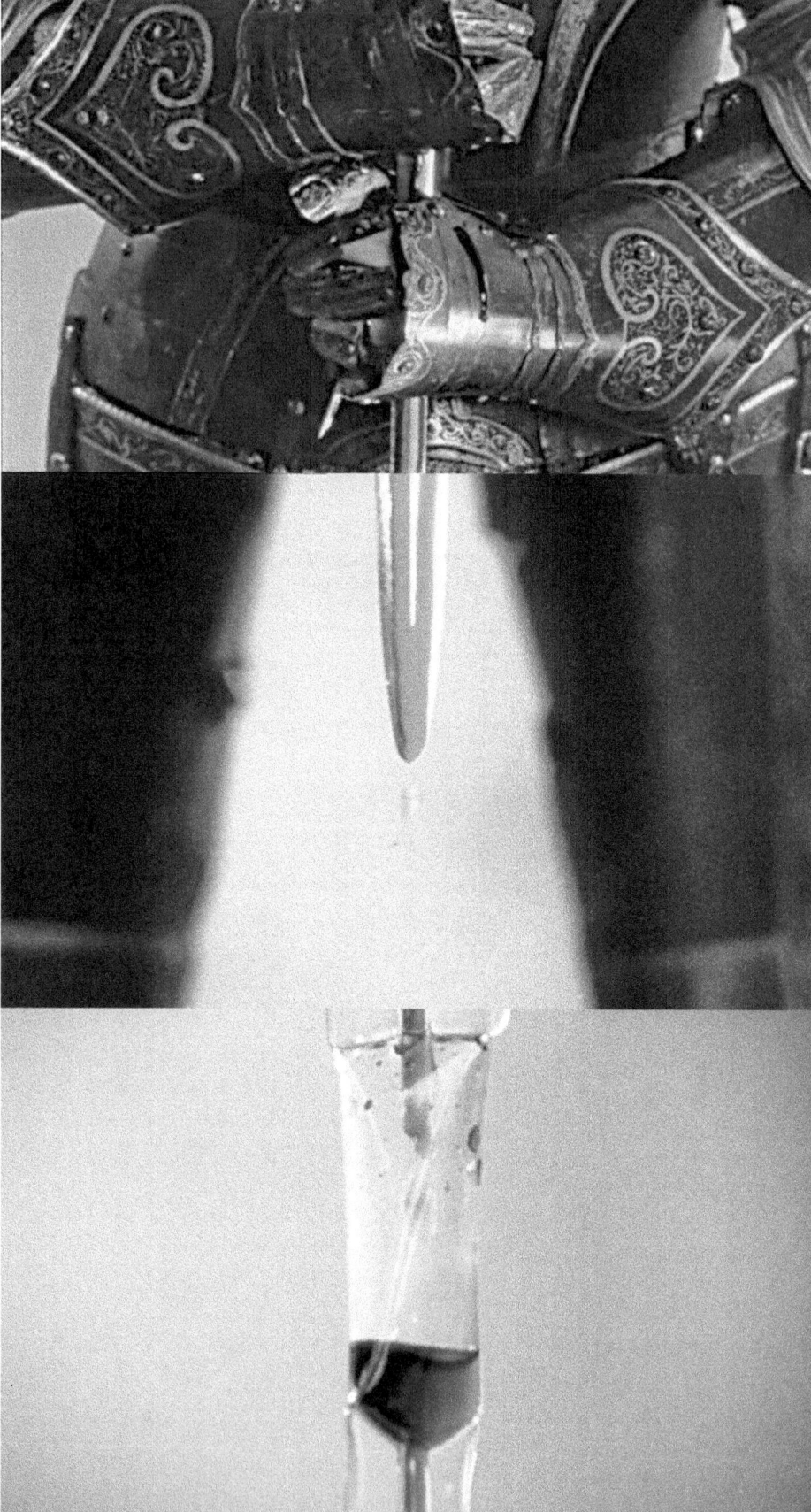

1 ▶ *No, or the Vain Glory of Command* (MANOEL DE OLIVEIRA, 1990). THE BLOOD THAT FLOWS ALONG THE CURSED SWORD OF THE BATTLE OF ALCAZARQUIVIR IS THE SAME AS THAT WHICH, AT THE END OF THE FILM, DRIPS FROM THE IV OF THE SECOND LIEUTENANT, WHO WAS FATALLY WOUNDED IN ANGOLA IN 1974.

2 ▶
No, or the Vain Glory of Command (MANOEL DE OLIVEIRA, 1990). THE FILM'S FINAL SHOT: A DOCTOR'S HAND INSCRIBES IN A REGISTER THE DATE OF DEATH OF SECOND LIEUTENANT CABRITA: APRIL 25, 1974, A DATE THAT ALSO MARKED THE BEGINNING OF THE CARNATION REVOLUTION. THE CYCLE OF PORTUGUESE HISTORY IS THUS MADE OF DEFEATS TO WHICH THE NATION IS RESIGNED, LIKE A HISTORICAL MELANCHOLIA ILLUSTRATED BY THE PROPHECY THAT INSPIRED THE TITLE: "A TERRIBLE WORD, THAT 'NO.' HOWEVER YOU TAKE IT, IT REMAINS ALWAYS THE SAME, ALWAYS A SNAKE, ALWAYS VENOMOUS. NOTHING CAN SOFTEN IT, NO WILL ALWAYS REMAIN BITTER."

▶ HERE THE FRENCH WORD *HISTOIRE* IS USED IN THE FULLNESS OF ITS DOUBLE MEANING, AS BOTH STORY AND HISTORY. THE READER SHOULD BE AWARE THAT THE FRENCH WORD OFTEN CONTAINS THIS AMBIGUITY. — TRANS.

lieutenant-historian, who was fatally wounded by Angolan rebels, and then puts down his pen. This is the ultimate moment of the historical chronicle, the last casualty of the last battle. But that date—April 25, 1974—also marks a historical event in Portugal: the Carnation Revolution. In the end this moment is also one of myth: the tipping point between the end of a world—which, in Portugal, is called the *ancien régime*—and the origin of a new one, that of contemporary Portugal in today's Europe, an undetermined shift in which, once again in the history of *portugality*, cataclysm and renewal meet. On that page of a military hospital's register, Manoel de Oliveira weaves together all the temporal threads of his story, his history.▶ This cinematographic form echoes the first sequence, in which all the ways of entering into history meet around the tree. On the page of the register can be discerned all the ways out of it (fig. 2).

CAMERA HISTORICA

INTRODUCTION ▶
THE CINEMATOGRAPHIC FORMS OF HISTORY

◀ 3
Poster for *Europa '51*
(ROBERTO ROSSELLINI, 1952). (PHOTO COURTESY BIFI)

IT WAS IN WATCHING, one after the other, Alain Resnais' *Night and Fog* and *Hiroshima mon amour*, and Roberto Rossellini's *Europa '51*, that a "cinematographic form of history" was first revealed to me. I had already seen the films, but not the forms. I would later locate others. In *Europa '51* a dolly shot captures several inmates of a lunatic asylum gazing intensely at the camera. These women were staring, and, all of a sudden, they were staring at me. I then replayed scenes from *Hiroshima mon amour*, and I encountered the same fixed gaze, at the beginning of the film: Japanese women were waiting for me at the doors to their hospital rooms, beckoning me in, staring me in the face so that I might bear witness to their suffering as victims of the bomb. I watched the DVD of *Night and Fog* again. In some of the archival documents selected by Resnais—the images shot by American, British, and Russian cameramen as the camps were being liberated—the same fixed gaze emerges: gaunt survivors, staring out at me.

Where did this gaze, this head-on intensity, come from? *From history*. Not specifically from the history of cinema—even though quite a few looks-to-camera had been cast at spectators in the days of silent movies, when burlesque films would wink in connivance with the audiences—but rather from a blind spot of twentieth-century history, its unrepresentability, which is, nonetheless, staring right at us. This look attests, from beyond the grave, to the fact that the survivors have seen extermination, have stared it in the face. There is a cinema after extermination, after images of the camps. Following Gilles Deleuze, I would venture that the true break in the history of cinema is embedded in the history of the century and that it illustrates the interpenetration of form and chronology.[1] It was the war, its violence, the resulting stupor, and the traumatic realization of the reality of extermination camps as the nodal point of the Nazi worldview that suddenly erupted onto the screen. The looks-to-camera—in Bergen-Belsen and Buchenwald, in *Night and Fog*, *Europa '51*, and *Hiroshima mon amour*—tell us that cinema had to change because nobody could remain innocent after these images, neither filmmakers nor spectators, neither actors nor characters. It is thus the history of the century that invented modern cinema, including one of the supreme forms of this new cinema, that which transgresses, that which enables us to see the inconceivable: the look-to-camera. It was re-presented by Rossellini and Resnais in the mid-1950s, but it was born in 1945, when cameras captured the horror of the "living dead coming out of the camps, with their wild-eyed look, from beyond the grave."[2] This look-to-camera, so direct as to be petrifying, was to take ten years to move from document to fiction, founding a part of modern cinema by penetrating into the mise-en-scène itself. This form—the look-to-camera—thus only became historical *and* cinematographic through the foreclosure that repressed it and caused its return, as a hallucination of history and a vibration of mise-en-scène. Hence, the eyes staring into the lens and at us are part and parcel of the century and of its films, the highest evidence of the encounter of history and cinema (fig. 4).

I then proceeded to identify, within the very form of certain films (these specific visual and narrative combinations) that I considered exemplary, similar moments of the irruption of history. A few filmmakers have tried to capture this sense of irruption, or at least have striven, through a particular mise-en-scène, to give form to history, whether the history of the past or the history unfolding before their eyes. It is these untimely irruptions that disrupt the very material of the film, this specific mise-en-scène, which I call *cinematographic forms of history*. I have endeavored to define, then locate, describe, and interpret, these very particular forms within seven distinct bodies of cinema: 1950s modern cinema, and the way in which it conjured up the morbid trauma of war; the French New Wave, which turned style into the negative imprint of the malaise of young contemporaries of the Algerian War; postcommunist Russian films, "demodern" works of *catastroika*; contemporary Hollywood films that attach themselves to the master fiction of 9/11; and, added to these, the characteristic *mise en forme* of Sacha Guitry, who filmed French history from inside its chateau in *Si Versailles m'était conté*; of Jean-Luc Godard, who conjured up history in his own museum memory of the century; and of Peter Watkins, who covered history like a war correspondent.

Working in this way on history and its cinematographic forms, I am fully aware of taking up both the stakes and objectives of Jean Starobinski's masterful books on the Enlightenment—*The Invention of Liberty* and *1789: The Emblems of Reason*—works that were originally published in 1964 as part of a collection, which its founder, Yves Bonnefoy, defined as "showing how the becoming of forms and developments in society condition each other."[3] Starobinski described his own ambition within this formal vision of history thus: "I was attempting to perceive and to understand, according to their mode of emergence, the experiences that become *figured* through the course of the [eighteenth] century and during the revolutionary crisis. In the same way as one reads physiognomy, I wanted to give meaning to the various *mises*

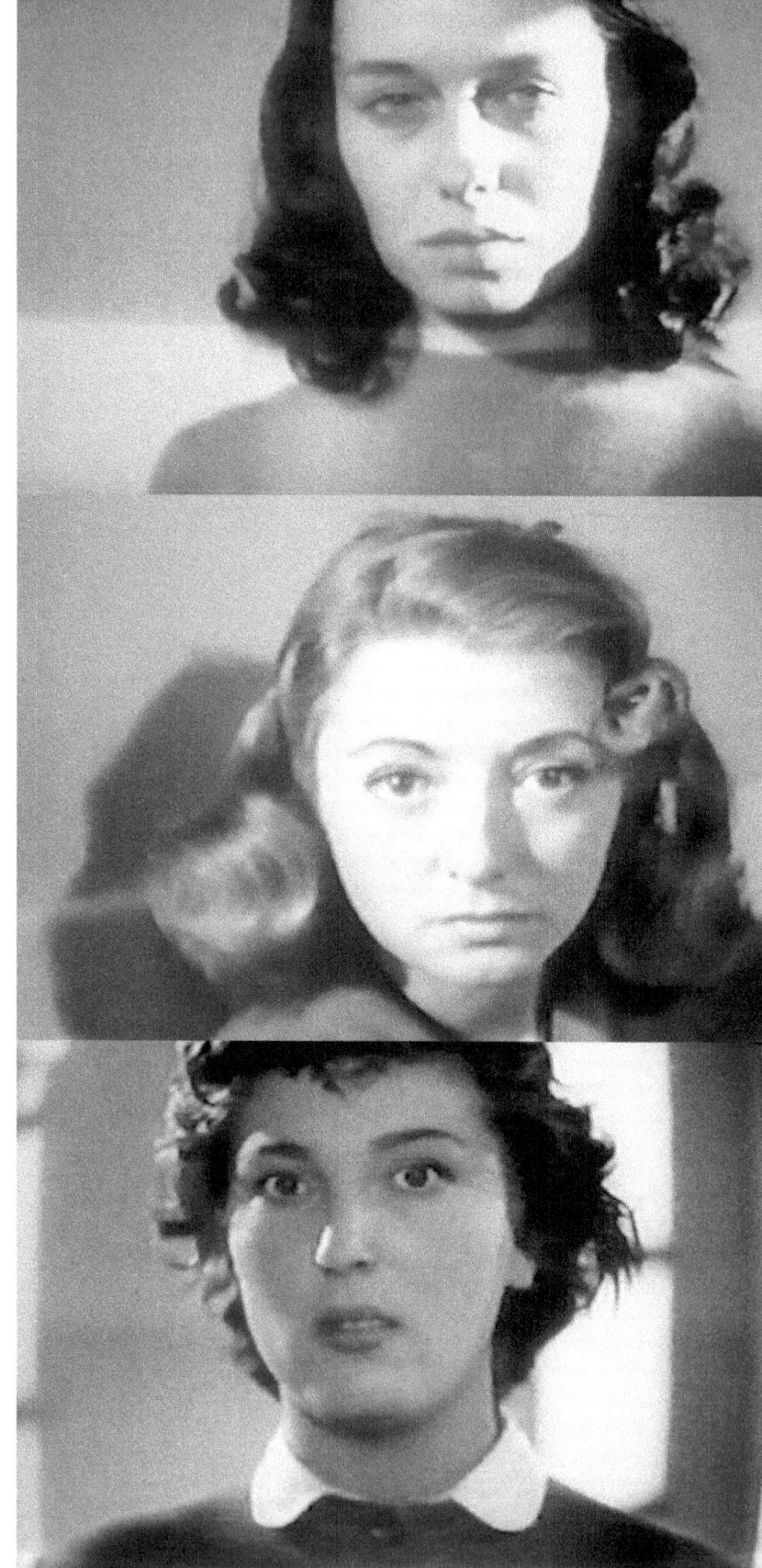

4 ▶
Europa '51
(ROBERTO ROSSELLINI, 1952). THESE WOMEN ARE STARING AT IRENE (INGRID BERGMAN), WHO HAS BEEN ADMITTED TO A LUNATIC ASYLUM, AND AT US, SPECTATORS, WITH HEAD-ON INTENSITY. THIS IS A GAZE COMING FROM HISTORY AS MUCH AS FROM MADNESS.

en spectacle produced by artists."⁴ For my part I will modestly endeavor—by substituting form for figure, the twentieth century for the eighteenth, and the mise-en-scène of filmmakers for the *mise en spectacle* of artists—to offer ways of thinking history by offering ways of seeing films.

Disciplinary Uncertainties

Since the late nineteenth century, cinema has been an object of study for historians. In a letter to the daily paper *Le Figaro,* published on March 25, 1898, Boleslav Matuszewski, an underappreciated Polish photographer, called for the creation of "a cinematographic archival museum for future generations of researchers and historians," which would constitute a "new source of history." And Germaine Dulac, one of the earliest female filmmakers, shot a film in 1935 that she entitled *Le cinéma au service de l'histoire*—a panoramic perspective on the history of Europe between 1895 and 1930 and an exhilarating archival montage. The question of the relationship between cinema and the history of its century, and of the fusion of the two within that history, did not take long to arise. During the Belle Epoque it had become a certainty for many that the new century would be the century of cinema, even if the latter had not yet been granted legitimacy as a part of cultural heritage. Thus, naked, trivial, primitive, popular, and—not to mince words—vulgar, cinema was all the better positioned to be the art of history. Here, for example, is Sartre's childhood intuition, as he later described in *Les Mots*:

> We blindly entered a century without traditions, a century that was to contrast strongly with the others by its bad manners, and the new art, the art of the common man, foreshadowed our barbarism. Born in a den of thieves, officially classified as a traveling show, it had popular ways that shocked serious people. It was an amusement for women and children. My mother and I loved it, but we hardly gave it a thought, and we never talked about it. Does one talk about bread if one has it? When we came to realize its existence, it had long since become our chief need.⁵

The idea that the history of the century could be represented by cinema, or better still, embodied by it, was soon advanced and defended by films, spectators, and historians alike.

Ever since, for better or worse, the powers-that-be have developed projects for cinema, and sometimes ideas in its stead. Stalin, for instance, appointed himself a script doctor and decided on the finale of *The Fall of Berlin,* directed in 1949 by Mikheil Chiaureli, and a number of other socialist realist productions; Roosevelt recommended that all men of goodwill watch Jean Renoir's *La Grande illusion*. Ministers had their plans for cinema, and nations had their policies and pantheons. The history of this art and the history of the century were intimately connected: as archival reflections, mirrors of the times, and ambitious reconstructions. That the Dreyfus Affair, the Crash of 1929, the events of May 1968, or the Gulf War should be most visible onscreen, perhaps more than anywhere else, has now become a truism. In this respect cinema has given form to the history of the twentieth century, using its own weapons: it constituted events (there is not a major landmark in this century that has not also been cinematographic) and furnished tools—constantly appropriated and recycled, as so many worldviews. By developing its visual processes, its effects, and its techniques, cinema soon became the century's *toolbox*. Special effects, framing, editing, Technicolor, superimposed images, slow motion, flashbacks, split screens, looks-to-camera, as well as the burlesque body, cinephilia, transparency, and title cards—all these tools have a history, which can be traced from their appearance to their resurgence, and all have also played a role in history: artists, writers, ideologues, and advertisers have made use of them, borrowing them from the screen and using them to live, write, think, and create in history.

The call was soon sounded to write a history of the century through the cinematographic arts. It began with the establishment, in the 1920s, of the first archaeology of the masterpieces of the new art, the constitution of a pantheon that "future historians" would be able to tap into. In the cine-clubs (Louis Delluc, Ricciotto Canudo, Léon Moussinac), at the Salon d'automne (Canudo again), and at the conferences held at the Théâtre du Vieux-Colombier (Jean Tedesco) in Paris, the first selections of "classic films" were made, imposing certain styles and schools, creating prejudices and historical narratives, bestowing and revoking reputations. These choices were always justified in writing, published in newspapers, reviews, and books, as well as in the first film anthologies. They were further sanctioned in the 1930s with the simultaneous creation, in Europe and the United States, of cinematheques, conceived as "archives" where the corpus of films and works necessary for the constitution of a true history of the cinematic arts would be preserved.

The project of writing this history was then undertaken, in the form of an ambitious synthesis, by Georges Sadoul. Begun in the late 1930s, and written in the early 1940s, it was published from 1945 onward in large reference volumes under the title *Histoire générale du cinéma*. It compiled archival and erudite syntheses recounting the story of the early days, then of the triumph and subsequent evolution of the new art form, through major moments of technical, economic, and even social ruptures. In the early 1950s Sadoul's history was taken up by French cinephilia, which was then in full swing, and reinterpreted, in light of contemporary cinephilic debates and discoveries, according to their respective schools, filmmakers, and stylistic evolution. Rife with filmographies, classifications, reassessments, devaluations, and genres, this history of cinema was experienced as autonomous, wary of society and its representations—disdained as *film à thèse*—and endowed with a brand new touchstone—the "auteur," now the principal reference—as well as a mode of writing—the polemic. Polemical writing fueled parochial rivalries, kindled clannish squabbles, and sharpened competing allegiances. Such and such lineage and such and such family of auteurs vs. another—*Cahiers du cinéma* vs. *Positif*, and so forth. This was how, through collections of monographs, through edited volumes of critiques and interviews, through aligned or antagonistic journals, the history of cinema in the 1950s and 1960s was written—a history that was lively, rigorous, erudite, and written in the present tense of the New Wave and its controversies but that distrusted the academic world, which it considered scholastic and supercilious, even desiccating. The identification of cinema and history was so strong in this moment that it allowed critics to confine themselves to discussing only films, since history was, anyway, entirely contained within them. Cinema embodied technical and political modernity for the communist Sadoul; it was an ontological recording of the century in the eyes of the mystic Bazin; it intimately and vitally resonated with history in the view of the cinephile Truffaut. The question of the relationship between cinema and history was, in a sense, moot. The connection appeared not only natural and appropriate but constitutive of cinema itself.

Despite general hostility and skepticism, it was from within academia, where this link between cinema and history did not exist or remained to be demonstrated, that new works emerged on the history of cinema or, rather, on cinema as an agent of history. Eccentric academics Marc Ferro, at the Ecole des hautes études en sciences sociales (EHESS), and Pierre Sorlin, at the Institut d'études et de recherches cinématographiques at the University of Paris III, who lamented the scant attention paid to film in historical studies, proposed to trace cinema images back to the world that had produced them, through historical interpretation. In 1973 Ferro thus declared, in a seminal article published in *Annales ESC*:

Go back to the images. Do not seek in them merely the illustration, confirmation, or contradiction of another knowledge—that of written tradition. Consider images as such at the risk of using other forms of knowledge to grasp them even better. Historians have already accorded a legitimate place to sources (both written and unwritten) that have popular origins: folklore, popular arts, and traditions. We need to study film and see it in relation to the world that produces it. What is our hypothesis?—that film, image or not of reality, document or fiction, true story or pure invention, is History. Our postulate?—that what has not occurred (and even what *has* occurred)—beliefs, intentions, human imagination—is as much history as History.[6]

Cinema thus brought "what has not occurred" into history, inaugurating the era of the world as representation. In *Cinema and History* Ferro focuses on two films, in which he locates and discusses cinematographic forms of history—what he himself describes as an analysis "based on a purely cinematographic process." In offering an affirmative response to the question—"Is there a filmic vision of history?"—Ferro provides a formal analysis of the historical functioning of two classic films: Eisenstein's *Strike*, which the *Annales* historian considered to be a filmic transcription of the Marxist conception of the capitalist mode of production in a pre-1905 Russian factory; and Fritz Lang's *M*, in which, through the story of a sexual pervert, Ferro deconstructs the "degenerate" functioning of the Weimar Republic and underscores Germany's fascination, as well as his own, with Hitler's personality and rise to power. Ferro ends the chapter by concluding that "films constitute a privileged form of history."

The Slovenian thinker Slavoj Žižek has reached a similar conclusion, though formulated in more philosophical terms, in an essay on cinema entitled *Lacrimae rerum*. In ancient Rome "public tears" (lacrimae rerum) shed at ceremonial sacrifices were acted, artificial, and yet served a purpose. They signified to all that the big Other was being mourned. Žižek sees in these tears the key to a decisive rupture in the films of Krzysztof Kieslowski. Indeed, the filmmaker said he had felt the "fright of real tears" as he was filming his documentary *First Love* (1974), in which a young father cries, holding his newborn child in his arms. Deeming the father's joy to be fake, almost obscene, Kieslowski abandoned the documentary form in favor of fiction, considering that the reality of subjective experience could only be conveyed in fictional form. In so doing, the director acquired his own cinematographic form, which Žižek interprets principally as a historical idea, a "fiction that recounts and produces history." In choosing fiction, the filmmaker in fact exposed the "sensitive" use of the documentary by communist propaganda and Polish television in the 1970s. The staged tears were a form of historical contestation, as opposed to the "true" tears in TV propaganda documentaries.

Conferences, symposiums, meetings, programmatic works, and collective publications have all tracked the moment when studies on cinema and history crystallized; they have allowed for a better understanding of both cinema and the social reality of specific key cinematographic moments: the Russian Revolution, the French Popular Front, France's occupation by and collaboration with Germany, Nazi films, representations of the French Revolution onscreen, and the works of Jean Renoir, Fritz Lang, Sergei Eisenstein, Abel Gance, Stanley Kubrick (fig. 5), and David Lean. Uncovering, through this confrontation with films, a "non-visible reality," Marc Ferro and Pierre Sorlin—and their disciples—not only broke new historiographical ground but also appropriated a history that had long been monopolized by cinephiles and thus needed to assert their differences and mark their distance. The "and" in *Cinema and History*—the title of a collection of essays published by Ferro in 1977, which quickly became a classic work and even the name of a new discipline in the making—was probably intended to signify this distance from the film-object that cinephiles considered the subject of life and polemics. The "and" served to keep a safe distance from these disputes, to back out and disengage. Historians are not cinephiles: what mattered to them was the development of a new epistemological method, a game of mirroring between film and the state of the society that produced it, watched it, and understood it. They thus built a new discipline, over the course of the 1970s and 1980s, that fueled the whole history of representations. But they did so at a cost: the absence, if not of cinema itself at least of the passion for it, and of the immanent and intimate, rather than historicized, knowledge of it.

This disciplinary field—long sidelined by historians themselves and dominated by other, more theoretical (linguistic, semiological, psychoanalytic), approaches to film—managed to establish itself only belatedly and with considerable difficulty. For work to get under way and proliferate, a context of "historical concern" had to develop, as Serge Daney pointed out in the early 1990s, stressing the fact that "questions of genealogy and of origins reassert themselves objectively" through the films that we see, or rather, re-see.[7] In the late 1980s Dudley Andrew noticed a "turn toward historical research" when he analyzed the paper and research topics submitted to SCS (Society for Cinema Studies) meetings, conferences, and seminars.[8] In 1989 almost

5 ▶
Spartacus
(STANLEY KUBRICK, 1960). IN THIS SCENE, SHOT IN SPAIN, TWO ARMIES MEET: THAT OF SPARTACUS, A KIND OF HISTORICAL EXTRA, AND THAT OF SPAIN, AS THOUGH ATTENDING A HISTORICAL SPECTACLE THAT IT TRIES TO SUPERVISE. (PHOTO © WILLIAM READ WOODFIELD; COLL. *CAHIERS DU CINÉMA*)

half the papers at the SCS annual conference dealt with the history of cinema, many of which followed Marc Ferro's approach. This trend was confirmed in the context of the centenary anniversary of cinema, which led to a sharp increase, circa 1995, in the number of retrospectives, publications, and conferences around cinema and its history. History as a discipline and as an approach to the filmic text was yet again the center of scholarly preoccupation, together with sociology (especially of culture and its artifacts), and took over the role of providing intellectual legitimacy, which had once been the province of semiology and anthropology. This stimulating epistemological turn spurred a rethinking of cinema as one of the engines of twentieth-century history—not only as illustration but also as agent and metaphor of human actions in society.

It is in this context that cinema gradually became one of the privileged objects of cultural history, since, among other reasons, this discipline often explored questions that were particularly relevant to cinema studies: the constitution of a public around moving images, the cultural legitimation of a long-scorned form of cultural activity, the impact of intellectual trends and political movements, the rise of the press, the relationship between mass culture and elite culture, the growing place of the culture industry in Western societies of the spectacle, and so forth. But the history of cinema is just as much that of a cultural practice as of a representation of society. In terms of methodology this *cultural history of cinema* called for embedding film in the widest possible variety of sources, for overloading it, in a way, with interpretations: the work would be "seen" together with texts that commented on it, accompanied it, and received it; with the ceremonial gestures that guided its reception; with the political events that informed its understanding, the social upheavals that changed its meaning, the economic transformations that determined its technique or its reception—in short, every possible historical register that had been neglected in its relation to film. The arrival of cinema in cultural history marked the inauguration of a renewed hermeneutic.

Cinema as Historian

Up to this point the relation between history and cinema had to navigate three potential pitfalls: Sadoul-style encyclopedism, cinephile auteur monographs, and the history of cinematographic signification—that is, focusing on what the cinematic art reveals about a society at any given moment, often at the expense of the film-object itself. How can we study history with films and yet not lapse into the increasing tendency to historicize them? The objective, in a way, is to answer questions raised by history through films, through figures that are specific to cinema, while avoiding the dissolution of either history or film into a purely illustrative conception of the relation between the two. Gilles Deleuze was saying precisely this when he explained, "It is not when one discipline begins to reflect on another that they come into contact. Contact can be made only when one discipline realizes that another discipline has already posed a similar problem, and so the one reaches out to the other to resolve this problem, but on its own terms and for its own needs."[9] History is always comparative: to write on and with cinema, when the historian's questions lead us to look for answers in films, even if these might trigger other questions specific to history.

In this sense the recourse to film may allow historians to enlarge their field of investigation and renew their narrative capacity in order to better approach past reality. "Cinema does not have to be summoned up," as Arlette Farge put it in 1998: "it is already with us, like all other artistic forms that organize our way of being in the world, and thus of writing history."[10] Film offers the historian a process for understanding and writing history that has certain points in common. Jacques Revel, for example, in an essay on Michelangelo Antonioni's *Blow Up*, demonstrated the extent to which the very form of the film and its work on image enlargement could be compared to the methodology of microhistory. It, too, shifts from an expected plot to an unexpected one, through a series of enlargements: "The successive enlargements in *Blow Up* make a different reading possible at each stage. Hidden elements, previously invisible, suddenly appear and can be studied. New details introduce new readings of the scene as a whole. By analogy, we find in this procedure illustrated in *Blow Up* an experimental method put forward and practiced by micro-history" (see fig. 6).[11]

Arlette Farge has recently emphasized cinema's capacity for history. The cinematographic technique allows for the historical process to take place under optimum conditions—to place a narrative of the past within its context of gestures, sets, colors, and landscapes. This process might be called *visualization*—of a fiction for the filmmaker or of an archive for the historian. Even though neither fiction nor archive constitutes historical reality, their visualization is a condition of historical experience. There are, of course, as Natalie Zemon Davis has pointed out, major discordances between the historical reconstruction approach to cinema and the essentially interpretative perspective of the historian working from archival material. Yet, as the prominent

6 ▶
Blow Up
(MICHELANGELO ANTONIONI, 1967). THE PHOTOGRAPHER (DAVID HEMMINGS) DEVELOPS A SERIES OF PICTURES, THEN PENETRATES INTO HIS SHOTS IN SEARCH OF A DETAIL THAT PUZZLES HIM. HE DISCOVERS IN IT A FICTION, A STORY, A WORRY, PROBABLY A MURDER. THIS IS A VISUALIZATION OF THE INVESTIGATION TECHNIQUE DEVELOPED IN MICROHISTORY.

American historian has brilliantly demonstrated, cinema's narrative mode has transformed—and increasingly transforms—the writing of history itself.[12] Whereas the historian painstakingly strives to approach this experience of the reality of the past and deploys elaborate ruses and considerable efforts to do so, the filmmaker manages it as a matter of course.

Indeed, the filmmaker possesses a kind of simultaneity, within a given time, from the beginning to the end of a fiction, with all the elements that compose the space, the meanings, and the bodies, as so many contrasted, and sometimes contradictory, elements that contextualize the characters and the story. "This is my dream as a historian," Arlette Farge has confided, "this diversity united in and by a context. Historical narrative has considerable difficulty articulating character, event, and archive with the larger world, i.e. the singular with the collective. Cinema, on the contrary, manages this rather easily." Through a multiplicity of perspectives cinema, technically speaking, can convey both distance and closeness at the same time, both the singular and the plural. In this respect cinema appears as a form of experimentation with history. "A bare landscape, simply recorded," Farge continues, "carries a historical depth that we, historians of archive and narrative, have a very difficult time reproducing with the same intensity." Cinema appears capable of capturing the historical event at the very core of what triggered and perpetuated it. Through its mastery of time it enables this dynamic integration within a fictional reality, bundling time, light, performance, bodies, and thought in order to create history. "Cinema offers, almost by definition, a comprehensive historical narrative that, in my opinion, will never be written," Farge concludes.[13] If neither the recorded document nor the archive holds any particular historical interest in itself, it is only the way the filmmaker or historian intervenes through it and stages it that attests to, and conveys, reality. It is this form, either visual or scriptural, that makes historicity happen. Because it *moves* and *temporalizes* images, cinema appears as a distinct material yet one that shares many affinities with history. It is not as a language that it should be understood here but as a historical material. According to Deleuze, "cinema is the visual reserve of events in the justice and complexity of their historical context. It is the cutting of images and sound that is history."[14] And it is precisely this Deleuzian "thought in motion" that appears most capable of visualizing history.

Various historians and theorists of history have attempted to think the indiscernibility of cinema and history—not in terms of the relationship that the one maintains with the other but, more profoundly, in the kind of stubborn homology, the dynamic interrelation, the constant cross-stimulation that occurs between the two. As Jean-Louis Comolli phrased it: "cinema establishes a scene that is never outside history, insofar as the history of this century is in large part made of cinematographic representations, and is therefore fabricated in relation to and in the form of cinematographic spectacle; it is, in any case, transmitted and diffused as such."[15] Walter Benjamin—in the seventeenth thesis of "On the Concept of History," one of his last writings (1940)—provided a more accurate metaphor for the intimate proximity of cinematographic and historic processes in invoking his fondness for leafing through films like historical atlases of a given moment. Benjamin enjoyed films as an amateur but was wary of them as a theorist of art. In "The Work of Art in the Age of Its Mechanical Reproducibility" (1939 version) he insisted, almost obsessively, on the "destructive, cathartic" character of this art, which he saw as "the liquidation of the value of tradition in the cultural heritage," a predatory image that seeks to possess the world in an imperial manner and from as close a proximity as possible. Cinema, in Benjamin's view, is the emblem of a culture that manages "to destroy the aura of the work of art" and that, through the infinite reproduction of the same, "succeeds in standardizing the unique."[16] He nonetheless acknowledged cinema's all-powerful presence, which historicizes reality by seizing it within the world. Thinking about cinema in relation to the German philosopher's theses on history, gathered together in "On the Concept of History," enables us to see it in all its historicity, as *the* art that captures the instant of history, and in a way preserves it, freezes it, conserves it. Cinema can be seen as "a messianic arrest of happening, or (to put it differently) a revolutionary chance in the fight for the oppressed past." In other words, it saves history by recording it: "blast[ing] a specific era out of the homogenous course of history; thus, . . . blast[ing] a specific life out of the era, a specific work out of the lifework. As a result of this method, the lifework is both preserved and sublated *in* the work, the era *in* the lifework, and the entire course of history *in* the era."[17]

As early as 1930, a historian ventured an epistemological challenge by comparing the historical method to the mode of temporal narration specific to cinema. This historian was Marc Bloch, who, in the foreword to *French Rural History*, posited the following, little known, hypothesis: "Since life is nothing but movement, could we not consider that grasping history through the regressive method is akin to unrolling the last reel of a film from its end, expecting to find gaps in it, but intent on respecting its mobility?"[18] Bloch compares historical narrative to an audacious experiment in scrolling images, as if, in its genealogical and chronological character, the historical process could be merged into the cinematographic process.

Cinema and History: An Analogy of the "Half-Cooked State"

The theorist who has tried most intensely to think cinema and history *together* in their essential homology is Siegfried Kracauer. Indeed, the recent translation of his *History: The Last Things Before the Last* (1969) into French is likely to rekindle efforts at the interpretation of cinema as a historical object in France. Kracauer himself embodies what a "history of the century through film" might look like. A journalist of culture and cinema critic for the *Frankfurter Allgemeine Zeitung* in Germany throughout the 1920s, he fled Nazism in 1933 and settled in Paris for eight years, where he continued as best he could to write reviews of films and art exhibits for German-language Swiss newspapers and magazines. In 1938 he met Iris Barry, the founder and director of the film archive at New York's MOMA, who had come to Paris to present a retrospective of American cinema and an exhibit as part of the event "Three Centuries of Art in the United States." This personal contact later earned him a job at MOMA's film department in New York, where he settled in 1941. Living on the cheap, without a stable position, supported by fellowships and grants, he worked there for twenty-five years and produced three major books on the relationship between cinema and history: *From Caligari to Hitler: A Psychological History of the German Film* (1947), commissioned by the MOMA film department; *Theory of Film: The Redemption of Physical Reality* (1960); and, *History: The Last Things Before the Last*, which was published three years after his death.

The first two are the better known, especially *From Caligari to Hitler*, which has become a cinema studies classic—on a par with Lotte Eisner's *The Haunted Screen*, dealing with German cinema confronted with, and bearing witness to, the rise of Nazism. In the posthumous work Kracauer developed his core thesis on the homological relationship to reality between the writing of history and the photographic image. Under the latter rubric Kracauer develops the concept of *camera-reality*, which encompasses—through the identical ontological process that links them—both the photographic and the cinematographic arts. Throughout *History* he refers to numerous examples from the history of both visual forms, quoting from Robert Flaherty's *Nanook*, Roberto Rossellini's *Païsa*, and several 1920s avant-garde films. In Kracauer's view the historian and the filmmaker stand in a similar position in relation to the archival and documentary material of reality. Their work is torn between a realistic definition—the ontological, quasi-ethical, and deontological demand for truth through faithfulness to the reality they are registering—and a "formative" tendency, which stimulates them by offering the possibility of "recreating the world," of transfiguring it into a specific form through the writing of history or the artistic development of a film. The imaginative power is never as intense and stimulating as when it manages to model a reality through aligning a sensation of truth and a sentiment of beauty. Kracauer writes, "History coincides with the camera craft in challenging its adepts to capture a given universe. The challenge is strict enough to rouse the urge for discounting it. To remain within the dimension of art, numbers of historical writings impress you as being determined by their authors' inherent form designs rather than the peculiar formation of their material."[19]

In the second chapter of *History*, entitled "The Historical Approach," the theorist of history further develops this specific homological relation. He confronts the two activities according to their "basic aesthetic principle" and finds "an exact analogy" between them:

> There is, then, a fundamental analogy between historiography and the photographic media: like the photographer, the historian is loath to neglect his recording obligations over his preconceptions and fully to consume the raw material he tries to mould. But this is not the whole story. Another basic analogy bears on the subject matter peculiar to the two fields of endeavor.... "Camera reality" has all the earmarks of the *Lebenswelt*.... Its grand theme is life in its fullness.... Small wonder that camera-reality parallels historical reality in terms of its structure, its general constitution. Exactly as historical reality, it is partly patterned, partly amorphous—a consequence, in both cases, of the half-cooked state of our everyday world.[20]

The historical operation—from archive to narrative—and the cinematographic process—through the aesthetic chain that transforms recorded material into a film—are like two stewpots of reality in a "half-cooked state," similar in their recipes and their flavor: to produce a sensible experience of reality, past or present, by giving it form. This sets up historiography and cinema as two parallel phenomena, at once intellectual *and* aesthetic. Thus, Kracauer ends on a striking vision of convergence between history and cinema in which the historical *continuum* is akin to a giant film recording the photography of time: "Historicism is concerned with the photography of time. The equivalent of its temporal photography would be a giant film depicting the temporally interconnected events from every vantage point."[21] Kracauer thus consecrated cinema as the paradigm of history in the century. Cinema is like history, history like a film: cinema is an allegory of history.

Thus, history and cinema alike are capable of giving the world shape. Kracauer calls this the "formative" resource of what he considers to be two arts of suggestion, two models of representation, two sensible narratives of the real. Kracauer clearly identifies historiography and cinema as two capacities for giving intelligible or artistic form to the material traces of a reality to which they attest. One might say, with him, that the historian and the filmmaker muster all their formal resources only to dissolve them into the substance of everyday life phenomena so that these phenomena may be read and seen in their ability to touch the imagination and the senses. Such formal power transcends life even while consigning it, a process that was best captured by Louis Delluc in his definition of cinema: "Art which transcends art, in being life."[22]

Cinema Pursues the Path of History to Reveal What Is Hidden Even from Memory

How are cinema and history to be related? The former can be made the object of the latter, which then describes its origins, its evolution, the conditions of its production or viewing, and the principal artists involved. Conversely, history can be turned into an object for cinema. Films narrate the events of a century, reconstruct a period, and illustrate a way of being in such and such a period. But the "and" that conjoins cinema and history opens up yet another door. The conjunction compels us to look elsewhere, to break free of the subject-object relation. Taking both terms together, it is about understanding, as Jacques Rancière put it, how these two representations of the world "mutually belong" and create what I have called cinematographic forms of history.[23] Cinema, then, acquires an intrinsic relationship to a certain conception of history. Each captures a past reality in its eternal documentary present and gives it form through a kind of writing.

In the eyes of many exegetes cinema is a *mise en forme* of the world. The cinema image is a form insofar as it organizes reality, in an essential sense, along rays of imagination. Yet in organizing this reality, the imagination imprints it with history. Conversely, while it is woven by imagination, reality leaves a historical trace—the imagination reifies it into a historical form as if the film form had lent itself, given its body over, to the history of the century. It is a body in all senses of the word in that it offers faces and movements, both individual and collective, and also in that it assimilates ideas, references, works, concepts, and practices to become itself capable of thinking and being thought and hence to create an event and develop a history of its own. Both an embodiment and a body of knowledge, cinema has been and remains for the century both a sensible surface and a way of knowing. In this respect cinema gives our time its form in the same way as the novel had done for the nineteenth century, theater for the seventeenth century, the encyclopedic dictionary for the Enlightenment, and the lampoon for the French Revolution. In a given historical moment a historical form becomes both most revealing of what is at stake, the tensions and sensibilities, and also most adapted to enabling people to signify their sense of living in their times. In his book on Jean-Luc Godard, Jacques Aumont describes this form as "a practice that reveals modes of thought (which it contributes to shaping), a practice most favorable to invention and to the new, one that 'sticks' to the life of the century and—its ultimate and supreme criterion—to its conception of reality."[24] Reality, in the nineteenth century, was literary—that is, describable, analyzable, and imaginable in the way literature affords. It is quite different for creatures of the twenty-first century, who imagine, analyze, and describe their times according to primarily cinematographic principles. Literature itself, as well as theater, performance, and contemporary art, has now adopted, first and foremost, a cinematographic approach to the world, replete with montage, framing, and other visual affects.

▶ ▶ ▶

THE PRESENT BOOK aims to connect aesthetics and history through cinema. I have selected films representative of cinema's capacity for giving form to reality. In the fall of 1938 Charles Chaplin was finishing a script he had been writing on the sly. Despite his efforts to keep it under wraps, rumors began circulating that the Tramp had decided to make his first talkie, in which he would play a character based on Adolf Hitler. Worries, circumspection, and even scandal surrounded the project. Two years later, in New York, on October 15, 1940, Chaplin screened *The Great Dictator*. In the interim, war had broken out, and the United States had kept out of it. By challenging Hitler with the weapons of the mustachioed Tramp he had invented, the filmmaker was getting personally involved in a burlesque film on the most serious of subjects. He was reconstructing history, whereas it had *not yet happened*, in the full magnitude of its traumatic impact. He gave birth to a "historical film" through premonitory laughter, most notably when, following the credits, a warning flashed: "Any resemblance between Hynkel the dictator and the Jewish barber is purely coincidental." Under pressure of historical events Chaplin turned historian (the archives show how rigorously he researched and documented his film) and offered his cinema and his Tramp, the most famous fictional character in the world, to the service of this historical demonstration, which was also a denunciation and a political statement (fig. 7). "*The Great Dictator* is my first film in which history is bigger than the little tramp," as the filmmaker himself recognized.[25] Chaplin inaugurated a new era of historical film, in which history speaks in the present tense of cinema and holds forth on the present tense of the world in which it is screened.

Beginning with *The Great Dictator*, most major historical films are also, and above all, newsreels—as much about the present of their shooting (their context) as about the past they attempt to reconstruct (their subject matter). This is what the present book will try to illustrate, in presenting various cinematographic forms of history. After an opening chapter on modern cinema as a return of the trauma of World War II, the second chapter focuses on Sacha Guitry, who shot *Si Versailles m'était conté* in 1953, a production that the writer-filmmaker held as his own personal revenge on history, the revenge of a victim of postwar purges. This film articulates a cinematographic form of history based on a few key associations. Versailles is featured as simultaneously time, body, and language—that is, a representation of French history. The elements of this representation are linked through a series of ceremonies and rituals, of which Guitry gives an acerbic depiction, both caustic and respectful, so that *Si Versailles m'était conté* constitutes a portrait—simultaneously faithful, anecdotal, literary, and inventive—of the civilizational process that erected this castle into a model of French civility. The author filmed his court society and reconciled himself with the history of his country, even as he alienated, and for some time to come, the majority of historians.

The Englishman Peter Watkins (chapter 4) elaborated a system that enabled him to reconstruct history in order to film it in the present, bringing together within the same shot all historical time frames: his films are located in the past, since they meticulously endeavor to situate themselves in history; they are also located in the present, since events are presented as though recorded live, in the style of reportage, complete with on-the-scene commentary; and, they also convey a strange sense of the future, readily projecting themselves toward anachronistic and prophetic techniques. Watkins offers an original and polemical mode of fabrication of historical film that he has refined over a dozen films—from *Forgotten Faces*, in 1960, in which the young director plunges into the heart of the Budapest uprising that has been "reconstructed" in a British factory, to *La Commune*, shot in 1999, which replays the Parisian insurrection over six hours in a vast warehouse in the Paris suburb of Montreuil, with live coverage by two rival TV networks of 1871, one pro-Versailles and the other pro-Communards. This sharing of history through film takes on two distinct characteristics in Watkins's work: on the one hand, he develops a very particular style, which gives the impression that the film is entirely devoted to the news, reportage, interviews, in short, "live" coverage; and, on the other hand, he meticulously reconstructs a historical milieu, through a characteristic method of rigorous archival and pedagogical work, often collective, which involves every aspect of the film. The British filmmaker has thus forged a form of *reportage within history*.

One of the many possible portraits one could paint of Jean-Luc Godard (chapter 5) is as an artist—both sorcerer's apprentice and high priest—who has fancied himself, and still fancies himself, a historian. From his 1960s productions—most notably *Band of Outsiders, The Carabineers*, and *Pierrot le fou*—to *Histoire(s) du cinéma* in the 1980s and 1990s—a four-hour-long opus that "cuts and puts together" fragments of cinema and fragments of the century—not to mention a recent exhibition at Centre Georges-Pompidou in Paris, Godard has evolved a lyrical form of montage designed to embody history as an intimate epic, a kind of confession of a child of the century who is also a child of cinema (*ciné-fils*). What we are dealing with here is a cinematographic form of *autobiography of all*, in which a filmmaker, looking for his personal logic in his personal history, ends up shedding light on the logic of history and even attempts to save it by conferring onto film, which has recorded it, a moral responsibility.

If "historical films" all strive, in one way or another, to reconstitute history through facts, events, mysteries, and atmospheres, filmmakers like the ones I have just described immerse themselves in history so as to submit their questions to it, to illustrate a period, to draw lessons from it, whether for the past or the present. Though the outward trappings of a historical film (sets, costumes, atmosphere, dialogue) may be recognizable to all—evidence of a genre and of a take on the past—the power of a film will most often depend on the relationship that the reconstituted past maintains with the present of the film's conception, production, and reception. All historical films are to be seen in the present, and it is this temporality that establishes the specific connection between cinema and history. It may also happen that the latter suddenly irrupts within a film, a series of films, or a moment of cinema. Then, another

7 ▶
The Great Dictator (Charles Chaplin, 1940). The final ceremony of the film: the dictator, Hynkel, has been replaced by the little Jewish barber, who himself looks like the Tramp, who himself plays Hitler, with the same mustache, body twitches, and vocal tics. The characters here are but pawns of history, which has for its part become cinema's favorite prey. (Photo © William Wallace; Coll. *Cahiers du Cinéma*)

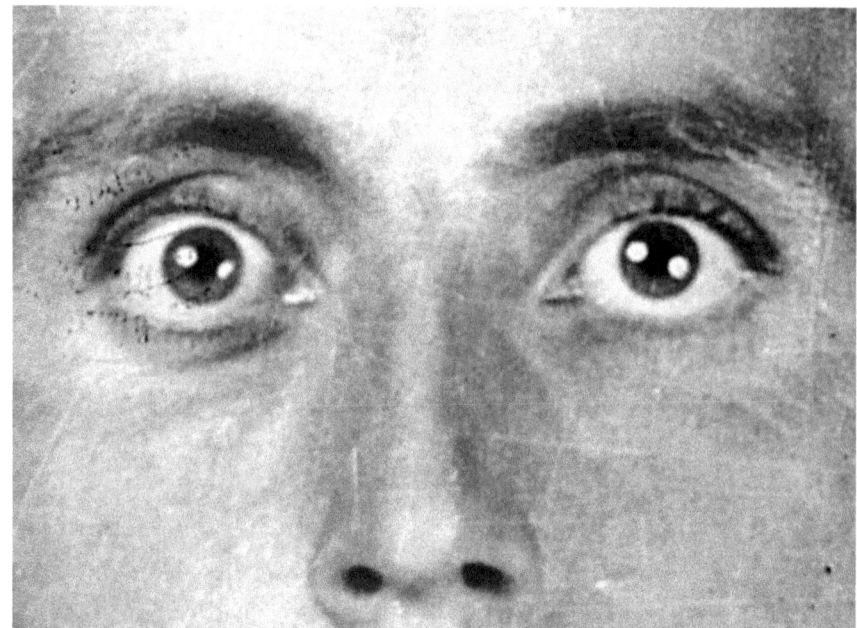

8 ▶
Night and Fog
(ALAIN RESNAIS, 1956).
"FIRST SIGHT OF THE CAMP: IT IS ANOTHER PLANET. FOR THE SAKE OF HYGIENE, THEY ARE DELIVERED TO THE CAMP STARK NAKED, THESE MEN WHO HAVE ALREADY BEEN HUMILIATED" (TEXT BY JEAN CAYROL, READ AS A VOICE-OVER COMMENTARY ON THIS IMAGE).

kind of relation between history and cinema arises: it is no longer a question of the latter attempting to reconstitute the former but rather of history impressing itself into the filmic material, into the mise-en-scène, into the specific visual and narrative combinations of certain films. Indeed, it is this very irruption that brings forth cinematographic forms of history. This book attempts to identify several examples.

The most convincing evidence of history bursting into cinema is given to us by the century's chronology. In my view the most significant rupture in the history of the cinematic art is not a cinematographic fact, per se—it is neither the invention of cinema nor the shift from silent to sound nor the generalization of color nor even the challenge of television. I would argue, instead, that the true break is related to history itself. In his preface to the American edition of *The Time-Image* Gilles Deleuze also located and defended the chronological break at work in his analysis—the shift to modern cinema resulting from World War II—in the rise of the jump-cut technique: "Images are no longer connected by rational cuts and links but reconnect through false-links or irrational cuts. Even the body is no longer exactly the motor, the subject of movement and instrument of the action. It starts to reveal time, to bear witness to time through fatigue and waiting."[26] The cinematographic form of the jump cut thus gave the historical moment its full depth—the rupture of war, the shift from classic to modern cinema. Deleuze seems to suggest that the jump cut has kept open a doorway into historical time, through which "the amnesiac characters of modern cinema plunge literally into the past or emerge from it to show what is hidden even from memory" (353). In the first chapter I focus on another formal figure of the irruption of that same history: the look-to-camera (fig. 8).

A few years later, as some have argued, the rejection of history appeared to be the main objective of the French New Wave (chapter 3). Considered in its historical context, that of the intellectual and cultural life of the 1950s and 1960s, the New Wave does indeed appear to have had strong political affinities with the Young Right, who advocated political "disengagement" while taking refuge in style, marking a sharp contrast with the political commitment of the progressive writers. Yet these young filmmakers were primarily trying to escape the obligatory political commitments of the age, regarding their times instead through the melancholy lucidity of those who are convinced history has passed them by. This was, paradoxically, a way of breaking new historical ground: New Wave directors were thus able to capture their times because they were uncomfortable in them. Moreover, these films were happening against an all-pervasive backdrop: the Algerian War. These directors chose to give reality a try, and each in his own way opted for an interventionist cinema, or at least for a cinema that was sensitive and responsive to the Zeitgeist— a cinema in which history often surfaced and sometimes irrupted. That the New Wave refused to deal with the Algerian War is a tenacious, and ultimately unfounded, myth. The New Wave's unique style and formal specificity enabled it to successfully embody history, to capture youth and its malaise in relation to its times.

To take another example, the fall of communism in Eastern Europe emerged in cinema (chapter 6) by generating a specific cinematographic form of history to capture the collapse. It may be characterized, in certain Russian and Eastern European films, as a "demodern aesthetic"—an attack on the very raw material of that which claimed to be modernity itself: the Soviet system. In a few films by Andrei Tarkovsky, Aleksandr Sokurov, Alexei Guerman, and Emir Kusturica, what had been posited as modern (the city, the new man, science, the army, the conquest of space, etc.) is denigrated and transformed into the "demodern": not through a rejection or a destruction of modernization but by exposing within it a regression, a mutation, a warped delusion. Their images exhibit the marks of a modernity that has been inverted against itself, diverted toward other ends, soiled, made ironic, and beset by aesthetic decay. In these films history itself is at work and imprints the very form of the film.

History is also present in contemporary American cinema. Many Hollywood films bear traces of forms that reveal history (chapter 7), especially genre films such as fantasy, horror, disaster, gothic, and trash comedies. It is as though, in Tim Burton's two *Batman* films, in the Farrelly brothers' *There's Something About Mary*, and in Steven Spielberg's *War of the Worlds*, for instance, a series of master fictions reveal, through identification and rejection, the values, beliefs, and anxieties of contemporary America. These master fictions should also be understood in the sadomasochistic sense of the term: they hurt America, put it in constraints, beat it, insult it, humiliate it. The emperor has no clothes; America is exposed. These fictions, because they are filmed at the same time as history, give a better sense of the state of the country than any sociological study or news bulletin. Cinema is, will be, and always has been a manifesto of the present, whose contemporary energy is continually refueled by its very realism. This capacity justifies the downstream limit of this study: American cinema, post 9/11, which transformed itself under the force of the event to accommodate in full frame the doubts cast by history.

The Sensible Fabric of the World

Cinema is the art that gives form to history because it is able to display the reality of a time by arranging fragments of it according to an original organization: mise-en-scène. It is in this way that cinema makes history visible. It is the art of a form sensible of history *and* sensible to history. As Jacques Rancière has put it, cinema "weaves this sensible fabric of the common world," embodying Mallarmé's "magnificence quelconque."[27] For twentieth-century history, cinema became the fabric of life, the bustling rhythm of the community, the collective plasticity of myth. Cinema incarnates history by combining a formal mode of its contemporary reality with the will to transform this reality—which is the posture of humanity in historical action. By the same token, it appears as a historical configuration itself: both "historicizing"—since it grounds fictions, characters, locations, and objects in history—and "historicizable"—since it is itself determined by successive contexts. This is a way to affirm, with Rancière, that cinema is "more than art"; indeed, it is history itself, or at least its most responsive incarnation. Aesthetics, with cinema, can become a historical regime. As Alain Badiou has suggested, turning cinema into the successor to classical tragedy and Christianity, it constitutes "the third historical attempt at the spiritual subjugation of the visible, available to all, without exception or measure."[28] One could say that the cinematographic form allows for the sculpting of a historical moment, that all films extract from the century a moving sculpture of a given historical time, because their mise-en-scène is a kind of digging into history.

At the end of his life Max Jacob had a poetic vision of the world split into two sensible surfaces—cinema, on the one hand, and history, on the other—while at the center, on the ground in between, as a mirror reflecting one onto the other, was death and its millions of ghosts: "We make cinema with the dead. We take the dead from history and make them walk. That is what cinema is all about."[29] In *History: The Last Things Before the Last* Kracauer obeys a vision no less poetic, and just as historical, in the sculpting of his form. In his view cinema hovers above history like a helicopter or a plane taking topographical photographs, yet not as high as theory, whose obsession with regular patterns and concepts blinds it to the contours of the landscape below. Cinema swoops down low enough to examine the landscape in detail and then climbs back up to obtain a perspective that seems better suited and more suggestive. Sometimes it comes in so low over history that it can get a glimpse of the films that are playing in the open-air theaters. Mesmerized by such a mise en abyme and metareflection of cinema in history, the historian may then cease for a second to consider the past as such and see it as a film, comfortably settling into history's open-air cinema.

FORECLOSED FORMS ▶
HOW IMAGES OF MASS DEATH REEMERGED IN MODERN CINEMA

◀ 9
Poster for *Hiroshima mon amour*
(ALAIN RESNAIS, 1959). (PHOTO COURTESY BIFI)

AT THE BEGINNING of Alain Resnais' *Hiroshima mon amour*, released in 1959, we are met by the gaze of Japanese women. They appear to have been waiting for us at the threshold of their hospital rooms. They are ill, no doubt mortally so, as a result of the radioactive fallout from the bomb dropped on Hiroshima on August 6, 1945. They greet us and calmly, almost serenely, fix their eyes on us. It is as though they capture our attention in order to direct it to the horrific images on display at the Hiroshima Museum, images that were recorded by Akira Iwasaki in the hours and days immediately following the detonation. Iwasaki was a Japanese cameraman whose footage was seized by American authorities when they occupied the archipelago soon thereafter (fig. 10).

The Look-to-Camera: A Modern Form of History

These horrific images, introduced by the looks-to-camera of the women, had not been seen for fourteen years when Resnais chose to use them in the opening montage of his first feature. "You didn't see anything at Hiroshima?" asks Marguerite Duras, in a phrase that is repeated like a mantra over the unbearable images. "Yes I did," responds the film's heroine, Emmanuelle Riva. Yes, she did see. Thanks to the gaze of the Japanese women. Through their gaze the heroine has seen, and every spectator is able to see, mass death. The fictional story can now begin, merging two temporal frames: the present of a love affair between a French woman and a Japanese man from Hiroshima, and the past of a love affair between the very same French woman—a *shorn woman of Nevers*—and a German soldier, fifteen years earlier, toward the end of the German occupation of France. Fiction may now begin, and cinematographic forms take shape; martyred women have looked to camera, thus interpolating every spectator into Resnais' film. History itself is staring at us.

Alain Resnais had already encountered this scene, these looks staring at him through the camera's eye. In 1952, in Roberto Rossellini's *Europa '51*, Irene, interned in a psychiatric hospital by her husband, roams from room to room and finally pauses in a kind of waiting area. There she encounters eleven women, most probably mad. They stare at her. For Irene this marks a moment of revelation after a long ordeal: indeed, the *grande bourgeoise* from Rome has seen her adolescent son commit suicide, the dead body of a man whom she hoped to rescue from poverty lying on a ghetto street, and a prostitute she wanted to help die of tuberculosis in her own arms. Her ordeal and ultimate redemption come through her being disowned by her family and interned in

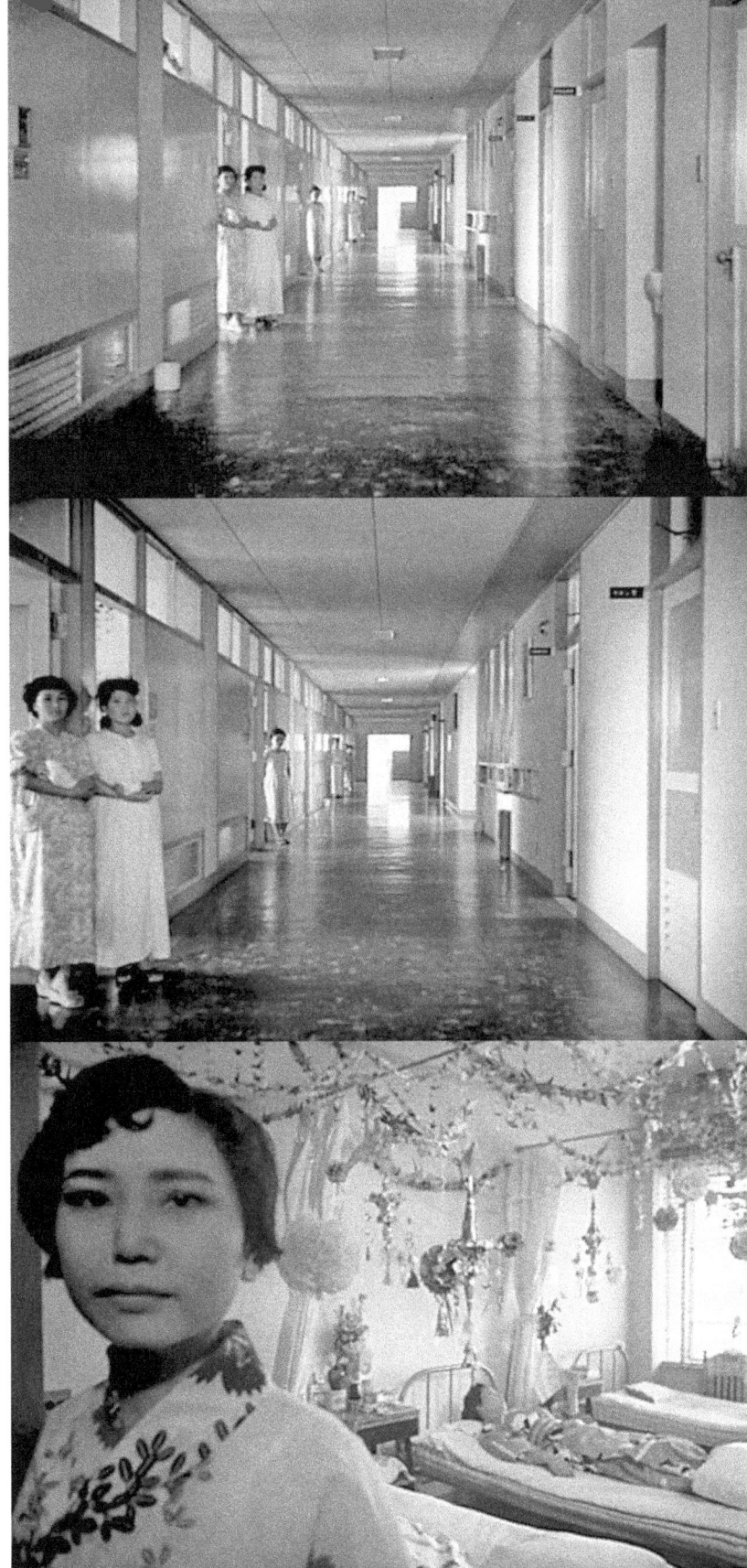

10 ▶
Hiroshima mon amour (ALAIN RESNAIS, 1959). ALAIN RESNAIS' FAMOUS TRACKING SHOTS: HERE, IN HIROSHIMA'S HOSPITAL, WE ARE ARRESTED BY THE WOMEN'S GAZE BECKONING US INTO THE ROOMS.

11 ▶
Monika
(INGMAR BERGMAN, 1952). THE SADDEST SHOT IN THE HISTORY OF CINEMA, ACCORDING TO JEAN-LUC GODARD. WHEN MONIKA DEFIES THE SPECTATOR'S GAZE, IT IS TO CONFIRM HER MORAL FAILING AND FLAUNT IT. WHO ARE WE TO JUDGE HER?

an asylum. When Irene enters the room, where the women appear to have been waiting for her, and they look her in the eyes, *Europa '51* turns into a nightmare and a revelation—a form of apoplexy. The camera records the gaze of the women fixed on that of Ingrid Bergman; it pans from one woman to the next in a whirling movement, which is that of madness—a little over a minute of film face-to-face with absolute otherness (see fig. 4). This shot, of exceptional intensity, is twice interrupted by reverse shots showing Irene staring back, in greater close up (see fig. 25). These reverse shots are also looks-to-camera. The madwomen stare at a woman as though she is a monster, and the latter confronts madness head-on. In these shots Ingrid Bergman's gaze and that of the mad women lay claim to the eye of Roberto Rossellini's camera. The madwomen stare at the camera, and they stare at us. Ingrid Bergman stares at the camera, and she stares at us. *Europa '51* thus institutes the look-to-camera as the very cinematographic form of challenging the Other, looking directly into the eyes of madness. Critics, following Jacques Rivette and *Cahiers du cinema*, were quick to label this form "modern cinema."

The looks in *Europa '51* were nearly simultaneous with another: the sustained look-to-camera of Harriet Andersson in *Monika*, the film Ingmar Bergman was making on the other side of Europe, as she seduces a man who is not her husband (fig. 11). This, of course, is one of the most famous shots in the history of cinema: the transgression shot. The character, Monika, opts in a single look for absolute freedom from all conventional values. This shot expresses the fact that she has deliberately chosen to sleep with the first man she sees in order to demonstrate her transgressive freedom. At that moment "she departs the fictional world and looks the spectator[s] right in the eyes,"[1] as though addressing them directly, calling them to bear witness to her act, provoking them. In *Arts* Jean-Luc Godard interpreted this blunt look-to-camera as an expression of "all the self-contempt this young woman feels as she chooses hell over heaven." He concludes, in moralizing tones: "it is the saddest shot in the history of cinema."[2] In his book *Images* Bergman described the shot in sexual rather than moral terms: an indecent look through which the actress suddenly leaves her fictional partner and seeks out, seduces, flirts with the spectator sitting in the dark, establishing a very intimate relationship.[3] The filmic creature shatters the fiction to turn everyone in the audience, with a single glance, into a john. Such is the power of this cinematographic form, one of the most provocative in all of cinema.

From whence does such head-on intensity emerge? *Straight from history.* Not the history of cinema, although quite a few looks-to-camera were thrown

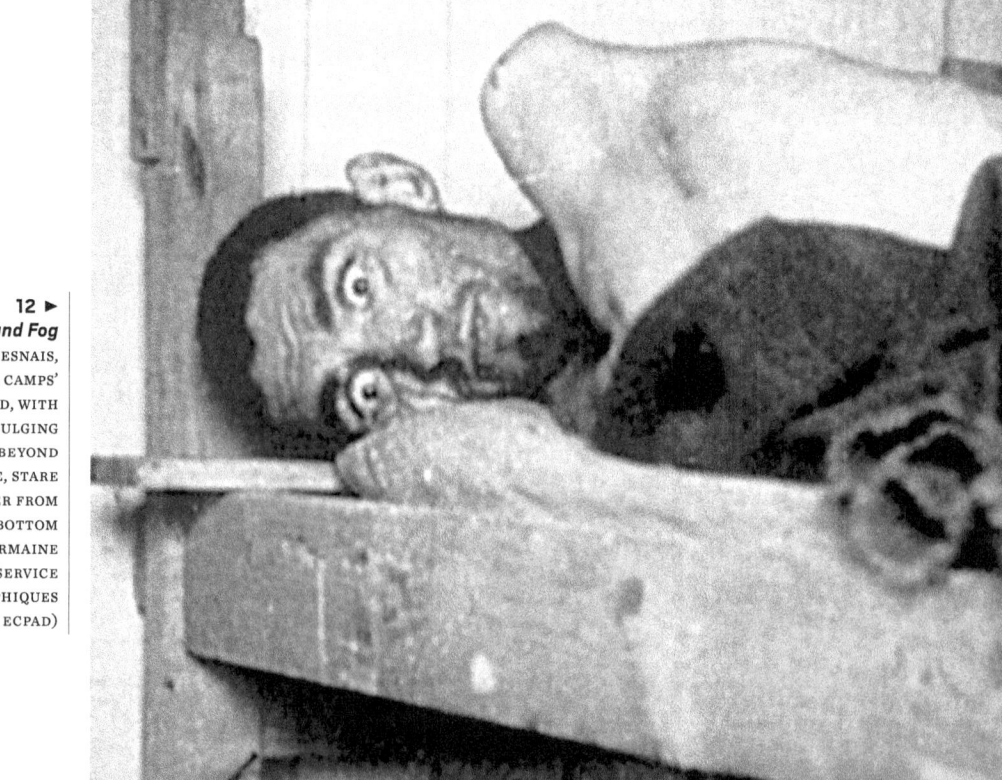

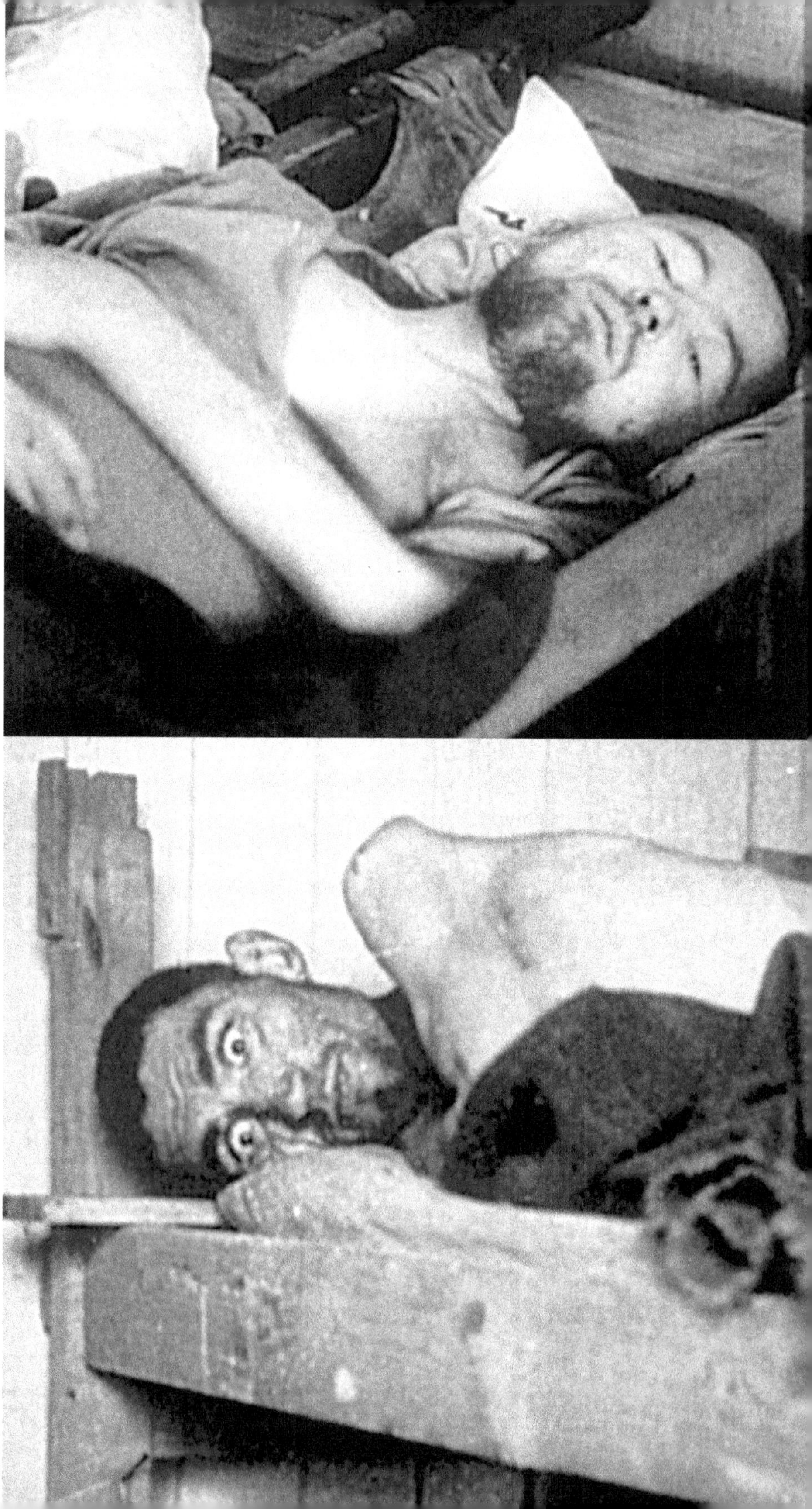

12 ▶ *Night and Fog* (ALAIN RESNAIS, 1956). THE CAMPS' LIVING DEAD, WITH THEIR TIRED BULGING EYES, FROM BEYOND THE GRAVE, STARE AT THE OTHER FROM DEATH. (BOTTOM PHOTO © GERMAINE KANOVA, SERVICE PHOTOGRAPHIQUES DES ARMÉES, ECPAD)

at spectators in the days of silent film, when burlesque actors, large and small, would wink in connivance with the audience. Comic actors—Fernandel, Louis de Funès, Bourvil, but also Guitry—deployed this knowing glance throughout their careers. Nor does it come from the looks of the Japanese women of Hiroshima, the madwomen in *Europa '51*, nor even the haughty woman in *Monika*. This direct and disturbing stare resurfaces in another Alain Resnais film, *Night and Fog*, which was made to commemorate the tenth anniversary of the liberation of the concentration camps. The film fixes us with countless stares, wrenched from the death camps by photographers and cinematographers—stares that bear witness to the Nazi horror of Bergen-Belsen, Buchenwald, Dachau, Thekla, Ohrdruf, and other camps (figs. 12, 13).

Through his use of these documents from "after," Alain Resnais accesses a blind spot of twentieth-century history: the unrepresentable, which is nonetheless staring right at us. These are the "mad eyes" of camp survivors, the closed looks, as though sealed off behind some impassable boundary, that bear witness from beyond death, which they have looked in the face, to extermination. There is cinema after extermination, after the camp footage. These looks-to-camera in *Night and Fog*, *Europa '51*, and *Hiroshima mon amour* signified that cinema had to change, indeed *had* changed, since nobody could remain innocent after these images. It is the century's history that invented modern cinema—and one of the quintessential forms of this new cinema, that which transgresses, that which enables us to see the insane.

Something was indeed filmed. Many saw it. Some remembered it as an inconceivable shock. François Truffaut, for instance, recalled a few minutes of footage inserted into a newsreel in May 1945, at the Cinéac-Italiens Theatre: the "mass graves," the "mutilated corpses," the "charred bodies," and the "living dead emerging out of their barracks," with their wild-eyed looks, from beyond the grave.[4]

The Gaze of Death in Action

The Allies liberated the camps over the course of the year leading up to the German surrender: Majdanek in July of 1944, Struthof in November, Auschwitz-Birkenau in January of 1945. The American, British, and Russian armies all made films, using small crews supervised by a small number of filmmakers. These included Lieutenant Colonel George Stevens, who was in charge of a "transmission unit" linked to the Allied High Command (led by Eisenhower); Sydney Bernstein, assisted by Alfred Hitchcock and Peter

13 ▶
Night and Fog
(ALAIN RESNAIS, 1956).
SURVIVORS STARING
AT US.

Tanner, working in the Film Section of the Combat Psychological Division of British Army Headquarters; and, for the Soviets, directors Voronzov and Setkiva. Hours of footage were quickly archived by military authorities, both Eastern and Western, and organized chronologically according to the progressive liberation of the camps.[5]

For several months these images were not shown at all, as they were deemed too disturbing, too sensitive to make any use of with a general audience, when hundreds of thousands of war prisoners and deportees had not yet made it back home. Annette Wieviorka quotes a telegram from the French ministry of the interior, dated April 12, 1945, ordering the "prevention by all means of press coverage and images on the liberation of Ravensbrück and the repatriation of the first women."[6] Military censorship adhered to the same line: "presentation of such documents must be deferred, due to the emotional reaction they would surely trigger in the families of deportees, many of whom have not heard from their loved ones. Will be approved for screening as soon as the situation of French deportees has been clarified."[7] The deliberate dissemination of filmic and photographic documentation that was simultaneously being undertaken in the United States by Eisenhower stood in sharp contrast to the gag order imposed by French authorities. In the winter of 1944–45 the mood in France was more inclined toward constructing the heroic archetype of the deported resistance fighter and to lamenting the fates of "prisoners of war" and "work deportees"—the "three million men whose return is still anxiously awaited."

In late April and early May of 1945 the veil of silence began to lift in official statements and circulars. For the first time, *France-Libre-Actualités*, which presented newsreels before feature film screenings, alluded to a massive death rate and invoked the possibility that deportees might not return, whereas officialdom was still clinging to the idealized promise: "all will return!" As Sylvie Lindeperg has demonstrated in her book on French newsreels, it was only later that the first images were brought to French screens, and they came as a shock even though they had been carefully selected from among documents sent by the film crews of the Allied Forces. On April 27, 1945, the first brief shots of only a few seconds appeared, selected from American footage: a mass grave in Ohrdruf full of bodies in striped prison garb, two close-ups of corpses, also in prison stripes, one frontal, one from the back. On May 3 the weekly newsreel presented a few images of Bergen-Belsen that had been filmed by the British: general overviews of the camp, shots of gaunt prisoners walking aimlessly among corpses, sharing a bowl of soup, a close-up of a corpse dressed in a ragged suit and a cap, a panoramic view of a mass grave full of naked bodies. On May 18 a piece on Buchenwald entitled *Les criminels* (The Criminals) dealt with the horror of the camps in a bit more detail: emaciated faces, charred leftovers in a crematorium, piles of bones, pyramids of naked corpses, piled up on the ground or crammed into train cars. The commentary invoked "the immense mass grave that has now become like a gaping mouth across Europe, crying out its implacable testimony." On May 25 images of an entire train full of corpses at Dachau Station were screened, as well as shots of bodies charred by flamethrowers in Thekla. The most unsettling images, notably those of medical experiments, were censored to maintain the taboo surrounding the representation of naked female bodies.

It is difficult to grasp today the wave of shock triggered by these images, though the recollections of cinephiles like François Truffaut, Jacques Rivette, and Jean Douchet give us some idea. In a special issue of *Cahiers du cinema*, in November 2000, Alain Resnais, who had been twenty-five years old at the moment of France's liberation, recalled: "I saw these images in May 1945. How could I forget? . . . I was a creature of France, like any other, and they shook me to the core. Rumors had been circulating about these camps, but being confronted with images was an entirely different thing. In the face of these images, you can't turn away, you can't ignore it anymore. It was a horrifying denunciation of human idiocy."[8]

We also have the testimonies of simple moviegoers, such as Jean Galtier-Boissière, who wrote in his journal in late May of 1945: "in the news, horrifying images: a train carrying skeletal camp inmates, who had simply been abandoned during the German retreat and had starved to death."[9] Jorge Semprun, a survivor of the Buchenwald camp, saw the images a few weeks later at a movie theater: "The eye of the camera explored the inside of a barrack: utterly exhausted men, collapsed on their bedsteads and agonizingly gaunt, stared with bulging eyes at those who were bringing them—too late for many of them—freedom."[10] This was, of course, a somewhat distorted representation, since the footage could only record the "aftermath" of extermination, a "horrific prolongation"—an "after-image," to paraphrase Joshua Hirsch.[11] Such a displaced image, to use the psychoanalytic jargon, of the reality of genocide is related to the spectacular effectivity of cinema. It bears witness for the conscious mind of the spectator to that which cannot be represented, following the Nazi intention not to leave any visible trace of Jews or their extermination. As Annette Wieviorka explains: "The destruction was that of people who did not have time to go hungry and who were killed *en masse*. It does not conform to our images of horror; there was no discourse on their dehumanization, no discourse of the limit. Only the killing on a mass scale of people who left home and who, a few days later, no longer existed. There was only life, and then death."[12]

The path from life to death disappears, since it cannot be represented, for lack of documentation and archives, to be sure, but also simply because it is unrepresentable, made up of a few rare "images in spite of all," as Georges Didi-Huberman has put it, images that were generally discovered and disseminated in a second or even third moment of Holocaust memory.[13] Mass extermination is the unsaid and unseen of the camp liberation footage, as emphasized by the lack of references to the Jews or the very site of genocide: the gas chamber. Indeed, the news of the spring of 1945 revealed to all the full extent of the horror, through the bodies, the remains (hair, clothes, objects), the mass graves, and the crematoriums but never the gas chambers, the key industrial link in the project to eradicate European Jewry.

Initially glimpsed only as fragments in newsreels, these films were soon edited into synthetic accounts, which were to be used as evidence against the perpetrators of mass death. On November 29, 1945, the ninth day of hearings at the International Military Tribunal at Nuremberg, at which twenty-two members of the Nazi leadership were on trial, a one-hour film entitled *Nazi Concentration Camps* was shown and entered into evidence in support of American allegations. This document, a truly incriminating piece of evidence, provides a sinister catalogue of cruelty, abuse, and torture inflicted at the camps. It was a montage of images shot by George Stevens, from the Normandy landing to the liberation of the camps at Penig, Ohrdruf, Hadamar, Nordhausen, Harland, Arnstadt, Mauthausen, Buchenwald, and Dachau. These images had such an impact that they can be said to have altered the course of the trial and lastingly influenced the behavior and attitude of the accused. Goering himself even said, with the arrogant cynicism of a man at a picture show: "this horrible film has spoiled everything."

Already in the spring of 1945, Robert H. Jackson—the American judge appointed by President Harry Truman as chief prosecutor of Nazi war criminals at Nuremberg—had ordered a "search and seizure" by the OSS (Office of Strategic Services) of all "film documents." The prosecution had to show evidence of crimes and hence created what Christian Delage has called an "audio-visual laboratory." Indeed, visual evidence proved crucial at the Nuremberg trial. It was the first time that the use of film as archive and evidence was deemed legitimate. This is how Judge Jackson described it in his opening statement at the trial:

> We must not forget that, when the Nazi plans were announced in all their arrogance, they were so extravagant that the world refused to take them seriously.... We will give you undeniable proofs of incredible events.... We will show you these concentration camps in motion pictures, just as the Allied armies found them when they arrived.... Our proof will be disgusting and you will say I have robbed you of your sleep.... I am one who received most tales of atrocity during this war with suspicion and skepticism. But the proof here will be so overwhelming that I venture to predict not one word I have spoken will be denied.[14]

This echoes Eisenhower's famous statement, which is now engraved on a plaque at the entrance to the Holocaust Memorial in Washington, D.C.: "The things I saw beggar description.... I made the visit [to Buchenwald] deliberately, in order to be in a position to give firsthand evidence of these things if ever, in the future, there develops a tendency to charge these allegations to propaganda."[15]

At the Nuremberg trial the authenticity of the films was essential. Two kinds of film documents were taken into consideration: the films shot by the Nazis themselves, which made clear their plans and actions, and those shot by the Allies in 1945, as the camps were being liberated. The film *Nazi Concentration Camps*, as Christian Delage puts it, "attests to what, at the most representative of these camps, the actual living conditions were."[16] Some of the main sequences had already been screened by Fox Movietone News, to a "rather incredulous" audience. Eisenhower had requested that the army organize filming visits to some of the camps the following summer, to be shown exclusively to Hollywood studio heads, members of the press, and members of Congress.

The Nuremberg judges were trying, for their part, to elicit a "particular effect" from the screening of these images. They had thought about placing a retractable screen at the center of the courtroom, between the accused and the judges' gallery, to ensure optimal viewing. On the eve of the screening it was decided that a neon light would shine on the accused while the room was darkened for the screening. The spectator's gaze would then focus both on the screen and on the faces of the accused, on which could presumably be read guilt, remorse, and responsibility for the horrors depicted. This goes to show how ingrained was the idea that film images provoked reactions that were impossible to dissemble or fake. Indeed, the screening had such a powerful shock effect that Joseph Kessel, who covered the trial for the French press, among several hundred international colleagues, wrote in *France-soir*: "All of a sudden, I realized that the resurrection of horror was no longer, at that precise moment, the main point. The idea was not to show members of the tribunal a document with which they were undoubtedly already very familiar. The idea was to suddenly confront the criminals with their immense crime, to throw, so to speak, the assassins, the butchers of Europe, into the mass graves they had organized, and to capture the gestures that such a spectacle, such a shock, was bound to trigger."[17]

The Nazi officials were thus forced to confront these incontestable images of mass death before witnesses. In France the ministry of information commissioned a somewhat similar film, on May 18, 1945, from the secretary general of *France-Libre-Actualités*. Entitled *Les Camps de la mort*, this cinematographic document designed to inform the public about Nazi atrocities was used as evidence at the exhibition on the camps organized in Pau, in southern France, in April 1946. Thus, cinema played its part: films of the camps, "the day after," showing theater audiences the traces of death recorded and presented as evidence.

At the center of all these films there is a singularly unbearable image, almost a formal signature, the ultimate damning evidence: the stare into the camera. It is as if these stares were saying, "I have returned from the dead. I have stared death in the face." To look into the camera is to present conclusive testimony (fig. 14). In *Les Camps de la mort* an initial shot of a mass grave of several hundred bodies is shown. The cameraman chose to zoom in and film a few close-ups of gaunt and naked corpses. This is followed by an eight-minute panoramic shot of a mass grave, another shot of bodies piled up like logs, and the whole thing ends on a sequence of three close-ups of the gaunt faces of survivors staring into the camera with their horrifying gaze, almost absent, an opaque sheen to their eyes. As for the French newsreel on Buchenwald, it opens with a selection of the footage shot by the Americans at the camp, a series of shots of the faces of survivors staring into the camera in a similar fashion. The commentary points out the petrifying aspect of death staring you in the face. It was as though those who had seen it, the survivors, could only communicate their experience through the strange fixity of their stare—the "beastly gaze," the "insane look," as the newsreels described them, or the gaze "impenetrable to interlocution," as Jacques Aumont puts it.[18] These faces

◀ 14
Photograph taken at the liberation of the Buchenwald camp, in April 1945, by Margaret Bourke-White for *Time-Life*. HERE, ELEVEN OUT OF SIXTEEN OF THE MEN ARE LOOKING AT US. (PHOTO © MARGARET BOURKE-WHITE, TIME-LIFE PICTURES/ GETTY IMAGES)

imposed themselves as the traumatic emblem of the camps and their liberation with the same force as the piles of emaciated corpses; and they have been staring down the history of cinema ever since, offering themselves up as a generic form for modern cinema.

How History Reemerges Through Cinema

After being screened at the Nuremberg trials, these documents disappeared from sight. *Nazi Concentration Camps* was shown exclusively at Nuremberg; *Les Camps de la mort* was only seen by limited audiences in the context of official ceremonies (tributes, commemorations, exhibitions). The newsreels, as with all the film shot at the liberation of the camps, were archived in boxes where they remained sealed for years. An official policy of forgetting was implemented to make these images "pass on" for fear they would turn into a repository of collective guilt and preclude Germany from ever reintegrating into the family of nations. Yet this did not spare modern cinema in the 1950s from being intensely wrought by these sights and stares—the visions, the unease and the trauma of "this actually happened"—and from being entirely recast, even, by these images, which were to constantly resurface and metamorphose into precise forms.

Throughout this long postwar period, until the end of the 1950s, cinema appeared to be picking up again. Of course, the crisis of the studio system in Hollywood, as well as to some extent throughout the world, had left the industry without the unified guiding principle that had characterized the classic period. There was now, more than ever before, a greater range of different kinds of movie theaters, filmmakers, and audiences. This modern turn, in the case of certain directors, grew out of an attitude of critical assimilation of the inheritance from the past: consisting both of the fact of the existence of extermination camps, as seen in the striking footage of 1945, and of a history of cinema whose affiliations—for Chaplin, Rossellini, Bergman, Hitchcock, Fuller, Resnais, and the French New Wave—were no longer straightforward and no longer consisted of direct genealogical lineages. These filmmakers were no longer innocent. They were now aware in their work that both their century and their art had a history laden with meaning and that they had to find a way out of this problematic inheritance through a practice of ideological doubt and methodological interrogation, a return to the real by getting out of the studio to film the world. They had to find forms that, in the films themselves, would give expression to the end of innocence and to experimentation with the modern. This fundamentally transformed the classic contract that had held, in the name of cinema, between the auteur and the cinematic system, the director and the world, among the characters themselves, and between the storyteller and the spectator.

This break can be seen as the *foreclosed memory of the camps*. These images, born of the war, which deeply marked cinema and filmmakers at the time, did a kind of subterranean work, a "reworking" so to speak, subconsciously—since they never actually appear in postwar films—and then resurfaced in films (often ten years later) in definite forms, like a traumatic memory that, little by little, had bored its way into the history of cinema. An art form had lost its innocence, and the great auteurs would no longer be making the same kinds of films. Ernst Lubitsch's *To Be or Not to Be*, Charles Chaplin's *The Great Dictator*, even the American series *Why We Fight*, or the images shot by George Stevens's team, sometimes in color, the very first American images of Europe in shambles, all these anti-Nazi classics, had become unthinkable by 1955. What was no longer possible, in fact, was to proceed as though it were the first time—the initial image, the founding narrative. According to Serge Daney, watching these films a few decades later, they still had "the almost immaculate beauty of a travel narrative," "a beauty that arose less from the fact of finding the adequate distance than from the innocence of their perspective."[19]

If, in 1945, innocence resided in the camp survivors' eyes, adequacy had to be "founded," that is to say, recomposed, reformulated, as in a process of formal sedimentation. Adequacy is the form that comes after innocence. The latter springs from simply setting the camera rolling; the former is a process of *formalization* that strives to overcome the impossibility of telling and showing. Thus, we cannot simply speak of these images in terms of forgetting, amnesia, or even repression and return, but of a veritable *foreclosure*. In its strict Lacanian definition foreclosure refers to the "hallucinatory return into the real of something upon which it had not been possible to produce a 'judgment of reality.'"[20] In other words, the filmmakers who "innocently" saw the images of the camps in 1945 would have put them aside, effecting their return in their films ten years later, through renewed and radical forms of mise-en-scène of the present. Cinema thus entered its adulthood through these "things that," as Jacques Rivette put it, "must be approached with fear and trembling."[21]

This is to raise a series of questions that have plagued the cinema since the camps, which an entire generation of filmmakers, and above all critics and spectators, have labeled "modern." The form that this cinema was trying to adopt mattered not merely to audiences but, above all, to the human race. Spectators in 1955 felt themselves suddenly seized, through these foreclosed forms, by a powerful sense of being part of humanity. This existential experience has been described by Serge Daney: "And then, I see clearly why I had adopted cinema: so it could adopt me in return. So it could teach me to relentlessly touch with my eyes how far from myself the other begins. This history of course begins and ends with the camps because they are the limit that was waiting for me at the beginning of my life as a spectator."[22] These forms thus became part of the history of cinema. Audiences, cinephiles, and critics noticed, with Jacques Rivette, that, from that moment, "films could not stay the same, since both cinema and history, ha[d], in a single movement, been toppled by the quake that we still had a hard time naming, but which we felt was irreversible."[23] Daney was saying nothing less than this when he described his induction into the order of cinephilia through Alain Resnais' *Night and Fog* (see figs. 15, 16), the modern film that rekindled the memory of death-camp images:

> The dead bodies of *Night and Fog* and four years later those in the first frames of *Hiroshima mon amour* are among those "things" that have watched me more than I have seen them. I was staggered—and I was not the only one—because I never

15 ▶
Night and Fog
(ALAIN RESNAIS, 1956). A PICTURE OF 1945: HEAPS OF SHOES, 'REMAINS' OF EXTERMINATED BODIES.

thought that cinema was capable of "that." It is because *Night and Fog* had been possible that Resnais was for me a seminal figure. He was revolutionizing the cinematographic language simply by taking his subject seriously and because he had the intuition, the luck almost, to spot this subject from among all the others: nothing less than the damaged and disfigured human species after the Nazi camps and the atomic trauma.[24]

Alain Resnais and the Editing of Time

How did filmmakers film the "things" and the "that" to which Daney refers? Through what images and camera movements did they manage to represent and communicate them to spectators ten years after 1945? In other words, what are the foreclosed forms in *Night and Fog*? The piles of corpses, shoes, eyeglasses, hair, teeth, as though wrenched from the archives in fragments? Or the way Resnais has in his films of settling on the edge of a twisted humanity?

Alain Resnais, although not normally an avid commentator on his own work, has provided some explanation of these specific cinematographic forms, forged for the most part during the editing of *Night and Fog*. The film was commissioned in 1954 by the producer Anatole Dauman and the *Comité d'histoire de la Seconde Guerre mondiale*, in anticipation of the tenth

16 ▶
Night and Fog
(ALAIN RESNAIS, 1956).
THE LATRINES AT
AUSCHWITZ, FILMED
BY ALAIN RESNAIS IN
1955, TEN YEARS LATER.
HISTORY, FOR THE
FILMMAKER, RESIDES
IN THIS TIME LAG.

anniversary of the liberation of the camps. It was to be the first French film to contribute to the remembrance of the "deportation dead," in the context of the implementation of a national policy of memory of the camps, which included the establishment, on April 14, 1954, of a "national day of remembrance for the victims and heroes of deportation," and, on November 10, 1954, of the opening, at the Musée pédagogique in Paris, of an exhibition entitled *Résistance-Libération-Déportation*. Resnais quickly shook off the commission and its official discourse—even though all of the commentary and images in the film were submitted to the commissioners for approval—as he sought to find a specific form for his film. "I viewed everything the film archives in Paris had at the time," he explained in 2000, "and I also went to Amsterdam, where I had a freer hand. I was very disturbed; the documents were strong, especially the footage shot by the British cameramen, and they constituted, in themselves, the documentary I had to make. So I proposed another form for it. And the meeting with Jean Cayrol changed the perspective. We went for a very different film."[25] Cayrol, himself a former deportee and the author of several essays and novels on the death camps, whose style has been labeled "lazarist" (in that it brings the dead back to the surface of words), wrote a text for the film. Read by the actor Michel Bouquet, it is a very distinctive narrative: neither a commentary on archival images nor a historical précis on the extermination of the Jews but rather a "literary" evocation of the challenge to humanity posed by the Nazi death machine, a song of grief, made more intense by Hans Eisler's singular score. This marked a decisive break from the traditional commentary offered in documentaries, especially historical ones. Resnais thus sought, in this way, the *distancing* that would enable the images of 1945 to make a hallucinatory return into the real of 1955, as though, ten years later, it was no longer possible to look into the head-on gaze emanating from the death camps; rather, it had to be inscribed into another medium: no longer the sensitive surface of a distressed public but rather cinema itself, as an antispectacular form of history.

Resnais thus worked from archival fragments, which were not always rigorously selected, and "edited" them into cinema, his cinema: "The archival footage of 1945 can only provoke reactions of horror. One could say my work started there. The footage had to be very strongly imprinted on my brain. But I went for something else. I am a film editor, and my concern was to match two very different kinds of images: the footage shot at the opening of camps, and images that I had myself shot at Auschwitz."[26] It is through the images of Auschwitz shot on location by Resnais and his team that, ten years after the liberation of the camps, history penetrates *Night and Fog*, through this specific form of distancing. In themselves the archival documents did not constitute history; neither did the nearly empty and peaceful images shot at Auschwitz. It is through the temporal distance at play between the 1945 documents and the 1955 images that history emerges.

Resnais invented "time-editing," the foreclosed form that tells of the human species' confrontation with extermination camps. Time is the cinematographic form specific to history in Resnais' films, time that is edited and evidenced in *Night and Fog*. The ten-year lapse between the stares and the bodies of 1945 and the buildings, fields, and barbed wire of 1955—a lapse that Resnais makes material through the formal juxtaposition of excerpts from British newsreels and his own dolly shots, confronting the "gaze gazing at us" with the "there is nothing left to see" of nature resuming its course, of derelict buildings—these ten years represent just so many traces of death abandoned to themselves. The adequacy of the film rests, precisely, on this *interval* and, above all, on the cinematographic form invented by the filmmaker to manifest it onscreen. The encounter between cinema and history across this interval occurs as the very precisely timed temporal and visual conjunction of the archival images emerging from the camps and Resnais' "nonimages," which refuse reconstruction and aestheticization. Such a form verges on an outright rejection of cinematographic spectacle and as a result contains within itself the new adequacy of cinema, which has processed the impossibility of direct representation of extermination, whether as archive or fiction. It presents the unrepresentable through a time-lapse, as a hallucination that is absolutely true.

Alain Resnais was for Serge Daney a seminal figure. The critic also named Rossellini, Hitchcock, and Fuller, all of whom experimented, in their films, through their characters, and on their audiences, with cruelty, fear, and terror, to reveal human nature. Orson Welles, yet another monster of modern cinema, could also be mentioned here, as the first to refer explicitly to extermination in *The Stranger* (1946), his postwar fiction film that conjured up images shot at the liberation of the camps. Franz Kindler (Orson Welles)—a Nazi war criminal who has fled to the United States, settled in a small town where he teaches history and has married a young American woman who is unaware of his past—is hunted down by an agent of the War Crimes Investigation Commission (Edward G. Robinson). To capture the Nazi, who hides but does not repent, the agent tries to enlist his wife's cooperation by showing her a documentary on the liberation of the camps. He thus literally attempts to open her eyes by showing her other eyes, the eyes of those who have survived mass death (fig. 17).

This sequence displays a striking historical sense. Taken from *Nazi Concentration Camps,* the images viewed in the half-light of the projection room are the very material of history on which the bodies of the actors are reflected, either through their silhouettes being cast on the images of the camps or through the latter being projected onto them. Welles thus renders visible the interaction between documentary and cinema, giving this effect of superimposition a key role in the plot. Indeed, it is through this process that the characters become aware of history and its trauma. Welles did not, however, invent any specifically cinematographic form to conjure up these images. He himself later insisted that nothing in *The Stranger* was his and that he had only made it to show the industry that he could make a conventional Hollywood film.[27] In the most classic and probably also the weakest of his films—as well as his one and only true box-office success—Welles remains straightforwardly pedagogical, more or less taking on the role of prosecutor at the Nuremberg trial. "I'm against that sort of thing in principle," he confided to Peter Bogdanovich, "exploiting real misery, agony, or death for purposes of entertainment. But in that case, I do think that every time you can get the public to look at any footage of a concentration camp, under any pretense at all, it's a step forward. People just don't want to know that those things ever happened."[28]

17 ▶
The Stranger
(ORSON WELLES, 1946). DURING THE PROJECTION OF A FILM WITHIN THE FILM, EDWARD G. ROBINSON SHOWS IMAGES OF THE CAMPS TO LORETTA YOUNG. IN THIS CASE SUPERIMPOSED IMAGES (IMAGES PROJECTED ONTO THE ACTORS, OR THEIR SHADOWS ON THE IMAGES) FUNCTION AS A REVELATION OF HISTORY.

Monsieur Verdoux, or
How Chaplin Puts to Death His Inner Wandering Jew

Charles Chaplin appears to have been the very first filmmaker to conjure up a foreclosed vision of mass death in a postwar movie—as early as 1947, in his *Monsieur Verdoux*. It is not so much the real-life serial killing spree of Henri Désiré Landru that enables Chaplin to invoke extermination as the way in which the most popular figure of the past half-century—the Tramp—is put to death. Taking meticulous notes on his victims, keeping careful accounts of the travel expenses necessary for his crimes, M. Verdoux is a kind of thrifty and diligent bureaucrat of serial death, in whom we might recognize—in whom some *have* recognized—a metaphorical representation of the war criminals who conceived and operated the camps. Verdoux is almost overly adept at murder: distant, cold, not quite monstrous, but worse than that, carrying to its logical extreme the fundamental law governing social interaction in entrepreneurial modernity: "business is business." Pushing the economic logic of a market in liquidation to its limit, Verdoux eliminates his victims in the same manner as mass murder was conducted in Nazi camps: in an orderly fashion, with bureaucratic accounting and a scientific suppression of evidence. His small business is a corpse-manufactory, managed by an accountant and operated by an engineer, just like the extermination camp was conceived, on a mass scale, as a corpse-producing factory. What is certain is that Chaplin—after directing *The Great Dictator* in the context of the rise of Hitler, Nazism, and anti-Semitism—conceived *Monsieur Verdoux*, beginning in November 1942, against the backdrop of the progressively unfolding horror of mass death. The original idea came from Orson Welles, who had suggested that Chaplin play Landru in a film he was going to direct "in almost documentary style."

The plot is set in 1930s France, but death lurks everywhere, as though some catastrophe for the human race had broken the back of the film and reconfigured the corrosive comedy as tragic despair. Chaplin made no secret of the fact that the context for the parable of Verdoux was the aftermath of mass death. "Out of catastrophe come people like [Verdoux]," was one of the aphorisms on which he built the script.[29] At a press conference in New York organized right after the film's release, in April of 1947, he commented that contemporary civilization was "creating so much horror and fear that we are going to grow up a bunch of neurotics."[30] The profound moral of *Monsieur Verdoux* is that modern society turns us all into mass murderers. The Breen Office, one of the American film censorship bureaus, was not so far off when it vehemently reproached Chaplin for M. Verdoux's philosophy, which Breen saw as asserting that it is "ridiculous, in fact, for anyone to be shocked by his actions when they were simply a 'comedy of murders' in comparison with 'the legalized mass murders of war.' "[31]

A very brief shot at the start of the film makes this clear: indeed, it may be seen as the subtle apparition of extermination, its subimage—in the same way as one talks of subtexts in literature—or its palimpsest, since the image is almost entirely covered by another, more ideal, image of Verdoux's "dear roses" in sumptuous bloom. Indeed, if the roses thrive in this delightful garden on the Riviera, it is because the crematorium is burning steadily, ostensibly to turn plant clippings into fertilizer, whereas it is in fact probably, at that very moment—just as the neighbors express their amazement at the lush blooms that are so impeccably maintained and superbly "fertilized," even if one of them confesses (in yet another example of coded subtext) that all this smoke "makes her nauseous"—consuming the remains of one of Verdoux's victims. Here the image appears almost fake, with the smoke in the shot given emphasis by a black, sooty coloration that was added for visual effect by the filmmaker. The scene harkens back to the hallucinatory truth of extermination on a far more massive scale than that practiced by Verdoux, the virtuoso craftsman, a foreclosed form embedded in the shot in a terribly disturbing way (fig. 18).

This form is one of ellipsis, or litote: the smoke from an incinerator signifying much more. The entire film rests on this artistry of shortcuts, both in the elimination of Verdoux's victims and the final death of the assassin himself, as the last shot follows him to the guillotine, which does not need to be shown to convey the elimination of the condemned man (fig. 19). Chaplin offers this formal principle to modern cinema through self-sacrifice, or at least through the sacrifice of the Tramp, who had been until that moment kept inside him, since what has disappeared in this film above all is gags. *Monsieur Verdoux* marks first and foremost the exhaustion of the Tramp's comic genius in the career of his creator. Indeed, about the film's tragic finale, André Bazin remarked, in a characteristically direct manner verging on cruelty, that at that very moment Verdoux resumes his identity as a comedian, Chaplin transforms into the Tramp for a final bit of burlesque. Verdoux is guilty, but it is the Tramp that they are going to guillotine. Upon the film's release, Bazin wrote: "This same road to nowhere, taken in every film by the little fellow with the cane, which some see as the road of the wandering Jew while others prefer to identify it with the road of hope—now we know where it ends. It ends as a

18 ▶
Monsieur Verdoux (CHARLES CHAPLIN, 1947). IN THE DELIGHTFUL TRANQUILITY OF THE SOUTH OF FRANCE, AMID VERDOUX'S ROSE BUSHES, SMOKE BILLOWS FROM THE OVEN THE SERIAL KILLER USES TO INCINERATE HIS VICTIMS. THE SMOKE, THE BLACKNESS OF WHICH LOOKS AS IF IT HAS BEEN ENHANCED, IS THE HALLUCINATORY TRUTH OF MASS EXTERMINATION.

19 ▶ *Monsieur Verdoux* (CHARLES CHAPLIN, 1947). THE MAN BEING LED TO THE GUILLOTINE, IN THE LAST SHOT OF THE FILM, SUDDENLY RESUMES HIS DISTINCTIVE GAIT. VERDOUX IS GUILTY, BUT IT IS THE TRAMP THAT IS GOING TO BE GUILLOTINED.

path across a prison yard in the morning mist, through which we make out the silhouette of a guillotine."[32]

The formal figure in *Monsieur Verdoux* is the ellipsis, and it is in this film that Chaplin excises the Tramp by submitting him to the knife-blade of ellipsis: he cuts him out. It is unquestionably the Tramp's body that Verdoux makes disappear in the pitch-black smoke of despair billowing out of his crematorium.

From the very beginning, the Tramp was a contemporary incarnation of the figure of the wandering Jew, the unloved yet famous vagabond, even if Chaplin himself was not Jewish. What is more, in *The Great Dictator* he was the poor barber from the Jewish ghetto with the same mustache as Hitler. And since the repeated anti-intellectual and anti-Semitic insults hurled at the filmmaker by an ex-mistress at trial in 1943 and 1944, he became the pervert of "loose" and "foreign" morals.[33] For all these reasons, ranging from the glory of the actor-turned-icon to the exposure of the maniac, as well as the political manifesto, putting the Tramp to death was to eliminate the Jew within Chaplin as much as the comedian. The Tramp could simply not survive in a world that had just experienced the extermination of the Jews. As he goes to meet his death and reprises for a brief moment his burlesque gait, Chaplin inserts in his film, in a supreme and foreclosed manner, a little hiccup that gestures to the mass death that had, a few years earlier, disfigured the twentieth century.

"Faces with Black, Rat-Like Eyes"

Samuel Fuller represents another case in point, another resurgence, and the same obsession with finding a form to express the trauma of the death camps. Resnais came to know this death by viewing the archives, and Chaplin felt it in his bones as the world embodiment of the wandering Jew, but neither of them witnessed it directly. Sergeant Fuller, of the *Big Red One*, saw it with his own delirious eyes, and filmed it. At age thirty-one, after Pearl Harbor, Fuller joined the Sixteenth Regiment of the U.S. Army's First Infantry Division. Having landed at Normandy in June of 1944, and started on his way across Europe, he asked his mother to send him a camera, which caught up with him in early 1945, in Czechoslovakia. It was a 16-mm Bell and Howell manual-advance designed for combat filming but would get most of its use recording corpses at the Falkenau camp. Fuller was filming for the first time ever, and it was like a secret and long-repressed prelude to the superb films he was to make ten years later. He filmed the liberation of the camp, at the request of his captain, Kimbald Richmond, and later, on May 9, 1945, the burying of the camp's dead. This film, which is around twenty minutes long, was shot with one overriding constraint in mind: "to avoid cuts in both the filming and the editing."[34] As it was designed to bear witness to a literally unbelievable truth, the long-take format was adopted to avoid any suggestion that the images were being manipulated, and slow pan shots were chosen as the cinematographic form "most respectful of the event being filmed." In the main sequence camp officials are forced by American soldiers to cover the corpses with a sheet, with the elites of the local town looking on, standing side by side on a hilltop. Corpses that had been hastily buried were dug up, examined by coroners, and then dressed by camp officials and local elites—who denied knowing anything about what was going on in their backyard—"so that their exit from this world would have some kind of dignity." Nazis and notables are then seen pushing a cartful of corpses from the camp to the town, under the gaze of Falkenau's inhabitants who, embarrassed and holding their noses, attend their burial in a mass grave.

A few months later, Samuel Fuller was back in the United States, resuming work as a journalist and writer, but he did not have the film processed. He rediscovered it only forty years later, with aching regret: "I would like to have shown my images at Nuremberg." It was in 1988, as the centerpiece of Emil Weiss's documentary *Falkenau, the Impossible,* that Samuel Fuller finally provided his testimony. Screened in front of the filmmaker, who offers commentary on it, the silent footage finally comes into existence through the eyes of its maker and of the public (fig. 20).

These images had profoundly marked Fuller, and it is probably for this reason that he never developed them in the first place: they were stronger on the photographic plate of his mind's eye than on the silver screen. "These faces and these bodies," he said, "they have always been with me. It's an impossible nightmare I'll never forget." In 1985 he confided in Jean Narboni and Noël Simsolo:

> What we saw were faces with black, rat-like eyes, weightless bodies. It is not horror. It is something that does not exist! You do not see that. But at the same time you do see it, and it is so impossible. It is beyond horror. It is the Impossible. We had never had this sense of the Impossible when we were fighting. Omaha Beach was Horror, but not Impossible. I could not watch my own footage: it was that night in Czechoslovakia, the end of the war, the Impossible. Not the Unbelievable, nor the Horrifying, but a simple word that everyone understands—one single word.

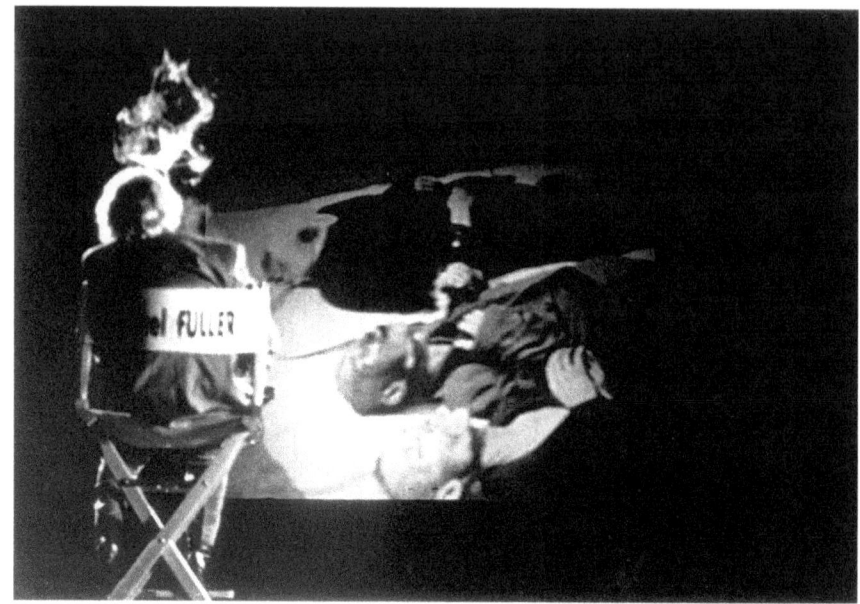

20 ▶
Falkenau, the Impossible
(EMIL WEISS, 1988). SAMUEL FULLER VIEWING THE FOOTAGE HE SHOT IN 1945 IN FALKENAU WITH HIS BELL AND HOWELL 16-MM CAMERA.

The important thing is that the Impossible shocked us, but not in the traditional sense of the word "shock." It was stronger than sickening or horrifying. It hypnotized. And the silence among our soldiers was heavy; for four or five days we remained silent.[35]

Before *The Big Red One* (1980), the film that recounts the story of Samuel Fuller's war (fig. 21) but in which he still did not use images drawn from the 1945 footage, the filmmaker had already subjected—in a series of very striking shots in *Verboten!* (1959)—his fictional characters to the hypnotic vision of the concentration camp. The film recounts the "denazification" of Rothbach, a small town in Germany, carried out by a former American soldier who has married a German woman and settled there after the war. The American, David Brent, must confront a new wave of activity by the *Verwolf*, the Nazi secret organization that attempted to carry on the fight by any means, including destabilizing the occupation authorities. In particular, he must deal with the rebellion of his wife's younger brother, Frantz, aged fifteen, who has been turned into a fanatic by the local small-time Nazi chief. To show Frantz the error of his ways, and convert him to democracy, Helga wants to show her younger brother "evidence of Nazi crimes" and so brings him to the Nuremberg trial, which they attend in the seats reserved for the general public.

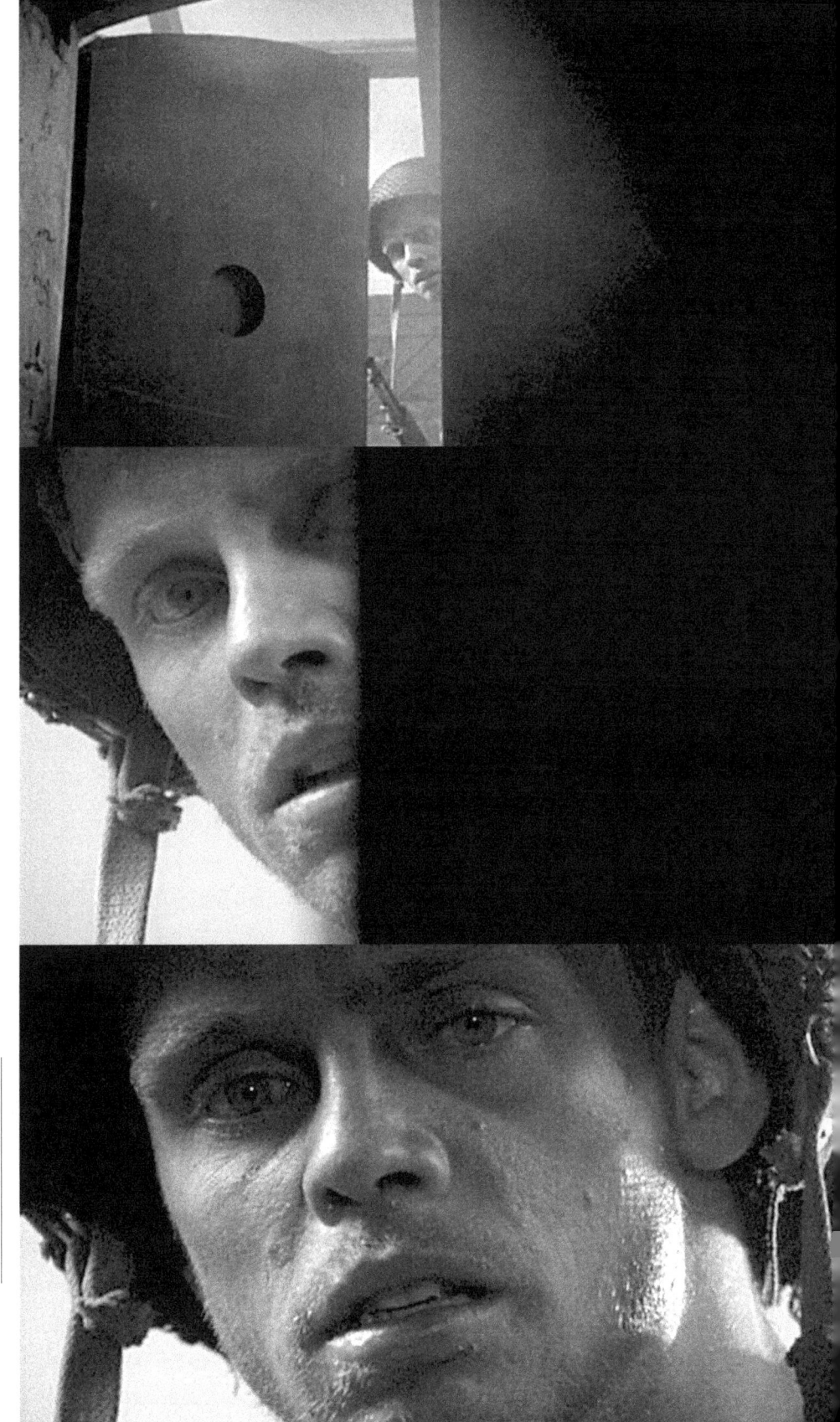

21 ▶
The Big Red One
(SAMUEL FULLER, 1980). "WE MUST LOOK; THE WHOLE WORLD MUST LOOK": THIS IS WHAT THE AMERICAN SOLDIER DISCOVERING THE CREMATORIUM IN FALKENAU SEEMS TO SUGGEST.

Toward the end of *Verboten!*—in a sequence that is edited into a series of electroshocks, a constant of his cinema of extreme violence—Frantz and Helga are sitting in a reconstructed dock of the international tribunal, when Fuller confronts them with images lifted from the American footage of *Nazi Concentration Camps*. The effect is rather crude. The 1959 faces and the 1945 images are not bridged very well, but the constant cuts back and forth from the one to the other—about thirty in total—serve another function: to overwhelm the Hollywood fiction with real images of mass death in order to provoke terror, anxiety, and shame, which can clearly be read on the face of the teenager, who progressively breaks down, while his sister howls: "We must watch.... The whole world must watch."

Fuller thus establishes a conversation, which takes the form of a reverse horror movie: it takes off from terror and works its way toward fulfillment, from the evil toward the good, suggesting that cinema and editing effects are, in large part, visual heirs of the archived death camp stock footage. Violence is the unifying factor of these images but a form of violence for the sake of the good, which turns the fanaticism of totalitarian evil into another kind of fanaticism, that of saving democracy. Fuller thus practices, through his shock cinema, a form of *salvation through excess* (of violence, of pain), trying to retrace the experience of the impossible he had when discovering the camp at Falkenau. The cinematographic evidence comes from the footage, which literally irrupts into the fiction, lunges for its throat, embedding itself in the characters, who then cry out their conversion in order to stop the torture by images of the truth.

The foreclosed form developed by Fuller thus resides entirely in the experience of the violent confrontation of images through which the truth is imprinted on the real, in the same way as the archival footage is superimposed on the fiction. Confronted with the archival footage of gas chambers, the young German's face breaks into a cold sweat. The image of yet another dismembered corpse being thrown into a mass grave is matched with tear-filled eyes. When his sister grabs his face and forces him to watch the ghastly images, he is converted, if not to democracy at least to anti-Nazism. *Verboten!*'s six minutes of terror delineate a pedagogy of concentration camp horror. The critic Luc Moullet wrote in *Cahiers du cinéma*, in June 1960, describing the shocks and double-exposures created by montage as "bolts of fury on which is superimposed the traumatizing archive of the revelation of truth"[36]

Hitchcock and the Indelible Corpse

According to Luc Moullet, this form made Samuel Fuller the alter ego of Alfred Hitchcock. Both filmmakers, as masters in hypnosis, used shock effects to frighten spectators, seize them, astound them and ingrain the filmmaker's ideas as deeply as possible in them. Hitchcock himself also experienced the death camps, at least through images of them filmed in 1945. Although he did not himself visit the sites, from as early as February 1945 he was in charge of supervising the editing of a documentary on Nazi atrocities based on the footage produced by British cameramen, notably at the Bergen-Belsen camp, under the supervision of Sydney Bernstein, chief of the film section of the British Command. Thanks to the British Ministry of Information archives and to the film made in 1985 for Granada TV, *A Painful Reminder*, it has been established that Hitchcock and Bernstein exchanged many letters about this documentary. The director of *The 39 Steps* had indeed taken this editing job to heart, until it was abandoned at the Foreign Office's request in August 1945, by which time the "images of atrocities" were out of step with the policy of the day, which was the "rehabilitation" of Germany.

Bernstein, Hitchcock, and their editor, Peter Tanner, had developed a very precise method for filming the atrocities, which was put in writing and sent as detailed notes to the British Movietone News camera teams, as well as to American technicians who were about to start filming at Dachau. The suggestions dealt with both what to film and how to film it. The aim was, in part, to demonstrate the complicity with the death machine not only of SS camp guards, soldiers, and Wehrmacht officers but also of German industry, and even civilians in neighboring towns, despite their denials. Sylvie Lindeperg mentions that the cameramen were instructed to take down the names of the soldiers and to film the army unit numbers, just as they were encouraged to record the names of manufacturers featured on plaques on the cremation equipment, or to film the reactions of civilians, local elites, and authorities who were made to visit the opened camps. Hitchcock himself asked for shots of rowboat promenades on Lake Ebensee, a nearby seaside resort, to highlight the proximity of peaceful German country villages to mass death. All this, as Bernstein explained in a memo, was to "prove that they had all seen it, and this was the evidence, since I assumed that most people would indeed try to deny that it had happened."

The second set of instructions aimed to define a comprehensive mise-en-scène for the filming of the atrocities, complete with instructions on framing, camera movements, and technical conditions. Camera operators were to give their names orally, as well as the date and location of the shooting, and introduce themselves facing the camera "in such a way that, behind the person who is speaking, the camp, its survivors and its dead are clearly visible." As for the other shots, and notably those of mass burials, Hitchcock suggested slow pans, with the camera moving right and left on a tripod to capture in a single sequence shot the SS guards carrying the dead, the German civilians gathered to attend the ceremony, and the burying of the bodies in the mass grave, amidst piles of other corpses. Peter Tanner, the editor who was selected for the documentary, later explained: "a panoramic shot running from a group of respectable citizens to the dead bodies and corpses assured us that nobody would suggest we had altered the print."[37] This filming technique is quite close to the one the novice filmmaker Samuel Fuller adopted instinctively at Falkenau. It was inscribed in the ontology of the filmic image, at precisely the same time, by André Bazin in his early critical writings: the sequence shot and the pan shot, which, by avoiding any cut in the take, and thus the pitfalls of editing, are the most ethical formal acts of cinema, in that they appear to be a mechanical copy of the real—"The Veil of Veronica," as the mystical Bazin put it—the least manipulated and least manipulable image that can render reality visible, and especially its supreme ordeal—the corpse, the work of death.

These corpses, so rigorously—and strikingly—staged, later became recurring features in Alfred Hitchcock's American feature films. He was, after all, the filmmaker who was most particular about the presence of death on-screen, staging murders and dying bodies in his films in an indelible and almost exaggerated way—through close-ups, long shots, and the "how hard it is to kill" shot. *Strangers on a Train*, *Dial M for Murder*, *Psycho*, many episodes of the *Alfred Hitchcock Presents* series, as well as the later works *The Torn Curtain* (1966), *Frenzy* (1972), and *Family Plot* (1976), are all films in which sadistic murder has become an all-pervasive obsession, which takes up, with increasing urgency and discomfort, more and more of the space and time of the films. In an early episode of the *Alfred Hitchcock Presents* television series, the master of suspense explains: "I have a predilection for dead bodies to conceal. You might not like some of these stories, and you might find them too awful, morbid, or macabre, but I am quite certain that none of them will be dull or boring."

Hitchcock went even further: despite its bawdy and impetuous, or even cynical, feel, *The Trouble with Harry* is entirely devoted to the filming of a corpse. The film strictly follows all the directives sent, ten years earlier, to the cameramen in the death camps who "worked for him." Shot in 1955, the film, in which the cadaveric form imposes itself as key, tells a seemingly benign if morbid story: a little boy playing with guns discovers a dead body under a tree in the countryside, and several of the village residents come to visit him, accusing one another in turns of being the murderer (Jennifer, the boy's mother; Captain Wiles, an inveterate hunter; Miss Gravely, a mythomaniacal spinster; and Sam, a painter obsessed with suffering), while the body is constantly buried and dug up, carried off and hidden away. A virtuoso stylistic exercise, the macabre comedy is a playful transposition, into magnificent New England countryside, of the discovery of mass death by the boys of the American army who made their way from camp to camp in early 1945, as well as the unresolved guilt from it accruing to the entire human race gathered around the insistent corpse. The film reads as yet another illustrated textbook on the mise-en-scène of this central body, a metaphor for a disfigured world and a concrete presence hypnotizing all those who come near (fig. 22).

In *The Trouble with Harry* Hitchcock directly introduces each of the protagonists involved in this game of death, who confront both the dead body and the camera when they first appear onscreen, and uses long pan shots, which confer on the corpse its authenticity, as well as its most trivial ponderous reality. From the opening credits—a long pan shot on a child's drawing which turns out to be that of a dead body with gigantic feet—to the conclusion—a final visit paid by the armed little boy to the dead man as the four "culprits" observe the macabre scene one last time—Hitchcock continuously expresses his fascination for this morbid form and the repulsion, guilt, and awe, as well as aesthetic stimulation and voyeuristic pleasure, it elicits in him. The filmmaker, thus, fully partakes of the hallucinatory resurgence of the foreclosed images of mass death, even if he draws from it the exact opposite life lesson, with playful manipulation being at the heart of the film. Ten years earlier, Hitchcock had watched the images that whimsically return in *The Trouble with Harry*—a great and underappreciated film about the disappearance of God and the tragedy of the human race thus left to its own devices—for hours on end, in a state of near-hypnosis. They were the images of abandoned corpses at the Bergen-Belsen camp, which the filmmaker's formal genius had adopted and transmuted into the McGuffin of a macabre Hollywood comedy.[38]

Man Alone in the Face of the Machine of Death

How can the experience of the depravity of the human race in the death camps be given a cinematographic form? Thus far we have isolated the look-to-camera, which reemerges in fiction films several years after the stares of the survivors of mass death are recorded in the documentary footage of 1945: the mad women and a cornered Ingrid Bergman staring into Roberto Rossellini's camera in *Europa '51*, the essential look that Jean-Luc Godard also pinpointed, in his film book *Histoire(s) du cinema*, when he captions a still photo of Ingrid Bergman's stare with the following words: "forgetting extermination is part of extermination."

Three years after *Europa '51*, toward the end of *Journey to Italy*, which many critics consider the first conscious manifesto of modern cinema, Rossellini consecrated another of these foreclosed forms of the tragedy of the human race. In that film Alexander and Katherine Joyce, a British couple in crisis, played by George Sanders and Ingrid Bergman, go on a (final?) trip to Naples. Nothing much happens—a few minor incidents, several secondary characters—except for the Neapolitan city and its surroundings. Ingrid Bergman is filmed as a sensory surface on which sounds and images are imprinted. The film appears to rest entirely on her reactions: her face in response to the city, to the art at the museum, to the countryside, to the final miracle of San Gennaro, to whatever she is supposed to be looking at. What she sees sometimes overwhelms her with emotion. Rossellini deliberately refuses to invent, to imagine; he refuses fiction. What happens, what occurs, is the real of the world, and this is what constitutes the story: *attesa*, the wait, aimless and circuitous, like taking leave of reason and the senses. It is this latency—"the wait that doesn't wait for anything," the absent, melancholic stare, gently alighting on the dispersed fragments of the real, at the limit of the legible—in which Rossellini is most interested (fig. 23).

A few minutes before the end of the film—as the modern day couple is taking a stroll, through an excavation site, on the slopes of Vesuvius, among the ruins of Pompeii—an ancient couple in full embrace emerges from out of the earth, revealed only gradually by archaeologists dusting it off with brushes

◂ 22
The Trouble with Harry
(ALFRED HITCHCOCK, 1955). THE CHILD WITH THE EVER-PRESENT CORPSE: IN A SINGLE SHOT HITCHCOCK IRONICALLY YET DIRECTLY CAPTURES THE DISCOVERY OF MASS DEATH BY AMERICAN ARMY 'BOYS' AS THEY SWEPT ACROSS EUROPE, FROM THE LANDING BEACHES TO THE DEATH CAMPS, IN 1944 AND 1945.

23 ▶
Journey to Italy
(ROBERTO ROSSELLINI, 1953). INGRID BERGMAN IS ALL GAZE—A GAZE WITH WHICH SHE STROLLS, BETWEEN NAPLES AND VESUVIUS, THROUGH THE STILL VISIBLE, OR SUDDENLY APPARENT, TRACES OF DEATH THAT HAUNT ITALY.

and small brooms. It is an apparition of bones, of porous white material, a plaster cast that gradually, faithfully takes the form of the ancient couple frozen in death by the erupting volcano in the midst of their lovemaking: a cast of the void left in the lava by the bodies of two lovers caught by surprise. At the moment of exhumation, which takes place under the spellbound gaze of the unsettled couple, something happens: a frozen image through which an embrace is captured for all eternity, like an image of death itself—one of these epiphanies of the real whose fullness in Rossellini's work was much admired by André Bazin. The Vesuvius couple is a bared surface, from before the birth of form, a time frozen two thousand years before. Everything in the film comes to a halt, as though succumbing to a sudden drowsiness, in a fictional void. Something senseless has appeared; the unformed has emerged, soon to take form and dramatically disrupt the lives of the characters who have laid eyes upon it. It arises as a challenge. The Pompeii cast takes form by giving meaning to life; something sacred arises in the world from death and nothingness.

Katherine Joyce (Ingrid Bergman) bursts into tears: she has seen the truth—of her story, of herself, of the world, of the human race—the tragedy that freezes everything in sudden death. The epiphany composed by Rossellini proceeds through a poetics of revelation, of apparition, when a dazzling vision alters the destiny of beings and transforms characters. How can this truth befall the film? This is the major question for Rossellini—as well as for modern cinema—which he himself answers in his book *Le Cinéma révélé*: "Cinema confronts people with realities, with things as they are. What fascinates me is the wait until this moment when, from inanimate matter, all of a sudden and mysteriously, consciousness is born."[39] Here Rossellini embodies—in a thoroughly modern way, through the void, in the negative—the neorealist theory of a cinema of epiphany, bringing to the screen aspects of blank reality that escape the passer-by, revealing an unsuspected, strange, autonomous reality that is fixed above, or beneath, the perceptible habitus of men and things.

From the void, from the slumber of the senses and of nature, emerges a form of tragedy—a somnambulant and hallucinatory phenomenon. As Alain Bergala points out, "For the first time on film, a shot that matches eye-line with a visible action does not necessarily mean it was seen, does not produce an organized, intelligible image that has already been filtered through an organizing consciousness; it may just as well trigger a seizure in the face of the unspeakable or the shapeless, which then takes the form of the inexplicable mystery of the world, its tragic sense."[40] It is the sudden emergence of the tragic that the Rossellinian wait enables and that overwhelms the actress, as well as the character, with emotion, as though the camera was just a representation of fate. Referring to this scene in *Journey*, James Agee talked about the "cruel radiation of what is,"[41] as the surfacing of the macabre horror of an always finite and ever impossible love. Maurice Blanchot, writing in *The Space of Literature*, may offer another key to understanding this apparition, as ghostly as it is gaunt, which punctuates Roberto Rossellini's film: "Death is ... truth's elaboration in the world."[42] However, the filmmaker himself should be called back to conclude this reading of his *Journey to Italy*, as a hallucinatory return of death, which, emerging from the extermination camps, has seized and seemingly disfigured the human race, thereby making traditional cinema inadequate to the task of transcribing the trauma of modern man: "man is a very small being who stands under something terribly lethal which dominates him and which will suddenly hit him at the very moment when he finds himself freely in the world, and does not expect anything."[43] Man is now alone in the face of the machine of death.

Modern cinema was born, in the work of all these great filmmakers, for whom Rossellini was the leading light, from images of mass death that worked steadily inside them and resurfaced in other, foreclosed, forms: the look-to-camera, the frozen image, documentary within fiction, the montage of fear, the emergence of macabre figures—all the specifically cinematographic forms that attest to the obsessive presence of a palimpsest of the concentration camp in the cinema of the 1950s. These modern directors are also united around a common refusal to "reconstruct" and directly represent onscreen the system of extermination, the reemergence of which they all nevertheless effected in formal traces in certain of their fiction films. The very presence of these foreclosed forms seems to have denied them the possibility of a direct mise-en-scène of extermination—a sentiment Alain Resnais, for one, expressed with considerable clarity: "It is not possible to achieve any *mise en scene* using these images. It is also impossible to recreate them in fiction. A fiction film on concentration camps sounds like an appalling idea to me. We all need imagination. But it is not incompatible with history, or with a rigorous treatment of archival material. The imagination is not the reconstruction of camps 'as they really were,' but rather the ability to distance oneself from archival footage."[44] Samuel Fuller voiced the same position in response to a journalist's suggestion that he "reconstruct Falkenau in a film." His brief but firm refusal was expressed in ethical terms: "I could never do that. How can you do it better than the Germans?"[45]

At the time, the only "modern" filmmaker to have seriously considered making a fiction film on an extermination camp was the very young François Truffaut, who was obsessed with the Second World War period and confided on several occasions that he had been spellbound by the images of the death camps he saw in 1945, at the age of fourteen. In the early 1960s, in New York, Truffaut met the writer and future Nobel Peace Prize recipient Elie Wiesel, a survivor of Auschwitz, who tried to convince the twenty-eight-year-old filmmaker to make a film on deportation and the extermination camps. Wiesel gave him the galleys of his novel *Day*, in the hopes that Truffaut would adapt it for the screen. The two men later considered making a film entitled *Le Dernier déporté*, which told the story of the very last convoy of French Jews sent to the death camps, on July 31, 1944, and of the return of a survivor. In December 1960 Wiesel wrote to Truffaut: "Now, if you want, or still want, we could start working on your film subject. *Le dernier déporté*: the scores to be settled with the men of the past and the future, the anxieties that overwhelm him, the doubts (did it really happen?), the silences—a subject overflowing with rich possibilities." And Truffaut began to research the subject, reading "many books on the final solution, on Hitler, and on Nuremberg."[46]

He also met with Alexandre Chambon, a survivor of the last convoy, who had by then become the French consul in Rio de Janeiro and had published a memoir on the Buchenwald camp, a horrific testimonial, whose title, *81490*, refers to his camp identification number. In the end Truffaut renounced the project, rejecting the idea of "staging the false reality of horror." He continued: "I couldn't accept having characters weighing 30 kilos played by 60 kilo extras, for here, the physical, visual and bodily reality is too important to be sacrificed."[47] In 1960, faced with the images of mass death, with the hollow and hallucinating eyes of survivors, with the gaunt bodies of these living-dead, with all these figures that, fifteen years later, still haunted Truffaut and his cinema like ghosts, the very idea of mise-en-scène was inconceivable. Aesthetic reconstruction in film had come to be seen as an ethical and visual defect, which modern cinema would consistently dread and denounce.

Mass Death: Neither Reconstruction nor Mise-en-scène

In June 1961, a few months after Truffaut decided not to make *Le Dernier déporté*, having carefully weighed the pros and cons, Jacques Rivette penned a scathing attack in *Cahiers du Cinema* on the first Western film to openly and fully reconstruct a death camp through mise-en-scène: Gillo Pontecorvo's *Kapo*. Rivette's principal objection to this film by the radical Italian filmmaker was not so much its subject matter—a terrifying depiction of a death camp "seen" from the inside—as its form: the attempt, in certain scenes, to reconstruct the horror of an extermination camp, and moreover to do so with a concern for aesthetics, thus turning death into something that could be "beautifully filmed." Rivette calls on his readers to attest to the abject character of a moment in the film: "In *Kapo*, witness the shot in which Emmanuelle Riva commits suicide and throws herself on the electric barbwire: a man who decides, at that precise point, to have the camera track in and tilt up at the dead body—carefully positioning the raised hand in a corner of the final frame—that man deserves nothing but the most profound contempt."[48] A simple camera movement, when it is done to capture mass death, might be better left undone, and a simple piece of cinema criticism might become one of the most renowned denunciations in the history of any art (fig. 24).

This criticism by Rivette would spawn a considerable progeny and end up defining the perspective on cinema, indeed the ethics of cinema, for an entire generation of critics and filmmakers—those who, throughout their adolescence in the early 1960s, read *Cahiers du cinéma* and who were later to identify with another famous text, written to mirror that of Rivette: Serge Daney's take on *Kapo*'s traveling shot, published in the periodical *Trafic* in the fall of 1992. From then on cinema became an ethical domain in which polemics might flare up whenever the issue at stake was filming death in process, and all the more so mass death. Taboo figures, contemptible aestheticization, criminal beauty, forbidden manipulation and montage—these were things that critics, as privileged spectators, would no longer tolerate on the screen and would not hesitate to denounce in writing, as Rivette had done in his June 1961 piece: "there are things which should not be approached but in the throes of fear and trembling—death is one of them. As one is about to film such a mysterious thing, how could one not feel like a fraud? And thus not forbid oneself to cast it in incongruous beauty." Pontecorvo felt no such shame. In *Kapo* he adorned death with this subtle camera movement, which revolted a generation of critics, who were therefore incapable of seeing and supporting the Italian director's following film, censored at the insistence of the French ministry of defense: *The Battle of Algiers*. In this film he denounces—again, through reconstruction—a brutal episode in the Algerian War: the fight to control the *casbah* of Algiers in 1957. A rejection of the obscene character of aesthetic reconstruction of the camp experience was also at the heart

24 ▶
Kapo
(GILLO PONTECORVO, 1960). THE FAMOUS "KAPO TRAVELING SHOT," WHICH IS IN FACT NOT SO MUCH A CAMERA MOVEMENT AS A CLOSE-UP ON EMMANUÈLE RIVA'S HAND AND FACE TWISTED IN AGONY.

of Claude Lanzmann's work in *Shoah*, in which the filmmaker shuns both archival footage and fictional reconstruction, opting for a composition based on the contradictory and multifarious remembrances of witnesses.[49]

In the 1961 essay, entitled "Of Abjection," Rivette condemns the aestheticization of mass death in the name of a cinematographic ethics, an ethics essentially linked to modern cinema, which in the works of Rossellini, Resnais, Fuller, Chaplin, and Hitchcock always opted for foreclosed form rather than reconstruction in its attempts to figure the trauma of the camps. This essay contributed to a debate on the morality of cinema, which had become very intense by the late 1950s and early 1960s. In the March 1959 issue of *Cahiers du cinéma*, Luc Moullet coined the following phrase, in reference to Samuel Fuller (a filmmaker accused of anticommunism, whom Moullet wanted to legitimize on artistic grounds, purely through mise-en-scène): "the question of morality is a question of traveling shots." A few months later, in July, at a roundtable on Resnais' *Hiroshima mon amour*, whose proceedings were published in *Cahiers du cinéma* (July 1959), Jean-Luc Godard, who would be a critic for only another few months, reversed the proposition: "traveling shots are a question of morality."

This inversion was, precisely, the intervention that signaled the denunciation of any and all aestheticization of images originating from the death camps. According to Godard's formula, all cinematic gestures are related, both beforehand and when screened, to the taking of a moral stand. For Moullet morality was a question of form: to use a traveling shot was to disengage from ideology, and none of Fuller's camera movements were anticommunist, even if the dialogues in his films were. For Godard it is both the view on cinema and cinema's view that, together, convey morality. Furthermore, in appropriating and inverting Moullet's proposition, Godard explicitly connected it to the representation of extermination, rejecting all aestheticism in this matter, by referring to Alain Resnais' exemplary approach in *Night and Fog* and then *Hiroshima mon amour*. Jean-Luc Godard is probably one of the first theorists of cinema—since the more technical and juridical considerations that prevailed in 1945 on the screening of films on the liberation of the camps at Nuremberg—to attempt to define and propose a "morality" of representation of the Shoah. What shocks him "is the ease with which scenes of horror are represented, since we are very quickly beyond the realm of the aesthetic." Taking the example of a contemporary American film, Stanley Kramer's *Judgment at Nuremberg*, he denounced the obscene character of the scenes that, in his view, attempt to "aestheticize horror"—either through a montage of archival footage or through nightmarish reconstructions of the camps. He compares this process—the *Kapo* traveling shot would surely have been included if the film had been released in 1959—to "pornographic images."[50]

Against the obscenity of editing archival footage that *spectacularizes* mass death, and in opposition to the realistic and ornamental reconstructions of the camps that aimed to "do it better than the Germans themselves" (in Samuel Fuller's formulation), the French cinema critics who were close to the New Wave—and who were soon to be called "modern," like the cinema they promoted—offered an alternative morality of images, that of a cinema that encompasses within its mise-en-scène a hallucinatory trace of the visual experience of extermination. The historical trauma is thus neither moral lesson nor inappropriate, superfluous, and thus contemptible ornamentation but rather a foreclosed form that, at work within the mise-en-scène, resurfaces through nonreconstructive, nonaestheticizing images of an unrepresentable experience. The point, then, is not to film as aesthetically or as convincingly as possible the experience of life and death in an extermination camp but to salvage history through cinema images, by being in the right place with a redemptive camera. Hence the exemplary career of George Stevens (who was a cameraman for the U.S. Army in 1945, before becoming a prominent classical Hollywood filmmaker), at least as summed up in a few shots in Godard's *Histoire(s) du cinéma*, which show images of Stevens's footage on the liberation of the camps, as well as a few shots from his subsequent films, notably the beautiful scene with Elizabeth Taylor in a row boat on the lake from *A Place in the Sun*. It is the fact of having been at Auschwitz with a camera, in 1945, that allows George Stevens to film sublime images of Elizabeth Taylor's bliss in *A Place in the Sun* ten years later: having "salvaged" history through film, the filmmaker can subsequently produce beautiful images, only not of the camps. Such a redemptive conception of cinema—originating, in Godard's case, in the indignation he felt on seeing, in the late 1950s, the first film reconstructions of camps, as well as in his careful and revelatory reading of some of Walter Benjamin's texts—is the exact antithesis of aestheticization and reconstruction of mass death. It rather pays homage to the *filmic palimpsest*, in which extermination is a subtext, a foreclosed form, in the mise-en-scène of something entirely different, which nonetheless takes on a traumatic coloration and is revealed precisely as a hallucinatory truth suddenly turned image.

"No poetry after Auschwitz," Adorno famously declared, before later retracting his statement. No reconstruction of the camps in cinema. One should add: nor any ornamentalizing of extermination through overly aesthetic ges-

25 ▶
Europa '51
(ROBERTO ROSSELLINI, 1952). ABOUT THIS WOMAN'S FACE—THAT OF IRENE'S, PLAYED BY INGRID BERGMAN—JOSÉ LUIS GUARNER WOULD WRITE: "THIS WOMAN'S FACE CAPTURES A MORAL CONFLICT OF CONSIDERABLE MAGNITUDE, WITH A SIMPLICITY THAT BORDERS ON ABSTRACTION. IN THE END, IT IS THIS FACE THAT GIVES COHERENCE TO THE FILM AS A WHOLE, AS AN UNWAVERING PROGRESSION TO THE COMPLETE ASCETICISM OF A SPIRITUALITY FINALLY ATTAINED OVER THE RAVAGES OF HISTORY."

tures. Five, ten, or fifteen years after Auschwitz, modern cinema was able to bring other responses to these prohibitions. The foreclosed forms that the major directors of the time brought into being—by reanimating them—from the visions that had marked them at the liberation of the camps in 1945, these once forgotten visions found figures and forms that haunted the new cinema, as the hallucinatory return of a disturbing and long obscure real. In other words, since the images of mass death were foreclosed, all these forms that, in the work of modern filmmakers, enabled them to reemerge in spite of everything, represent various attempts at "disclosure." It is this dynamic of foreclosed images and disclosed forms that made a series of films *visible* in the mid-1950s as emblems of the modern in cinema. To this day we still watch *Europa '51, Night and Fog, Journey to Italy, Monsieur Verdoux, Verboten!,* and *The Trouble with Harry*, whereas, if not for texts by Rivette and then Daney, we would have forgotten *Kapo* long ago.[51]

2
FROM VERSAILLES TO THE SILVER SCREEN ▶
SACHA GUITRY, HISTORIAN OF FRANCE

◄ 26
Poster for *Si Versailles m'était conté*
(SACHA GUITRY, 1954).

VERSAILLES IS NOT an ideal film studio, even if the chateau and its adjoining gardens, now a national monument, have made no small effort to attract film crews and their financial resources. Sofia Coppola shot a part of her recent *Marie Antoinette* there, on a big American production budget.[1] But Patrice Leconte, speaking about his *Ridicule*; Bertrand Tavernier, who shot a few sequences of *Let Joy Reign Supreme* there more than three decades ago; and Alain Corneau, who depicted a famous monarch in *All the Mornings of the World* all claim to have terrible memories of their hours, or days, of shooting at Versailles:[2] limited access to the building and gardens, difficulties in obtaining the necessary authorizations, numerous prohibitions, and multiple constraints. All this should hardly come as a surprise: Versailles is a place of power and ceremony, which was not conceived for film. And the conservation work is not exactly photogenic either.

Yet, in addition to the four films mentioned above, many films and film scenes have been shot there—a dozen or so over the past three decades, including Jacques Demy's *Lady Oscar* (1978), Ariane Mnouchkine's *Molière* (1978), two parts of Roberto Enrico and Richard Heffron's *The French Revolution* (marking the bicentennial celebration), Nina Companeez's *L'Allée du roi* (1994), James Ivory's *Jefferson in Paris* (1995), Edouard Molinaro's *Beaumarchais* (1996), and Vera Belmont's *Marquise* (1997). In each the seasoned spectator senses the problem: the few scenes shot there overdo the "on location" effect. Often, a view of the chateau signals Versailles, in the same way American films flash a shot of the Eiffel Tower to indicate Paris. As a result, shooting on location at Versailles often just means shooting the scene that will "sell" Versailles—like a bond to increase the legitimacy of the period piece (a shot of the gardens, or a famous interior, will usually do)—while most of the scenes supposedly set in Versailles are shot elsewhere. This is particularly glaring in *Ridicule*. In 1995 Patrice Leconte's crew shot on location a part of the stairs, a view over the gardens, and then proceeded to shoot the majority of the court sequences at Vaux-le-Vicomte, under more favorable and less constraining conditions. Versailles onscreen is a disappointing subject when treated as such, since the chateau, which can be seen in more than thirty films, appears only so as to meet the minimum contractual requirement of French period pieces.

The essentials are indeed shot elsewhere, in a parallel and mimetic space, which raises an interesting question with regard to the history of representations—that of the artificial reconstruction of the Versailles Chateau. What should Versailles look like when one cannot, or does not want to, shoot there? The challenge is to represent an image of Versailles *in absentia*. That much is clear in *The Man in the Iron Mask*, an implausible American blockbuster shot at Vaux-le-Vicomte in 1998, in which the young king, played by Leonardo DiCaprio, reigns over a kind of toy castle that is both barbaric (torture is committed in basement dungeons) and wondrous (a never-ending party). In Patrice Leconte's *Ridicule* the chateau becomes a maze, divided up into discreet compartments, the right wing housing the court, the left wing the ministries, while circulations, humiliations, and hierarchical spaces (corridors, waiting rooms, receiving rooms, ballrooms, and staterooms) convey a sense of the palace's inner workings, simultaneously bureaucratic, ceremonial, and courtly. This palace reflects the ways of *ancien regime* society, yet 80 percent of it was reconstructed outside Versailles. One is tempted to see it as an ironic and paradoxical turn of history, the disgraced Fouquet's posthumous revenge on Louis XIV: it is Vaux-le-Vicomte that now stands for Versailles. The chateau at Vaux, which remains in private hands, sustains itself in large part on the proceeds from major French and international productions.[3]

This used not to be an issue: the period piece could do without the "evidence" of authentic Versailles shots. The countless early fiction films on French history won their audiences over through other means. It was most probably Renoir, with *La Marseillaise*, who inaugurated the trend of minimal realism, which requires that a scene set in historic Versailles look at least a little like it was shot at the chateau. Indeed, this constitutes one of the core values in Renoir's cinema, which is explicitly based on a sense of authenticity, where the contract with the audience rests on this precise mode of believability.[4] Later on, especially during the 1950s, and the age of so-called French quality (technical quality and quality of the script, more than historical quality), around thirty films contained sequences shot at Versailles: films such as Marcel l'Herbier's *Queen's Necklace* (1945), Fernando Cerchio's *Count of Bragelonne* (1954), Henri Decoin's *The Poison Affair* (1955), Christian-Jaque's *Madame Du Barry* (1954), Jean Delannoy's *Marie-Antoinette* (1955), Jean Dréville's *La Fayette* (1961), and Bernard Borderie's *Angelique and the King* (1965). All of these films, it must be said, have long ago passed into oblivion.

"Doing Versailles": Controversial Project and Historical Polemic

Is representing Versailles onscreen a dead end, then? It most likely would have been, were it not for *the* Versailles film, feverishly shot over two stifling

27 ▶
The Rise of Louis XIV
(ROBERTO ROSSELLINI, 1966). ROBERTO ROSSELLINI DIRECTING A SCENE FROM HIS PERIOD PIECE, A KIND OF ABSOLUTIST COUNTRY-STYLE PICNIC ON THE BANKS OF HISTORY, QUITE FAR FROM THE CHATEAU. (PHOTO © GEORGES LECLERC; COLL. *CAHIERS DU CINÉMA*)

summer months in 1953, under the omnipresent, though already wavering, direction of a great madman named Sacha Guitry. To this day *Si Versailles m'était conté* remains the one and only work that justifies, and justifies fully, charting the path, as a historian of cinematographic forms, that leads from Versailles to the silver screen. This applies to the film itself, as well as to the context in which it was shot, the polemics that surrounded it, and unquestionably also the historical intuitions of its auteur. Sacha Guitry, in his inimitable fashion, seized the challenge of filming Versailles and making a story out of this challenge. He is the only true cineaste of the chateau, even if others have, in the course of shooting scenes at Versailles, raised real historical questions: for instance, Roberto Rossellini about Louis XIV, his power, the court, and the classical sensibility, in his incredibly riveting film, *The Rise of Louis XIV* (1966) (fig. 27), even if it deals only in passing with Versailles; and Jean Renoir on the way to film revolutions. These works involved filming Versailles but never with the scope, magnificence, charisma, and megalomania displayed by Sacha Guitry, who endeavored to become the chronicler of the chateau and France's history both. The filmmaker's identification with Versailles is manifest from the opening credits: opening the great "book of the chateau," written in his own handwriting, indeed in his own words, Guitry himself launches *Si Versailles m'était conté*, a three-hour epic film that was entirely shot in the chateau's halls and gardens (fig. 28).

Shooting began on July 6, 1953, and ended the following September 6. "We gorged ourselves on overtime," Guitry later wrote in an account of his improvisational frenzy, which began a few weeks earlier, in London, from June 5 to June 22. By night he would act in *Ecoutez bien, messieurs*, while by day he wrote the dialogue for his future film, then still entitled *Ce soir à Versailles*. The excitement reached a fever pitch during the shooting, however, with the constant bustle, the intensity of the crew, and the steady flow of movie stars, each of whom had only one scene, or sometimes even just one line, in the film.

In a twelve-episode radio show entitled *Et Versailles vous est conté*, designed to introduce the project to listeners a few weeks prior to the film's theatrical release, Sacha Guitry described the genesis and ambition of his work:

> So, to pretend to be Louis XIV, in principle, was not an option. But to do Versailles, in principle, was. And the opportunity presented itself to me three times. The first was during the German occupation. Glorifying France right under the nose of the occupier, with the support of the ministry of fine arts, nothing could be more tempting. However, the producer who called upon me, a sweet man if ever there was one, was quite unsophisticated. This vastly complicated our exchanges.... The project, as a result, did not go anywhere. The second offer, during that same period, brought together ten producers to do Versailles. The idea, this time, was mine. It was a brilliant idea, but not a good one: one cannot make ten men in the same business agree with one another. The third opportunity—and this time it was the right one—was presented to me last April, one night, on the telephone. Yet it was serious. Producers Gilbert Bokanovski and Clément Duhour jointly asked me to make this film on Versailles, with the consent of the ministry, and the next day we had an agreement.[5]

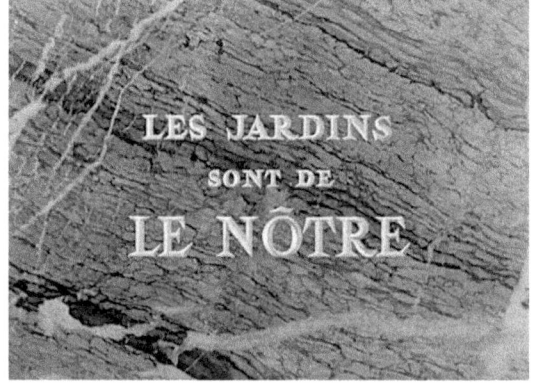

28 ▶
Si Versailles m'était conté
(SACHA GUITRY, 1954). IN THE STYLE OF THE CREDITS IN HIS PREVIOUS FILMS, GUITRY'S OPENING CREDITS HERE (OF HIMSELF, AND OTHERS) FLASH AN IRONIC WINK.

The Versailles Chateau was in need of restoration work. Money was short. The ministry of fine arts, headed by André Cornu, was inclined toward making a film whose proceeds would go to financing the first phase of the restoration.[6] The deal was as follows: private financing for the film, ministerial authorization for complete access to the chateau for shooting, and the making of a film celebrating the glory of Versailles by Sacha Guitry—with the state hoping that the proceeds, to be shared with the producers, would be substantial. In the end all parties held up their end of the bargain, including the paying public. Guitry, who was thrilled at having realized his longtime dream of having Versailles for a set, summoned sufficient energy to pull off the strenuous challenge of making a film with hundreds of actors and extras. Then, the 685,075 moviegoers who turned up for the exclusive Paris release made *Si Versailles m'était conté* into a great box-office success, providing the financial resources for the restoration of one of the symbols of the *grandeur* of France.[7]

The ambitious project also triggered a fair amount of controversy, however. It started on August 3, 1953, as the film was still being shot, when the daily *Combat* published a brief article asserting that the film was being "financed with taxpayer money." Dubbing the film an "official work" and Guitry an "official artist," *Combat* condemned both, because of the license that Guitry was likely to take with French history, because of his scant involvement in the Resistance and general lack of heroism during the war—"to say the least," was the writer's impish rejoinder—and because of the lack of any control by legitimate historical and civic authorities over the script and editing of the film. As early as August 14, Clément Duhour, Sacha Guitry's assistant producer, had to deny any state involvement in the production of the film:

> Quite the opposite, it is my company that is contributing ten million francs to the fund for the restoration of the Versailles château in exchange for the right to shoot, plus an additional 20 percent of the film's international profits. The great work of art, when used as part of a set, is under the constant surveillance of specialized Versailles personnel. Members of the national museum guard service, as well as a team of firefighters, are permanently on set during shooting, and neither the Petit Trianon nor the chateau itself have ever been closed to the public to accommodate the needs of the crew.[8]

But these clarifications were to no avail: *Si Versailles m'était conté* was to retain its reputation as an official film, and rumors of its state funding continued to circulate.

The second polemic was historiographical, having to do with Sacha Guitry's own take on French history. When the film was released, the filmmaker was attacked from both the right and left: the royalists saw a lack of sufficient majesty in this ironic take on Versailles, and the communists criticized the banal story, which lacked the lyrical quality usually conferred on popular uprisings—the French Revolution was thus "reduced to a riot organized by dancing shrews at Trianon."[9] The Duke of Brissac, royalist historian and president of the Friends of Versailles, fired the opening salvo in *Le Figaro*'s literary supplement on December 26, 1953, a few days after the film hit theaters:

> I expected, if not quite propaganda (a term I dislike), at least a principled work that did justice to our history, our art, and Versailles itself. We would have been happy to distribute it as widely as possible beyond our borders, and to invite schoolchildren in France to see it, as well as all our compatriots who rightly feel a sense of pride in their past. But the film is unsuitable, in every sense of the term. The film is embarrassingly and obsessively fixated on the boudoir. It emphasizes the dubious, trades in the scandalous, travesties our kings, those great servants of our country, and even reduces the French Revolution to a masquerade. The filmmaker's personal responsibility is all the more acute in light of reports that both the conservation and architecture departments tried, on several occasions during the shooting, to draw his attention to this deliberate contempt for history. I would venture to respectfully reproach the ministries of education and the fine arts for not containing and orienting a work that they sponsored, their claims to the contrary notwithstanding. And now, what are we to do? Distribute the film, on the basis that any revenue brought into the restoration fund is good for Versailles? As President of the Friends of Versailles, I cannot reconcile myself to this. Let us rather pursue a more constructive approach: the film is made, the ship has been launched. But I insist that such a ship is unworthy of the French flag. It must be brought back to port, put into dry dock, carefully overhauled and, with such careful attention, we would remedy its lapses and redress its excesses.

To grade Guitry's history essay—this was the ambition of the schoolmasters who, as François Truffaut later decried, "were ever so eager to play the prig, moved by their perpetual seriousness and misplaced awe for the idea of grandeur, looking down on the qualities of childhood, such as charm, frivolity, mischievousness, insolence, and fantasy, which Guitry has managed to preserve."[10] Jacques de Lacretelle, member of the Académie française, rallied to the side of the Duke of Brissac, describing passages in the film as "episodes worthy of the Marx Brothers at best."[11] The Countess Pierre de Fleurieu ("let us fight to eradicate the vulgar attitudes and sentiments that threaten to become the image of France"), the Count Antonin de Mun, as well as Jean Dufour and Edouard Van Dievoet, members of the Friends of Versailles, all simultaneously denounced the "false images that insult and vulgarize the symbol of the grandeur of France."[12] *Le Figaro*'s literary supplement maintained the hostile campaign for a considerable time, publishing on February 24, 1954, a series of very unfavorable reviews by historians André Castelot, Adrien Dansette, Charles Kunstler, Louis Hastier, Jules Bertaut, Georges Mongrédien, and Victor Tapié. Erudition was thus mobilized against Guitry's phantasms, to catalogue the errors and anachronisms with which the film is indeed riddled, notably the famous scene where Marie Antoinette, the princess of Lamballe, Lavoisier, André Chénier, and Robespierre are all sitting together around a table chatting, just before the revolution, and the filmmaker has the conversation turn tendentiously toward a most anachronistic subject: their common fate under the blade of the guillotine.[13] The guardians of national grandeur demanded cuts and insertions of new scenes more representative of French glory, such as "those unforgettable episodes which coincided with the victory of 1918: the meeting between Saint-Cyriens and the Alsatian mayors in the Glass Gallery, as well as so many other events that have been recounted in words and pictures, which would do honor to both the truth and national grandeur."[14]

The communists and guardians of the French Revolution, for their part, were no less virulently hostile to *Si Versailles m'était conté*. They decried its contempt for the people's role as agent of history. Georges Sadoul, in the February 12, 1954, issue of *L'Humanité*, accused the film of looking at history through the small end of a telescope: "Mr. Guitry views the men of Versailles from the perspective of their valets. He reduces French history to the secrets of the boudoir, or worse, of the chamber pot. The engine of history is located, in his view, in the lower bowels of great men. Versailles was a brothel. And had Louis XVI not taken several months to consummate his marriage to Marie-Antoinette, the French Revolution would almost certainly not have happened." In Sadoul's view Guitry was nothing but a "decrepit boulevardier, who fancies himself Louis XIV, Madame de Pompadour, Napoleon, Racine, and Moliere all rolled into one"; moreover, his view on the French Revolution was utterly unacceptable: "Mr. Guitry's crass ignorance also betrays a contempt for the French Revolution, whose constructive dimension he would cast into oblivion. For him, 1789 was driven by Voltaire's antipopulist egotism and the hatred of drunken tarts who bared their bosoms against the beauty and virtue of Marie-Antoinette." These accusations, further elaborated three days later in *Les Lettres françaises*, triggered a severe attack against the state's management of the Versailles landmark: "this priceless French treasure is falling apart; the ministers and their undersecretaries, the Maries and the Cornus, would not dream of drawing on state resources to save it but prefer to rely on private initiative. Rather than forgo a few bombers and their napalm payloads, or a kilometer or two of the 1954 version of the Maginot Line, to restore the roofs of Versailles, the governing authorities go, hat in hand, begging to Mr. Rockefeller and M. Sacha Guitry." Sadoul thus pointed out that, for the state, the restoration of Versailles could only proceed through the promotion of a narcissistic filmmaker who confused France with his personal interests: "While 'saving Versailles' for his own promotion, Sacha Guitry did not renounce his share of the profits. He was given the palace as a studio, installed canvas sets in disregard of security issues, used troops as free extras, and proclaimed to anyone who would listen that he had agreed to sacrifice his time and energy for France's glory. Yet he did accept a few million, as compensation or royalties."[15]

Finally, on March 18, 1954, in *L'éducation nationale*, Henri Michel—a great authority among historians of the Resistance, and the president of the Committee for the History of the Second World War (*Comité pour l'histoire de la Deuxième Guerre mondiale*)—refused, in the name of the history teaching profession, to confer the designation of "historian," or even "historiographer," of Versailles on Sacha Guitry:

> The conception of history deployed in this film is both ridiculous and puerile. The first major critique that must be raised against the film is that it clearly demonstrates the incapacity of the medium to seize something more than the anecdotal or the stereotypical, and that the author's imagination has led him to casually reverse the course of history, make up entire dialogues, bring characters together who have never met, etc. In short, once again, commercial success crowns a work whose impact on the mind can only be harmful, since it promotes error. What are we left with after three hours? Not much, as the advertising poster says: "a three-century long history, a three-hour long film, 90 stars"—in other words, a spectacular show which turns the Versailles staircase into a music-hall set. Above all, we are left with Sacha Guitry, always present, as a narrator when not as an actor, pontificating, all the more grave in his tone that he is empty of thought. If Louis XIV regretted not having been a writer (*sic*), it is no doubt because he felt that some day Sacha Guitry would come along. Alas for us.

Several months earlier, the polemic had made the rounds of officialdom when, on January 16, Deputy Speaker of the National Assembly Gaston Palewski—who considered that "the film in no way fulfills its role as an instrument of national commemoration and propaganda"—submitted a motion in the National Assembly requesting that the secretary of state for fine arts provide clarification on "the extent of the state's financial participation in the affair" and on "the guarantees provided in exchange for this participation as regards artistic and technical questions, as well as the level of historical faithfulness required to ensure the film's release both in France and abroad."[16] At the same time, the General de Bénouville, deputy for Ille-et-Vilaine, sent a written inquiry to the secretary of state for fine arts, asking how "the ministry could possibly authorize the film's export, given the fact that it ridicules our history," and what measures might be taken to remove or replace the passages that do particular violence to the truth.[17]

André Cornu was summoned to explain the situation before the National Assembly on March 19, 1954. He denied that the state had made any financial investment in the film's production and reminded the representatives that the only contractual arrangement that had been made relating to *Si Versailles m'était conté* was an authorization to shoot on location at the chateau in exchange for a percentage of the box-office proceeds, which were to be spent on the renovation of the buildings. He specified the amount that had been thereby raised for the restoration of Versailles—fifty-six million francs—and refused to comment on the "historical polemic" triggered by the film, as part of the "age-old feud between art and truth."[18] In André Cornu's view *Si Versailles m'était conté* was not an official film, insofar as the state, while it helped to make it possible, did not contribute any subsidy of any kind, nor did it exercise any oversight over its historiographical decisions—it was a Sacha Guitry film. He then reluctantly consented to venture an interpretation: "this film should not be considered as a representation of our history, but rather as a tale, as indicated by the very title chosen by the filmmaker." Cornu was particularly keen to remind the deputies of the state's responsibilities as regarded the restoration of national heritage: "let us please see this project in the broader context of initiatives that have been undertaken to restore the Versailles Chateau, a project for which two billion have been committed over the past two years." Palewski was quick to reply, with the backing of both right- and far-left-wing deputies: "the government was both mistaken and wrong to grant support for this film. Mistaken, since the historical value of the film is nil. Wrong, since the moral value of this affair is low. Eroticism and the glorification of banal human depravity is all this film can offer French families and foreign audiences. The case that you have pleaded, Mr. State Secretary, is that money has no odor. But France is not an accomplice of Sacha Guitry."[19]

Guitry and the Revenge of History

Although Sacha Guitry himself enjoyed the public success of the film—which he saw as his own revenge on history, an acquittal, handed down by audiences, in the case brought against him in the court of public opinion by a number of figures of the Resistance—he was deeply affected by these polemics, especially given the fact that he had never attained any real intellectual or artistic recognition. But he did not personally respond to the attacks until a few weeks later, in a preface to the complete edition of the script of *Si Versailles m'était conté*:

> In the "literary" branch office of some obscure daily, I was literally assaulted by people whose opinions of my work it never occurred to me to ask—which thus spared me from having to read their attacks. These were aimed at the anachronisms. Indeed, they were simply nitpicking. The following week, they were at it again. Clearly, they wanted to spoil my pleasure. But one should never take too seriously people who take themselves seriously. Am I a historian myself? Yes. But in the way a painter might be. I am a historian in the way Louis David was when he painted his magnificent painting entitled *The Coronation of Napoleon*, which features, right at the center of it, Mrs. Laetitia—whereas the Emperor's mother was notoriously in Rome on that day. Her absence is a fact—and it even qualifies as a historical fact. Did she not indeed disapprove of her son's coronation of Empress Josephine on that day? As for me, I cannot say. And David, well aware of it, might very well have thought: the issue is neither here nor there, this is not the subject of the painting. I am not painting the mother's presence or absence at the Emperor's coronation—and I would rather her absence did not distract the viewer's attention. Her presence is normal, logical—and I do not wish to be considered, a hundred years from now, as an inattentive painter.... This leads me, quite naturally, to the formal declaration of Paul-Louis Courier, who set things right on the issue: "Plutarch could not care less about facts and only took what suited him from among them, only caring about being seen as a skillful writer. He could have had Pompey win the Battle of Pharsalus if it helped him round out a sentence ever so slightly. And he was right. All the silliness we call history is worthless unless it is tastefully adorned." Versailles contains an astounding error that nobody has pointed out to me yet. It is in the final shot of the film—a shot that definitively ensured its success.

In that moving shot of French history, on this majestic flight of stairs, stand both Louis XIV and Clemenceau—who, if memory serves, never met.[20]

This long reply is more serious than it appears—after all, people who do not take themselves seriously should be taken seriously. One of the advertisements published in the press at the end of January 1954, as the film was playing at the Marignan Theatre, read: "Yet another historical inaccuracy: Louis XIV triumphs at Marignan!" Guitry claims full responsibility for his historical inaccuracies. Indeed, as he himself said, they precisely reveal his manner of being a historian: as a painter of history, and as the dunce of Versailles history. This attitude, which was entirely conscious, even intentional, was a way to offer, through Versailles and its chronicle, a cinematographic form of history.

It thus warrants a closer look, to try to consider *Si Versailles m'était conté* not as a series of gems, anachronisms, and errors but rather to attempt to think of the gems, anachronisms, and errors that adorn the film as forming a coherent and revealing discourse. This was indeed the project of "Sacha Guitry, historian of France."[21] The interpretative challenge had, it must be said, already been taken up by a few independent critics at the time of the film's release in 1954. It was taken up, however, by cinema critics, not historians—for this constellation of gems, anachronisms, and errors was understood by a minority of fervent supporters of Guitry the filmmaker, as the aesthetic manifestation of his peculiar talent as an auteur. In articles published in *Cahiers du cinéma*, François Truffaut and then Jacques Audiberti attempted to defend *Si Versailles m'était conté* not as a history book but as an auteur film, in which Guitry's personality shines through with all his wit, sarcasm, and, above all, the supreme elegance of his nonchalance. Its special way of punning on history, of taking liberties with the national pomp and glory, of banishing all solemnity, appeared to Truffaut as the absolute opposite of the "republican airs" and of the "parade of overdressed maids" that usually stand for historical reconstruction in French films.[22] He saw Guitry's attempt at incarnating the country's history all by himself, through his protean body and virtuoso punning, and to turn it into a chronicle that is at once urbane, moving, and original but whose principal quality is elegance, a quasi-instinctive style that inhabits all Sacha Guitry characters. There was also the complete rejection of historical reconstruction, which struck Jacques Audiberti. The writer and critic supported the film, which he liked "for its foul language and bare bodies," in the name of an ahistorical vision of history: "he manages, in my view, through wit, taste, documents and a noble desire, to signify the past while not, even for a second,

29 ▶
Les Perles de la couronne
(SACHA GUITRY, CHRISTIAN-JAQUE, 1937). SACHA GUITRY AS FRANÇOIS I.

bringing us into it."[23] There is a kind of distanciation in Guitry, which turns *Si Versailles m'était conté* into both a piece of entertainment and a narrative *based on* the history of France. In 1977 Truffaut reaffirmed, in more polemical tones, his attack on the "puritanical intellectuals of the left bank": "Our solemn pedants have the nerve to declare, all by themselves and without further ado, what is 'cultural' and what is not. They are the ones who invented the mutually exclusive notions of 'reflexive products' and 'entertainment products,' as though the three hundred novels of Simenon, the five hundred songs of Charles Trénet, and the plays and films of Sacha Guitry did not stand precisely as demonstrations that truly entertaining works also offer food for thought."[24]

A Certain Vision of History

What gives us food for thought while also entertaining us is precisely a certain vision of history, a vision that informs decisions regarding mise-en-scène and the direction of actors, and that manages to turn history into a particular cinematographic form. The first element of this mise en forme of history is time. The three hours of *Si Versailles m'était conté* consist, literally, of the passing of a certain amount of time. And to look at this time, to organize it, is to film history. Sacha Guitry's political stance has triggered many questions.[25] His

30 ▶
Si Versailles m'était conté
(SACHA GUITRY, 1954).
SACHA GUITRY AS
LOUIS XIV.

principal position in the film was not to take any, even at moments of history when it was demanded of him. Of course, Guitry was a man of the *ancien régime*[26]—he felt most comfortable in royal regalia and in the company of princes, steeped in the witticisms of aristocratic culture. Guitry was, in this respect, a direct descendant of the seventeenth-century royal historiographers—Perrault, Racine, Félibien—and he reprises, in this "film-lecture" on the history of Versailles, the principle of the guided tour wholly dedicated to the glory of the king, as Le Nôtre had illustrated through his gardens, Le Brun through the royal painting collections, and Félibien through the portraits of the king. There was something in the royal function, in the way it was commented on and elevated, a sense of pomp and decorum, not to say of mise-en-scène, which undoubtedly appealed to Guitry. He was, after all, the great, narcissistic, and obsessive organizer of rituals of his own presence on the stage and screen—a kind of spoken and gestural superabundance. Yet Sacha Guitry, aside from this ceremonial form of power, appears comfortable with any regime. He, himself, felt very much at ease interpreting kings: Louis XI in *Si Paris nous était conté*, François I in *Les Perles de la couronne*, Louis XIV in *Si Versailles m'était conté*, Louis XV in *Remontons les Champs-Elysées*. But he also played Napoleon several times (Napoleon I in *Le Destin fabuleux de Désirée Clary*, Napoleon III in *Les Perles de la couronne* and in *Remontons les Champs-Elysées*) (figs. 29–34).

31–34 ▶
Remontons les Champs-Elysées (SACHA GUITRY, 1938). NO FEWER THAN THREE SOVEREIGNS IN A SINGLE FILM: GUITRY AS LOUIS XV (SMILING, THEN IN AGONY), AS NAPOLEON I (SPEECHIFYING), AND AS NAPOLEON III (DANCING). THE ACTOR DISPLAYED AN IMMODERATE PENCHANT FOR PERSONIFYING FRANCE.

In fact, Guitry's conception of history is as a form of successive engenderings: the various moments reproduce one another while generating novelty through the reproduction process itself. It is not a *grand* history, insofar as everything is seen through the lens of historical love affairs, or tales of "bastard children," since each historical entity, such as France for instance, results from the secret gestation of historical moments. In *Remontons les Champs-Elysées*, which was shot at the end of 1937, Guitry narrates the wedding between Jean-Louis, an illegitimate grandchild of Louis XV, and an illegitimate daughter of Napoleon, born in St. Helena. But Jean-Louis himself is the offspring of a certain Ludovic (the king's bastard son) and an illegitimate daughter that Marat had with a horrible *tricoteuse* of the Terror. This politically fanciful dynasty leads to Guitry himself, who, in the film, narrates French history to his pupils—the historian-narrator-filmmaker becoming, through this imaginary lineage, the offspring of some unorthodox historical admixture, made of a bit of monarchy, a bit of Terror, and a bit of Napoleonic fervor.

The poster for *Diable boiteux* reveals a similar conception of historical time. The poster features graffiti on a wall that reads: "long live the king!" crossed out, "long live the Republic!" also crossed out, "long live the Emperor!" again crossed out, and, below, "long live France!" in block letters, of course, not crossed out. The chateau at Versailles, because of its long succession of political ceremonies, which are also seductions and love rituals embedded in historical continuity, was for Guitry the archetypal location for this conception of time, that of a national *continuum* made of the birthing of the successive stories that compose the nation. Versailles, more than any other place, is imbued with the temporality that turns Guitry into a historian of French lineage. The filmmaker is quick to indulge in his taste for perverted genealogies and for the names of families whose misdeeds and depravity he ceaselessly recounts. *Si Versailles m'était conté* records these interlinked circles of time—linked to Versailles and linked at Versailles—circles that Guitry makes vicious by lacing them with dirty stories and chronicles of royal love rituals. Through its historical caprice the film is constantly searching for a kind of "chronological ubiquity." The aim is, quite literally, to be everywhere in time at once. All the discrete frames of space-time thus offer sketches of meaning that, in their juxtaposition, recompose a complex and problematic unity: French identity. The historical discourse of *Si Versailles m'était conté* resides in this principle, both modern and exciting, of temporal *collage* that generates a synthetic and complex national identity.

Moreover, for Guitry, Versailles was also a body. Not only did he conceive of his project as the ultimate gallery of the faces of his time, with an impressive cast, drawing on celebrated as well as lesser known actors of early 1950s international cinema, who together form a kind of tremendous multiheaded and many-gestured cinematographic body, as though the hydra of the box office was reflected through Guitry's casting in the historical hydra that is Versailles. But he also offers an anthropomorphic, or at least corporeal, vision of French history. This vision is narcissistic, auteurist, and megalomaniacal, since the entire history of the chateau passes through the representation of the body of Guitry himself, a body that is staged, from the beginning to the end of the film, in the various roles played by the filmmaker, as well as through his presence, spoken or embodied, at all the key moments of the work, at each narrative turning point. The identification of Guitry with the personages that embody France (Louis XIV, Louis-Philippe) is essential: he derives from it the quasi-magical power to resurrect, through his voice and his presence, a "certain idea of France." But this incarnation, which constitutes the central project in *Si Versailles m'était conté*, is at the same time infinitely somber, melancholic, sickly, even morbid. Guitry's body, he made no secret of it, was a sick body, run down, that of an old man who was to pass away less than four years later,[27] embodying and encapsulating in a direct manner the physical state of the Versailles building—the chateau was also ill, run down, destined for partial dilapidation if intensive restoration work was not quickly undertaken. Thus, the body of Guitry as an aging Louis XIV expresses the project of the film itself: to save Versailles, whose prestige no longer serves to conceal its decrepitude.

The appearance of bodies in the film—which are simply shown frontally, according to a minimalist theatrical technique—further contributes to the sense of frailty, weakness, and sometimes defeat of bodies caught in history. The end of Louis XIV, especially, is lugubrious, captured in an image of greenish tones. "I am dying alone, almost abandoned," whispers the old man as Louis XIV, aware of his physical degeneration ("Quick, my wig," he whispers, "and please don't let the child see me. He doesn't need to see me this way. It is not a pleasant sight..."). The body is then opened up: "next came the autopsy, attended by Maréchal de Montesquiou, the dukes of Moretemart, of Villoroy and of La Rochefoucault, and Prince Charles of Lorraine. Horrible pieces—the King of France was reduced to pieces." The body is finally dispersed, fragmented: "His entrails were carried to Notre-Dame de Paris.... His heart was committed to the Jesuits' convent by the Duke of Sully. As for his body, it was carried to Saint-Denis." Guitry, who attends each of the stages of this decomposition as Louis XIV, first in the flesh, then as a voice, gives his own body to history, going so far as to play, he confides, the specter, the ghost, resulting from such physical degeneration:

> One day as I was alone in the King's bedroom, an extraordinary little event happened. On that day, we were shooting the last moments of Louis XIV in the Bull's Eye Room. They were installing the lights and as I was feeling a little tired, I went to sit in the sumptuous and moving bedroom where the Sun King passed away. I was sitting in a very large armchair, dressed as Louis the XIV himself, in full regalia, with my wig on, my eyes closed, haggard, in the dark. A door opened, and a museum attendant leading a group of about thirty tourists announced: "We are now entering the room in which Louis XIV died. . . ." There followed a moment of silence; and I looked up to see thirty dumfounded people staring at me.

The chateau at Versailles, then, is the only character capable of competing with this historical and cinematographic demiurge. It is Guitry's alter ego, and it, too, is filmed like a body, not so much in all its glory as in all its frailty, its fragmentation and variety. All the rooms are visited in the course of the film, with an emphasis on the spaces of relative intimacy of the royal body (the king's commode and chamber, the Diane Drawing-Room, Louis XV's work space) and on those of courtly life (the *Salon de l'oeil-de-Boeuf*). The spaces of ceremonial pomp are relatively somewhat sacrificed (the Hall of Mirrors, the *Galerie des Batailles*), but all these spaces find a place in the architecture specific to the film, as if to show, through them, the organs of an immense body, in which French history takes place and is incarnated.

The Spectacle of Court Society

Si Versailles m'était conté ends on a long sequence, still famous, in which all the characters, of all the periods and styles, walk together down the One-Hundred-Step Staircase, while the French flag gradually rises on the screen: "The hundred steps of the grand stair, coats of arms crowning its top. The music breaks out. At the very top appears Louis XIV, first, and in no particular order, six or seven hundred lords, soldiers, kings, queens, clerics, minions, ministers, magistrates, and then Jacobins, sans-culottes, and then the Emperor Napoleon and his grenadiers, and then Clemenceau leading a regiment of veterans of the Great War, and then flags of all countries, and then finally ours which rises up to the heavens."

The king is dead—Guitry embodied him through his own sickly decomposition, through the lugubrious and morbid atmosphere surrounding his personal appearance. But here comes the great body of France, spectral and majestic, carried by the national community united in its descent down the great marble stair. This doubling, this substitution of the king's body, humble and mortal in his glory, for a symbolic body, whose durability and reconstituted appearance embody the continuity of French history, had probably never been better expressed cinematically, nor better filmed. Indeed, by filming this head-on, Sacha Guitry was acting as a historian, "gropingly," so to speak, but with considerable intuition, since it was at the very same time that Ernst Kantorowicz and then Ralph Giesey elaborated the theory of the "king's two bodies" in French history (fig. 35).[28]

Versailles, finally, is a language—a classical French language haunted by Sacha Guitry's highly particular style, writing, and diction, whose lingual omnipresence appears as the principal element of the film. Fully 40 percent of *Si Versailles m'était conté* is "spoken" by the voice of Guitry, and the film is written entirely by the hand of the dramatist, who modeled it on the "film-lecture," ever-present in his work. As early as 1915 Guitry had shot *Ceux de chez nous*, featuring Rodin, Rostand, Monet, Anatole France, Degas, Renoir, Sarah Bernardt, and many others as a gallery of artists and writers become silent silhouettes, while the voice of the auteur, reading a written text, offered commentary on the work of each. This parallel structure, in which the image is left to the cinema figures and the sound is captured by Guitry, was used constantly in *Si Versailles m'était conté*—a highly sophisticated yet very simple narrative mode, in which the story is told to the audience directly by the narrator's voice while it is acted and embodied by what we might call figurines. This narrative mode is not just an ingenious technique of embellishment; it directly informs the film's substance: a stroll through the time of history, a tour of the bodies of history, guided in a lively manner, with sudden shifts in tone, ellipses, parallels, resurgences, but where the central presence, the constant link, the subject matter being filmed, is given by the language itself. The chateau at Versailles thus becomes a book, and French history a language that is written and spoken by Guitry as "a historian in the text."

This is the metaphor with which the film begins and ends: Guitry as himself, in contemporary dress, opens the film by opening the "great book" of Versailles and starting to read (fig. 36). The film is thus presented to all its spectator-listeners as a representation of the pages of French history, which Guitry is leafing through, naming, and commenting on—the singular trait of a

35 ▶
Si Versailles m'était conté (SACHA GUITRY, 1954). THE FILM'S CLOSING SCENE: FRANCE DESCENDING THE HUNDRED STEPS OF HISTORY. BOURVIL, THE CHATEAU'S KEEPER, DREAMS OUT LOUD: "AND SO WHAT IF *I* FANCY THEM ALL DESCENDING THE MOST BEAUTIFUL GRAND STAIR IN THE WORLD!" FROM THE KING'S MUSKETEERS TO THE POILUS OF THE GREAT WAR, FROM THE COURTIERS TO THE SANS-CULOTTES AND THE SOLDIERS OF THE GRANDE ARMÉE, FRANCE DESCENDS, AS ONE SINGLE BODY, UNDER THE PROTECTION OF THE TRICOLOR FLAG, AN EMBODIMENT OF THE ENTIRE NATION.

36 ▶
Si Versailles m'était conté (SACHA GUITRY, 1954). GUITRY'S HANDS OPEN THE GREAT BOOK OF VERSAILLES: THE FILM PENETRATES THE BOOK, THE CAMERA TRAVELS WITHIN THE TEXT, AND HISTORY IS EMBODIED. GUITRY "READS" HIS FILM AS MUCH AS HE SHOWS IT.

national culture where the book tells the truth of political power. Guitry puts this representation of history as an open book, as an affirmation of the French language, into the mouth of Louis XIV, played by the filmmaker, at the peak of his glory, vehemently addressing his minister Colbert:

> The more it will have cost, my beautiful chateau, the more it will yield. And I am quite convinced that in a hundred years, two hundred years, three hundred years, the one who rules France will see to it that it is protected from the assaults of time, since it will stand as a testimony to my country's *grandeur*. It will read as an imperishable book that tells the story of the immortal heroes of the most beautiful country on earth. Indeed it is a book—it is my own book—for me who has, alas, no talent for writing. And I want my chateau to be modern. I do not want this old furniture I find boring. Do you like these buffets, these dark-wood wardrobes? I don't. And for many reasons. I find them to be full of grammatical mistakes.

There is, indeed, a cinematographic form of history present in Guitry's film, governed by a few master associations: Versailles here is simultaneously time, a body, and a language—that is, a representation of French history. There was, thus, no better subject than Versailles to enter French history into representation. Guitry fancied himself the spectacle of the chateau and of its successive inhabitants, which amounts to filming all at once the chateau-as-power, the chateau-as-city, and the chateau-as-society. He fully succeeds in this endeavor: the kings are always visible to all; the monument is visited in its various aspects, as though they were the neighborhoods of a multifaceted city; and the courtesans—who encompass all social classes, in the end, from aristocrats to intellectuals, from parvenus to the humble folk who tend the gardens, gates, and offices—constitute a gallery that quickly comes to appear as a form of France in motion, even if it maintains the old-fashioned appearance that endears it to the filmmaker.

The various elements of this representation of history are linked by a series of minutely ordered ceremonies and rituals that Guitry chronicles from a perspective both biting and caustic but also respectful, to the point that *Si Versailles m'était conté* may be compared to a painting, both faithful and inventive, of the civilizational process that gradually erected the chateau and its court into a model of French civility. In Guitry's film Versailles is thus a place of submission—of the courtesans to the absolute power of the king; of the actors to the desires, or even whims, of the director; and of cinema itself, which has become his thing, absolutely domesticated. But it is also a place of revelation, since, from the monarch to the lowliest of servants, from the princes to the lesser nobility, each can and must learn from it what French civilization is. This theater of history is in many respects close kin of the court society described by Norbert Elias in his now classic book. No matter that Guitry has not read it, could not possibly have read it: he filmed, at Versailles, his very own court society.[29]

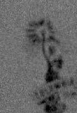

3

"ME? UH, NOTHING!" ▶
THE FRENCH NEW WAVE, POLITICS, AND HISTORY

◀ 37
Poster for *Band of Outsiders*
(JEAN-LUC GODARD, 1964).

THE FRENCH NEW WAVE has sometimes been labeled right-wing, even fascist, given the personal ties connecting François Truffaut to the collaborationist and anti-Semitic writer Lucien Rebatet, and Claude Chabrol to the leader of the National Front, Jean-Marie Le Pen. Neither Truffaut nor Chabrol, more recently, has ever made a secret of these ties.[1] These friendships did not constitute a politics for them but rather a provocation. To shock the sensibilities of self-righteous leftists, to scandalize—this was what the Young Turks of the French New Wave were going for. In the virulent polemics of the time, *Cahiers du Cinéma*, the principal organ in which the New Wave's conception of cinema was articulated, was called a "fascist publication,"[2] and the films themselves were charged with exuding a spirit of "right-wing anarchism."[3] The exuberance of the polemical context would suggest that these attacks were largely unfounded, however, or at least overblown.

Yet they warrant closer attention since, returned to the intellectual and cultural context of the 1950s and 1960s, the French New Wave and the critical movement that gave rise to it had a strong political impact, triggering fierce disputes: Was it just a kind of "hussar" dandyism? Or the cinematic arm of Gaullism, which had just come to power? Or was it a provocative celebration of youth broken free of moral constraints and traditional values? The ever-present backdrop to these often heated exchanges, as well as the texts and films that were soon to become famous, was the Algerian War, contemporaneous with the ebb and flow of the French New Wave. Often keen to remove themselves from this context, even if this refusal of commitment was in itself a politics of sorts, the Young Turks were gradually forced to confront reality, and they opted, in diverse ways, for an interventionist cinema, or at least a cinema that was sensitive and reactive to the signs of the times. That the New Wave ignored the Algerian War is a tenacious myth. Quite the contrary, in responding to a history of the present that included soldiers, as well as the subjects and spectators of cinema, it got involved in a conflict that it marked through its manifestos, as well as its original and intimate gaze. In the end it is clear that this intellectual movement, which had an unquestionably rightward orientation, swerved to the left when confronted with the realities of its times, without ever disavowing, to either the right or the left, that which gave it its formal specificity: an inimitable style.

Hussar Thought

Cinephilia and cinema criticism were the intellectual training grounds of the New Wave. Culturally speaking, traditional academicism, on the one hand, and militant progressivism, on the other, were equally repulsive to them. Politically, both the traditional right and communist left felt equally alien. It was in movie houses, watching the many masterpieces of the immediate postwar period, from Hollywood to neorealist, that these young men were schooled in a dandy, offbeat, provocative, and Americanophile (counter)culture, which quickly came to define the identity of these critics who, at age twenty, took over the new cinema journals that had been founded in the early 1950s.

In *La Gazette du cinema*, and later in *Les Cahiers du cinéma* and *Arts*, Alexandre Astruc, Eric Rohmer, Jacques Rivette, Jean Douchet, François Truffaut, Jean-Luc Godard, and Claude Chabrol articulated their sweeping defense of film and its auteurs in the name of a radical conception of cinema: an auteur's thought takes cinematographic shape through mise-en-scène, and this "thought that takes form / form that thinks"—according to Jean-Luc Godard's formula[4]—constitutes the film's beauty. Modern cinema criticism revolved around this idea, which had the advantage of rejecting the old form/content dichotomy and of offering an original synthesis: the content of a film *is* its form. Luc Moullet and Jean-Luc Godard, each in his own way, famously summed up this view, a few years later, as we have already seen in chapter 1: "the question of morality is a question of traveling shots," in Moullet's formulation of March 1959; "traveling shots are a question of morality," in Godard's inversion of July 1959.[5] In other words a film's moral position (its content, its message, its politics) is entirely contained within the cinematographic form the auteur chooses to employ (traveling shots, as well as framing angles, camera movements, montage, etc.) (fig. 38). Of course, to say so out loud, at the time, constituted a provocation, bad taste, utter nonsense or an ill-considered subversion of recognized values. Critical opinion (as represented by the majority of newspapers, journals, and cine-clubs) looked down on most American films on account of their manifestly superficial content—stories of murder, love, and suspense—or worse, their disengagement from politics. This same legitimate critical establishment held French, Italian, and Soviet films in the highest esteem (especially communist critics, in the latter case, of course), precisely because they had "something to say" and made this clear through their lofty subjects, explicit political commitments, and clear messages.

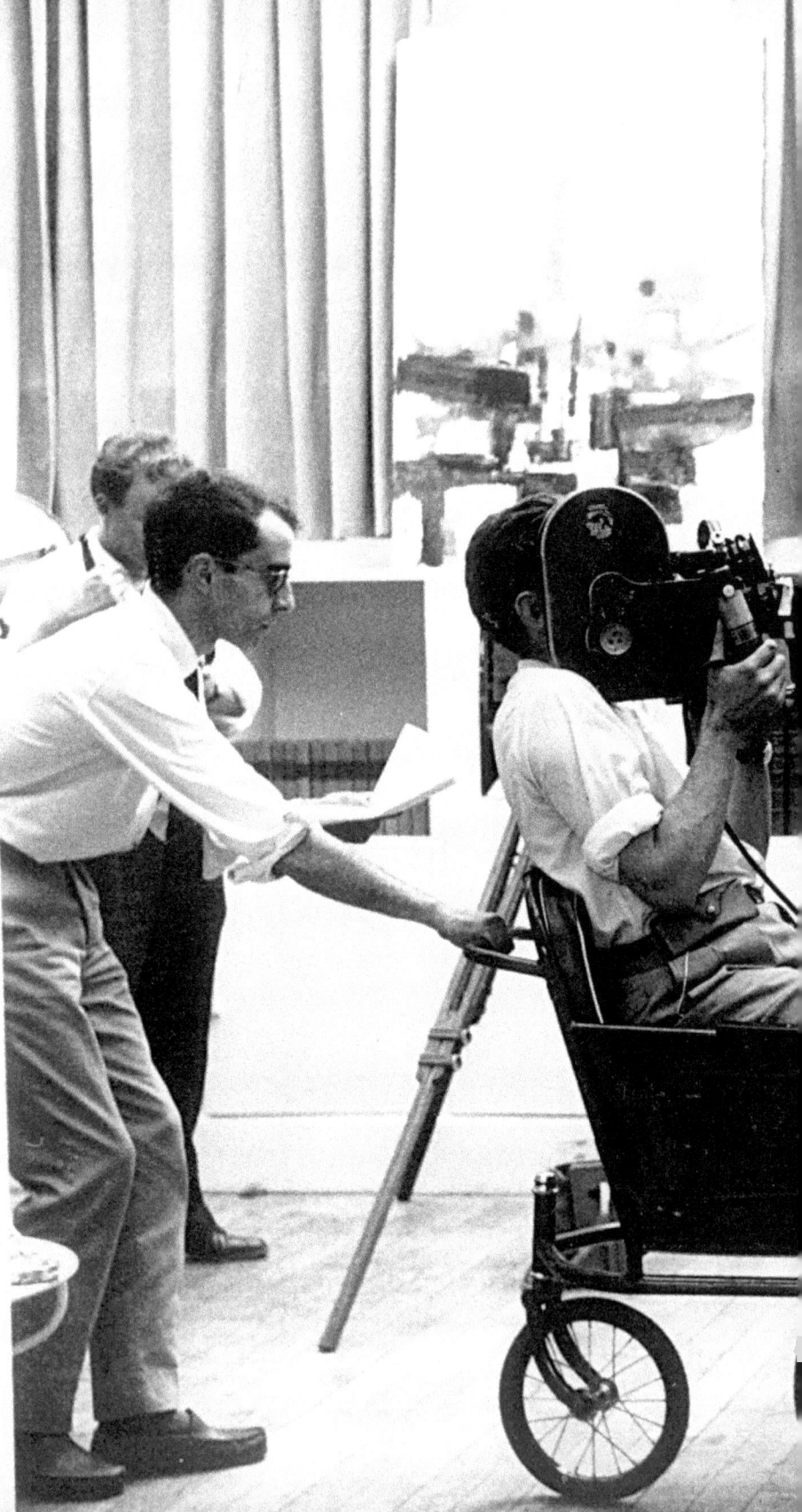

38 ▶
Breathless
(JEAN-LUC GODARD, 1960). ON THE SET OF *BREATHLESS*, IN THE PHOTOGRAPHER'S STUDIO, AT THE END OF THE FILM. THE WHOLE PHILOSOPHY THAT GOVERNED THE NEW WAVE WAY OF MAKING FILMS IS AT WORK HERE: LIGHTNESS, SPEED, IMPROVISATION, THRIFTINESS, AND RESOURCEFULNESS. IN FRONT OF ACTORS JEAN SEBERG AND JEAN-PAUL BELMONDO, JEAN-LUC GODARD PUSHES RAOUL COUTARD, WHO SITS WITH HIS LIGHT CAMERA IN A WHEELCHAIR, AN EASY-TO-HANDLE VERSION OF THE TRAVELING SHOT. (PHOTO © RAYMOND CAUCHETIER; COLL. *CAHIERS DU CINÉMA*)

The defense of form and style articulated by the Young Turks, in the overwhelmingly dominant cold war and progressive cultural context in France, was a political provocation aimed at the intelligentsia. But provocation was precisely the weapon of choice for the new critics. Their first provocation was to write in journals and newspapers that were considered right-wing, and under clear hussar influences: Rohmer's *La Gazette du cinéma*, *Cahiers du cinéma*, which they took over, the weekly *Arts*, where Truffaut officiated, the monthly journal *La Parisienne*, and even *Le Temps de Paris*, a short-lived daily started by Philippe Boegner to challenge *Le Monde* from the right. This network of periodicals maintained multiple ties to that of right-wing writers, which was mostly oriented around *La Table ronde*, *La Parisienne*, *Liberté de l'esprit*, and the weeklies *Opéra*, *Carrefour*, and *Arts*. *La Table ronde* had been founded in 1948 with the avowed purpose of countering Sartre's *Les Temps modernes*; it was the first literary refuge for the collaborationist writers who had been purged after the war—Marcel Jouhandeau, Jacques Chardonne, André Fraigneau, and Paul Morand—and a home for younger apolitical writers—Roger Nimier, Jacques Laurent, Michel Déon, Antoine Blondin, Laurent Laudenbach, Bernard de Fallois, and Jean-Louis Bory (winner of the Goncourt prize in 1945 for *Mon village à l'heure allemande* and later a cinema critic at *Nouvel observateur*). *Liberté de l'esprit*, founded in 1949 by Claude Mauriac, brought together members of the Gaullist intelligentsia, who were sidelined at the time—Malraux, Roger Cailloix, Denis de Rougemont, Max-Pol Fouchet—and claimed to be the spearhead of anticommunism in France. *La Parisienne*, run by Jacques Laurent and François Nourissier, published a combination of short stories, reportage, and analysis of current events. This is where the principal manifesto for this entire literary world was published in 1951: Laurent's "Paul et Jean-Paul," a pamphlet attacking Sartre and his progressive politics, in which he is compared to Paul Bourget, suggesting that the two shared the same spirit of academicism and commitment to didactic literature. As for Roger Nimier, he directed *Opéra* in the early 1950s—the "journal of Parisian life," an irreverent and dandyish society weekly—and took over *Carrefour* in 1953, laboring unwaveringly to rehabilitate Rebater and Céline and soliciting contributions from Max-Pol Fouchet, Jacques Laurent, and Antoine Blondin.

But the principal platform for this motley group, and the gathering point for the new cinema criticism, was unquestionably *Arts*. A rather heteroclite weekly in the immediate postwar years, *Arts* took a rightward turn in 1951, with the arrival of Louis Pauwels as its editor-in-chief, Nino Franck as its cinema critic, and André Parinaud as reviewer of literature and the arts. In 1954 Jacques Laurent had assumed stable direction of the journal and brought over the Young Turks: first Jean Aurel, a cinema critic close to *Cahiers du cinéma*, then François Truffaut at the end of 1954—after the publication of his famous polemic "A Certain Tendency in French Cinema," in *Cahiers du cinema*—and, finally, Rohmer, Godard, and Douchet. The alliance between the two periodicals was sealed by a commercial agreement—the cultural weekly was discounted for the cinema monthly's subscribers—as well as by the converging strategies of its writers—the "angry young men" of the "criticism of the catacombs," who all derived from their participation in *Arts* a rebellious energy and style, as well as a circulation (of about seventy thousand) with the potential to make their angry denunciations known to a wider readership than the meager five thousand subscribers to *Cahiers*.[6] From then on, the pages of *Arts* buzzed with their condemnations of self-righteous French "quality cinema," their exhilarating cult of Hollywood B-movies, and their scathing polemics, initiated for the most part by François Truffaut, against the official French cinema establishment.

In their vivid, elegant, provocative, sometimes sophomoric but always highly literary, texts, which readily and with relish resorted to insult, the influence of right-wing literature, and its call for political "disengagement," is palpable. The historian Emmanuelle Loyer has shown how this "literary constellation"—labeled "hussar" by Bernard Franck in a December 1952 article in *Les Temps modernes*—had formed through the postwar period and the 1950s into a refuge for those who exalted style and promoted an "art of writing" that was apolitical, or even antipolitical.[7] The intellectual paradigm of political engagement, imposed by a combination of Sartrean authority and communist cultural hegemony, was indeed contested, timidly at first, then more and more noisily, by this small literary group, who pulled out all the stops, banding together hussar literature (with Nimier riding point) and the Young Turk critics (led, guns blazing, by François Truffaut). These troublemakers, hastily labeled "fascistic" by their adversaries,[8] mounted a kind of rebellion, elegant and nonchalant, that fueled the revolt of style against a moralizing, progressive, utilitarian, and didactic literature that occupied most of the literary landscape at the time, flaunting a revolutionary messianism and declaring itself in a state of political engagement with its times.

In Sartre's view, particularly as articulated in *What Is Literature?* (1947), writers, artists, and intellectuals must be politically engaged as a function of an existential imperative, a necessary condition for any creative act aiming at an effective transformation of reality. The philosopher of *Les Temps modernes* pleaded for a "literature of praxis . . . which should not be mystical communion any more than it should be masturbation, but rather companionship."[9] In a similar vein Julien Benda wrote, in a revised preface to his 1927 book *The Treason of the Intellectuals*, which he adapted, in 1946, to the postwar context: "From now on, betrayal is the refusal to make a choice." Betrayal—an obsessive theme in hussar literature, and then in New Wave films, to the point that it is vindicated as a heroic and tragic form of sacrificial and generational "disengagement"—constituted the perspective of history's losers, the forgotten and accursed writers, the intellectuals purged after the war, the exiled or imprisoned literary figures, or simply the young and idle dandies overcome with the spleen of the 1950s: precisely all those whom the new republic of letters of the young right claimed as its own. This cluster of writers—who, together with the "aptly named hussars,"[10] were crossing swords with the intellectual left—propounded a spirit, a set of literary concerns, and a lifestyle that was affirmatively iconoclastic.

Indeed, it was all a matter of style for these young hussars of film criticism. As Bernard Frank pointed out: "as with all fascists, they despised discussion, which was invariably too drawn out, as well as ideas. They took pleasure in short sentences, a style which they tended to think they themselves had invented."[11] Incisive phrases, brilliant conclusions, elegant formulations, a vigorous style and stimulating narrative, a fascination for bodies and feminine beauty, the despair of vanity, the pleasures of seduction, the sad intoxication of depression—all these were turned against the utilitarian logorrhea of militant discourse.

The hussars were descendants of Julien Gracq, who published a pamphlet in 1950 entitled *La Littérature à l'estomac*, against what he called the "dictatorship of metaphysics" and the postwar ideologization of letters: "the truth is that literature has fallen victim, in recent years, to a formidable campaign of intimidation on the part of the non-literary." He called for "dislodging" the "poetic fact" from its rut in the "literature of the pedant," where it is covered over by "a certain metaphysics of the flesh," colonized by jargon, overloaded with the novel of ideas, and disoriented by the vagaries of cold war stakes and affiliations.[12] To get a better sense of Gracq's aspiration, Emmanuelle Loyer suggests rereading the texts collected by René Etiemble in *Hygiène des lettres*, especially the second volume, which is entitled precisely *Literature Dislodged*.[13] "Dislodged" here means outside of any and all dogmatism, rid of the literary-existentialist jargon, free of the demonstrative idea, of the clear message, of utilitarianism, all of which were reproaches to Sartre himself, as well as his disciples. These modes of "dislodgement" specific to Gracq and Etiemble were internalized by the hussar generation and were pushed, overdone, politicized, sometimes even caricatured, at any rate transformed into "disengagement" and even "anti-engagement." Nimier openly campaigned against "reigning ideas," exposing "king Sartre" and "vice-queen Beauvoir" as the "existentialist Bouvard and Pécuchet"; Jacques Laurent published his lampoons in *La Parisienne* and *Arts*; and André Parinaud derided the novel of ideas and the "Saint-Germain-des-prés night-school literature."[14] Disengagement became a genuine cause and counterattack in the last years of the Algerian War, when the hussars replied to the "Manifesto of the 121," which called on French draftees in Algeria to desert, with an openly pro-French Algeria countermanifesto, published in *Carrefour* in October 1960.

Throughout the 1950s the writings of the Young Turks of cinema criticism remained in close stylistic, editorial, and ideological proximity to hussar literature. The kinship was based on shared space in the newspaper columns, shared dinner parties, and a parallel and simultaneous sense of disengagement as the true politics of the day. This was further reinforced by a network of links and a series of broadly shared reactionary ideological views: Truffaut, with his fascination for the then embargoed literary figures of the collaboration—Rebatet, Brasillach, Drieu la Rochelle; Truffaut, again, with his close hussar connections—Jacques Laurent, André Parinaud, Roger Nimier; Rivette, with his adherence to a mystical conception of cinema as the "imprint of grace"; Chabrol, with his anti-Semitic and Nazi-enthralled "evil genius," Paul Gégauff; Godard, with his pro-French Algeria iconoclastic tendencies; and Rohmer, with his defense of an unadulterated Western cinema, in which "white blood flows through the veins" of the characters.[15]

In the ultimate provocation they asserted style and form as the only criteria for cinematic taste and judgment. This "neo-formalist" critique—as André Bazin, editor of *Cahiers du cinema*, put it while inducting his new recruits, often lecturing them from a tolerant and progressive Christian left perspective[16]—aimed primarily to disengage critical judgment and writing from any notion of content (no more hierarchies between worthy and unworthy subjects, good and bad messages) and container (blissful ignorance of a film's economic, political, historical, and technical contexts), in order to focus the defense and analysis of films on their style, and their style only, which mirrored the singular personalities of their makers. When Bazin attempted to define the neoformalism of his junior associates, he invoked their sweeping praise of mise-en-scène, as though it were the "open sesame!" that would unlock all doors to the Young Turk aesthetic and its "hitchcocko-hawksian" sensibility: "If they make such a big deal about mise-en-scène, it's because they detect in it the very stuff of film, an organization of works and things, which is in itself its meaning, both moral and aesthetic. . . . This is a conception of cinema as a purely formal thinking of the world."[17]

Their love of style fastened onto a pantheon of directors that was particularly provocative, in political terms, either because openly anticommunist (Fuller, Sternberg, McCarey, Becker, Gance, Guitry) or simply Hollywood (Hitchcock, Hawks, Lang, Ray, Minnelli), and only exceptionally on the left (Rossellini, Renoir, Aldrich). In the context of the cold war, rampant anti-Americanism, and the cultural conformism of postwar French intellectuals, this set of choices was strongly frowned upon. On the face of it, *Cahiers du cinéma* knew no other politics than that of *auteurs*—a term the Young Turks coined to discredit and dismiss all other forms of militancy. But there were unmistakable signs that everyone picked up on—signs that enabled Bazin to declare that Rohmer, Truffaut, and Rivette were "not exactly writers of the left."[18]

This neoformalism was tantamount, in the postwar literary and intellectual context, to a declaration of right-wing affiliation, or at least it was recognized as such by all of the combatants and observers on the battlefield that was French culture. To be "disengaged," in the mid-1950s, also meant being "engaged" in a battle against anything and everything that constituted left-wing culture, in all its diversity: Sartre, *Les Temps modernes*; Camus, *Combat*; Vilar and the National Public Theatre; Bazin, Travail et Culture, *Esprit*; Sadoul, Aragon, *Les Lettres françaises*; and the communists. The evidence leaves little room for doubt: modern cinema criticism—that which was clever enough to view film through mise-en-scène, which boldly postulated that an auteur's thought is essentially formal, and which constituted a pantheon of filmmakers in support of these arguments—was born and raised on the political right. This affiliation was almost never expressed in terms of overt political commitment but rather almost always present formally, through a penchant for polemics, political disengagement, and elitism, through a defense of style, dandyism, neoformalism, mysticism, nonconformism, and provocation—all hallmarks of a certain set of right-wing writers and thinkers. More than a full-fledged ideology, it was a "right-wing aesthetics," as François Truffaut defined it in an article on *Jet Pilot*, Josef von Sternberg's anticommunist film: "The right wing has often been defined by its flippancy, its casualness, its lack of qualms (the ends justifying the means), its high culture, its style, and its refinement; the left wing appears conversely as ponderous, awkward, simplistic, militant, full of good intentions, and always conscientious.... Indeed, my view on the matter is that it was not until Alain Resnais turned to making feature films that we finally got to see 'left wing' films that were good and beautiful."[19]

The general provocation of Hollywoodophilia—that is, exaltation of the minor and the quirky over good taste—was coupled with provocative acts: flaunting collaborationist acquaintances, behaving intolerantly, and disparaging humanism and any kind of progressive good conscience. The paradox here lies in the fact that this approach, which involves discovering and describing cinema only as form, enabled a group of critics to see and understand, and even to sublimate, films for which they were far from the target audience—films that were manufactured through a mass industry for mass consumption by artists who, working in the belly of the Hollywood system, and forced to respect and abide by its rules, could only engage in barely perceptible stylistic deviations. It was precisely these barely perceptible deviations that the hitchcocko-hawksian critics saw. And it was all they wanted to see. This is also how they were able to rewrite the history of cinema, dislodging it while disengaging themselves. No doubt, the right-wing penchant of the young critics should be somewhat qualified. Anticonformist dandyism did not necessarily entail taking on the entire ideological program. As for their neoformalism, this was an aesthetic posture that was to be adopted a few years later by structuralists, whose political commitments were on the left (Jacques Rivette, who directed *Cahiers du cinéma*, is a good example of this trend).

Form, for the Young Turks, was most likely less the expression of a conscious political ideology than an ethics of cinema. Neoformalist critics staked out ethical ground that was inherent to cinematic form itself. "Morality is a question of traveling shots"—and is thus neither of the right nor of the left but simply cinematographic. Still, did they not have to be right-wing—some consciously and provocatively, others only unconsciously—to make the modern turn in cinema criticism in the mid-1950s? It was not a sufficient condition, of course, but it sometimes seemed a necessary one. Tribute must be paid to the artistic and literary right for developing a gaze that actively distinguished form, style, and mise-en-scène from commitments, causes, and important issues. The New Wave school of criticism thus rests on a most unlikely political paradox: while most of the "modern turns" in midcentury France were born of the left—from literary criticism (both *Nouveau Roman* and Roland Barthes' mythosemiotic analysis), to theater criticism (Bernard Dort's "Brechtianism"), to, of course, structuralism—only cinema criticism, or at least its most innovative strain (the *Cahiers du cinéma* tradition), rested on an ideological, stylistic, even dandyish foundation, which was identified as right wing.

A Cinema "That Has Nothing to Say"

Many observers of French cinema spotted the reappearance of this hussar spirit and distinctive young right style in the early productions of the New Wave. Michel Mardore, for instance, wrote in 1960:

> This fear-mongering disease, which the young generation of critics had turned into its bacteriological weapon, and which now targets the young dabblers in return, is in fact, under cover of the New Wave, a particular trend in French cinema that, for the sake of convenience, we shall call "right-wing anarchism." In the world of right-wing anarchism, the hero has seen it all, society is corrupt, and love—that egotistical lie—and death—the imposture of creation—have become good bedfellows. Everyone is vile, sometimes innocently so, in a pleasantly hopeless world, the bitter fruit of hatred which calls for dismissive apocalypse. These selective criteria were those of the young right's literature. They resurfaced in Astruc, Malle, Vadim, whose atmosphere paved the way for Chabrol, who, with the help of his scriptwriter Paul Gégauff, raised it to a high degree of perfection . . . and lack of charm. We have only to recall that in 1960 this state of mind, this style, was epitomized by *Breathless*, which is rightly considered the very essence of the New Wave.[20]

Others, however, simply pretended the New Wave was on the left—most notably Georges Sadoul, the communist paragon of cinema criticism who defended the New Wave with energy, talent, and influence in the pages of *Les Lettres françaises* and *L'Humanité*. Without Sadoul on its side the New Wave would undoubtedly have found itself isolated. Characterizing this new cinema, Sadoul resorted to a rather simplistic but eminently progressive syllogism: the New Wave is youth, youth is progress, and progress is on the left. But at the time, the new directors were mostly criticized for situating themselves elsewhere, outside the social and political field, which was deemed irresponsible, both morally and politically, at a time when the French army was committing torture in Algeria and when, owing to the first media coverage of gang activities, youth was becoming perceived as a social problem and demands for change and social justice were mounting. A cinema "that has nothing to say"—this was the gist of the attacks leveled at the apolitical French New Wave: "The young directors refrain from any challenge to the social or political order.

Their politics does not go much further than a vaguely anarchistic and confused reflection on the Algerian war"; "the New Wave has nothing to say, but it says it well. No wonder, then, if Godard's films feel like a manic depressive who rambles on and on and has no idea what they are talking about."[21]

Because of its political disengagement, the New Wave was severely attacked, often by peers (journalists, filmmakers, actors, scriptwriters) who, only a few months earlier, had appeared to accept the movement, had sometimes even supported it, and had at any rate tolerated it. These violent, and generally condescending, "politically engaged" slaps in the face did hurt the young filmmakers, who subsequently had a very difficult time overcoming the charge of being "irresponsible petty bourgeois."[22] In a letter dated September 26, 1960, Truffaut thus spoke of "a movement that gets insulted on the radio, on TV, and in the papers, every single week." "I am not persecuted," he added, "and I am not saying there is a plot against us, but it has become very clear that these days, young people's films that stray from the norm, however slightly, run into roadblocks erected by the industry and the press. There certainly were a lot of old-style big budget French films released this year. This stinks of Old Wave revenge."[23] Truffaut located this shift—from the praise of young people who spoke up, to the systematic denigration of his discourse—in the press campaign that accompanied the release of Denys de La Patellière's film *Rue des prairies*, which featured Jean Gabin as a gruff hero of the anti–New Wave movement and scriptwriter Michel Audiard as the champion of the fight against this idle and depressed generation's petty bourgeois attitudes and dandy postures. The film's tagline was, "Jean Gabin settles his score with the New Wave." In *Arts* Audiard railed against "futile and incoherent youth":

> Ah, rebellion! Big deal! Truffaut's been through here no doubt. A charming boy. One eye always on the perfect little anarchist manual, and the other riveted to the *Centrale catholique*, one hand clenched toward the future, the other concealing his bow tie. Messieurs Truffaut, Godard, Chabrol and company would like to convince the diners at Fouquet's that they are scary and dangerous people. It makes the experts laugh, but it impresses poor Eric Rohmer. For if young people who had nothing to say used to meet around a teapot, now they meet in front of a screen. Truffaut applauds for Rohmer who, the week before, applauded for Pollet, who next week will applaud for Godard or Chabrol. For these people like to keep it in the family.... This is where they are at now, or rather where they were at. For it makes no sense to keep talking about them in the present tense. The New Wave [*Vague*] is dead. And what we realize is that, in the end, it was much more vague than new.[24]

Henri Jeanson, another successful scriptwriter—a profession that particularly had it out for the young filmmakers who relentlessly challenged their domination of French cinema—railed against the "young cheaters-*en-scène*" in *Cinémonde*, *La Croix*, and *Le Journal du dimanche*, while Jacques Lanzmann, in *Arts*, solemnly pondered whether "the future of young French filmmakers is behind them." Jean Nocher, on France Inter radio, denounced "gloomy movies." Jean Aurenche, the leader of the old guard scriptwriters, very polemically invoked, in a corrosive interview in *Cinema 60*, the "trendy pseudo-talents."[25] The journal *Positif* followed up, in early 1962, with an entire issue devoted to attacks on the New Wave as the symbol of a youth that enthusiastically denied history. In it Robert Benayoun singled out his bête-noire, the "fascist" and "zombie" Jean-Luc Godard: "It is well known that the program of this rickety junkshop of the New Wave was established by the zombie Jean-Luc Godard, who has at last found a way to surprise me. Indeed, I thought it was impossible to distinguish between various degrees of worthlessness, to decide which of his films was the worst. It has now become possible. He has just surpassed himself, crashing through the lowest level of even his own insignificant clutter. Jean-Luc now [with *Alphaville*] digs below the ground, in a pellicle of narcissistic and dehydrated bullshit."[26]

Another cinema journal with a clear leftist affiliation, *Premier plan*, devoted two issues (May and June 1960) to a dismantling of the "new French cinema." Raymond Borde's editorial set the tone: "snug and self-satisfied France gets the young cinema it deserves." He added, "A product of their times, the sheep of the New Wave are political caution personified. They take up received ideas with stunning ease. Nothing matters more to them than that their souls be at rest. They have peaceful prejudices: Gaullist monarchy constitutes their golden age, in the end. And they fight for it in style."[27] In the same issue Bernard Chardère characterized *Breathless* as embodying "a kind of anarcho-fascist ideal." As for François Nourissier, in one of the antiyouth diatribes that he made his specialty during these New Wave years, he tried to foil "the trap set by a small band of youngsters in order to cleanly gun down their elders" by ironically turning the young filmmakers into champions of right-wing academicism: "the heralded revolution looks rather like the reasonable coming to power of the next generation. And, surprise, surprise, they are not all rabid fanatics. All this feels, how to say, a little mild. In a nutshell, the generation that showed up on the Champs-Elysées in 1959 already has its Bressons, its Renoirs, its Cléments, as well as a new Charles Spaak, Marc-Guilbert Sauvageon, Delannoy, and Autant-Lara."[28] *La Parisienne*'s ex-chief was making an argument about the New Wave filmmakers that was to be constantly reiterated: their imminent, or even already completed, sellout to a "cinema of quality" that they had previously denounced. The syndrome of betrayal and disavowal was hovering over these filmmakers who had, it must be said, never rejected the French cinema system and had often used it to preserve their independence.

More vehement still, because more sincere, more raw, and closer to artistic and literary youth, the journalist and writer Jean-René Huguenin, nauseated by the young New Wave hero portrayed in some of the films, contributed his own satirical piece. In an article entitled "Dénonçons le mythe de la Nouvelle Vague" (Let's Expose the Myth of the New Wave), published in *Arts* on March 22, 1961, he lambasted the young cinema for the pointlessness and frivolousness of its subjects and situations:

> Girl meets boy; she likes him. He has everything going for him. A bitter smirk and a sullen smile, slightly stooped shoulders, weighed down by precocious experience of the world's vanity—and his weary eyes open reluctantly.... He is beautiful. He is a composite photo of Maurice Ronet, Alain Delon, Jean-Paul Belmondo, Jean-Claude Brialy, Jean-Louis Trintignant, and Mastroianni, the male replica of Brigitte Bardot, the man-child. She sighs and asks: "What shall we do?" He sighs and responds: "Make love?" They undress a little and embrace. They smoke a cigarette. After a while, they sigh and say: "What shall we do?" This cliché of modern love has been endlessly repeated for the past five years, by the shrewd salesmen of cinema, of the press and of literature, who are not really interested in raising a scandal but who are interested in raising themselves. In 1957, *L'Express* announced that youth were about to change. It was good news, but uncertain news, and it was indeed called vague news [*nouvelle vague*].... The New Wave [Nouvelle Vague] is a myth. It does not represent today's youth. It is dated; it has just lasted too long.

In a more paternalistic vein Jean Cau, Sartre's former secretary at *Les Temps modernes*, a former man of the left who was soon to become a champion of traditional values, "watched a few new French films for *L'Express*" and offered his amazed, sorry, worried, and discouraged account of them in the pages of the weekly that had coined the expression "New Wave":

> For ten years, the "young people" whined: "ah, if only they'd put a camera in our hands!" Then we took them at their word, and gave them cameras. And what did they say? Shockingly, nothing! What do they have in their heads? Surprisingly, a pea! And in their hearts? Woefully, water! I must admit I am flabbergasted, both

stunned and saddened. They talk of Saint-Tropez, race cars, whiskey, ski resorts, the age-old game of love and chance, the heavy gallantries of boys and girls who sleep together on command like Pavlov's dog. To see, on the screen, a France reduced to a bed on which a couple lies with arms and legs entangled—how soothing, how intoxicating, how lethal! We are realizing that the young filmmakers have more or less nothing to say.[29]

For the right it was their loose morals and libertine world that scandalized. For the left it was the gratuitousness, the pointlessness, and the political disengagement.

Heroes of the New Wave and Militants of Disarray

It is no easy task to politically categorize the various attitudes the New Wave and its heroes have been assigned. Attacks came from all camps, and the same films could give rise to radically opposite interpretations—the movement was alternately deemed right-wing, left-wing, and as having "nothing to say." Yet many New Wave films bear traces of an uncomfortable relationship to the present and to history, which itself signaled a historically unresolved self-questioning. This is what Bruno Forestier, the hero of *Le Petit soldat* (*The Little Soldier*, 1960) played by Michel Subor, very aptly expressed in the final confession of a young political recruit, disillusioned and disenchanted, who had become the diffident, cynical, wisecracking witness to his own downfall:

> It is terrible, nowadays. If you keep quiet and do nothing, you are told off, precisely because you are doing nothing. So you do things half-heartedly, and I find it a shame to make war half-heartedly. There's a very beautiful quote, who is it by again? I think it's Lenin: "Ethics is the aesthetics of the future...." I find this phrase very moving. It brings right and left together. What do right-wing and left-wing people think about? Whenever a reactionary government comes to power, it implements left-wing policies, and conversely the other way around.... Around 1930, young people had a revolution. For instance, Malraux, Drieu la Rochelle, Aragon. There's nothing for us anymore. They had the war in Spain; we don't even have our own war.

Forestier, a right-wing anarchist steeped in the culture of the left, a desperate kind of dandy, is looking for an ideal. He will not find one. "Maybe, in the end, asking questions is more important than finding answers," he concludes. Godard has often been asked to explain the shady politics of his little soldier from Geneva, who works for a far-right underground terrorist movement and is tortured by Algerian FLN activists but who also reads and clearly loves on the left. Godard explained in 1962 in *Cahiers du cinéma*:

> I wanted to achieve the realism that was lacking in *A Bout de souffle* [*Breathless*], the concrete. Films must contain signs of their times. Politics are discussed, but it is not oriented to either political side. My way of being political was to say: the New Wave has been accused of only showing people in their beds, I am going to show a few who are political and don't have time to sleep with anyone. Politics, in 1960, was Algeria. Personally, I don't take sides. I am rooting for both the left-wing girl and the right-wing soldier. I have told the story of a right-wing agent, but I could just as well direct a movie about the life of Djamila Bouhired. Besides, the soldier is a right-winger who is also left-wing; he is sentimental. Similar to both Drieu La Rochelle's Gilles and Aragon's Aurélien, he is a romantic character who "thinks on the left" in a "right-wing situation." If he had to choose, he would probably be on the "other side." I find it easy to identify with him. When I look at myself in a mirror, I feel the same way.[30]

It is indeed rather difficult—and this is an understatement—to make political sense of *Le Petit soldat* or, more generally, of Godard's thinking at the time, which vacillated between political bravado and provocation. The "other side" Godard talks about includes all those who were in the wrong in relation to the massive and progressive political commitment of French intellectuals at the time: that is, former collaborationists of occupied France, who had been purged after France's liberation; the hussars who had been dubbed "fascist writers" in the parlance of the progressive and militant *Les Temps modernes*; and far-right soldiers, a source of romantic and picturesque fascination since they were targeted by both de Gaulle's police and the anticolonial fighters. More than a clear political stance on the issues of the day, they expressed a general temporal confusion in relation to the world and its history.

Jean Collet's analysis of *The Little Soldier*, published as early as 1963, reads as a generational manifesto of the New Wave heroes, young people ill-suited to their times:

> Being twenty in 1950, and being born in an old world. We had a world to consume, and nothing to conquer; everything had been invented for us; the war had been fought for us; everything had been thought for us, examined, weighed, destroyed, and built for us. All we had left to do was to inhabit, admire, thank, sleep, and dream. To each century its ills, and to each generation too. Some suffer from not knowing

39 ▶
Le Petit soldat
(JEAN-LUC GODARD, 1960–63). FORESTIER'S REFERENCES, FROM GENEVA 1960 TO BUDAPEST 1956, AND A PROVOCATIVELY "REARMED" HITLER: THE WORLD OF A YOUNG RIGHT-WINGER.

their fathers, and arriving in an empty world. Others suffer for the opposite reason: because they land in a world that is too full, too made, because their fathers are all too present. In short, for good or bad reasons, we no longer had to invent our lives, only to let ourselves live. To inherit everything our fathers had written, thought, filmed, for us. We were a generation of spectators.[31]

What characterizes the spirit of the New Wave is not an absence of political context—quite the opposite, it was probably more palpable than in the French films of the two previous decades—but a rejection of the simplifications necessary for an effective politics. The idea that the world is more complex than politicians and militants claim was key to a movement that, politically, was always intent on defying interpretation. As though the New Wave, which was never very keen on its times, chose to romanticize it, chose to turn it into a black-and-white tale through the sovereign style of an all-powerful cinematic form (figs. 39, 40).

Half a dozen New Wave films thus offer a very direct illustration of these heroes of melancholia—whether political, aesthetic, or existential—a portrait gallery of dark and cynical dandies and desperadoes, which aptly characterizes the oxymoronic style of that provocative and childish political posture, right-wing anarchism. Think, for instance, of the writer whom Patricia interviews at the airport in *Breathless*. The author of *Candidat* wears sunglasses, talks in riddles, and does not believe in anything but love, which he appears to confuse with eroticism. He flaunts his "profound pessimism" and yet venerates France as the "country of intelligence," and he finally confesses, when prompted by Patricia's question, that his greatest ambition in life is to "become immortal, and then die." A series of questionable syllogisms and glib provocations captures the hussar style quite well, further enhanced by the fact that the novelist, "an admirer of Casanova and Cocteau," is played by the mannerist director Jean-Pierre Melville and is called "Parvulesco," a cryptic underground reference to the young fascist of Romanian descent, Jean Parvulesco, whom Godard had met at a Latin Quarter cine-club, and whose radical positions had fascinated the director.[32]

Claude Chabrol's second film, *Les Cousins* (*The Cousins*), released in 1958, also features a hussar: the flamboyant Paul, a mixture of nonchalance and vigor, played by Jean-Claude Brialy, whose sparkling verve, punctuated by sudden fits of despair, offers a powerful screen rendition of the "young right-wing style." Urbane Paul, who puts up his country cousin Charles (Gérard Blain), who has "come up" to Paris to study law at the Sorbonne, in his Neuilly

40 ▶
Le Petit soldat
(JEAN-LUC GODARD, 1960–63). ANNA KARINA, OR THE FREE AND NATURAL BEAUTY OF A LEFT-WING YOUNG WOMAN.

apartment, is unquestionably a young right-winger, even though he does not ever talk about politics. His acquaintances say it all for him: racist jetsetters, who consort with the mafia and shady characters. Indeed, everything about him obeys a certain style and logic: his immoderate taste for firearms and trophies, of which he has assembled an impressive collection; his manicured look of an elegant petty aristocrat; even his club in the Latin Quarter, "Association," where girls sitting at the bar celebrate his arrival by laughing and giggling; and of course his masterful sense of repartee and penchant for crafted phrases: "I am the living picture of the inanity of work." Last but not least, his love of decadence: crisscrossing the city from party to party, he comments, while stepping over the tired bodies of alcohol-ravaged guests, "It's Babylon here, it's Babylon..."

His extremely provocative use of German culture completes the picture. A mere fifteen years after the end of the war, a large part of his vocabulary is German, and he revels in quotes from Goethe, Nietzsche, and especially Wagner. The highlight of the party at his place is a Wagnerian ritual, a scene that gave rise to great controversy when the film was released in early 1959: Paul, in a Wehrmacht soldier's hat, dimly lit by the fire of a pagan torch, with the Bayreuth master's *Tetralogy* playing in the background, recites lines in German about a "poor lonesome fighter," while casually stepping over the bodies of his guests lying on the ground. At the break of dawn, in the ultimate joke of questionable taste, Paul howls, "Gestapo," and feigns torturing a young man who suddenly wakes up looking frightened and promptly runs away, yelling, "You scared me..." This reaction and the extent of the joke is later explained to us when Paul tells his cousin: "Marc is Jewish, so it gave him a shock, and sobered him up instantly." This Aryan fascination is rather typical of the iconoclastic gestures favored by Paul Gégauff, Chabrol's scriptwriter: this presentable young man was perfectly capable of showing up at a costume ball dressed as a Nazi officer holding a leash with a friend wearing the striped outfit of a camp inmate on the other end of it. It is also reminiscent of the beginning of one of Roger Nimier's novels, which reads: "When I was in the Waffen SS...," just as the hero of *Hussard bleu*, François Sanders, proclaimed it—as if the *jeunesse dorée* felt free to do whatever they pleased. In *The Cousins* Paul ends up killing Charles, in an unfortunate gun accident, after having stolen his fiancée away from him, but for no reason, gratuitously, "so as not to die of boredom." A pointless, stupid, disengaged death (figs. 41, 42).

The true far-right activist of the New Wave, though, is to be found in Alain Cavalier's *Le Combat dans l'île* (*Fire and Ice*, 1962). Jean-Louis Trintig-

41 ▶
The Cousins
(CLAUDE CHABROL, 1959). JEAN-CLAUDE BRIALY, FIRST OF A LONG LINE OF CHABROL "PAULS": AN ELEGANT, DECADENT, PROVOCATIVE DANDY. (PHOTO © GEORGES PIERRE; COLL. *CAHIERS DU CINÉMA*)

nant plays Clément—a cold, meticulous, jealous, racist, sometimes violent, but intelligent, subtle, handsome, dogged, and attractive character, walking, straight and stiff, on the verge of madness. Through a so-called hunting club, he regularly meets with a group of men in an isolated house where he undergoes strict brainwashing and training in the handling of firearms. It is a small fascist group whose name is not OAS to avoid censorship. It plans and carries out a bazooka terrorist attack on a left-wing deputy. Clément's young wife (Romy Schneider), who understands what is going on, leaves him, and the latter, hounded, must hide out in the countryside for a while and then go off to Spain and South America, where he tracks down a traitor whom he assassinates in cold blood. On his return all he wants to do is take revenge on his wife's lover, Paul, a humanistic and idealistic printer, whose child she is expecting, and challenge him to a duel. A shoot-out ensues, on a small island, and Paul ends up shooting Clément. Cavalier points out how the violent threat of

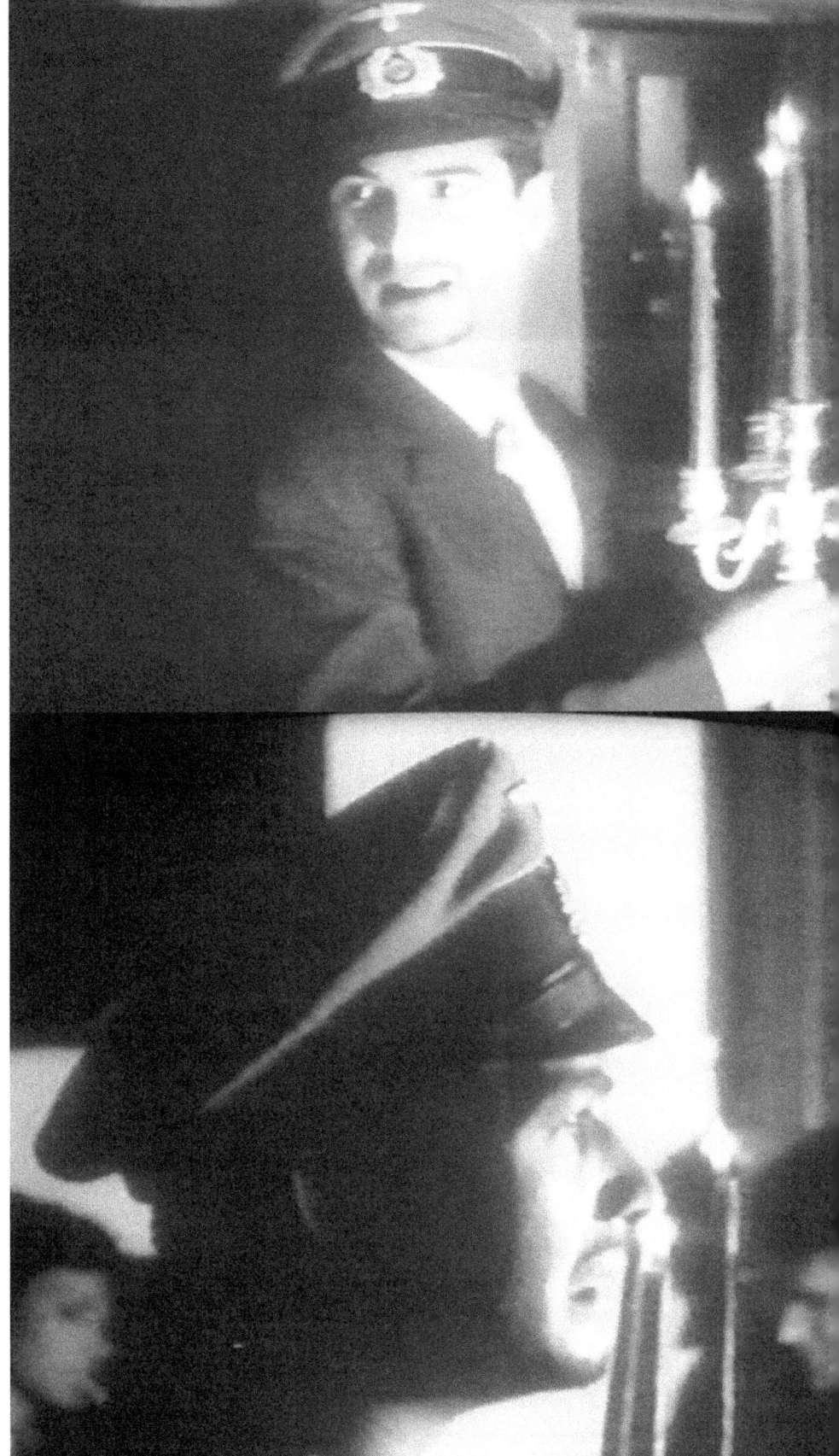

42 ▶
The Cousins (CLAUDE CHABROL, 1959). THE WAGNERIAN RITUAL IN WHICH BRIALY APPEARS LIKE A GHOST, SUDDENLY RESURFACING FROM A FUNERAL CEREMONY IN HONOR OF THE WEHRMACHT.

right-wing terrorism forces democracy into a protective, defensive position and into adopting the other side's violence, the very weapon of the opponent. It is a left-wing film, of course, but the detailed depiction of the life of this lost young soldier of the OAS—hounded, menacing, distraught, and yet rigidly single-minded—is deeply moving. While undoubtedly an antihero, Clément carries the logic of history's losers to its end and by so doing highlights the New Wave's attraction for misfits and outcasts, those rebels of defeat. *Le Combat dans l'île* was received as a left-wing film at the time—"the most blatant refutation of the accusations of irresponsibility leveled at the New Wave of Godard, Chabrol, and Truffaut," wrote Robert Benayoun in *Positif*.[33] Yet Jean-Louis Trintignant/Clément may be seen as the most accurate depiction by a contemporary of the ambiguities of young right-wingers reacting to "Western decadence" and ready to err on the side of "national regeneration."

Yet the most magnificent hussar hero of the New Wave, whose drift is less toward terrorist action than alcoholic daze, who is characterized by a tragic fate and sickly charm, and yet who manages it all with style and elegance, is unquestionably Alain Leroy, the unhappy hero played by Maurice Ronet in Louis Malle's 1963 adaptation of Pierre Drieu La Rochelle's novel *Feu follet* (*The Fire Within*). Alain is unhappy—this is a given. He writes but mostly crosses out his words. From time to time he leaves the Versailles clinic, where he has been in rehab for four months, and wanders through Paris at night with women who fall under the spell of his sad beauty and desperate charm. He is endowed with several of the requisite attributes of the hussar dandy: he, too, likes guns, women, death, literature, and he, too, lives in a time warp where the present pales by comparison with a past in which Alain "used to command" and "was in the army." There, he experienced firsthand, in action, intoxicating pleasure and the making of history—probably the colonial adventure, but this is never made clear. Since then, everything has come undone, thoughts as well as life, creation as well as action, and Alain Leroy has decided to commit suicide, on July 23, in forty-eight hours. He walks around in Paris—the Paris of the New Wave, on the left bank, between Odeon, the rue de Buci, and Saint-Germain-des-Prés; he encounters women (Jeanne Moreau, Alexandra Stewart); he meets up with a few dubious friends at Café Flore (unquestionably OAS activists raising funds among them). His final hours are spent in an alcoholic stupor, debauchery, and depressive broodings. "Life doesn't move fast enough in me"; "I've had it with mediocrity, I quit, I've had enough, I don't want to grow old"; "I have a taste for risk and death, it is in my blood"—all these statements are delivered in voice-over by an inspired and demoralized Maurice Ronet,

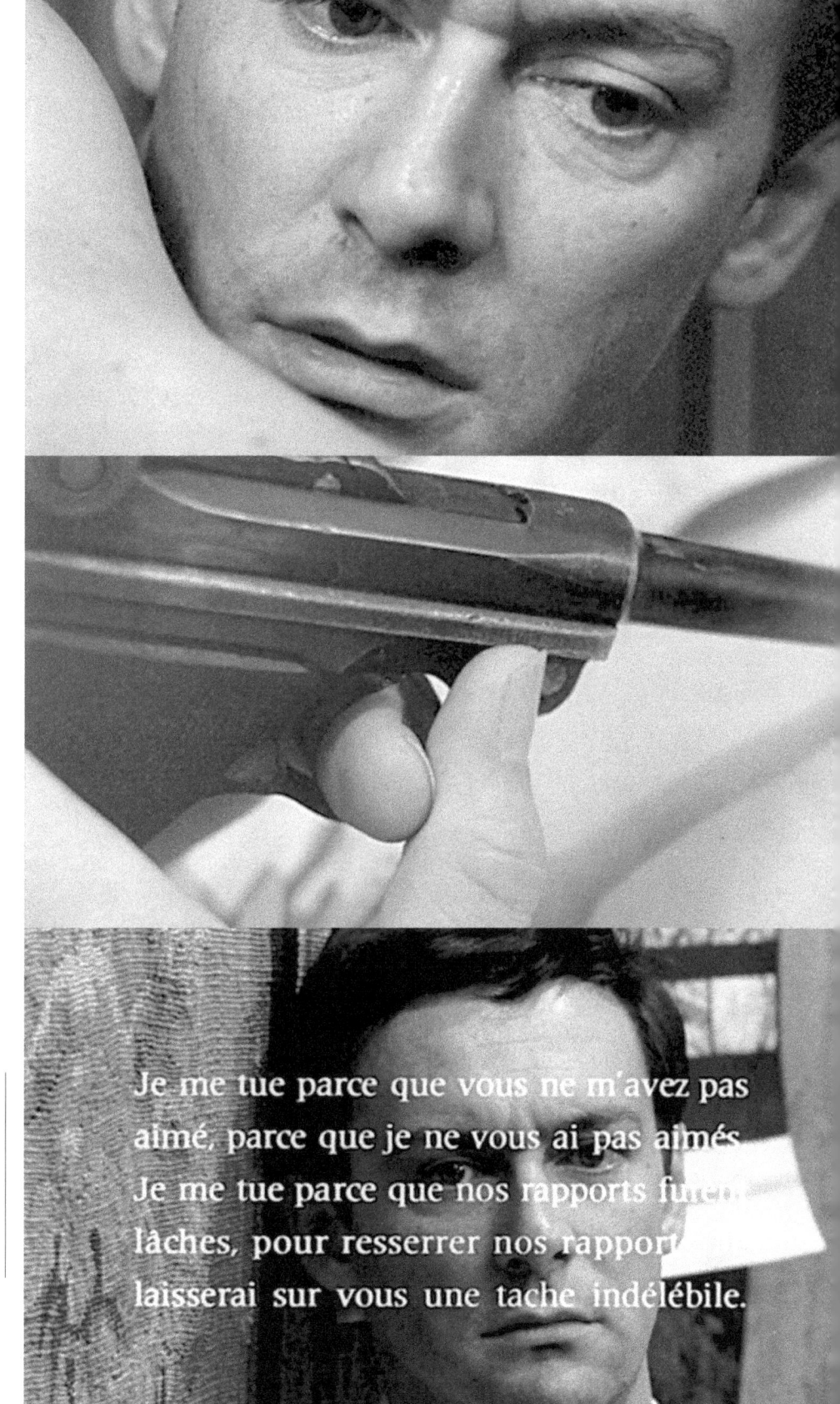

43 ▶
The Fire Within
(LOUIS MALLE, 1963).
ALAIN LEROY (MAURICE
RONET)'S SUICIDE,
IN *THE FIRE WITHIN*:
THERE IS NOTHING TO
BE EXPECTED OF THE
FUTURE IN A WORLD
THAT IS TOO OLD.

while he wanders through Paris under the rain through the sometimes bright and sometimes dim lighting of Ghislain Cloquet, director of photography for both Louis Malle and Alain Resnais. His inspiration is depression, the kind that is "experienced" in the suicidal mode (a colt bullet through the heart, in the end, at the break of a pale dawn) but with style. A hussar all the way, not the least in his political disengagement—"*utterly apolitical*," he says to define his position at a dinner where he is expected to take sides—Alain Leroy has the same bitter grin as Roger Nimier's *Hussard bleu*, the grin of *Enfants tristes (Sad Children)*, who "turned twenty in the Hiroshima haze that taught them the world was neither serious, nor lasting," the generation who "turned twenty at the end of civilization."[34] There is no nonchalance nor action nor politics nor creation, only despair. Nimier is the writer who enabled Malle and Ronet to adapt Drieu La Rochelle in the early 1960s, with his heroes "detached from the world": "Our detachment would not be so profound if it were not for this final cause: there is nothing to be expected from the future."[35] In contrast to the political intellectual, the New Wave hero stands against the spirit of seriousness: his incapacity to take part *in* his times makes him the most stylish being *of* his times (fig. 43).

Politicization via Malraux

The politicization of the New Wave was encouraged in the late 1950s by an encounter, a sudden passion, an affair. For not only were the critics lying in wait for the young filmmakers, but so was politics. As early as 1959, André Malraux, de Gaulle's newly minted minister of cultural affairs, felt blowing from the films of the young filmmakers the breath of fresh air that might signify the kind of renewal in the domain of culture that the new administration was otherwise trying to impose on the political, economic, and social life of the country. There was a striking synchronicity between the rise of these young filmmakers and the coming to power of the Gaullists. Not that the former should be read as, in any way, an illustration of the latter, but insofar as various resonances echo between the two contexts, between culture and politics.

The Young Turks had been fascinated by the literary, artistic, and political figure of Malraux for a long time. In the spring of 1958, when the author of *L'Espoir* was attacked severely in the left-wing press of the dying Fourth Republic, they supported him vigorously. Thus, in May 1958 Jean-Luc Godard published a brief text in *Cahiers du cinéma* that was openly political, whereas the journal was not: "without further ado, no doubt to prove that his name sounds like blinkers [œillères], Billières, just before he fell with the rest of the Gaillard government, thought it wise to declare that Malraux was a bad Frenchman.... Speculation is rife as to the exact reason for his veto... since Malraux remains the most fascinating figure in modern French literature."[36]

Likewise, the young filmmakers eagerly tapped into funds provided to promote the making of short and feature films that were set up in the early 1950s but whose resources and efficiency were immediately increased by the new Malraux ministry. In September 1948 the TSA (*taxe spéciale additionnelle*, or special additional tax) was created by the Centre national de la cinématographie, and levied on all box-office tickets sold in France, to endow a "development fund," later renamed a "support fund." This compulsory self-funding system was designed to boost national production—with the TSA applying to all box-office receipts, including for foreign films. It would remain a pillar of the French system of film subsidies and protectionism. In 1953 a new law further strengthened and expanded the TSA, maintaining the original principle but instituting for the first time a special premium for quality French films that "serve the cause of French cinema, and open new perspectives for the cinematographic arts."[37]

The impact of the new quality premium was felt from 1955 and reinforced the position of the more recognized productions of French cinema, those that the Young Turks had relentlessly bashed in their columns under the ironic term "French quality." But the fund also played a sometimes decisive role in the productions of the other side of French cinema, which as early as 1956 and 1957 had come to be known as the energetic "young cinema." In December 1956 Jacques Flaud, the influential CNC director, condemned the "negative impact" of the policy of automatic support for all French films and increased the targeting of quality cinema, insisting in particular on the young cinema.[38] He thus sealed an objective alliance between institutional authorities and the New Wave. This funding program for young cinema, officially announced in *La Revue du CNC* at the beginning of 1957, was thus perfectly synchronized with the rise of the New Wave. This was probably the first time in cultural history that an innovative artistic movement received official institutional support from the outset. On January 11, 1957, the industry weekly *Le Film français* emphatically announced—under the title "A New Youth for our Cinema"—the reform of the development fund. To the utter dismay of the professional film guilds, who protested against what amounted in their view to a "misappropriation of subsidies," and a means of "circumventing the quality standards in favor of dangerous amateurism,"[39] the new technical requirements were designed to make it easier for very young filmmakers to obtain special dispensations to shoot their first films. The allocation of premium subsidies was determined by guidelines that were favorable to first and second films, as well as to a few auteur films, which were to benefit the producers who financed the early efforts of the New Wave.

In 1956 several films were recipients of the premium, most notably Robert Bresson's *Un condamné à mort s'est échappé* (*A Man Escaped*) and Juan Antonio Bardem's *Grand-rue* (*Main Street*). In both cases Georges de Beauregard and Pierre Braunberger pocketed the subsidy, which later enabled them to produce Godard's *Breathless* and Truffaut's *Shoot the Piano Player*, as well as many of the young directors' short films, without much difficulty. In 1957 Chabrol's *Handsome Serge* was the first New Wave film to directly receive a premium, in the amount of thirty-five million francs (toward a total cost of forty-two million) for this first film, which was immediately invested in the production of his second film, *The Cousins*.[40] That same year, three other films that were part of the New Wave cluster received similar subsidies: Pierre Kast's *Girl in His Pocket*, Louis Malle's *Elevator to the Scaffold*, and Jacques Barratier's *Goha*. In the spring of 1958 Jacques Flaud published a lyrical text in *Le Film français* entitled "Common Youth," which promised effective support for new filmmakers, while defending the idea that French cinema could only benefit from such an influx of new blood: "I like youngsters with a past and men with a future," he concluded.[41] Finally, in another very political text, published on June 20, 1958, Flaud outlined a strategy that confirmed the CNC's allegiance (and that of its funds for young filmmakers) to the new regime in power: Charles de Gaulle and his future minister André Malraux. Indeed, Flaud expressed a "Gaullist" aim for cinema: to support the development law favoring a quality premium that would more and more obviously benefit young filmmakers.

Malraux acknowledged the validity of such a policy when he personally committed to cultural activities in support of film and oriented his own ministry in a direction that, with regard to cinema, was largely that charted by Flaud, whom he encouraged and reconfirmed as the head of CNC. As early as 1959, the richly symbolic transfer of responsibility for film from the ministry of industry and commerce to the ministry of cultural affairs served as official recognition of cinema as an art form in its own right. Malraux quickly expanded the policy of supporting high-quality French films—a policy that, as we have seen, benefited the New Wave first and foremost—through the adoption of new measures, even though box-office figures had begun to decline: a selective funding system in the form of loans against box-office receipts, tax deductions for experimental and art film theaters, increased funding for the French film school IDHEC (Institut des hautes études cinématographiques) and the French Cinémathèque, and construction of a second screening facility for the Cinémathèque at Chaillot Palace.

Malraux expressed his personal support for the emerging New Wave by providing a helping ministerial hand when it came time for the ministry to select the films that were to represent France at the 1959 Cannes Film Festival, contributing a great deal to the daring choices of François Truffaut's *The Four Hundred Blows* and Alain Resnais' *Hiroshima mon amour*, as Godard did not fail to note in *Arts*:

> The screening [of *The Four Hundred Blows*] had ended and the lights had gradually come back up in the small projection room. The audience remained silent for a while. Then Philippe Erlanger, foreign affairs envoy, leaned toward André Malraux: "Is it really necessary for this film to represent France at the Cannes festival?"—"Yes, it is, quite necessary!" Thus did the minister of cultural affairs endorse the selection committee's decision to send to Cannes, alone, officially, in the name of France, François Truffaut's first feature film, *The Four Hundred Blows*. What matters is that, for the first time, a young director's film was officially selected by public authorities to show the world French cinema's true face.... Malraux made no mistake. Deep in the eyes of Truffaut's Antoine, nervously adjusting the hat on his head before stealing a typewriter in the dead of a Paris night, the author of *La Monnaie de l'absolu* was bound to see the glimmer of the inner spark, an uncompromising glow that he recognized, since it was the same as had gleamed twenty years before on Tchen's dagger, on the first page of *Man's Fate*. The creator of *L'Espoir* was best placed to know just what this meant: the vital talent nowadays, in cinema, is to grant greater importance to what is before the camera than to the camera itself, to respond first to the question "why?" so as to be later in a position to respond to the "how?" In other words, content is also form. If the first is wrong, then inevitably the latter will also be wrong.[42]

This homage was, in fact, a declaration of mutual love: indeed, the quintessential Gaullist minister and the New Wave did share a special moment at the beginning of the Fifth Republic.

An Intrinsically Political Cinema: Filming Life with Style

The New Wave was neither "Gaullist" nor "fascist" nor even "right-wing anarchist." The fling with Malraux was short-lived and rapidly degenerated into mutual recrimination, culminating in a sensational divorce with the scandal around *Suzanne Simonin, la religieuse de Diderot*—a Jacques Rivette film censored by the government in 1966, which prompted Jean-Luc Godard to publicly attack the "Minister of Kultur" in *Le Monde* and *Le Nouvel observateur*.[43] Two years later, in February 1968, it was Truffaut's turn to bash the "man with the short anti-memory"—with the eruption of a new scandal around the dismissal of Henri Langlois, the head of the French Cinémathèque, which was carried out blindly and clumsily, with Malraux's personal approval—marking the definitive break between the New Wave filmmakers and the minister of cultural affairs.[44]

More fundamentally, politics was at the very core of the New Wave project, that is, the concrete implementation of principles forged in the 1950s through a theory of apolitical cinema. Thus, the New Wave and politics were joined in this unexpected way, when ideas about cinema articulated by an apolitical criticism were taken up and applied. And they were applied in the name of style, the founding principle, which was, for cinema criticism à la Young Turks, the principal token of the artist's personality. In one of his early texts, "In Defense of a Political Cinema"—which he published in *La Gazette du cinéma* in September 1950, at age twenty—Jean-Luc Godard called on uninspired and unimaginative French directors to film the history of their country naturally, "to film as though they were shooting newsreels for Soviet propaganda"; "French filmmakers in need of scripts, poor wretches, how is it that you haven't made films about tax distribution, the death of Philippe Henriot, the wonderful life of Danielle Casanova?"[45]

A few years later, the young apprentice filmmakers of the New Wave shot their own "newsreels," filming the young bodies of their times, who spoke, loved, rambled, even if they did it all with a detached elegance rather than a true political commitment. Consider, for instance, the first short films, the early dabbling in filmmaking: Jacques Rivette's *Le Coup du berger* (*Fool's Mate*), Eric Rohmer's *Charlotte et son steak* (*Charlotte and Her Steak*), Jean-Luc Godard's *Charlotte et son Jules* (*Charlotte and Her Boyfriend*), François Truffaut's *Les Mistons* (*The Kids*)—all intentionally eschewed "great" subject matter. These films are all sheer stylistic exercises and direct illustrations of the neoformalism of which Bazin was suspicious: set in apartments or the countryside, they focus exclusively on the soap-opera musings of young people in love. A far cry from Claude Autant-Lara, who, at the time, offered a singularly biting depiction of the cowardice and spinelessness of the French during the occupation (*La traversée de Paris* [*Four Bags Full*]), or from Cayatte's didactic *films à thèse* (on the death penalty, the justice system, abortion), Allégret (prostitution), not to mention the highly political films of Louis Daquin and Alain Resnais, who directed *Les statues meurent aussi* (*Statues Also Die*), against colonial crimes, and *Night and Fog*, against the Shoah's fading from memory. These are genuinely political works. Yet the light love stories of the New Wave are as political as the rest of French cinema during the 1950s. But they are political in a different way, almost inherently, through their style.

The short films of the New Wave offered a brand-new form of experimentation, of a highly fragile and ephemeral nature, whereby the films' very form (the shooting, the technique, in other words, the gaze they impose) becomes a means of recording politics onscreen. It is no longer the script or the message, the lines or the subject matter that present us with a politics but quite the opposite. It is a way of filming, of lighting, of locating places, of moving bodies, which seizes politics precisely where it could not be captured by traditional films: in the youth of the time as seen through a personal style and perspective. In this sense the New Wave was able to grasp its time because it was uncomfortable with it. Being uncomfortable enabled these filmmakers to capture it, while maintaining the distance that is necessary to appropriate its complex contemporaneousness. All the New Wave heroes and heroines have an uncomfortable relationship with their time—Godard's uneasiness, Truffaut's nostalgia, Chabrol's decadence, and Resnais' sense of guilt. Their behavior is quirky, their perspective is off-kilter, which in turn allows for style and their ability to capture the real. To be contemporary, in the New Wave sense, is to be resolutely out of sync, but this also affords an angle-shot that truly captures people and things. The New Wave does not illustrate its time; it captures it and offers an uncomfortable commentary on it. And this constitutes its politics.

Truffaut's 1957 declaration of faith with regard to "first person" cinema and a cinema of "small subjects" should thus be read as a political tract: "it seems to me that future films will be even more personal than a novel, as individual and autobiographical as a confession or a private diary. Young filmmakers will express themselves in the first person, and recount what has happened to them. . . . They should be excessively ambitious and excessively sincere. Tomorrow's film will resemble the one who has shot it."[46] The point was to film something else, some other way, and politics was located precisely in that otherness: it was the formal economy of what invaded the screen when the rules of the game of cinema had suddenly changed. In a similar way Truffaut's plea in defense of *And God Created Woman* and of Brigitte Bardot—a New Wave icon, as "the first young woman of her time to appear in French cinema"—should be understood as a political declaration:

> As far as I'm concerned, after seeing three thousand films over ten years, I can't stand the saccharine and stilted love scenes of Hollywood films, nor the filthy, bawdy, and no less fake ones of French cinema. This is why I am grateful to Vadim for filming his young wife engaging in everyday movements in front of the camera, innocent gestures, such as playing with her sandal, and less innocent ones, such as making love in broad daylight—that's right! But just as real. Rather than imitating other films, Vadim has attempted to forget cinema and "copy life," true intimacy, and, except for a few scenes that end somewhat complacently, he entirely succeeded.[47]

The New Wave became political when it thought it had found its modern Danielle Casanova in Brigitte Bardot. The Joan of Arc of the firing squad victims suddenly wore her nakedness skin deep, the nakedness of "a girl who drives men insane."[48] The joint discovery of Vadim and Bardot was key: they constituted a formal and political manifesto, political because formal. More than an auteur, Vadim appeared as the catalyst of the crisis, the very embodiment of what films should be all about: to show a 1956 woman, while French quality films concealed the modern body under period costumes, psychology, "performance" acting, "beautiful" lights, and pseudo ideas. Politics became the presence of the present in itself, the intuition that capturing it would be, in itself, a manifesto.

In April 1957 *Cahiers du cinéma* devoted its cover to *No Sun in Venice*, Roger Vadim's second film, with the following comment: "Our readers already know how important we think *And God Created Woman* has been." In July of that same year, still in *Cahiers*, Jean-Luc Godard acknowledged the decisive nature of the phenomenon: "Roger Vadim is 'with it.' This is a fact. Most of his colleagues are still shooting 'in the dark.' This is also a fact. Yet Vadim deserves our admiration because he is doing as a matter of course what should have been the ABC of French cinema for a while now. What is more natural, in fact, than to breathe the *air du temps*? Thus, there is no need to congratulate Vadim for being ahead of his time, for it so happens that if all the others are late, he is right on time."[49]

44 ▶
And God Created Woman
(ROGER VADIM, 1956).
A DOCUMENTARY ON LOVE?

45 ▶
And God Created Woman (ROGER VADIM, 1956). AT LONG LAST, A FRENCH FILM FEATURING A YOUNG WOMAN OF HER TIMES.

Being "right on time" meant to film the Paris of 1957 in 1957. A few months later, the young critics would bring cameras down onto the streets, up narrow flights of stairs, and film real apartments; they would lose the heavy sound equipment to practice an on-the-fly postsynchronization that was both light and economical. The highly asserted realism of the New Wave amounted to a technical revolution that brought cinema back to a more primitive form, but the way had been paved politically by the revelation of *And God Created Woman* (figs. 44, 45). It was in the name of the realistic quality of attitudes and mannerisms that Jean-Luc Godard took the French quality filmmakers to task: "Your camera movements are ugly because your subject matter is bad, your actors are no good because your dialogs are worthless, in a word, you can't make films because you don't know what it means anymore.... We cannot forgive you for never filming girls as we love them, boys as we meet them every day, parents as we despise or admire them, children as they amaze us or leave us indifferent, in short, things as they are."[50]

Suddenly, the reality of a radically changed France erupted onscreen. It was no longer made up but was ready to be captured by a light camera in streets and homes. Truffaut made *Tirez sur le pianiste* (*Shoot the Piano Player*); Chabrol *Les Cousins* (*The Cousins*), *Les Godelureaux* (*The Wise Guys*), and *Les Bonnes femmes* (*The Good Time Girls*); Godard *Breathless*, *Une femme est une*

46 ▶
Band of Outsiders
(JEAN-LUC GODARD, 1964). CAUGHT ON THE SPOT, STYLIZED, BUT SO PRESENT: LIFE, MOVEMENT, BODIES—THE MOODS AND CODES OF A NEW WAVE PORTRAIT.

47 ▶
Band of Outsiders
(JEAN-LUC GODARD, 1964). RUNNING THROUGH THE GALLERIES OF THE LOUVRE AT TOP SPEED: A TRANSGRESSION RITUAL FOR JEAN-LUC GODARD.

femme (*A Woman Is a Woman*), and *Bande à part* (*Band of Outsiders*); Rivette *Paris nous appartient* (*Paris Belongs to Us*); Rohmer *Le Signe du lion* (*The Sign of Leo*) and *La Boulangère de Monceau* (*The Baker of Monceau*). None of them were directly engaged in making political films, but all conceived of filmmaking politically, that is, as a way to reveal the truth of a present that was, at long last, truly contemporary (figs. 46, 47).

The New Wave looked at the world through the lens of its own simplicity, its straightforwardness, its poverty almost, and these economic and technical constraints were the very conditions of its "politics." The availability of film stock that was more photosensitive, the technology of postsynchronization (that enabled them to lose the constraining recording equipment), their cult of speed, which became a dogma, their refusal to be enclosed in costly sets of reconstructed reality, the spontaneity of their actors, the devotion of their young crews that were not constrained by guilds in the number of hours they could work—all of these factors enabled, fostered, and soon obligated filmmakers to go out onto the streets, into apartments, in the fields. There was no radical novelty here—Italian neorealist films and Hollywood westerns had already practiced this method, each in their own way—but there was an intensity of action and a principle of survival that gave these films both authenticity and solutions they could not have found in French studios. In a 1959 interview Truffaut confirmed the highly political aspect of the new method:

> When a seasoned director would routinely shoot fifteen takes of the same scene, we would shoot only two or three. This stimulates actors, who must give it their all. The photography in our films does not have that glossy picture-perfect quality that French films usually have and the public has been moved by their spontaneous feel. All this confers on our films a new authenticity. For instance, in normal films, when a scene is shot that takes place inside a car, it is done in the studio by superimposing already filmed images of the scenery, which are projected behind the car. It is clear that the actor is not driving, and he says his lines while not paying attention to the road. Spectators must wonder why the car never hits a tree. What we did, for the first time in years, was to affix the camera onto the front of the car. The result was that we obtained greater authenticity of the streets and of the actors' performances, and these car scenes really captured the public's attention. Traditional cinema had lost all semblance of authenticity. The actors' costumes, for instance, were always impeccably ironed, their hair always flawlessly done. I also deeply believe in coincidences that happen on set. A lot of things happen on set. Shooting outside provides a further impetus. And it enables us to be perpetually on the lookout for these accidents, and sometimes to improvise.[51]

Director of photography Raoul Coutard—who was a key figure of this cinema and worked with Schoendoerffer and Godard first, then with Truffaut from his second feature, *Shoot the Piano Player*—shared the same perspective: "I immediately came to like the shooting constraints on low budget films. I arrived on the scene with the bad habits of a photojournalist. I like working on the spot and quickly. The slick and glossy doesn't appeal. I began with eliminating in all of my films all the so-called artistic effects that cameramen revel in, and instead of demanding a whole arsenal of lights, I used natural daylight. As a result, we shot fifteen times faster for ten times less money, and our laid back and lively films offered more atmosphere."[52]

The New Wave offered a stylized universe, with its rituals, gestures, words, attitudes, and looks, and that universe was the one in which audiences lived day-to-day. What was really new was the extent to which an entire generation thought it recognized itself in the mirror, often identifying with, sometimes rebelling against, the reflection. The New Wave filmed young people, captured their habits, the way they spoke. It offered to its young viewers young actors who told the stories of young directors. Something quite unique resulted: a double-identification. A whole generation of French people—who were labeled "new wave" in newspapers, surveys, and magazines—found itself more or less in sync with a certain theory and practice of cinema—called "New Wave." Only such a recognition, which was almost too much, but also ephemeral, could turn a specific moment in the history of cinema into a mythology of modern times. It was this cinema that the New Wave infused with style. It did not just record life as it was lived in front of the cameras; it shaped it, and the various forms it produced informed the range of possible approaches to the realities of the day. If the New Wave almost immediately forged a myth, it was because it was the first school of cinema that successfully captured with such precision a snapshot of history. The New Wave politics inheres in this film form, which transformed the reality of youth into a modern French mythology.

The Algerian War: The Intimate Drama of the New Wave

The conception of cinema specific to the New Wave, put to the test of reality in the late 1950s and early 1960s, increasingly led the movement of young directors to become politically involved. No matter how "disengaged" they wanted to be, or how much they aspired to hussar provocation, confronting contemporary reality head-on in film anchored their cinema in politics. And politics, at that moment, mostly meant the Algerian War. Notwithstanding widespread and persistent misconceptions, the Algerian "events" are present in New Wave films, if not as they were happening in Algeria itself, nor explicitly commented upon—until 1962, the French censorship board kept a careful watch—nor even strongly denounced. Indeed, the New Wave never claimed the mantle of "martyr" or *art maudit* for its own films and even less that of militant or political cinema. Yet in more than twenty films the Algerian War almost naturally figures as the traumatic horizon of youth drafted to serve twenty-seven months and twenty-seven days in Algeria, or returning therefrom. The characters do not talk much about it, yet their destinies, bodies, love affairs, and even sometimes words, are suddenly infused with the conflict that was waged by adults but fought by their children. The heroes and characters of *Le Petit soldat, Les Parapluies de Cherbourg, Adieu Philippine, Muriel, Chronique d'un été, Le Joli Mai, L'Insoumis, Combat dans l'île, Cléo de 5 à 7, Les Oliviers de la justice, Demain l'amour,* and *La Belle vie,* to name only the feature films, carry within them, on them, traces of the war, whatever discourse they articulate—or do not articulate—on it. These traces are political, and

New Wave cinema managed to capture and show them better than any other. The war was, thus, "not so invisible," even if it remained "not much seen," to borrow two expressions from Laurent Gervereau.[53]

The war, which imposed itself on the New Wave as something that could not be ignored, was made very clear in *Chronique d'un été*, the experimental "laboratory-film" shot by Jean Rouch and Edgar Morin in the summer of 1960, which follows the preoccupations of a dozen young people going about their daily lives. The film asks a simple question of these young people: "How do you live?" They each proceed to relate their living conditions, their aspirations, their love affairs, their studies, and their personal life-courses. In these face-to-face interviews there is little mention of the Algerian War. But when Rouch and Morin, halfway through the film, gather together this group of young people for a dinner, at which "we are going to talk together about the fact of being twenty in the summer of 1960," the war is all the participants can talk about. And, as in the famous Caran d'Ache cartoon of the Dreyfus Affair, *Ils en ont parlé*, they are not in agreement. When one of them (Marceline Loridan) exclaims, right from the get-go, "this absurd war must be stopped," another answers, "but France has rights over that country!" All, however, maintain that the dirty war has lost direction, and they express their common passivity, their own sense of *malaise*, in the face of the bad news coming out of it: "we have settled into this habit and consented to it. Crimes take place there, and we accept them." The two directors, dabbling in direct cinema, end this dinner gone awry on an inconclusive note, with Morin exclaiming: "France is very muddled," while Rouch prophesies (quite rightly): "There will be extraordinary film subjects to come out of the Algerian War." The sequence ends with a flurry of headlines from the Paris press, all on the Algerian War, to further highlight how much the event dominated the spirit of the times. Any film that claims to be attuned to its times is bound to record some of its elements.

Censorship, of course, placed certain constraints on this expression. The 1954–62 period was one of the most tightly controlled in the history of French cinema. There was a total ban in place until 1958, and allusions to contemporary Algeria in films were few and far between. In Algeria itself two French filmmakers working on the side of the FLN—René Vautier and Pierre Clément—shot documentaries among the resistance fighters of the ALN (National Liberation Army)—such as *Algérie en flammes* (1957–58), *Sakiet-Sidi-Youssef* (1958), and *L'ALN au combat*, which was begun in 1958 but interrupted when Clément was imprisoned by French forces. In 1955 René Vautier, Jean Lods, and Sylvie Blanc shot the anticolonial film *Une nation, l'Algérie*.

However, this kind of militant cinema remained, both in spirit and in form, very foreign to the New Wave.

From 1958 on, French cinema produced several films that were more ambitious and daring. Claude Autant-Lara, for instance, a long-standing opponent of the New Wave, who was himself willfully iconoclastic, began shooting his pacifist antiwar manifesto, *L'Objecteur*. Presented at the 1961 Venice Film Festival, under the title *Tu ne tueras point* (*Thou Shalt Not Kill*), and under the Yugoslav flag, it was vehemently denounced by French authorities. Banned from French screens until 1963, it was finally released with thirteen scenes excised. The other famous banned film was Godard's *Le Petit soldat*, shot in 1960 and ready for release in September of the same year. The censorship board justified its decision thus: "At a time when all French youth are called upon to fight in Algeria, it hardly seems possible to sanction depictions of the opposite course of action, illustrated and ultimately justified through the story of a deserter. The fact that the character is paradoxically engaged in antiterrorist action does not change anything for the core issue at stake. Finally, the lines of one of the characters in the film, in which France's intervention in Algeria is presented as ruthless while the rebel's cause is defended and glorified, in themselves constitute sufficient grounds for a ban."[54]

The film was, indeed, banned for three years. The case of *Secteur postal 89 098*—the medium-length film that Philippe Durand began shooting in 1959 and finished with no financial support in 1961—is an even clearer example. It recounts the story of a couple shattered by their son's departure for Algeria. It was banned "due to the provocative and intolerable nature of its message, which incites military insubordination."[55] Alain Resnais experienced another form of censorship, which operated further upstream, taking financial form. In 1959 and 1960 he endeavored to make a film on the Algerian War, based on a script by Anne-Marie de Villaine, entitled *A suivre à n'en plus finir*, but he never managed to obtain the necessary funding. Michel Marie, Jean-Luc Douin, and Benjamin Stora, all of whom have offered overviews of "Anastasia's scissors" in that period, point out that in the year 1960 alone ten films were banned outright, forty-nine others were "restricted" to people over the age of eighteen, and thirty-one were partially censored and had to be recut. Not all of these films dealt with the Algerian War, but the tally speaks volumes about the frenzy of the French censorship board at the time. The eighteen French medium- and full-length films censored in various ways between 1958 and 1962 for showing or mentioning the Algerian War were all released after the summer of 1962 and the Evian Accords, with most of them (*Le Petit soldat*,

Muriel, La Belle vie, L'Insoumis, Adieu Philippine) benefiting from the buzz generated by their "martyr" and "censored" status.

There were several possible stances in response to this censorship. First, there was explicit confrontation, which required going underground. This was the case for *Octobre à Paris*, a film on the massacres of October 17, 1961, shot by a collective of directors led by Jacques Panijel for the Maurice Audin Committee and the newspaper *Vérité-Liberté*. The film recorded the testimonies of several Algerians who, because they had demonstrated on that day, had been tortured by French policemen. It even staged a reenactment of the beginning of the demonstration from the Nanterre slums, combining the reconstruction with archival footage. It was shown, through the efforts of militant networks, and especially that of *Vérité-Liberté*, at underground screenings in 1962. The police seized a print on October 9 of that year, at a Ciné-Club Action screening.[56] A second possibility for responding to censorship was to outsmart the censors, rendering it inoperative for lack of explicit censorable images or lines. This was the attitude adopted by many New Wave filmmakers: between 1959 and 1963 the Algerian War was present throughout their filmography but never provocatively so, with *Le Petit soldat* standing as the counterexample of total censorship to be avoided.

In filming young people New Wave films naturally dealt with soldiers who were either coming back from Algeria, on leave, or about to deploy. In Jacques Rozier's *Adieu Philippine*, shot during 1960 and 1961, two young television stagehands enjoy their last two months of freedom—at work, at home in the suburbs, meeting two girls during their last summer in Corsica—before going off for two years of military service in the French army fighting in Algeria. Through his treatment, at once funny and melancholy, Rozier realistically depicts the gestures and words of the young working-class protagonists reacting to the Algerian War—even though the words *war* and *Algeria* are never once uttered at any point in the film. When, at a family dinner, a friend who has just come back from the war, Dédé, is urged to talk about it ("What about you? Come on, you haven't said a word"), he cannot manage a single word—at least not the ones that can be read in his gaze, the gaze of a soldier who has been hunted, who has known fear—and he just sighs: "Me? Uh, nothing!" These three words capture the discomfort of a whole generation. His quasi silence is emblematic of the New Wave in general and its relationship to the Algerian War in particular: to say as little as possible, maybe, but to mean a lot (fig. 48). In the last sequence of the film, in which the two friends leave Corsica from the port at Calvi, the final farewells—waved from the boat, on one side, and

48 ▶
Adieu Philippine
(JACQUES ROZIER, 1963).
THE FAMILY DINNER
SCENE, IN WHICH
DÉDÉ, URGED TO
"TELL" ABOUT ALGERIA,
SIMPLY ANSWERS:
"ME? UH, NOTHING!"
(PHOTO © RAYMOND
CAUCHETIER; COLL.
CAHIERS DU CINÉMA)

while sprinting along the jetty, on the other—are of heartrending beauty. They evoke the end of innocence, the last moments of happiness, and the beginning of national tragedy. The Corsican song that accompanies their departure acts as a kind of coded narrative of their destiny as soldiers and is harrowing in translation: "if you fail to put a ring on my finger before leaving for duty, may a shower of bullets burn your brain."[57] Death hovers over the immaculate images of these young people who love and lose each other, with the Mediterranean Sea as the only backdrop. Jacques Rozier's film leads from the waterfront to the war front.

Agnès Varda's *Cléo de 5 à 7*, shot a bit later, ends on an encounter in Montsouris Park in Paris between Cléo (Corinne Marchand) and a young man in uniform on leave (Antoine Bourseiller). The latter, who must return that very night to Algiers, accompanies Cléo to the Pitié Hospital, where she is waiting for medical test results. Here again, death hovers over the protagonists. They are scared together, she of illness, he of war, and try to ward off the morbid feeling by huddling together as they wander through Paris, from Montsouris to Boulevard de l'Hôpital, via Place d'Italie. But we already know, ever since the tarot sequence that opens the film, that the outcome will be fatal: they are both "on leave" from death. Cancer for the one and war for the other will claim these young and beautiful bodies like so many sacrificial lambs. The contrast between youth and beauty, on the one hand, and lurking death, the war that perpetually returns, on the other, makes Varda's film moving and just—morally, aesthetically, and politically (fig. 49).

The Algerian War is present in these films as a diffuse anxiety, a lethal threat, but whose effects are seen from France. It was not until René Vautier's *Avoir 20 ans dans les Aurès* (*To Be Twenty in the Aures*)—a 1972 film adapted from *Le Désert à l'aube*,[58] the narrative of a young deserter, Noël Favrelière, who refuses to carry out his "wood-gathering detail" (i.e., the execution of a young Algerian prisoner)▸ and subsequently joins the ranks of the ALN—that a French film actually documented the dirty war in its former theater of operations. Jacques Demy's third film, *Les Parapluies de Cherbourg* (*The Umbrellas of Cherbourg*), which received the *Palme d'Or* at the 1964 Cannes Film Festival, is a perfect example of this kind of geographical displacement from the terrain of the Algerian War to a young draftee's agony in an intimate drama set in metropolitan France. The film's dramatic turning point is Guy's departure for military service in Algeria. When Guy leaves Geneviève, in a poignant scene of *adieu* on a train platform at the Cherbourg station, a parting made even more heartrending by Michel Legrand's music and lyrics—"But I'll never be able to live on without you / I won't / Don't leave, or I will die / I'll hide you

▸ THE EXPRESSION *CORVÉE DE BOIS*, LITERALLY "WOOD-GATHERING DETAIL," BECAME A EUPHEMISM FOR THE EXTRAJUDICIAL EXECUTION OF ALGERIAN PRISONERS BY FRENCH MILITARY PERSONNEL DURING THE ALGERIAN WAR. PRISONERS WOULD BE SHOT WHILE ALLEGEDLY TRYING TO ESCAPE DURING WOOD-GATHERING DETAIL. —TRANS.

49 ▶
Cléo de 5 à 7
(AGNÈS VARDA, 1962). ANTOINE BOURSEILLER AND CORINNE MARCHAND TAKING A STROLL THROUGH THE MONTSOURIS PARK IN PARIS, AS IF TO FORGET ABOUT WAR AND DEATH. JUST AROUND THE NEXT TREE, HOWEVER, BOTH WILL IMPLACABLY RESURFACE. (PHOTO © TAMARIS; COLL. *CAHIERS DU CINÉMA*)

and I'll keep you / But my love, don't leave me"—it is a whole world he leaves behind (a pregnant fiancée and a love story, an aunt who has raised him and taken care of him, a small town made to look like a fairy tale), which he will never find again. Indeed, when he does return, not only is he physically crippled and mentally destroyed by the war, but he has lost everything: his aunt Elise has died; his fiancée has married another man, Roland Cassard, who has acknowledged paternity of the child; and the couple has left town and moved to Paris. Guy, now a wrathful alcoholic and social misfit, soon loses his job as a car mechanic. The experience of war is a disaster and effects a profound transformation of *Les Parapluies de Cherbourg*, from sentimental comedy to tragic opera. Rarely has the havoc wreaked by this conflict received such representation in film, through its very form, as in Jacques Demy's "en-chanted" musical.

Several short films also tackle the war through this same prism of intimate drama. For example, Guy Chalon's film, shot in 16-mm format for the Jean-Vigo Group in 1957, whose title, *58 2/B*, refers to the registration number of a group of draftees that year. "The boy in my film returns completely crippled from Algeria and is utterly incapable of readapting to normal life,"[59] explained the filmmaker in introducing his work. The same theme is explored in Daniel Goldenberg's *Le Retour* (1960) and Paul Carpita's *La Récréation* (1959); the latter follows a schoolteacher who, back from the war, recalls childhood memories while thinking of his best friend, killed in Algeria. Also in 1960, Jean Herman shot *Actua-Tilt*, a film about young people's confusion regarding the war, then *La Quille* the following year, in which he filmed two soldiers returning from Algeria, one of whom is "seized by the dizzy spells that struck those who had been discharged."[60] Finally, in 1959 Ado Kyrou, one of the lead writers at *Positif*, shot *Parfois le dimanche*, which follows a young couple living under the weight of the man's imminent departure for Algeria. All these films are proof that, for the New Wave, the war was neither a remote nor an ideological issue but an intimate one that shaped and sundered the lives of individuals. The personal and subjective treatments offered in these films strove to steer clear of both militant films and Hollywood historical epics.

The lead character in all these films is the common draftee, the private soldier, in short, cannon fodder, though always depicted outside the combat zone, in France, with his life bracketed in parentheses: his way of coping with his departure or return; his experience of taking leave, from the military and from his life; his now complicated and anxious relationships with his friends, his lovers, his family, and with a society that does not know quite what to think of him. The scene of the Algerian War, itself, may well have remained the unfilmed of the New Wave, but their films constantly explored—sometimes to the point of cliché—the existential tempest that struck those leaving, returning, and leaving again. This attests to a profound sense of *malaise*, which is a far cry from the reputation for nonengagement that weighed on these films, films that have often wrongly been said to reflect a failure of French society, and of French youth in particular, to face up to its political responsibility. In fact, such a failure to take on the war and its impact was far more characteristic of official "quality" French films, which, in the second half of the 1950s, never dared to confront the Algerian taboo, despite the financial means, the power, and the prestige these supposedly political and cultural films enjoyed. The war, for the New Wave, was no taboo. Quite the contrary, it informed a specific cinematographic form, which may be dubbed "zero-degree cinema," on the model of "zero-degree writing" pursued by the new generation of novelists in the 1950s, according to the theorist Roland Barthes[61]—a kind of empty neutrality, as if this aesthetic could politically exhaust the strikingly blank character of its own light, so as to film the very absence of the Algerian War, thus turned into more than a war: an anxious parenthesis, a traumatic blank.

Algeria, in the eyes of the New Wave, was first and foremost a war of antiheroes: of former and soon-to-be soldiers who do not have much to say. Shot in 1964, *L'Insoumis*, Alain Cavalier's third film, starring Alain Delon and Lea Massari, tells the story of a lost soldier of the French Foreign Legion, who rejects the Gaullist Algerian policy and deserts to join the ranks of the far-right Algiers putsch of 1961. Thus, following up on *Le Combat dans l'île*, Cavalier focuses once again on a fascist character engaged in violent action. Thomas, the deserter, carries out his plan, just as Clément, the amateur terrorist, did, when, together with a group of rebels and hotheads, he abducted a female attorney who was defending FLN militants. But whereas Jean-Louis Trintignant remained politically and psychologically constant against all odds, living and dying as a militant for the cause, Alain Delon is transformed, won over by the personality, the ideas, and the love of the woman he has abducted. From then on the film turns into a frantic getaway, with Thomas being chased by killers from both the OAS and the FLN while he tries to meet up with the attorney and then, once wounded, to make it to his mother's house in the Ardennes. It is there, in his childhood home in the middle of a French forest, that he finally dies. The entire film's architecture rests on his escape, in successive stages, like a degenerative condition that gradually saps a defeated body: the Algerian war, even if minimally depicted through a few early shots of combat in Kabylia, is the cancer that is gnawing at French society from within.

L'Insoumis is thus not so much a film on the Algerian War as the chronicle of a young man who experiences the conflict, flees from it, and whose life is dramatically transformed by it.

Inspired by a true story—the abduction by the OAS of Mireille Glaymann, subsequently freed by one of her legionnaire paratrooper guards—Cavalier deliberately deviates from it and follows a more experimental and intimate path: that of the diary of a desperate man, a man who mistakes both his cause and his times, a wanderer in history who experiences an epoch he does not get as if in a stupor. "I opted for a non-classic form," the filmmaker explained, "of fragments that are abruptly juxtaposed, as it happens when we are half asleep. No reflection, a few detailed descriptions of objects, lyrical patches, enlargements, distortions, and constant action, experienced by an intoxicated consciousness."[62] When the director confessed, in another interview, that "to [his] naive mind, this was a symbol of France at the time,"[63] the intention of the film, as well as that of most New Wave films dealing with the Algerian War, became clearer: to avoid classic representations in favor of a mental image of a society and its youth, to eschew war epics in order to explore the more intimate territory of the diary, to remain disengaged so as to better capture bits of the reality of confused and puzzled youth.

In its French cinematographic form the Algerian War is not the scene of national historical drama—as Vietnam was for American cinema—but that of a fragile and bewildered individual's doubts in the face of history. It is a war with no front, in which the battlefield dilates and contracts all at once, according to the scale of intimate psyches and individual behaviors, a war whose combat is over nothing, emptiness. "No battles, no hand-to-hand, no confrontations, is the enemy even in view? Never, heaven forbid!" wrote Benjamin Stora about representations of the Algerian conflict.[64] These New Wave heroes caught in the Algerian war can only be lost soldiers, devoid of any motivation, any ideal, sullied; they are scared and try to pass on to others the burden of a confrontation without cause. This is true of Bruno Forestier's disabused attitude in *Le Petit soldat*—when his lover, Veronica, is naively asked, "Why do you work for the FLN, out of political conviction?" The demystifying answer echoes in his head, like a revelatory boomerang: "It's hard to say. In any case, I find that the French are wrong. The other side has a cause, not the French. It is important to have a cause, very important. Against the Germans, the French had a cause; against the Algerians, they don't. They will lose the war." The Algerian War, in New Wave films, is the comings and goings of boats and trains, itineraries that symbolize absent battlefield action, but whose cuts are deeper than wounds inflicted in combat: the lesions of moral defeat in a war that does not make sense.

Torture: The Limit Experience of the New Wave

Following the Evian Accords, the political and cinematographical context changed. Censorship became somewhat more lax, enabling Chris Marker to shoot, in May 1962, *Le Joli Mai*, which contained an explicit sequence depicting the February 8, 1962, demonstration and the carnage at the Charonne metro station in Paris. At the 1963 Venice Film Festival, two French films dealt with the Algerian question: Alain Resnais' *Muriel* and Robert Enrico's *La Belle vie*. In the latter, Frédéric, a discharged soldier, is reunited with his girlfriend, whom he marries. Their happiness is soon spoiled by the palpable tension in the Parisian air: OAS attacks, police roadblocks, paratroopers patrolling the capital, and the sudden eruption into daily life of the fear experienced in war. Our somber hero falls into depression, brooding with dark thoughts. His life becomes an empty promise undone by traumatic memories of combat *over there*, which resurface in his personality and his life *back here*, as the shockwaves of war become increasingly visible in the city around him.

Resnais takes up the exact same theme and plays in his own way with this traumatic memory: "I am so scared of demagoguery, pathologically scared of militant cinema, that I prefer to resort to an elliptical style."[65] Bernard, Hélène's son-in-law, returns from the war and settles in Boulogne-sur-Mer, and the entire film strives to show viewers how difficult it is for him to now exist in the present. Resnais invents a complex, fragmented, contradictory, almost kaleidoscopic, cinematographic form that signifies the painstaking reconstitution of a personality by drawing a parallel between the reconstruction of a town laid waste by World War II bombing, and the rebuilding of a life that was devastated by Algeria and its obsessive memories. Chief among these memories is Muriel herself, who is most likely Bernard's girlfriend but remains mysteriously absent while he dates another woman, Marie-Do. In response to the latter's question—"Do you want me to tell about Muriel?"—Bernard says: "Muriel can't be told." He dabbles at filmmaking, "compiling evidence," as he tells Marie-Do, by filming the way Boulogne looks and feels in 1962, as France is about to vote on a referendum introducing the direct election of the French president.

Muriel turns out to be a young woman who was tortured by a group of soldiers in Algeria, a martyrdom that Bernard witnessed. He has thus almost "adopted" the victim; and she pursues him. Most of Resnais' film consists in the abrupt and precise juxtaposition of almost abstract shots of the city of Boulogne—its architecture, its streets, its empty lots, its construction sites—with the complex and elliptical telling of sad and nested love stories, narratives filled with confusion, imposture, shams, and painful experiences of dilating lives, from which all the characters suffer—as if the point was to bring together the scattered fragments of a destructive experience. This frail, failing, and painful memory might be labeled the "return from Algeria" syndrome except that in Resnais' view neither Bernard nor anybody else ever manages to return from Algeria. That past never passes, nor does the present ever come fully into focus. One does not ever come back from the Algerian War; one remains there, even from afar.

This impossible return does not only convey the painful experience of war's end. It also presents the trauma that, for many, resulted from being confronted with torture—sometimes as victim, sometimes as perpetrator, often as witness. How are we to go on living after witnessing this, carrying this experience inside, bearing this horrible secret? "You are returning from Algeria," a man in *Muriel* says to an ex-soldier; "I would like to talk with you; it's true, we know precious little about the question." The phrasing is cruel, since it alludes to Henri Alleg's exposé, *The Question*, published in 1958, a decisive moment when the fight against the Algerian War in France became increasingly synonymous with exposing torture. The silence of New Wave films on the Algerian War should be heard as a direct allusion to this nagging question. The allusion was sometimes more indirect. In *L'Insoumis*, for instance, the simple series of bathroom shots—a bathtub, a sink, a radiator—and the scared eyes of the FLN lawyer who has been abducted by an OAS commando, points to the obsessive presence of the theme. The lieutenant almost need not explain when he turns to the young woman: "you are afraid we're going to dunk your head, but you have a one-track mind, don't worry." The deep fear that torture inspired, and the shame of having perpetrated it on a massive scale, both opened and closed this historical-cinematographic episode—from *Le Petit soldat*, in 1960, to *Muriel*, in 1963.

Once they have abducted Bruno Forestier, the underground FLN supporters torture him to obtain a telephone number, and they use the methods developed by the French army (water-boarding, electrocution, suffocation under a wet blanket, precision blows, burning of the hands and arms, psychological pressure). The film devotes more than fifteen minutes to such scenes in the bathroom of a typical building in the suburbs of Geneva (fig. 50). From without nothing can be seen or heard: the revolutionaries have organized torture like a bureaucracy of horror (indeed, while torture is going on in the backroom, a secretary is typing in the lobby, and people are having banal conversations). Forestier manages to escape by jumping from a window, but Veronica, the young Danish woman whom he photographs and with whom he is in love, and who is an FLN accomplice, is tortured to death by a small group of fascists. Godard deliberately chose to focus the film on this theme: "I originally meant to focus on an old idea, that of brainwashing. But events in Algeria led me to replace brainwashing with torture, which had become the big issue."[66]

In *Muriel* the key is finally provided by a short 8-mm film of innocent scenes shot by a soldier in Algeria (soldiers' rations, shots of mosques, Arabic children), over which Bernard's voice tells the story of Muriel's torture at the hands of draftees. A whole series of concrete and insignificant traces—the short 8-mm film, a photo album, audio recordings of the torturers' laughter, Bernard's sobbing—suddenly become powerfully meaningful through the hero's confession. Resnais' film itself is suddenly reorganized around the belated revelation, around the missing piece of a puzzle the filmmaker deliberately made almost incomprehensible until these final memorial images and confession. The two films carry the political experience of the New Wave to its extreme: to achieve through style and mise-en-scène (dandy nonchalance with Godard, elliptical memory with Resnais), a cinematographic form capable of capturing the crucial debate of a historical moment, quite simply its question.

A Political Janus-Face

The New Wave constitutes a political paradox. The very same cinematographic form, precisely defined by both the texts that inspired it and the major films that represented it, could be successively right- and left-wing. This form—the auteur form, which manifests a highly personal writing or directing style—is politically Janus-faced: when it is a style, it leans to the right; when it is a form of realism, it gestures to the left. The praise of mise-en-scène—the powerful weapon of young critics who were looking to break free from didactic films that conveyed a clear message, and the linchpin of political disengagement—was not unreasonably suspected of right-wing hussar tendencies, or even fascistic dandyism, in the 1950s. But a few years later, the same directors, now putting their theories into practice, were perceived through the prism of

50 ▶
Le Petit soldat
(JEAN-LUC GODARD, 1960–63). SCENES OF TORTURE LED BY LASZLO SZABO, AN FLN MILITANT WHO, SITTING ON THE EDGE OF THE BATHTUB, IS READING HENRI ALLEG'S *LA QUESTION*, A BOOK THAT DENOUNCES TORTURE IN ALGERIA.

realism, the direct capture of the minutiae of the lives of French youth. And this highly stylized cinema was deemed to be left-wing, communing with the desire for change expressed by the young people it made its own, as well as with their fears concerning the Algerian War, and even their revulsion at torture.

To the formal mix was added a genuine historical realization that developed in stages. First, the last months of the Algerian War struck the New Wave, together with the scandal of the systematic torture perpetrated by the French army. Then came the concrete impact of cultural censorship, which culminated in the ban of Jacques Rivette's film *Suzanne Simonin, la religieuse de Diderot*, imposed by Minister of Information Yvon Bourges in 1966. Finally, there was the Langlois affair, triggered by Malraux himself, in February 1968. These events turned the New Wave filmmakers against the Gaullist government and the right-wing policies to which they were not entirely hostile in 1958. This political paradox, which tracked a rise to historical consciousness, was impeccably expressed by Jean-Luc Godard, who had been the most vocal Malraux enthusiast, in an article published in *Le Monde*, on April 2, 1966, just as *Suzanne Simonin, la religieuse de Diderot* was banned:

> At the time of Munich and Gdańsk, I was playing marbles. At the time of Auschwitz, Vercors and Hiroshima, I had just begun wearing long pants. At the time of Sakiet and the Casbah, I was flirting with girls for the first time. In short, as an intellectual debutant, I was all the more naive being also a beginner filmmaker, and I only knew about fascism from books. "They took Daniel away, they arrested Pierre, they are going to shoot down Etienne": all these stock phrases of the Resistance and the Gestapo might have struck me with increasing force, but they never struck me in my flesh and blood, since I was lucky enough to have been born too late. Suddenly, yesterday, everything changed. They arrested Suzanne. Yes, the police went to the lab and they seized the prints. Thank you Yvon Bourges for showing me the true face of the prevailing intolerance.

The New Wave thus shifted from right to left, leading to the political paradox that gave rise to the major mythological construct of French culture: the New Wave as the highest expression of the spirit of May '68. If this cinematographic movement had been considered right-wing in the early 1960s, by 1968, as if through a resetting of French memory, it was reconsidered as left-wing. This historical shift in New Wave identity is a peculiar phenomenon that began in the early 1960s and culminated in 1968. Two recent films, illustrating this updating of memory, even try to recreate the cinematographic

51 ▶
Regular Lovers
(PHILIPPE GARREL, 2005). MAY 1968 RECREATED BY PHILIPPE GARREL IN A CREPUSCULAR BLACK & WHITE.

52 ▶
The Dreamers
(BERNARDO
BERTOLUCCI, 2003).
BERNARDO BERTOLUCCI
CONFRONTS THE MAY
'68 LEGEND HEAD-
ON AND INSERTS A
SERIES OF NEW WAVE
REFERENCES THROUGH
HIS CINEPHILE LOVERS.

53 ▶
The Dreamers
(BERNARDO
BERTOLUCCI, 2003).
THE CINEPHILE TRIO,
HERE IN THE GREAT
GALLERY, REENACTING
THE SCENE AT THE
LOUVRE SHOT BY JEAN-
LUC GODARD FORTY
YEARS EARLIER IN
BAND OF OUTSIDERS
(SEE FIG. 47).

ambience of the times, thereby marking an important stage in the representation of May '68.[67] Bernardo Bertolucci's *The Dreamers* (2003) and Philippe Garrel's *Les Amants réguliers* (*Regular Lovers*, 2005) are both successful films in that they reconstruct, in almost opposite ways, the particular texture of the spirit of May 1968 (figs. 51–53). Yet, even more than through these two films that "remake" May '68, the resurgence of the atmosphere of those times operates through a return to an imagination of the times activated by cinema, the cinema of the New Wave. If cinema in France has played such a major historical role in the construction of the revolutionary mythology of 1968—whereas objectively it played only a minor political one, and barely filmed the events of May themselves, or the leftist saga that followed—it is because it had already permeated the spirit of the times. Young people who took to the streets, just like those who subsequently dreamed of revolution, were, in a way, the children of the New Wave as much as those of anti-imperialism. The shots in *Les quatre cents coups* (*The Four Hundred Blows*), in *A Bout de souffle* (*Breathless*), in *Le Mépris* (*Contempt*), in *Hiroshima mon amour*, in *Les Parapluies de Cherbourg* (*The Umbrellas of Cherbourg*), and in *Adieu Philippine* haunted the minds and imaginations of the times: the people had adopted their perspective, the winds of protest blew thanks to them, even though at the time of their release they were understood as manifestos for a cinema out of history.

This is precisely what *The Dreamers* shows in a rather moving manner—and in this way the New Wave films come to have a politically devastating impact. When a new, parentless world was born—as a counterculture of images—when the New Wave left the movie houses and took to the streets, May '68 was taking cinematographic form. For that cinema of the 1960s offered the youth of 1968 a collection of images of a proud and youthful beauty, fragments of film through which to see a different world and to try to rebel in black and white. Indeed, political rebellion, which in the Anglo-American world had taken its cues above all from music, revolved in France around moving images—and this was the New Wave's legacy. After all, did not one of the slogans scrawled on the walls of the Sorbonne read "Vive Pierrot le fou!"?

LA BOMBE
THE WAR GAME x

OSCAR 67

*La Presse mondiale:
Le film qu'il FAUT
avoir vu !*

Un film de **Peter WATKINS** Une production **BBC** Présentée en association avec le **BRITISH FILM INSTITUTE**
La version française est commentée par Jacques PAOLI et Alain GÉRÔME
Une sélection LES GRANDS FILMS CLASSIQUES et CYTHÈRE FILMS

Interdit aux moins de 13 ans

DISTRIBUÉ PAR LA SOCIÉTÉ
LES GRANDS FILMS CLASSIQUES

4

PETER WATKINS, LIVE FROM HISTORY ▶

THE FILMS, STYLE, AND METHOD OF CINEMA'S SPECIAL CORRESPONDENT

◀ 54
Poster for *The War Game*
(PETER WATKINS, 1965). (PHOTO COURTESY BIFI)

"THIS GUY IS A GENIUS," said Ingmar Bergman of the English filmmaker Peter Watkins, in January 1974, as he was coming out of a screening of *Edvard Munch* in Stockholm.[1] Having seen *Edvard Munch* at the La Rochelle film festival in the summer of 2004, after it had languished in purgatory for thirty years, and then again on its rerelease in France in February 2005, I cannot but agree with Bergman's pronouncement. There was certainly considerable genius in this nonconformist narration of the Norwegian painter's early years, struggling under the Puritanical conventions of his time. In this film, shot in Norway in 1973, Watkins revisited the visual and narrative techniques that had enabled him, ever since his initial work fifteen years earlier in England, to invent a new form of historical cinema. Edvard Munch takes on a fictional body and image: an actor in Belle Epoque costume reenacts his youth, his love affairs, his travels, and his work as a painter, during the last thirty years of the nineteenth century, in Christiansen, Oslo, and in Germany. He also addresses the camera directly, to share with the spectator his problems, hopes, and musings (fig. 55). He thus becomes a "documentary being," who might have been featured in cinema newsreels, or even TV newscasts, had they existed at the time. Similarly, his intimates—his mistresses, masters, and rivals—are at once personages in the story *and* people providing "live" commentary on their actions and relationships with the painter.

A subtle admixture, the film is entirely dedicated to the delirious recording of the dynamic of individual creation, reinserting it in its rich and contradictory context, at once social, intellectual, sentimental, and familial. The Watkins system can be defined as a way of reconstructing history so as to film it, thus bringing together in a single shot all moments in time: the film is set in the past, and meticulously places itself in history, but also in the present, since the events have the appearance of being recorded (and also often commentated) live, and conveys a certain sense of futurity as well, since it is rife with anachronisms, such as speaking directly to camera, in 1880. This striking technique for producing an original and polemical cinematographic form of history has been explored in more than a dozen films, from *Forgotten Faces* (1961)—during some twenty minutes of which the young director places himself at the center of the Budapest uprising of 1956, which he recreated in an English factory—to *La Commune* (1999)—which reenacts the Paris Commune during nearly six hours of film in a large warehouse in the Paris suburb of Montreuil, in front of two competing television networks of . . . 1871, one pro-Versailles and the other Communard.

55 ▶
Edvard Munch
(PETER WATKINS, 1974).
THE ARTIST MUNCH
SMOKING AND LOOKING
AT US: THROUGH
WATKINS'S HISTORICAL
REPORTAGE FILM STYLE
HE HAS BECOME OUR
CONTEMPORARY.

Peter Watkins—who has been oft misunderstood, even if now, at seventy-plus years of age, he enjoys broad recognition[2]—has described his own distinctive project, style, and method in the foreword to his book, *Media Crisis*, published in a French edition in 2003.[3] What is most striking in this sometimes insistent plea is the coherence of his intertwined conceptions of cinema and history. From his early experimentation with "newsreel style" in the late 1950s to the relatively recent *La Commune*, Watkins has tried "to substitute the artificiality of Hollywood and its high-key lighting, with the faces and feelings of real people." His profound ambition has been "to offer a way of countering the effects of soap-opera historical reconstructions and TV news broadcasts, by sharing with the public an alternative exploration and presentation of history—and especially their *own* history—be it past or present." This *sharing of history* through cinema thus takes on two aspects with Watkins. First of all, he adopts a very special style—as though the film were given over entirely to current events, to live coverage, to interviews—leading to an aesthetics of pure capture, of the cult of the "live," of the revelation of truth in action. Second, he adheres to a consistent method: the reconstruction of a historical milieu—long past, recent, or futuristic—through intense archival and pedagogical work, often conducted collectively by everyone involved in making the film. From the filmmaker to the actors, everyone takes part in this documentary research, experienced as an act of both historical and political commitment. "My work," says the director, "with (mainly) non-professional actors has always been driven by a desire to add a dimension and a process to television and cinema, which they still lack today: that of the public directly, seriously, and in depth participating in the expressive use of the medium to examine history." Watkins is thus simultaneously both absolutely on his own—an isolation that sometimes borders on paranoia—frantically creating an original art form, controlling and creating his own world in which he can express his own vision of history, and radically communal, since he is intent on using a method that is both participatory and collective. His strength lies in his dogged determination: for almost fifty years, through about fifteen films, he has been systematically searching for a cinematographic form of history. As he himself has declared: "cinema and history constitute our vital forces."

Making War Through Making Films

Born in 1935 in Norbiton, Surrey, in the South of England, Watkins studied acting at the Royal Academy of Dramatic Arts (RADA) in London and discovered filmmaking by chance when he saw an amateur film on a socialist demonstration in Kent: "Someone lent me an 8mm camera and it changed my life. I was fascinated by the object and its possibilities." He went on to shoot short films with young actors from the amateur theater group Playcraft, in Canterbury, Kent, while making his living as an editor at a small documentary production house, George Street and Company. Watkins did not come to cinema via cinephilia, as did the young French filmmakers of his generation but via the practice of making a film—through amateur films, of which he shot a large number, as well as his work as an assistant and an editor, in a country where the social documentary tradition had been well established since the war, with Humphrey Jennings and John Grierson's Crown Film Unit.[4] The young man enjoyed the recognition of his fellow producers of amateur films, a genre that was nurtured at the time by the Amateur Film Movement, supported by *Amateur Cine World* magazine, and promoted through London's National Film Theatre competition, which conferred amateur film awards.

It was as part of this world that Peter Watkins shot his first short films, which were from the beginning focused on history. *The Web*, made in the fall of 1956, is about a German soldier who tries to escape from French underground Resistance fighters at the end of World War II. The young German manages to make his way across the French countryside (scenes that were shot in the fields of Canterbury) but eventually gets caught by the *francs-tireurs*. They waver, decide to let him go, and then shoot him in the back. This was the first appearance of what would become a major theme in the filmmaker's work: the implacable figure of the *deathblow*. *The Web* won several prizes at amateur film competitions. In 1958 Watkins shot, this time in 16-mm format, *The Field of Red*, on the American Civil War, and, the following year, *The Diary of an Unknown Soldier*, which takes place in the trenches in September 1916 and for twenty minutes follows a young English soldier in the Great War.[5] A narrator tells his story over scenes of the soldier's daily life—attacks, retreats, deaths, executions, and the long interludes of waiting. With the help of friends and a few actors the filmmaker recreated a bit of the front in Kent and "made war" with his mobile, inquisitive, and unforgiving camera.

In the early 1960s Peter Watkins began shooting an even more ambitious nineteen-minute short film, *Forgotten Faces*, in which he reenacted, in the industrial suburbs of Canterbury, several episodes of the Budapest uprising of 1956, "played" by Playcraft Group actors, supported by a few nonprofessional extras. In this film Watkins definitively broke with a number of rules governing fiction and also freed himself from the documentary ethics of truth—through interview scenes, in which the actors break out of the roles they are playing, look into the camera and address it directly, as well as through spectacular rioting scenes that are filmed as though they were being shot live. Camera movements become wobbly as the film closely follows the action and crops the movements and faces of the protagonists—all of this constitutes a deliberate mise-en-scène to "recreate" the newsreel-style realism of news footage. It is the fictional, then, that appears to gesture to a form of historical truth.

The film begins with a shot of a young man's dead body, a bouquet of flowers lying on his chest. Violent street fighting ensues, and the camera freezes on the faces of the partisans who "took up arms on October 29, 1956." A demonstration is coming together, but at no point is it ever made clear what kind of document we are dealing with, so that each spectator is confronted with these images as though they had been captured "on the scene" by a camera that just happened to be present in the right place at the right time: the preparations leading up to the Budapest uprising. But soon the partisans kill a soldier, and the retaliation is severe: a high school student is shot down by the police. His mother has come to identify the body when an English voice-over breaks in on the images and introduces the various protagonists: Thomas, a young rioter, aged twenty-seven; his fiancée; a journalist friend; a nurse; a pair of crying orphans, aged twelve and seventeen. Watkins lingers on the faces of the insurgents, as in Soviet silent films, when, suddenly, a few seconds later, two captured policemen are beaten to death by a crowd, their bodies dragged through the streets, and then hung by their feet. After several symbolic acts (smashing red stars, burning propaganda, putting up protest posters) the tension builds as night falls—communist army tanks are said to be on their way. Campfires, tributes, hugs, singing, and readings—the insurgent band is in the streets, gravely and anxiously waiting. In the early morning a radio voice rises over images of still-deserted streets strewn with rubble and traces of the uprising: "the Soviet army attacked our people this morning." The scene suddenly cuts, and the end credits roll over graffiti renderings of the faces of insurgents. It is not until the very end of the film, then, that the "fictional" key to the entire historical narrative is given—the film recreated the revolt through a cinema that, using artifice, managed to produce, four years after the events, a historical "truth" of the Budapest uprising of October 1956. When the television critic Milton Shulman suggested that Granada TV broadcast *Forgotten Faces*, the network's vice president watched it and turned it down, fearing that airing the film may create credibility issues for his regular news broadcasts. This gives a good sense of the ambiguities of the "fictional/real" at work in Peter Watkins's films and of the radical critique of the media that they mount. *Forgotten Faces* was, however, selected by several amateur film competitions, winning a few awards and ultimately getting aired on the BBC as a result. This earned the director a job as a production assistant for British television in 1963.

At the end of that same year, during this apprenticeship in British television, Watkins directed *La Gangrène*—a now lost adaptation of a banned book, published in France in 1958, that depicts in minute detail the ordeal of five Algerians who were arrested and tortured by the French police—using the same principles of faux documentary. He immediately submitted several other film ideas to the BBC, and in particular to Huw Wheldon, the documentary unit director, including one on the Sharpeville massacre in South Africa and a newsreel version of the crucifixion, adapted from the Nikos Kazantzakis book *The Last Temptation of Christ*. In 1964 he obtained BBC support for *Culloden* and proceeded to shoot the film.[6] Watkins mounted a documentary reconstruction of the famous battle, which took place on the moors of Scotland's borderlands on April 16, 1746. Elite English regiments, under the command of the Duke of Cumberland, crushed the last remaining supporters of Charles Stuart, the Catholic pretender who, during the Jacobite rebellion of 1745, had tried to overthrow the Hanover dynasty in London. The battle itself, in which twelve hundred Highlanders and fifty English soldiers perished, turned into a merciless pacification of the Scottish highlands. The combat degenerated into a massacre before ending in the repression of a people and its culture, colonized by the English occupier.

The filmmaker used approximately two hundred nonprofessional extras recruited in the Lowlands and in London, backed up by a few of his regulars from the Playcraft Group. The film was a shock, both stylistically and politically. In Watkins's films the actors—made-up and dressed with careful attention to the minutia of historical reconstruction—look to camera, provide "live" commentary on what they are doing, and are constantly shown in close-ups. The filmmaker, camera in hand, confronts the horror head-on, gathering the testimony of the combatants, exploring the kernel of repression, and offering an incriminating portrait of the mythical Charles Stuart (a.k.a. "Bonnie Prince Charlie"), who sent his men to be massacred without qualms. Opposite the naive prince was the superstitious and unimpressive Duke of Cumberland, "the butcher" who committed "the worst atrocities in the history of the English Army."

56 ▶
Culloden
(PETER WATKINS, 1964).
THE TERRIBLE ORDEAL
OF THE SCOTTISH
FIGHTERS, FINISHED
OFF ON THE CULLODEN
BATTLEFIELD BY THE
ENGLISH ARMY, WHICH
KILLS MERCILESSLY,
PROFESSIONALLY,
OUT OF DUTY...
AND IN SUBJECTIVE
CAMERA SHOTS.

Culloden spares its spectators none of these deeds, filming the clashes in close-up—the dead, the dying, the wounded, finished off by English soldiers with their bayonets or with a shot fired at point-blank range, and the massacres of civilians in villages, the rapes of women on farms. Executioners and victims recount the horror and the violence to the camera, their eyes staring into the lens that records them. A surgeon describes an amputation; an English officer defends summary execution; an exhausted Scottish prisoner invokes his pain, rage, and sense of humiliation. The film is at least as much a political tract as a rigorous reportage, as if Watkins, the "image reporter," had found himself at the very center of events—cinema's special correspondent from the eighteenth-century battle, a metaphorical position assumed in the film by a period chronicler who provides "live" commentary on the battle and principal troop movements, holding a map in one hand and a spyglass in the other, and standing just a little apart from the theater of operations. The last shots of *Culloden* focus on the faces of children, women, and Scottish combatants, capturing their desperate eyes, with the voice-over defiantly declaring: "The English government gradually eliminated everything that made these people unique individuals. The English have created a desert and called it peace." The film was broadcast on BBC One, on December 15, 1964, in prime time and was a success, shocking and thrilling British audiences. The BBC rebroadcast the film several times in the 1960s, and *Culloden* received the British Screenwriters Award of Merit and the prize of the Society of Film and Television Arts (fig. 56).

On the strength of his success and acclaim Peter Watkins proceeded to make, again for the BBC, a forty-five-minute "newsreel" that represented, with as much rigorous realism as possible, a thermonuclear attack on Great Britain—that is, showing the event, now become a filmic fact in the present, in all its terrifying impact. The "mockumentary" was originally entitled *After the Bomb*, a title that explicitly declared the chief objective of the film: to record the immediate and multifarious consequences of the detonation of sixty-eight Soviet nuclear missiles on British soil. Watkins focused on the county of Kent, around the towns of Gravesend, Tonbridge, and Dover, laid waste by a bomb that had obliterated an airport forty-three kilometers away, and on the daily lives of several families of various social backgrounds in the countryside and in cities. In the end the film was called *The War Game*, a new title that gestured to two other objectives: on the one hand to suggest that, despite the objective and convincing quality of the often grueling images presented here, this was just a fictional game, a tragic supposition, a dystopian horror

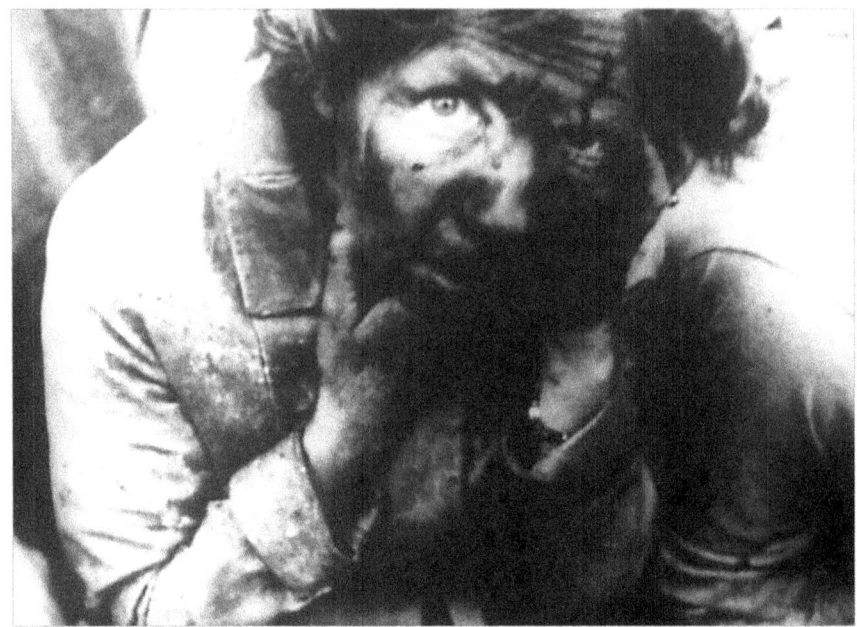

57 ▶
The War Game
(PETER WATKINS, 1965). "THIS WOMAN IS GOING TO DIE; IT IS IRREVERSIBLE," SAYS THE VOICE-OVER IMPLACABLY.

and could still be avoided if Britain renounced nuclear arms (this is the film's thesis); and, on the other hand, to denounce the strategic "game" of nuclear destruction adopted by the cold war superpowers at the time, as well as to show how a democracy, like Great Britain, could play games with fear and transform itself, pursuing perfectly logical and constitutional processes into a form of fascistic regime governed by laws of exception in order to deal with the emergency of nuclear war. Watkins added a first part to his film, showing, in parallel editing, on the one side, the escalating international tensions, and, on the other, the race for the bomb leading to the launching of missiles by the Soviets, and the simultaneous mobilization in England: psychological, defensive, and medical preparations, evacuation of millions of civilians, forced roundups, rationing and implementation of civil defense—with the operations being organized by increasingly militarized authorities. The events are accompanied with commentary by the realistic and slightly overbearing voice-over of a well-known BBC newscaster, Michael Aspel, himself parodying another famous British presenter, Dick Graham, who officiated during World War II. Even though everything for the film (sets, costumes, makeup, performances, special effects) was reconstructed by Peter Watkins on location in tranquil Kent, *The War Game* is terrifyingly realistic: it turns England into a postnuclear wasteland through a combination of processes of objectification used by the director: voice-over commentary, handheld camera reportage, talking-head interviews with experts, eyewitness testimonies, frequent looks-to-camera (fig. 57), and so forth.

Twenty minutes into the film, there is suddenly an interminable five-second blank. It is the flash of the nuclear detonation itself. Twelve seconds later, forty kilometers from impact, everyone is in a state of shock. The retinas of a child who happened to be looking up at the sky are burned. The film then shifts to a negative print: a couple with children, a simple Kent family, is screaming in their modest home. Somewhere else, a firestorm has erupted, with a burning wind blowing at one hundred miles per hour and carrying people along in its wake like straws. A fire captain and then a scholar offer expert testimony: "this is a firestorm, and these people are dying. Death comes within three minutes. This is nuclear war." Images of the wounded, of children with second- and third-degree burns, rush past. "Some of these people are just falling apart," comments a nurse in tears, while a doctor confides to the camera that is following him through a makeshift hospital: "For these it's just hopeless.... They'll be asking me to kill them.... Policemen have been shooting dying burn victims in the head." The voice-over announces: "between one third and one half of the population of the country is dying," while an excruciating dolly shot shows the bodies of dead women, most of whom have been disfigured (fig. 58). This horrifying sequence ends with a bucket full of wedding rings that have been salvaged from the bodies and the following terse comment: "This is a possible part of nuclear war." Two days later, the police begin to arm themselves to respond to the protests that greet their necessary efforts to retrieve bodies from families. For epidemics are spreading. A few weeks later, with most of the population interned in camps, the first food riots erupt. A policeman is stoned to death in Kent, and the scene is captured "live" by the camera, while the voice-over announces that many have died at a demonstration where the police opened fire on the crowd. Two looters are executed by army firing squad. When the image freezes on the executed men as they collapse, the voice-over predicts: "It is very likely that such a scene would happen within a short time after a thermonuclear attack has been launched on Britain." Finally, over images of the faces of children disfigured by the bomb, a short explanatory text scrolls down the screen before the end credits: "Much of the film that you have seen was based on information obtained from the bombings of Dresden, Darmstadt, Hamburg, Hiroshima and Nagasaki; on information obtained from 1954 Nevada Desert Nuclear tests; on information supplied by an advisory panel of three members of Civil Defence; two

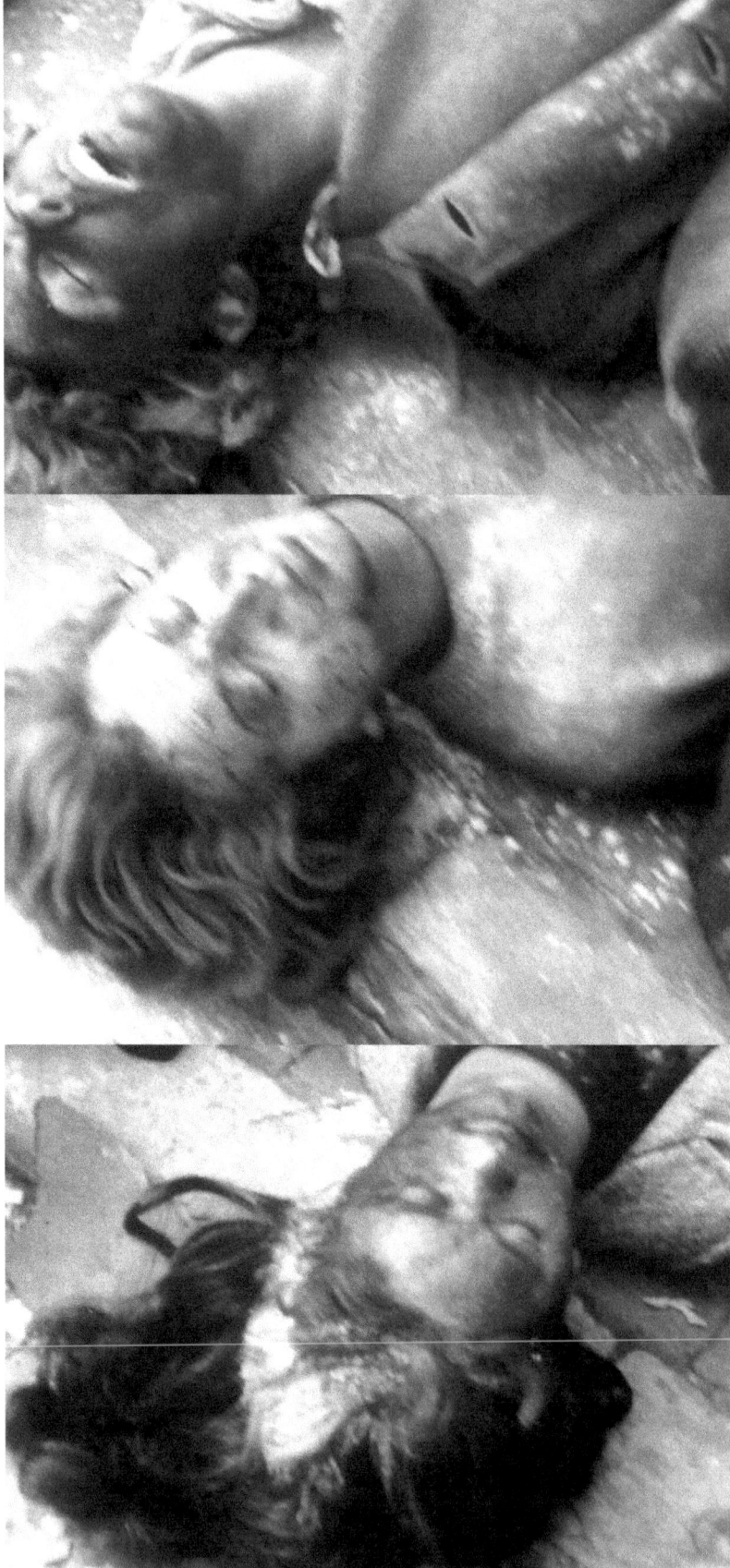

58 ▶
The War Game
(PETER WATKINS, 1965).
ONE OF THE MOST
UNSETTLING SHOTS
IN THE HISTORY OF
CINEMA: THE DEAD
BODIES OF WOMEN
ALIGNED ON THE
SIDEWALK, IN A SOUTH
ENGLAND TOWN
LAID WASTE BY THE
NUCLEAR EXPLOSION.

strategists; a doctor; a biophysicist and a psychiatrist." The end credits then supply the "key" to the fictional reconstruction—or rather anticipation—directed by Watkins, in mentioning the various collaborators involved in "make up," "costume design," "action sequences," and "special effects." The filmmaker has thus taken up, in a determined and insistent manner, the traditional crafts of action, entertainment, and escapist films so that they might participate in his denunciation film: he uses artifice to tell his truth more effectively. The weakest of the weak has thus seized the weapons of the strong to mount its own cinematographic guerilla action.

In the middle of the cold war this fictional disaster, filmed "live" as a newsreel, was deemed so realistic that it was awarded the Oscar for Best Documentary Film. Ironically, this also marked the beginning of Peter Watkins's difficulties with the censorship board. After viewing the film, Harold Wilson's government requested that the BBC not broadcast it, for fear it would trigger panic among the population, similar to the terror that spread among Americans when the Orson Welles radio "documentary" *War of the Worlds* was broadcast in 1939.[7] In both cases audiences were given live coverage of the end of the world, and authorities failed to appreciate the ultimate chaos staged and captured "in action." The ban on the film triggered an extensive debate within the British Parliament. In the end *The War Game* was shown only in movie theaters, first in England under the aegis of the CND (Campaign for Nuclear Disarmament), then in Europe and the United States. To protest the BBC's decision not to air his film, Peter Watkins resigned his position at the studio at the end of 1965. The British television ban on *The War Game* was maintained for twenty years.

The Time of Filmed Reportage

From the very beginning Watkins used hyperrealist techniques to capture images halfway between documentary and reportage, simultaneously formed by and reformulating the British documentary tradition founded by John Grierson and the groups he led in the 1930s and 1940s: the Empire Marketing Film Board, the GPO Film Unit, and later the ONF in Canada, together with filmmakers such as Alberto Cavalcanti, Humphrey Jennings, Paul Rotha, Harry Watt, Basil Wright, and Maurice Proulx.[8] This documentary school, which had considerable influence in England, was simultaneously realist and politically and socially engaged, striving to "turn cinema into a weapon at the service of the people while not falling into propaganda." As Grierson wrote:

"from beginning to end, the documentary movement was an adventure in reality, which consisted in observing the daily life of people. It could just as well have been a school of journalism, radio, or painting. Its essential force was social not aesthetic."[9]

What Watkins retained of it, however, became profoundly "aesthetic": a form and style that relied first and foremost on the lyrical quality of a cinema of testimony and vitality, of documents and veracity. Grierson and his disciples—whether they were filming workers, deep-sea fishermen, communication networks, factories, specific social problems, or the civil rights struggle—all deployed a politically engaged style, which Watkins adopted, following the ideas of the head of the GPO Film Unit: "The documentary idea is all about bringing onto the screen, by any means necessary, the concerns of our times, striking the imagination with as rich a quality of observation as possible. This vision may translate as reportage at some level, as poetry at another; and at yet another level, its aesthetic quality resides entirely in the lucidity of its exposition."[10]

This kind of political commitment is characteristic of another decisive influence on the way Watkins perceived the world: the Soviet school of documentary, which, following Dziga Vertov's inspiration, was represented by the "epic" work of Roman Karmen, which one of Watkins's early films, *Forgotten Faces*, echoes at times.[11] In this sense Peter Watkins's objectives were rather close to those of Lindsay Anderson and Karel Reisz, his contemporaries in the British Free Cinema movement who worked on more straightforwardly fiction films, training their cameras on history in order to restore the political consciousness of *homo britannicus*, as Anderson explained in 1956: "The filmmaker's role is not to directly encourage political action—which, given the current advanced state of embourgeoisement in England, would be particularly futile—but rather to make possible an awakening of the working classes by restoring their sense of their own human worth, their importance in past and present history, and their dignity."[12]

The medium that was, and remains, the true "contemporary" of the work of Peter Watkins is, of course, television—both his cross to bear and his modernity. The filmmaker may have denounced, in the harshest if not always most convincing terms, and with increasing vehemence, the "media crisis" and the degeneration of television into a "monoform," itself part of a standardizing "mass audiovisual media" system that obeys a "universal clock" that is globalized and conformist.[13] Yet Watkins has never been as effective as when borrowing for his own ends the very form he denounces, using its most spectacular techniques against the system for which it was originally conceived. In this way Peter Watkins's cinema has been nurtured and formed by BBC and American network styles of television reportage and news.

The growth of filmed journalism was one of the striking aspects of Anglo-American television in the 1950s and 1960s. On the radio, from the 1930s onward, sound reportage, with journalist commentary, had developed into a genre, of which Orson Welles's broadcasts of 1938 and 1939 constituted the fictional apex. As for film reportage, World War II precipitated a rapid change in the techniques, formats, and even the style of visual news.[14] American and Canadian correspondents, especially, took advantage of the lighter, sturdier, and easier to handle 16-mm format to record footage at the center of the action. Similarly, in the early 1950s portable tape recorders enabled faster sound recording. From then on, a small team comprising a cameraman, a soundman, and a journalist/director could produce field reports of considerable effectiveness and increasingly compete with the foreign correspondents of the print media. The movement toward film reportage marked the end of the traditional cinema "newsreel," which disappeared from theaters in the 1950s, and opened up new territory for dissemination, namely television. In the United States small companies specializing in film reportage were created, notably Drew Associates, founded by Robert Drew and Richard Leacock, which produced the most famous example of the genre at the time, *Primary*, a documentary on the Democratic primaries of 1959 and 1960, featuring John Fitzgerald Kennedy.[15] The context of the Vietnam War, from the escalation of U.S. intervention in 1964 onward, also gave rise to a flurry of war reportage of a new kind, very close to the combatants, sometimes candidly showing the fear and horror that soldiers endured—using techniques enabled by light cameras, direct sound, and on-the-scene commentary—in a way that was both authentic and spectacular.

American politics and the Vietnam War were the two principal topics around which the documentary genre was revitalized. Forging ahead, reporter-filmmakers established themselves in a genre that the critics called "newsreel" in the United States and Britain, "direct cinema" in France and Canada:[16] the Leacock-Pennebaker tandem (*Primary*, 1960), the Maysles brothers (*Gimme Shelter* and *Salesman*, 1969), Jean Rouch (*La Chasse au lion à l'arc*, 1966), James Blue (*The March*, 1963, on the civil rights march on Washington), Robert Young (*Sit In*, 1964, on the antisegregation actions by African Americans in Alabama), Carole Lucia Satrina and Eugene Marner (*Phyllis and*

Terry, 1964, on two young girls in Harlem), Emile de Antonio (*Point of Order*, 1964, on Senator Joseph McCarthy; and *Rush to Judgment*, 1966, on Kennedy's assassination), as well as, several years later, Robert Kramer, who made three political-fiction films in newsreel style (*In the Country*, 1967; *The Edge*, 1968, on a group of American anarchist intellectuals; and especially *Ice*, 1970, on the mechanisms that might lead to fascism in a country like the United States).[17] All of these films can be compared to those of Peter Watkins on several points. As Gilles Marsolais puts it in his now-classic book *L'Aventure du direct*: "From all corners of the globe, reporters were sending in short pieces that were filmed right there and then, illustrating events with eloquent and often compelling footage. Quickly put together, these newsreels enabled theater audiences and television viewers to receive fresh news and, even more important, trained them to decipher darting, chaotic, ill-defined images appearing in rapid succession, disjointed, and hastily edited. The audience was learning to read the 'live' style" (93).

Peter Watkins intervened in a world of visual representation that was beginning to recognize this form of reportage as authentic and enriching and was learning how to make use of it. His approach consisted in displacing this new form and applying it to filmed historical time, either past (the Battle of Culloden, the Great War, the Budapest uprising) or future (nuclear war), which was the traditional province of the most classic, and even academic, of studio genres (period films, war films, science fiction). However, this intersection of reportage and history was unheard of. The decisive influence on Watkins was that of British television's "new reportage."[18] From the early 1950s onward, through the auspices of Paul Rotha and then Norman Swallow, who presided over the documentary department at the BBC, there were many successful reportage programs: films on the arts and on artists; on magazines, such as Stephen McCormack's *London Town* series—which was broadcast from 1949 onward and provided a lively chronicle of daily life in the British capital; and, above all, Robert Barr's "semidocumentary" series *It's Your Money They're After*, which involved studio reconstructions of historical events and recent news items in order to artificially "dramatize" the reportage, punctuated by presentations and commentary. Watkins also resorts to some of these narrative tricks in his "semidocumentary" reconstructions. But the one series that probably had the deepest impact on Watkins was Anthony de Lotbiniere's *Special Enquiry*, which aired once a month between 1952 and 1957. Each broadcast focused on an important grassroots issue drawn from everyday English life (housing shortages, problem teenagers, education, food poisoning, the handicapped, car traffic, racial minorities, etc.). The forty-five minutes devoted to the issue included a presenter's introduction, which was followed by discussion with a guest who analyzed the images, documents, and testimonies shown in the reportage. *Special Enquiry* radically transformed British television journalism by giving investigative reporting center stage and by inviting a wide range of ordinary people to speak up, while also calling on legitimate expertise. Following in the footsteps of *Special Enquiry*, several other television documentary series marked their times deeply. Those, for example, by Denis Mitchell—*In Prison* (1957), *Night in the City* (1958), and *Morning in the Streets* (1959), filmed on location with a light camera and a small crew—declared their aim to "film the world in which people live." In the early 1960s, when Norman Swallow and Denis Mitchell began working there, Granada TV became the main outlet for the most exciting reportage: the *Look in on Life* series ("The Sewermen," "Road Sweepers," and "Tramps," to name only the most striking), and *World in Action*, with its characteristic news reportage, shot using handheld 16-mm cameras, live sound, and a direct "on-the-ground" style. This was the initiation for such major filmmakers as Donald Baverstock, Huw Wheldon, Jack Gold, Ken Russell, and John Boorman. To borrow a phrase form Norman Swallow, the decade from 1955 to 1965 was "the golden age of television reportage."[19]

What enabled Peter Watkins to redefine filmic representations of history were these techniques developed for television reporting—techniques he had himself developed during his apprenticeship at the BBC. From then on he made tireless excursions into the past, in the style of a foreign correspondent, using the cinematographic forms he had developed at the intersection of documentary, reportage, and political fiction. The filmmaker recognized his debt to these influential genres, acknowledging, in reference to *Culloden*, that he had "employed the style used in Vietnam War news broadcasts" like *World in Action*—a kind of collage of anachronism and heterogeneous technique, which was the only way "to bring a sense of familiarity to scenes from an 18th century battle, in the hope that this anachronism would also function to subvert the authority of the very genre [he] was using."[20] In a kind of poetic justice or supreme historical irony, the U.S. Army long used excerpts of *Culloden* as part of its training in military strategy, especially scenes of soldiers executing Scottish wounded on the battlefield, in order to put U.S. Army officers into a state of extreme savagery.[21]

The Trials and Tribulations of an Exiled Filmmaker

In 1966 Peter Watkins directed his first "fiction" feature film, *Privilege*, outside of the BBC framework in which he had been working. Universal Studios, the Hollywood major that produced it, was at the time looking to attract European directors to its London studios. Watkins accepted the studio's offer and chose to employ his distinctive pseudodocumentary mode, casting only two stars: singer Paul Jones and fashion model Jean Shrimpton. The script was an allegorical fable about contemporary decadence and brainwashing, which follows the rise and fall of an English pop idol, Steven Shorter (Jones), who enthralls fans with his charismatic power but who is himself manipulated by the British authorities and the Anglican Church into indoctrinating his public and diverting it away from any form of political consciousness. The first part of this ambitious film looks like uncompromising reportage, filmed with a handheld camera, on the world of pop music and its practices, with Shorter becoming, in his concerts as well as his private life, the maestro of a kind of orchestrated violence. The second part proceeds in a more satirical and science fiction vein (the film is set "in 1970," that is, three or four years after it was actually shot). Shorter has become a Christlike bard, singing pop hymns, and the Church organizes mass events around him, events whose similarities with Hitler's Nuremberg rallies were not lost on contemporary audiences and were received with some trepidation. *Privilege* begins as a clinical anatomy of the pop music world but then turns into a manifesto against state manipulation and perversity. Forty years later, however, the film plays mostly like a documentary of the "new tribal age"[22] of pop youth—its mores, its enthrallment with drugs (especially LSD), its induced dementia—and the manufacturing of an idol (fig. 59). *Privilege* was screened as an Out of Competition selection at the 1967 Cannes Film Festival. Released in England a few weeks later, it was a flop, receiving minimal distribution from Universal. From then on Peter Watkins followed the path of a *cinéaste maudit*.

Watkins did not, however, give up on a Hollywood project with Marlon Brando that he tried to make happen in 1967. The film, *Proper in the Circumstances*, was about the savage wars waged by the United States against the Sioux Nation. Through this film and this actor Watkins wanted to provide a denunciation of the Native American genocide. Universal did not follow through, and Watkins remained very bitter about it: "I wanted to make a film on the Indians and Indian elimination, the massacre of the Sioux tribes, and the peace process that was imposed on them: the deportation, poverty, and brutality of confinement. How American imperialism was built on that particular ferment. With Brando, we also discussed the possibility of a film on Kit Carson, the serviceman who organized the Navajos' deportation. Brando was really into it, but Richard Burton and Elizabeth Taylor began to interfere in these projects, and then all their lawyers, and I, the young British filmmaker, did not stand a chance."[23]

Gone from the BBC, estranged from Universal, and hurt by the negative critical response to *Privilege*, both at Cannes and on its London release, Peter Watkins decided to leave England. A protracted period of restless wandering followed, during which the filmmaker successively settled in the various countries that produced his films: Sweden, the United States, Norway, Denmark, Australia, France, and Lithuania. He never lived in England again, defining himself as a "filmmaker in exile" or, in the words of the critic John Cook, a "gypsy filmmaker,"[24] even if, in his spectacularly political, authentic, and satirical style, he remained faithful to the British political and social documentary tradition.

In late 1968 Watkins reached the first stage of that long exile, Sweden, where he settled with his wife and children. This is where he shot his second feature film, *The Gladiators*, whose original title, *The Peace Game*, gave a better sense of the project: it was no longer the nuclear war game that Watkins recreated and filmed in his pseudodocumentary style but the peace game, or rather the peace *games*, a sort of Olympic games that, in a near future, would enable warring parties all over the world to confront each other at a given time and place, and according to a set of predefined rules, through champions that they would train and appoint. In *The Gladiators* the governments of the world have agreed to replace war, costly in terms of both blood and treasure, with these "Peace Games"—which are, of course, reminiscent of the mortal combat of the Roman arenas—between national heroes who have been isolated in a deserted zone, in Sweden, on neutral territory. Sponsored by a brand of pasta, the combats are broadcast on TV the world over and are conducted, overseen, and arbitrated by a complex electronic machine that selects the order of events and the opponents and keeps score. The whole operation is closely monitored by a multinational military force. Watkins chooses to focus on two particular groups—Anglo-Saxon Westerners, on the one hand, and communist Chinese, on the other (see fig. 63)—who compete in a race to the control center, across rivers and ditches, through abandoned factories, corridors, trenches, and ruins, all the while under the constant threat of enemy ambush. Maoist indoctrination, on the one hand, and nationalism and the

59 ▶
Privilege
(PETER WATKINS, 1967).
A RITUAL THAT IS BOTH
RELIGIOUS AND POP:
A GIANT GATHERING
AROUND THE IDOL AND
CHARISMATIC SINGER
STEVEN SHORTER,
FILMED LIKE A NAZI
RALLY IN NUREMBERG.
PETER WATKINS
ENGAGES IN VIOLENT
POLEMICS AGAINST THE
MEDIA SOCIETY.

cult of money, on the other, are thus pitted against each other through these contained combats between trained fighters and avid mercenaries (fig. 60).

In the fall of 1969 Watkins's first professional film, *Culloden*, premiered in the United States on the campuses of UCLA and UC Berkeley. The film was such a success that a small left-wing distribution company, Red Star, decided to include it in the American campus film distribution network. Many critics saw it as an allegory for the Vietnam War and made the link—which readily suggested itself, since the filmmaker himself acknowledged he had been influenced by Vietnam War footage filmed by Western correspondents—between the Battle of Culloden, symbol of the violent extension of English rule in the eighteenth century, and the "pacification" campaign of the United States in Indochina, emblem of imperialist aggression two centuries later. Given this favorable reception of his earlier work, the thirty-three-year-old filmmaker decided to make a film of political fiction in California, with the financial and human support of Students for a Democratic Society (SDS), which was very active on U.S. campuses at the time. In the middle of the California desert, with an American flag planted in the ground as the only landmark, the filmmaker created the Bear Mountain Punishment Park, where two dozen pacifist students, chased by a pack of highly trained policemen, were to "suffer" and "die" under the gaze of his handheld camera.

Watkins was inspired by the context of violent confrontation between political authorities, police, and various leftist student groups at campus demonstrations against the Vietnam War. In May of 1970 four students were killed during a confrontation with the National Guard at Kent State University, in Ohio. A year earlier, in March 1969, there was the trial of the Chicago Seven—the young political activists who protested against the Vietnam War and were accused of conspiracy and of instigating the riots that had erupted at the Democratic National Convention in August 1968. In the face of rising protests against the increasingly intense bombing of Vietnam, President Nixon proclaimed a state of emergency in February 1970 and began to enforce the 1950 McCarran Act. This is the starting point for *Punishment Park*, which was shot in the early summer of 1970: to depict, in an intensely realist style, the conditions under which such a rigorous enforcement of this law of exception transforms the United States into a totalitarian regime that interns, judges, and punishes its own children. The film opens with shots of the desert being traversed by a small group of exhausted men and women flanked by policemen. At that point the text of Title 2 of the McCarran Act (September 2, 1950) scrolls down the screen: "The President of the United States of America is

60 ▶
The Gladiators
(PETER WATKINS, 1969).
IN THIS FILM PETER
WATKINS'S SHOTS ARE
CLEARLY REFERENCING
NEWSREELS OF THE
EVENTS OF 1968 AND
THE ANTI-AMERICAN
DEMONSTRATIONS OF
THE YOUNG REBELS.

authorized—without further approval by Congress—to determine the occurrence of insurrection within the United States and to proclaim the existence of an 'Internal Security Emergency.' The President is then authorized to apprehend and by order detain each person as to whom there is reasonable ground to believe that such person probably will engage in acts of espionage or of sabotage. Persons detained shall be given a hearing, without right of bail and without the necessity of evidence, and shall then be confined to places of detention."

The film cuts back and forth, through sometimes rather didactic parallel editing, between, on the one hand, scenes of the sentencing of a series of young activists, Group 638, by emergency tribunals charged with dispensing summary judgment in makeshift tents (we are successively shown seven trials, of students, black militants, hippies, a philosopher, artists, and such), and, on the other hand, the wanderings of Group 637, already convicted, who have been dispersed within Punishment Park, which was defined at the beginning of the film as "a training camp for the police and National Guard to discipline elements intent on overthrowing the United States government through violent means, and a punitive deterrent for such subversive elements." Indeed, rather than receiving long prison sentences (of five, seven, or ten years), the activists found guilty may choose to spend three days in this novel form of detention center, where the rules of survival are very severe. To win their freedom, the detainees of Punishment Park have three days to reach an American flag that has been planted in the mountains, fifty-three miles from their starting point, without food or water, under conditions of scorching sun by day and freezing cold by night, and while evading the law enforcement officers pursuing them.

The visual, political, and fictional force of Watkins's film resides, of course, in the spectacular representation of a "punishment park" that never actually existed in the United States, combining various cinematic references, from the initiation rituals of westerns to the ordeals endured by the protagonists of certain war movies, not to mention Count Zaroff's ferocious hunts in Ernest B. Schoedsack and Irving Pichel's masterpiece *The Most Dangerous Game*. The police officers have been trained to suppress rebellion using the most brutal means available, including lethal force. The camera constantly cuts between the depiction of these draconian methods and the fate of the rebels, who are never presented as heroic or even individualized, as they become divided or sometimes try to survive by being more violent than their executioners. *Punishment Park* does not offer leftist heroes, who are both victimized and combative, with whom the public could comfortably identify. Inside the park all are both victim and victimizer, young activists and their pursuers alike—all are ready to do whatever is necessary to survive, reduced to a condition of abjection and cowardice, the one devoid of conviction and blindly enforcing the rules and the other trying to save their own skins by any means. Once again, it is Watkins's pessimism that is most striking, as well as his ability to film at the closest range while rendering in an intense, spectacular, and vivid manner the processes by which ordinary individuals descend into barbarity, an ordered society slips into a state of emergency, and a civilization of compromise and comfort slides into rituals of punishment and humiliation—with no hope of return. Indeed, the four youths who do manage to reach the American flag, representing their longed-for sanctuary, are beaten to death by enraged policemen. When confronted by Watkins's camera, and in response to direct questioning, these men in uniform express either shame for having perpetrated such atrocities or pride for having defended the purity of the national flag.

As always with Watkins, the majority of the film's cast consists of nonprofessional actors, supported by a handful of professionals. The members of the tribunal, for instance, were all played by ordinary citizens of the small California desert town where these scenes were shot. When the film was released in a few American theaters in late 1970, it provoked a scandal and drew the wrath of conservative groups, who protested against this "immoral" work that "does not promote love of the flag."[25] *Punishment Park* was pulled from American theaters a mere four days after its release for fear of the demonstrations and riots it might trigger. The release gave rise to a flurry of fierce criticism from commentators who rejected the comparison of the United States with a totalitarian regime. Since then, the film has been rarely screened in American theaters and never on American television. Watkins, who had no choice but to pick up his pilgrim's staff once again, exiled himself anew in Scandinavia, where he remained, between Norway and Denmark, from 1972 to 1976.

The Deathblow as a Stylistic Form

Peter Watkins's style, his sensationalist—in the journalistic sense of the term—manner of capturing history, may be defined by the very presence of the camera, jostled by the movements of bodies and emotions, by the authentic feel of the reconstructed scenes, all of which are based on carefully researched and presented archival material, by a frontal confrontation with events (staged through a variety of realistic effects), accompanied by testimony of various kinds. The director's images literally assault us even while the characters move through a different time period, separated from ours by many years or even centuries. Their faces gaze out at us, their words engage us, their costumes have become clothing again, their physical bearing is no longer burdened by the past they are trying to recreate, the shots are haunted by a strange sense of presence. To all this Watkins generally adds a voice-over, which introduces distance, often an ironic distance, from this counterfeit historical objectivity.

His is a confusing cinematographic form of history, whose temporal markers have been turned upside down, whose truthfulness is ambiguous, whose status is double, if not triple, similar in this way to the world offered up to the chaos of *Culloden*, *The War Game*, *Punishment Park*, and *Edvard Munch*. When watching a Peter Watkins film, spectators find themselves placed in front of a representation of history about which they are led to wonder if it appears real because it is fictitious, or if it intends to be real while being fictitious, or even if it appears fictitious in order to convey a more essential sense of the real. These questions are raised by Watkins's world and, indeed, they have been raised by the critics. Contrary to the filmmaker's own claims, in his sometimes self-pitying writings, the films—or at least those released in theaters (*The War Game*, *Privilege*, *The Gladiators*, *Punishment Park*, and then *Edvard Munch*, *Force de frappe*, *Le Voyage*, and *La Commune*—that is, most of his work)—have received considerable attention in the press from critics who have consistently grappled with the questions they raise: what is this strange form of cinema, this hybrid style of mise-en-scène, this unique combination of rigor and spectacle in the representation of history?

Watkins himself has made fun of the critics' urge to develop taxonomies and semantic categories for his films: "articles about me are all obsessed with labeling me, maybe because my films are still unsettling."[26] Indeed, his films do seem to throw critics off, to elicit a kind of panic, to confuse them with a cinematographic and historical chimera they cannot make sense of. Watkins himself has a knack for aggravating this stylistically sensitive point by adamantly vindicating the contradiction that is inherent to his cinema:

> I have always attempted to establish links with the audience and escape Hollywood manipulations, while remaining aware of the power of that cinema and of television. One day, I was struck by the photos of the Budapest uprisings of 1956 that I saw in *Paris-Match*, and this is when I began to look for another representation of historical facts: to represent without it simply being fiction, and to create a cinema that challenges cinema. My films thus contain passages in which the public is of

course brought into a distorted reality, but also interviews in which people say the actual words of declarations or of archival texts and documents. Where is reality in film and in history? On the one hand, interviews that feature all the characteristics of cinematographic artifice, but which are based on exact quotes; on the other hand, scenes that appear real, but are entirely recreated and fake. What is more real? When confronted with that, the concept of "reality" loses its meaning: is our world a reality or a nightmare? These are the kind of questions that my films raise.[27]

In an attempt to define Watkins's style, Hubert Damisch and Jean-Pierre Rehm coined the phrase "mock live" to describe this chimera that combines live footage—which serves to reveal history reconstructed and recorded as if it were happening live, in front of the camera—and a form of "reportage of yesteryear," which is in itself debased, borrowing as it does from what is often considered the worst of television genres—the "docudrama," a blend of documentary and fiction, of television and cinema, that is characteristic of an English tradition "that has managed to reduce all destiny to soap opera."[28] According to Damisch and Rehm, the live footage is "minced to pieces and freed of its instantaneous ideology"—that is, set up only to be "deconstructed," "defused," and transformed into "chaos." It is this chaos that seals a pact between the spectator and the representation of the world: to venture into a mode of *disjunction*. The point is to deconstruct the cinematic and media system itself, and especially the documentary genre, if not the very concept of document and the system of historical representation, disrupting the homogeneity of the historical scenes to open up a radical reverse shot: the present, not the present of history but *our* present, the present of spectators being watched by the past. In so doing, Watkins not only reveals history through the cinematographic form he develops but interrogates it and challenges its representation.

This "documentary reconstruction," or "fictional documentary," has been taken up by critics, most notably by Guy Gauthier, from the moment *The War Game* was screened at the Venice Film Festival in September 1966 and then released in France in April of the following year: "Borrowing from the documentary form," wrote Gauthier, "to present a textbook example or a limit point of history is akin to having vice pay homage to virtue, and fiction to documentary, by acknowledging its specific form. This kind of technique is most masterfully deployed in Watkins' *The War Game*, which describes as an actual fact, through techniques of documentary and reportage, the detonation of a nuclear bomb in England. Having ruled out all manipulation through its subject matter and warnings, the filmmaker demonstrates here that the documentary form can be imitated and that this form is no guarantee against manipulation."[29]

Observers noted when seeing *The War Game* that the film rests on a paradox: the scenes of nuclear disaster appear the most realistic, whereas those of British daily life before the explosion have a distinctly unreal quality. The fictional future is real whereas present reality is fictitious. It is this "unfamiliar representation," this trap set for the real by the imagination, which is of course deliberate in Watkins, that gives the film its force.[30] How can we characterize what Peter Watkins shows us in *The War Game*? "A glimpse onto cataclysm" and "a dramatization of horror," as one critic wrote in 1967, claiming to be both impressed and perplexed by such an "onslaught of primal images"?[31] Or is it, rather, a "documentary of the future," as Georges Sadoul put it in one of his last chronicles in *Les Lettres françaises*? Sadoul immediately welcomed Watkins's works into his own pantheon of films that are both progressive and aesthetic: "The mise-en-scène in *The War Game* is exemplary. No pompous effects, everything is shown in newsreel style, relying on impeccable scientific and historical documents."[32]

In *Le Monde* Jacques Isnard identified this "reality-fiction" style as the source of the "at times unbearable sense of reality, as if the atrocious horror of nuclear cataclysm had just hit men and women whose paths we had only just crossed on the street."[33] Another critic from the same newspaper likened the film to a "manual for young servicemen, or an instructional film like the ones shown to medical students before they are sent to a lab or a hospital."[34] The terms vary, but it is the same strange game that is consistently described: that of a fiction that passes for reality all the more effectively by presenting itself as fiction and denying it, at the same time. In *Télérama* Claude-Jean Philippe identified this aspect as a "cinema of catharsis": "We are all children who are afraid of the dark. It is thus necessary to project onto the screen the most glaring and clear light, forcing us, sitting in the dark, to look danger in the face. Watkins' cinema draws its concrete strength from this fascination for violence, since in order to crush the fascination itself, one must trace it back to its source and demonstrate, as he does, the mechanism of nuclear apocalypse."[35] Jean-Louis Bory, for his part, attempted, in *Le Nouvel observateur*, to investigate the status of historical truth in Watkins, which arises in his films precisely because "all time frames appear to merge into the present": "the conditional and the future are nothing but grammatical figures, stylistic clauses. In fact, everything is of the present, of the unquestionable present of cinematographic evidence. A sense of the present that is all the more unbearable that it rests on experience, on a historical past. Here is what would happen, what will happen, what happens, because it has already happened like this. In Dresden, in Hamburg, in Hiroshima, as so many pasts on which Watkins carefully rests his case, with documents to back it up."[36] The film's dramatic efficiency is thus identified as its principal virtue, in the present, the virtue of bringing us "into it," which masks the fact that the work rests on "a bit of trickery, an obscene disguise,"[37] that is, nothing but a historical reconstruction, a hoax. It is its effectiveness that saves the film and constitutes its only moral: Watkins films the past and the future giving them the substance of the present.

Describing *Privilege* in the communist daily *L'Humanité*, the critic Samuel Lachize wrote of "social-fiction"—a film that transforms the society of a given moment into a laboratory for its own research, an instrumentalization that gives rise to a cinematographic form capable of capturing the "collective hysteria" that precedes the "rise of fascism," which remains the central subject of Peter Watkins's cinema. Is the filmmaker then nothing more than "a pure provocateur," a "purveyor of anxiety,"[38] or simply, as *Télérama* put it as early as 1967, "the first pamphleteer that cinema has ever produced: passionate, unfair, excessive, as if we had never seen, before him, films that call on us to take sides, and shake us up so violently"?[39] Is this "dissection of every fact and gesture on the operating table of historical documentary" itself not also susceptible to manipulation?[40] To achieve a truth of historical representation, Watkins was ready to manipulate not only his spectators but also his film and history. This could not but raise problems, and the notion itself was denounced by Jean Collet, as early as September 1967, in a long text published in *Etudes*, which envisioned Watkins's style as a mystification born out of the inexorable tendency, inherent to the medium of cinema as well as to the system he condemns, to one-upmanship—an accusation that Jean-Louis Bory also leveled at *The Gladiators*: "the spiritual game that is staged by Watkins is as systematic and mechanical as the System and the Machine he denounces." In other words, the very filmmaker who claimed to be immune to co-optation could himself succumb to "political-fiction" and become compromised by a form he reviled.[41] This is in a way the test to which he is put, leading to a reversal of roles: fiction then becomes an extrapolation of truth, a way of imagining what could be in order to better denounce what is. Watkins can thus be seen as pushing to their limit the principles and processes he is targeting, playing provocatively and with a degree of perversity on this ambiguity. This form of pedagogy rests on a complex dialectic that is constantly out of sync, playing on the interfacial and precarious balance between fabricated pseudodocuments and nonliberating fiction, rejecting identification. For Watkins it is from imbalance and discomfort that analysis and genuine thinking on history and its cinematographic form can arise.

These considerations inspired more precise definitions of Watkins's style: as Ignacio Ramonet put it, the director makes "imaginary documentaries" or "documentary allegories."[42] The fictional effects of his films have such dramatic and narrative force that they combine to produce a crystallization of truth—a truth that has effect in the past or in anticipation—and to trigger a critical reflection—whether it be on society, on the media, on cinema as a whole, or on Watkins's films in particular. Through his stylistic parody of the standard form of television reportage in Western democracies, Watkins offers the highest critique of these democracies themselves: the cynical image, because it is overly realistic, carries reality to its most absurd and also its most plausible end point, to its possible and implicit violence, that is, onto the path to fascism followed by any system of liberty that transforms into its opposite, the deprivation of liberty. Peter Watkins thus gives a cinematographic form to the historical nightmare of democracy: its slow, mechanical, and always latently possible evolution into its exact opposite. This is why he made fundamentally paranoid and pessimistic films, shooting in detail and in the present tense—as though they were bound to happen, even as though they had already happened—the processes of democratic degeneration, arming us mentally for the at once heartrending and exhilarating spectacle of the betrayal of democracy.

The trope of democratic betrayal through the proclamation of a state of exception takes its paradigmatic form in Peter Watkins's films in what may be called the *deathblow*. In almost every one of his films—as though it were its decisive event, its revelatory moment, its unsettling obsession—the mechanisms leading to the suspension of the rule of law in the name of emergency and the proclamation of a state of exception all culminate around a victim who is killed off in the name of reason and of the rule of right that has metamorphosed into the rule of might—that is, a regime of suspended liberties that ceases to recognize its own children and, in putting them to death, ceases to recognize itself. Many are executed in this manner: the pitiful Scottish warriors lying on *Culloden*'s battlefield who are finished off in various ways—clubbed to death, shot in the head, garroted—by English soldiers who no longer abide by the laws of war; the rioters of the apocalypse in *The War Game*, shot by policemen acting under a state of emergency made possible through the suspension of civil liberties; the bearded activists and girls in hippie frocks of *Punishment Park*, bludgeoned to death by an armed militia in the name of an America that no longer recognizes fundamental constitutional rights; the lovers in *The Gladiators*, who get a barrage of bullets in the back; and, later, the Communards, at the mercy of Versailles firing squads who crush the utopian moment in insurgent Paris with bullets to the head. This act, this "deathblow," gives rise to truth in an irremediable way, bonded by death. It is an act that can only be filmed in the present, even if it happened two centuries ago or will only happen in a contemplated future; an act that television reportage never, or only very exceptionally, filmed, either because its cameras were too far from the scene or because it refused to, deeming the content unwatchable; an act that Watkins, for his part, recreates as the apex, the culmination, of his films, their invisible suddenly made visible; an act that signals the final perversion of liberty, since it is most often performed in its name. Peter Watkins thus furnishes his cinematographic form of history with the supreme trope of the deathblow.

Edvard Munch, or How to Resist the Passage of Time

When shooting *Edvard Munch*, during 1972 and 1973, Peter Watkins thought he was opening a new chapter in his filmography, entering a new stage in his career. After his "English period," in which he had laid the technical, stylistic, and methodological groundwork for his films, and his second phase, devoted to political anticipation that helped him construct a critique of the debasement of the media and democracy, a third stage was dawning, which was to be devoted to historical biographies of artists, a form of reflection on the nature of genius. In a recent interview, the filmmaker made this clear:

> *Munch* was originally designed as the first part of a trilogy on "creative genius." A second film was to follow, on Scriabin, the composer and piano virtuoso. Vladimir Askenazi, who was one of the first interpreters of Scriabin, had agreed to play the part. But German television killed the project. The last part was to focus on Marinetti, another pure genius of style, a futurist poet, a young rebel who turned into a Mussolini fascist. It was to be a reflection on the madness of writing, but in this case it was Italian television that dropped me. The film was to focus on the creative process together with political commitment and social neurosis.[43]

This phase, which kept him busy from the middle through the end of the 1970s, does not occupy a significant place in his filmography, even if it does in his life, since the filmmaker spent most of the period preparing for each of these films. *Edvard Munch* now appears as the only surviving evidence of a larger project that was hindered, killed—censored, the filmmaker himself would say. But it is a quality piece of evidence nonetheless, where history is embodied—flesh in the painting.

Invited to a screening of *Culloden* in Oslo, Watkins discovered the paintings of the creator of *The Scream* at the beginning of the 1970s in the great hall of the Munch Museum. "I was so struck by them that I decided there and then that I would make a film of it," he explained. But Norwegian television was wary: Watkins was British, and his reputation as a highly political individual did not inspire confidence, while Munch had become the Norwegian national painter. It took three years of negotiations between Swedish and Norwegian television to reach an agreement on the project. Meanwhile, the filmmaker moved to Oslo with his family, at the end of 1972, in order to conduct archival research on Munch and to prepare for the shooting. *Edvard Munch* was shot during almost the entire year of 1973, in Oslo and in a small Norwegian town called Christiansen, where the painter was from. "If Peter Watkins' *Edvard Munch* was an art history article, it would be considered quite lame," the critic Philippe Azoury has rightly commented.[44] In light of more recent aesthetic approaches, Watkins's obsession with elucidating the mysteries of the work and explaining the power of the art by the man—Munch, both the suffering subject and passenger in time, a pure product of a century that he did not transcend but rather espoused—undoubtedly appears more dated than the film, shot in 1973 and briefly released at the end of 1976. But the film succeeds, thanks to the Watkins touch, at making palpable, sensual, and physical a young rebel of the 1880s, a painter who promoted free love and provoked society. "What struck me most," Watkins admitted, "is his incredibly direct way of looking at the world, as the characters in his paintings often do. I tried to recapture this frontal gaze at the spectator, which was a constant in my film. I have never seen another artist do the same thing with the same intensity."[45]

This approach in *Edvard Munch* presented several difficulties: Norwegian television, for one thing, was horrified at the idea of candidly depicting the sexual life of the young Munch, or his intimate biography. But Watkins drew support from the findings of a young art historian who shed new light on the painter's life, revealing the existence of his first mistress, Mrs. Heiberg (fig. 61), and of the notebooks he kept, written as intimate fragments. These

61 ▶
Edvard Munch
(PETER WATKINS, 1974).
THE TWO LOVERS,
THE ARTIST AND HIS
MISTRESS, APPEAR TO
IMPLICATE US IN THEIR
PASSIONATE EMBRACE.
PLUNGING INTO THE
HISTORY OF BODIES
AND SENTIMENTS,
WATKINS OFFERS A
"DREAM-HISTORY
OF MENTALITIES,"
ACCORDING TO
HISTORIAN
ARLETTE FARGE.

fragments offered up characters, facts, and phrases that had become historically irrefutable—even for Norwegian television—and that punctuate the film throughout. The film thus places Munch in a context of intense social violence, constantly stirring up in its discourse—in voice-over, a technique Watkins relished—class struggle and the rivalries and tensions that existed in the artist's milieu and in his life. Munch was an antibourgeois militant who lived in a bohemian world, whose atmosphere was as feverish as it was sensuous, as political as it was macabre. "He did not differentiate between all these levels; he lived his life to the fullest," said the filmmaker. "This is what was scandalous, and it is this mix that constitutes the fabric of the film." Watkins devotes very little time to the painter at work (*The Scream* takes up only a few minutes of the two-hour-and-forty-five-minute film), with most of the film devoted rather to groups of friends, dancing bodies, diseases (tuberculosis), walks in the park, informal meetings in cafés, and depictions of an international bohemian world that stretched from Paris to Berlin. Slowly but surely, the true subject of the film, however invisible, emerges: the intimate whispers of the wind of modernity blowing across all Europe.

But Norwegian and Swedish television considered this magnum opus to be "out of control," and thus a failure, declaring in particular that it did not work because the language spoken by Munch was not the Norwegian of the period. Their rejection also betrayed their reluctance to step outside of the already standardized format of television productions. Nordic television networks thus refused to broadcast the film in 35-mm format and blocked its screening at the Cannes Film Festival, even though it had been selected, and confined it to "B program" broadcasts on local networks. It was released in theaters for a few weeks only, in Poland, Czechoslovakia, and France. "Then the curtain fell on this film," as the filmmaker bitterly lamented. "The Scandinavian television networks buried it. It was not the right Munch." Only very recently did the team's technicians find the 16-mm prints, which had been thought lost, in an American lab. They were thus able to print new copies for a new French release in February 2005 that sounded the film's—as well as its director's—rehabilitation.

The Watkins Way: History in Common

How does Peter Watkins work? His relationship to cinema and television is essentially polemical—he uses their techniques only in order to abuse them—but his relationship to history appears more genuine, at once sensitive and rigorous, entailing immersion and archival research. He is not exactly a historian, since his way of recreating the past in order to update it, or even instrumentalize it, is far from academic and even runs counter to the epistemological principles of the discipline. No historian writes about the past as though it could be conjugated, or envisioned, in the present tense, whereas the live reportage of history developed by Watkins is closer to that of a camera exploring time in a state of emergency, in a state of belligerence. This temporal collage does pose a problem in that it sometimes turns Watkins's films into mere militant denunciation. Yet the sensitive relationship this cinematographic form maintains with history is nonetheless real, and its method merits close examination.

The filmmaker has not commented much on his interest in history, but he has sometimes said how important the process of archival research was to him. For instance, in reference to the period when he was preparing to make the trilogy on Munch, Scriabin, and Marinetti, he said: "I spent a lot of time on these projects, during the 1970s, since each one required six months to a year of research in the archives and documents. This work was very exciting but very demanding. I can't imagine making 'historical' films without this preparatory work of research and understanding." And earlier, notably in preparation for *Culloden* and *The War Game*, he had collected quite a large number of documents. For the former these included precise depictions of the 1746 battle—represented in the film by the historian-chronicler who observes the combat and offers commentary on it, as an expert and correspondent from the front lines, directly addressing the camera while watching the movement of the troops—and period testimonies and memoirs on the savagery and asymmetry of the fight. In the end Watkins decided to emphasize the antipapal and anti-French character of Charles Stuart's decisions, based on his writings and narratives left by the prince's entourage. For *The War Game* Watkins himself has said how important the documents on the experience of massive and deadly bombings that he consulted had been for the making of the film. Thus, all the statements in the film are referencing specific sources, and even though they are delivered by actors, they are cited as coming from reliable sources, often gathered by pacifist organizations promoting Britain's abandonment of nuclear weapons, such as the CND (Campaign for Nuclear Disarmament), which was the group with which the filmmaker had the closest ties.

A large part of Watkins's methodological work is carried out collectively: he has always insisted, ever since his early career in "history reportage," on involving as much as possible the many nonprofessional actors he hires to play the masses that are depicted, observed, and even scrutinized by his camera. The method was developed and tested on *Forgotten Faces* and *Culloden* in the early 1960s. First, with the help of a few close collaborators, Watkins selects the nonprofessional actors on the basis, first and foremost, of their interest in the story they are going to enact—in the case of *Culloden* some of them were even descendants of warriors who had died on the eighteenth-century battlefield. He then organizes seminars and meetings with the cast around the documentation and historical texts he has found. Watkins's films are *peopled*. From *Forgotten Faces* to *La Commune* his films offer collective heroes—soldiers, militants, city dwellers, citizens, men and women—played by groups of committed amateurs who constitute the foot soldiers of his "filmic battles." In each case the historical event was anticipated or reenacted by those who were committed to joining the director in teasing it out, following a theory of libertarian and collective reappropriation of history that harks back to the people's universities created at the end of the nineteenth century; committed to the progressive sound and light spectacles by figures like Romain Rolland, Jean-Richard Bloch, and Firmin Gémier, based on a culture of pride in historical filiation; and committed to the historical concepts developed by the Annales School, in which the representation of history is structured around large collective entities—social groups, classes—and not around the lives of individuals as the principal actors in history. Watkins's historical approach achieves, de facto, a synthesis between a "military" history of the event and a collective history of the rank and file of a given period. It operates at the crossroads of the chronological and the common structure. The Watkins approach aims to create a historical dynamic of the common people.

In a chapter of his book *Media Crisis* the filmmaker dwells at length on his methodological approach. First of all, he specifies that it developed in reaction to the standard processes and practices of global cinema, that is, Hollywood and all the films that fit his somewhat coarse category of the *Monoform*. Watkins defines the *Monoform* as "the internal language-form (editing, narrative structure, etc.) used by TV and commercial cinema to present their messages." He further explains: "It is the *densely packed and rapidly edited* barrage of images and sounds, the 'seamless' yet fragmented modular structure which we all know so well. . . . It also includes dense layers of music, voice and sound effects, abrupt cutting for shock effect, emotion-arousing music saturating every scene, rhythmic dialogue patterns, and endlessly moving cameras."[46] Even though it would be easy to demonstrate that Watkins's style, especially in the films of the early 1960s, is itself a variant of the Monoform that he so denounces nowadays (sound effects, shock effects, endlessly moving cameras, everything that, indeed, contributes to making his historical reportage so spectacular), the filmmaker claims to combat two principal processes used in mainstream cinema: historical reconstruction (involving manipulation of emotions, victimization, nationalism, fear of the other, and desire for revenge) and "the personalization of history" (the need for heroes or even icons). This entails the adoption of what might be called an alter-method, which Watkins sums up in his book and which I will outline here:

1. The filmmaker and community need to work together as colleagues—not as [one] expert showing lay people how to do things.
2. The filmmaker needs to be prepared to share decisions with the community/individual regarding the central focus of the film, and the methods used to achieve it.
3. The entire group must be prepared to discuss various aspects of the media crisis to collectively ascertain from the subject *their* feelings about the Monoform.
4. Everyone should be involved in researching the project. This is an excellent way to enrich and decentralize the information presented in the film.
5. During the filming process and editing stage, try to involve the feelings and opinions of everyone involved (filmmaker[s], community, technicians). This is not easy, as multiple and conflicting opinions arise, which if not handled carefully, can create chaos instead of consensus.
6. Be prepared to show the film to as many participants as possible while the editing phase is still open to change.
7. Screen the project for the wider community, and organize discussions around the work, which should influence the final editing.
8. Be prepared to have the work go onto DVD or VHS for accessible local screenings. Initial screenings are only part of a sustained process of change and development.
9. The community group must be prepared to share the struggle of getting their work onto TV.
10. Discuss with audiences—communities—the need for the media to become local and more participatory.[47]

All these imperatives aim, in a resolute, almost Icarian, fashion, to transform the experience of filmmaking into a collective and solidaristic adventure, to pool experiences, skills, and expertise, in order to conceptualize and actualize a project as a self-governing cooperative. These "commandments" also betray Watkins's authoritarian tendency, which is somewhat at odds with his call for harmonious debate. This "genuinely pluralistic form of cinema" is an experimental foray on the very Brechtian path that leads to the documentary recreation of history according to Watkins.

The filmmaker was bound, at some point, to film this "process of sustained protest"[48] itself, and to incorporate it into one of his stories: indeed, this was precisely the project of *La Commune*. The idea was as much to film the 1871 Paris Commune as a collective work-in-progress in the Paris of its time, as to record the collective making of the film as a contemporary resurgence of the Communard spirit. It was in the spring of 1999 that Watkins—commissioned by the Franco-German cultural television channel Arte, with the support of a small French production company, 13 Productions—set about shooting this highly ambitious project, which gave rise to a six-hour film. It was shot over three weeks in a large warehouse in the Paris suburb of Montreuil, which had been turned into a theater by playwright Armand Gatti and given the name "La Parole Errante." It took several months of preparation to select the 220 actors—for the most part nonprofessionals who were recruited from among the workers and denizens of the district of Popincourt, in the eleventh arrondissement of Paris—and to give them a sense of their responsibilities, immerse them in the historical period, and rehearse them.

Throughout this process Watkins lived among the communities that constituted his film's subject matter. He then endeavored to film lyrically—with a handheld camera, in long sequence shots—the unfolding of life in another age, reanimated in the Montreuil studio. All participants, in appropriate costume, learned about the specific texture of their roles, which were to be social rather than individualized, almost allegorical (the baker and his wife, the workmen, the soldiers, the head seamstress, the bourgeois, the newspaper writers, etc.), and all gathered together for the scenes of collective action (vigils, mobilizations, distribution of arms, demonstrations, riots, repressions). Dozens of faces come forward to relate, in a free, spoken form close to improvisation, their experience of life and politics, their daily sufferings, their misery and hunger but also hopes and disappointments, speaking indiscriminately of both the contemporary present and the historical past. The historical narrative and the process of filmmaking unfolded together: everyone talked, bustled, moved about, and circulated between 1871 and 1999, and the camera followed everything in a *continuum* of live reporting. All the more so as—and this was Watkins's key idea—his own camera was backed up by two others—openly anachronistic, out of sync, even provocative—that both constituted the film and criticized it, an integral part of the process that introduced the necessary distance to liberate speech: TV Versailles and Communal Television, competing organs "of 1871," which reported live on the development of the situation in Paris—deemed "worrying" by the conservative TVV, under the influence of French provisional president Adolphe Thiers, and "exciting" by the militant Communard TV (fig. 62).

Everything is artificial in the film, which flaunts its own "offstage," so to speak, and the fact that it is shot in a studio, and yet the speeches ring true and the physical movements feel authentic: the film plunges into an unorganized reality with which it must gradually come to terms. "The spectator," as Stéphane Bouquet wrote in *Cahiers du cinéma*, "takes away the strong impression that the Commune must, indeed, have happened more or less in this way, out of disorder and circulating speech, in this state of simultaneous improvisation and mobilization."[49] Watkins thus knotted together artificial and real, erudite and naive, historical and contemporary, cinematic and televisual, the misery of workers in 1871 and that of undocumented immigrants in 1999, his vision of the Paris Commune and that of the community that took it on and incarnated it. The effect is as if the Paris Commune were suddenly seen through a camera carried by Jules Vallès and Eugène Varlin and as if these two men of 1871 had not been writers and journalists, the authors of *L'Insurgé* and *Chroniques d'un espoir assassiné*, but rather two reporters sent on location by Commune Television.

The preparation for the project was typical of the Watkins method. The filmmaker and his close collaborators (his wife and son, Patrick, who was both his assistant and his chief collaborator) first contacted several leftist organizations, antiglobalization activists, and advocates for undocumented immigrants and the homeless, as well as Co-errances, an organization that campaigns "for a different cinema." "The idea was to recruit people who would have an active interest in participating in a film on the Paris Commune," explained Patrick Watkins.[50] Around three hundred people would regularly take part, behind or in front of the camera, in the development of the project. In April 1999 Watkins organized several screenings of *Culloden* at La Parole Errante, which served as a kind of breviary and handbook for his cinema, "after which we handed out questionnaires to better understand the profiles of the public interested in the project." In June work sessions began, in groups of ten to fifteen, during which Peter Watkins would explain in detail his idea for the film and discuss it with the various protagonists. The project carried on over the summer of 1999 in the form of workshops, at which the "actors" developed their own period characters while maintaining their contemporary

62 ▶
La Commune
(PETER WATKINS, 2000). REPORTERS FROM TV VERSAILLES AND COMMUNARD TELEVISION, "LIVE" FROM HISTORY IN THE REBEL PARIS DISTRICT OF FOLIE-MÉRICOURT.

personalities. Grouped by roles (the women's union, the bourgeois who were opposed to the Commune, the National Guard soldiers, the Versailles officers and soldiers, the Communard elected representatives, the artisans of the Popincourt District, etc.), they would gather and debate about the characters they were interpreting, write their own dialogue, and think about the links between the events of 1871 and contemporary society. This was a way for the actors to have direct input into the narrative of their own story, blending past and present commitments, and to develop a sense of belonging that went well beyond their role in the cast. "The aim," Patrick Watkins explained, "was to confront the actor-volunteers with the political, historical and moral dimensions of their characters. They were asked questions such as: 'would you be capable of seizing a gun and killing your enemy?' and 'What is your relationship to violence as a political solution?' This level of involvement was necessary for the shooting." The idea was thus not to train actors but to reveal citizens, in the revolutionary (and communard) sense of the term, to break the traditional relationship between "filmer" and "filmed," and to take performance as a form of political and active participation in the film, which in turn explicitly incorporated the personal experience of every member of the cast. This entailed a kind of distance from the act of performance, which revealed a commitment to the project that was more political than theatrical. Watkins and his team simultaneously carried out the same kind of work with those who were to represent the forces of Versailles in the film, the conservatives and the bourgeoisie. They deployed a different information network this time, and mobilized different kinds of people: personal ads in the conservative daily *Le Figaro* enabled them to get in touch with people who openly considered the failure of the Commune in positive terms. The film's preparation was thus explicitly indexed on the political links between past and present opinions.

The next stage involves the historian's craft to a greater extent. Before the actual shooting Watkins encouraged his actors and technicians to conduct their own research and learn about the history of the Commune, a relatively well-documented moment that had been a focus of French historiography since the 1970s. Documents, studies, conferences, books, and articles were made available, and all members of the project were encouraged to consult, read, and circulate them within the various preparation workshops. Professional historians working on the events of 1871 were also mobilized, and Watkins, his team, and the entire cast were invited to attend regular seminars given by academics like Alain Dalotel, Michel Cordillot, Marcel Cerf, Robert Tombs, and Jacques Rougerie, a Sorbonne professor and the undisputed authority on the period in French academia. The historical and historiographical work, which delved into classic and recent interpretations, focused specifically on the personages of the Commune and the Versailles government; the debates at Paris city hall and in Parliament; the role of women, of the church, and its educational system; the issues of sanitation, potable water, lighting, and food; military history; the question of clothing and period costumes; and finally the importance of music, songs, and the Communard press.

History was the very stuff of the film, and every participant assimilated it, individually and collectively, both with a professional guide and on their own. It is no less certain, however, that the political views held by Watkins and his actors—whether for (largely) or against the Commune—prevailed over the interpretations of historians. What was to be seen on the screen was this fusion, or even effusion, with its passions, lyricism, and emotion—what might be called "a sense of history"—rather than the academic's disinterest, with its sources and objects of study, giving rise to hypothesis and interpretation—what might be called "a critique of history." For all these reasons Watkins's *La Commune* provokes adherence or rejection, with spectators taking sides for or against it, a historical moment experienced anew, following a Manichean and obsidian logic, but carried by the hope that it will not have been in vain: contemporary echoes suggest the future dimension of a class movement, pictured in the film as highly antibourgeois, finding in the France of 1999 a strong current of grassroots movements mobilizing in support of undocumented immigrants and homeless people, through the critique of liberalism and existing democracy, and through protests against globalization. The Commune of the academic specialists of the period is of course something quite different: emphasizing the archaic character of the protest, questioning its logic of pitting class against class, and reading in its violence a fondness for an older, and sometimes primitive, form of politics and culture, which constantly references the Republic of 1793 and the Terror. These professional interpretations also offer a reading of the motivations of Versailles as political as much as social, which points out that among those who turned against the Commune were most of the founders of the Third Republic. In other words, where Watkins was filming a fusional embrace, a tragedy and a hope, historians describe, with more distance, the last of the revolts of revolutionary France, whose disappearance enabled the founding of a democratic and republican modernity.[51] It is clear that Peter Watkins's film is more interesting for its methodological and formal aspects (its manufacture and its mise-en-scène) than for the vision of history it offers—which is militant and forced.

The preparation, the debates, and the research later emerged rather dramatically in the shooting phase, and Watkins recorded this form of permanent improvisation, this historico-political happening, in long half-hour sequence shots that followed the chronological order of the events of the Commune, thus breaking away from the usual fragmentation that characterizes most traditional filmmaking. The film, which is made of about twenty of these long sequence shots, instigates and follows a group dynamic that conveys a sense of the emotion of history itself: the rise of the movement, the revolt, the organization of the Commune, the hope for better days, the wait for the other party's reaction, the fear and anxiety, the defeat of Commune troops, and finally the Versailles repression. All this is imprinted on the film through a sense of time, an attention to the words and their circulation, the bustling and then weary bodies, the involvement of the actors, the movements of a camera on the lookout for live reportage, especially when it follows the two journalists, a man and a woman, of Commune Television. Watkins films both his own film and the story of the Commune, as they are being made and unmade. And it is precisely in this fusion, organized yet free, that he develops a cinematographic form of history.

The Besieged Citadel and the Martyr Figure

At the end of 1999, Arte, the main sponsor of Watkins's film, informed the filmmaker that his work would be broadcast once, toward the end of the evening schedule. This amounted in his eyes to a declaration of war, a "Versailles" decision, which he considered a clear act of censorship: "Arte decided that all of the contemporary questions raised in the film (undocumented immigration, globalization, and especially the critique of the media) should be visible (if one can call it that) only to the chronic insomniacs and night watchmen, between 1 and 4 a.m."[52] Watkins protested, threatened, and tried to rally supporters, causing Arte—through the agency of Thierry Garrel, who was in charge of the documentary unit at the channel and who had initiated the project—to sever ties with the filmmaker, while also pulling out of the VHS edition of the film, as well as the book that was to come out simultaneously, *La Commune de Peter Watkins, l'aventure d'une création*, to be copublished with the Orsay Museum, in Paris, where an exhibition on the Paris Commune was opening. The film was aired on May 26, 2000, at 10 p.m.

Peter Watkins saw this not only as a waste but also as part of a veritable plot against him, fomented by his two coproducers—Arte, a symbol of media corruption, even and especially since it "serves as a cultural alibi," and 13 Productions, "a company that belongs to an arms dealer"[53] (80 percent of it is owned by the Hachette-Lagardère group)—and linked to his previous difficulties, starting with the ban on *The War Game* by the BBC in 1965. Yet Arte's "censorship," described as "subtle" by Watkins, was not really censorship, even if the filmmaker deeply resented what might better be called a kind of marginalization. Arte and Thierry Garrel were probably disappointed with the film—Watkins mentions criticism about the "overly loose editing" and the "unfinished character" of the work—and annoyed by its length (five hours and forty-five minutes), which served to justify broadcasting it in the late evening: "the nature of the work made this decision necessary."[54] But this was mostly just a disagreement between an artist and a program director. The film was broadcast—duly advertised on the channel, which adequately promoted the event—and hailed in the press. As Watkins writes, with the exception of himself, his team, his actors, and his technicians, "nobody raised a scandal," which he interpreted as a much more subtle form of conspiracy than in 1965 and evidence of the degeneration of a society that had definitively accepted "soft forms of censorship as a way of exercising self-censorship."[55] This marginalization led, on the initiative of some of the actors and technicians, to the creation of an organization, "Rebond pour la Commune," which managed to distribute the film in some of the independent theaters and alternative networks (squats, festivals, works councils, etc.), and later helped the film gain release on VHS and DVD, in January 2003.

Scathing accusations against the political and media "other" and permanent suspicion of a conspiracy being fomented against him have come to constitute Peter Watkins's discourse of martyrdom. It is part and parcel of his style and method, which can be seen as paranoid. The besieged citadel is the central figure of his films and also informs their making, as well as his cinematographic form and his recurring discourse of inside/outside. The filmmaker has systematically sought to mobilize teams and nonprofessional actors following this precise modus operandi: partisans in revolt against the powers that be; victims of history, the weak, the small, the unknown, the despised, those ostracized by the powerful; handfuls of resistance fighters and restorers of hidden truths. Peter Watkins can be considered both the victim and the perpetrator of his own martyrdom, and that makes his world all the more fascinating, his films all the more thrilling. For he inhabits this position fully, from character to method, from his worldview to, of course, his cinema.

The Alter-Filmmaker

In one decade, between *Culloden* and *Edvard Munch,* Watkins developed a cinematographic form of history that combines fiction and reportage and challenges the documentary genre with insolent and libertarian violence. But it took another thirty years for the significance of his work to be fully recognized, by the British Film Institute for instance, which ended a long period of ostracism and began to belatedly publish his films on DVD. Peter Watkins, who is now in his seventies, remains intractable. He also seems indefatigable. He has survived everything: Luftwaffe bombings over the Kent countryside of his youth during the war, repeated assaults of censorship boards, and, most of all, his own system, which reproduces, in its own paranoid way, the violence of the outside world. Rigid, vigorous, accusatory, and ascetic, he is and remains a heretical filmmaker.

Retrospectives, tributes, and festivals have contributed to turning Peter Watkins into one of the leading figures of the antiglobalization movement, a new militancy that recognized itself in his lampoons, as illustrated by the network in which his films and writings circulate. Rebond pour la Commune, the organization dedicated to promoting that film, is a case in point: it aims to "continue a process of which the film was only the beginning, and to investigate more deeply and broadly the ideas, the themes, and the debates that were raised during the preparation phase."[56] In March 2000 almost three hundred people participated in a weekend of meetings and screenings in Montreuil around Peter Watkins. Two documentaries in a row were made about the filmmaker and his work: Canadian Geoff Bowie's *The Universal Clock, or Peter Watkins' Resistance,* and *La Commune* actor Jean-Marc Gauthier's *Peter Watkins-Lithuania,* in which the filmmaker, filmed against the striking backdrop of a theme park abandoned by the Soviets a few miles outside Vilnius, speaks about his conception of cinema and the media. Finally, the broadcasting cooperative Co-errances has supported Watkins's films, restoring and rereleasing *Edvard Munch* in independent art theaters and organizing in 2004 and 2005, with the support of an independent organizational network, a series of conferences and debates around Peter Watkins and his films, the "Media Crisis Tour," which mostly aimed to involve spectators in Watkins's critical approach.

There is, thus, a historical paradox presiding over the twilight of Peter Watkins's career: the filmmaker, who has long claimed to be a martyr, who

63 ▶
The Gladiators
(PETER WATKINS, 1969). THE CHIEF GENERALS WHO ARE SUPERVISING THE GAME ALSO MASTER THE GAME OF HISTORY. AS THEIR CONTEMPTUOUS FACES SHOW, THEY ARE NOWHERE NEAR READY TO SURRENDER THEIR POWER.

has experienced exile, social isolation, and critical marginalization, is now at the very center of a militant movement and the focus of political and critical attention (through articles, publications, rereleases, and conferences) as a symbol of "alter-globalization" cinema. Watkins is experiencing a Renoir-like utopia, that of an ordinary director turned civil-society hero. And resting on this experience, he ventured a few suggestions to his fellow filmmakers, as a cinematographic form in action: "in my view, filmmakers should climb down from their pedestals, and walk the streets, with everyone else. We must regain a true sense of humility, stop kidding ourselves, and film more directly, at the level of the pavement."[57]

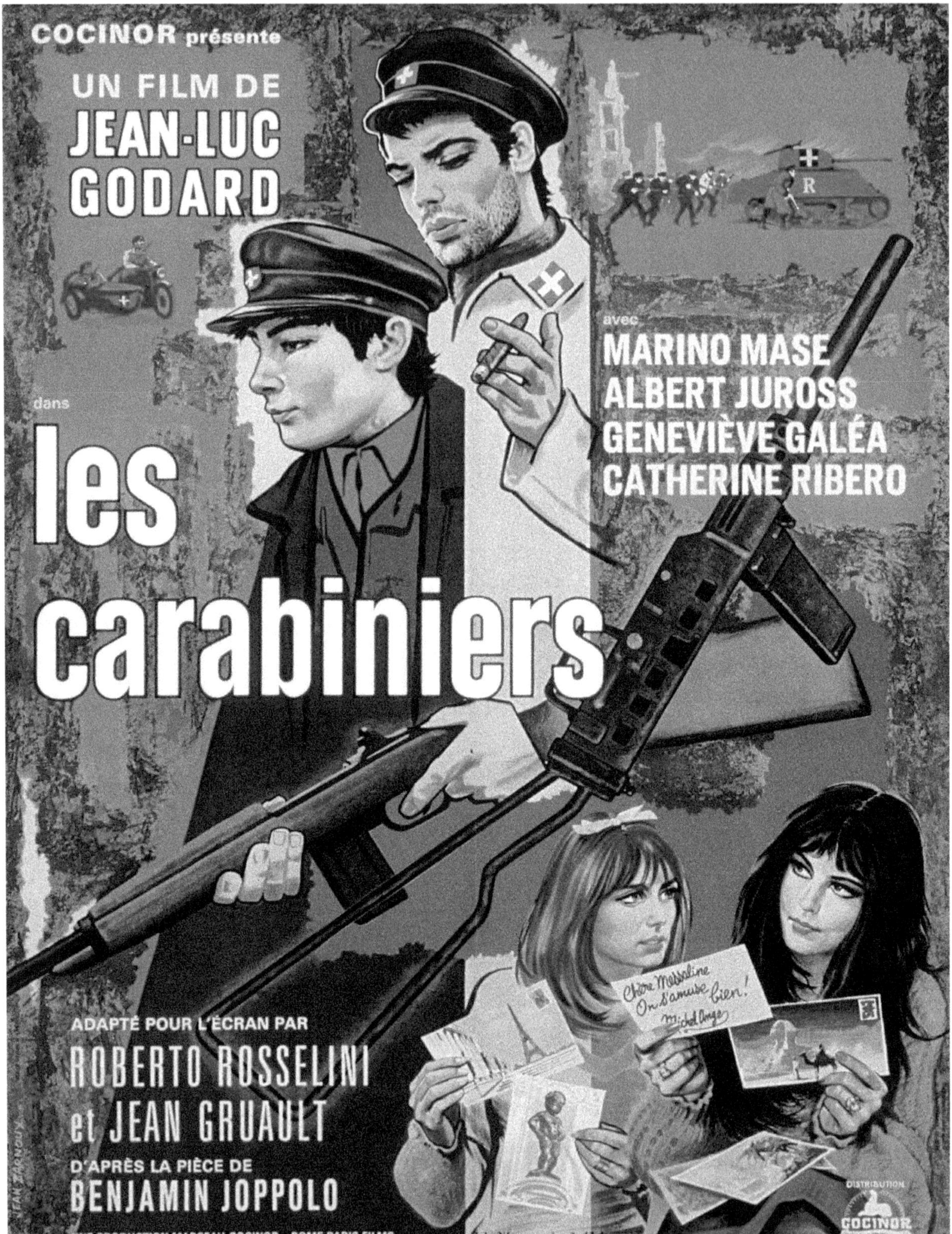
COCINOR présente
UN FILM DE
JEAN-LUC GODARD
dans
les carabiniers
avec
MARINO MASE
ALBERT JUROSS
GENEVIÈVE GALÉA
CATHERINE RIBERO
Chère Messaline
On s'amuse bien!
Michel Ange
ADAPTÉ POUR L'ÉCRAN PAR
ROBERTO ROSSELINI
et JEAN GRUAULT
D'APRÈS LA PIÈCE DE
BENJAMIN JOPPOLO
UNE PRODUCTION MARCEAU-COCINOR - ROME PARIS FILMS
Interdit aux moins de 13 Ans
DISTRIBUTION
COCINOR
JEAN ZARNOUX

5

THE THEORY OF SPARKS ▶
A HISTORY IN IMAGES, ACCORDING TO JEAN-LUC GODARD

◀ 64
Poster for *Les Carabiniers*
(JEAN-LUC GODARD, 1963). (PHOTO COURTESY BIFI)

ON SEPTEMBER 17, 1995, in Frankfurt, Jean-Luc Godard received the Adorno Award, an honor he held dear—indeed, more so than all the accolades he had received from what he called the "professionals of the profession."[1] His acceptance speech in Frankfurt, entitled "About Cinema and History,"[2] was a kind of double manifesto. On the one hand, it was a manifesto of what might be called a particular place in history—that of Godard himself, which he summed up concisely: "I exist today in profound solidarity with the past. I refuse to forget because I do not want to debase myself." On the other hand, it was a manifesto for a way of making history with images, moving images, but moving images that summon up painted images. In this lecture Godard referenced *Histoire(s) du cinéma*, the series of eight films he was then in the process of making on the relationship between history and cinema. According to Godard, cinema is the only art form that can "make history visible." He explained: "My idea, my extremely ambitious idea, an idea Michelet himself did not entertain while he was finishing his magnificent *History of France*, is that history is standing there, on its own, and that only cinema can make it visible." Indeed, this is cinema's historic role: "it has been nothing but a peddler of these cheap signs of history." The filmmaker explained the relationship between cinema and history, and more specifically between *his* cinema and history, through reference to his own position within a double and overlapping history (individual and collective), to his generational position, and to the biological incarnation of historical time. It was as if *Histoire(s) du cinéma* could only have come from a filmmaker of the New Wave, "perhaps the only generation to have found itself at the heart of both its century and cinema."

Godard seems to have recognized, and accepted, the power of such an incarnation: "To know that one comes before something and after something else, being in the middle of the century like this, to be the maker of one's own history oneself, of the history that follows you, is the only opportunity to make history." It was as if the junction of personal history and that of the century, at that precise moment called the New Wave, was the springboard from which to make history visible. This mission was at once intellectual, intimate, and historical, an appeal to take responsibility for the history of cinema and that of the century through his own fate, which the director formulated as early as the second episode of *Histoire(s) du cinéma*: "cinema was the only way to go, to tell, to realize, for myself to realize, that I have a history as myself, within the history of us all. Had it not been for cinema, I would not know that I have a history, or that there is such a thing as history."³ The only way to recount history, to produce history, is cinema. Godard boldly affiliates the historical mission of cinema, or at least the filmmakers of his generation, to that of an entire historiographical tradition—he invokes Michelet but also Marc Bloch, Fernand Braudel, and the Annales School: "only the French have been interested in history. At least, more than any one else, they have had the intuition that they were part of a history; they tried to find out what that history was, theirs within the larger and the larger within theirs."⁴ It was as though he himself had fallen heir to a legacy that transcended him in part, while also entrusting him with a promise to fulfill: to topple the (hi)story of the century over into the (hi)story of cinema, and vice versa. And, in this way, to "save" them both, now intimately connected.

If cinema now embodies the century, it is because it is the only art that can supply the theoretical and practical tool capable of making history visible. And that tool is *montage*, the true cinematographic form of history. In the second part of his Frankfurt lecture Godard marshaled examples in support of his thesis: montage, by bringing together two objects, two people, two periods, or two ideas, manufactures a historical image:

> If one points out that Copernicus raised the idea, circa 1540, that the sun no longer revolves around the earth; and if one points out that Vesalius published *De Corporis humanis fabrica*, then you have Copernicus in one book, and Vesalius in another—in one, the universe and the infinitely large; in the other, the interior of the human body and the infinitely small. And then, four hundred and fifty years later, the biologist François Jacob wrote: "in the same year, Copernicus and Vesalius..." Well, then, Jacob was not doing biology; he was making a film. History is nowhere else but here. It is the linkages; it is *montage*.

Thus, montage all at once initiates, justifies, and makes possible Jean-Luc Godard's historical work, by constantly bringing together clips, shots, and words:

> The gaze moves from one to the other, and thus you get a story, you get history, that of the dreaded Hegel, if you want, or of the amiable Benjamin. Not a spoken (hi)story, nor one that is told, but rather seen. This is why I entitled the first chapter of my work on cinema "All the (Hi)Stories," and continued on with "A Single (Hi)Story," and then "Only Cinema"—which is to say, only cinema can do this.

Godard ends his guided tour with a visit to his own filmmaker-historian's workshop, defining both the function and (historical) range of his principal tool:

> There is thus this thing that remains strictly within cinema, like an arrested chrysalis that will never become a butterfly, this thing that is montage. What does montage strive for? A linkage between something far and something near, especially in time. . . . My idea, as a country doctor or gardener of cinema, was that one of the purposes of cinema was to invent or discover montage in order to produce history.

It was as though cinema had discovered and developed montage so that the century may be made visible to everyone: "Here we have montage; here we have a moment of history; here we have a moment of cinema."

Although several historians were shown Godard's historical/cinematographic essay—the author himself showed a few episodes to Pierre Vidal-Naquet[5]—little is known of their reactions to his narrative, except for that of François Furet. Indeed, the specialist of the French Revolution, whom Godard invited to his Paris office, watched the first four episodes of *Histoire(s) du cinéma* and discussed them with the filmmaker before sharing some of his thoughts on what he considered "a lyrical and sacred vision of history" with *Cahiers du cinéma*. This occurred in June 1997, only a few weeks before Furet's death. The interview was published three years later in a special issue of the periodical aptly entitled "Le siècle du cinéma" (Cinema's Century). According to the author of *The Passing of an Illusion*, Godard's films appear to be animated by a dynamic in sync with that of the century's revolutions and dislocations: "Only films can still make us believe in the beauty of a revolutionary movement, can grasp something profound about the great assaults of history. Godard's films are genuinely powerful because they take account of the century as epic."[6] He also recognized montage as a historiographic tool offering truly essential resources and recalled the images "thrown on top of one another with a great sense of tempo as well as a mastery of balance and imbalance," which gave the filmmaker an enhanced power as a historian: "this cinema acts as a cosmological chaos that tells the story of our century. I have great admiration for this ability to create meaning through excess and the epic form, for there is an evocative power here that no historian will ever achieve."

Yet François Furet also pointed out that this form, while certainly that of a historian, disturbed him because of its very vitality, its historical drive—what he called its "ideology." Assuming adherence or defiance, polemical to its core, Godard's essay is lacking in a certain critical distance in relation to the history of the century and its illusions: "It is necessary to break from the enchantment of these magical, tragic, enthused invocations. This is why the lyrical power of images scares me, in their relationship to history, especially twentieth-century images, which have retained a memory that is emotionally charged. These images, their juxtapositions, and hence their ideas, are not mine: indeed, they offer themselves first and foremost as a sacred vision of history. And I find Godard's images lack a critical sense. They operate according to the same principles as the century's great illusions."

While fundamentally sound, Furet's interpretation requires some qualification, since these images seem to be *both* offering a critique of the century—through their commentary, their juxtaposition, their slow motion, freeze, and fast-forward effects—*and* taking part in the illusions of the century, those very illusions that crashed in on history. Jean-Luc Godard, as François Furet has shown, can certainly be regarded as a historian of sorts, whose work represents a visionary and epic attempt to forge a cinematographic form capable of making history visible through the combination of images.

This perspective on Godard's work is possible because the filmmaker, from the very beginning of his career, always considered films to be more than the sum of their traditional parts (script, actors, shooting, sets, lights, etc.): they also had to take into account the legacy of images, all images, their commentaries as well as their fabrication, their traditions as well as their ruptures. Godard, as a young critic and then as a filmmaker, always invoked a lineage that placed him within a *long durée*, that of art and image criticism. "Cinema, in France, is the history of art," he explains in the third episode of *Histoire(s) du cinéma*. "It's Diderot, Baudelaire, Malraux, and I would place immediately after them Truffaut, in a direct line. Baudelaire talking about Edgar Allan Poe is the same as Malraux talking about Faulkner, and Truffaut talking about Ulmer and Hawks."[7] Godard has also always been keen to return the images of this tradition to history, the history of the present, through which he was evolving in the initial phase of his career, and the history of the past, a past to which he felt compelled to remain faithful in the later phase of his career. One might even say Godard means to "displace" these images, with all the deliberate, dynamic, and even polemical translation that this required, and still requires. He probably saw this sidestepping movement as opening the possibility of initiating connections that are, in his view, the very source of all historical vision. The cinematographic form of history in Godard's films, indeed, requires a mixing of images in the century—of images with the century and of images with each other. In Godard's view, to produce history with images—film images *and* art images—has always consisted of montage that displaces cinema toward history, and the arts toward cinema and history. This historical form requires the translation of images, which are pulled out of film, as from books or museums, where they are kept. This amounts to what can be called a critique of the museum or, better still, its "exit," since montage—from the filmmaker's very first historical effort, *Breathless*, in 1959—has been for him a way of recreating an aura around the work of art, not by isolating and sublimating it but by displacing it into cinema, that is, into history.

Taking Art Out of the Museum and Projecting It into History

Godard developed a polemical relationship with art museums, which in his view are trivial and conservative places, sites of inherited and academic culture. This polemical relationship was made clear as early as 1964 in the famous scene in *Band of Outsiders* where the three main characters—Frantz, Arthur, and Odile—run at full speed, to the utter dismay of the helpless museum guards, through the great painting gallery of the Louvre. These three youths, consumed by life and living on the edge, take their museum visit at top speed to kill time and calm their nerves just before they are about to rob a bank at gunpoint. They belong to life rather than to a museum, or, more accurately, they bring life, speed, anxiety, and passion—the zeitgeist of 1964 history—into the world of tourist artifice and the death of art. It was a challenge, in fact, that Godard's voice-over commentary introduces thus: "They had to wait until night before they could do the job, thereby respecting the tradition of bad B-movie crime thrillers. What could they do, then, to kill the time that seemed to stretch on forever, Odile asked? Frantz had read in *France soir* that an American had managed to visit the Louvre collections in nine minutes and forty-five seconds. They decided they could beat that." It takes them nine minutes and forty-three seconds. In the film their frantic race takes exactly twenty-four seconds, during which we catch glimpses of David's monumental paintings and the Winged Victory of Samothrace. This ironic wink immediately places Godard within a certain French tradition—from Diderot to Alie Faure and Michel Leiris, from Quatremère de Quincy to Baudelaire and Dubuffet—which is hostile to the museum, both as a place where art is conserved and as a political institution. In the belly of the beast of academic culture, whose history seems to have frozen, the three dandyish bandits play the fool, organize their own rodeo, and act out their own western, for the benefit of passersby. They "speed up time for the sake of killing it,"[8] punching holes in the space of the Louvre in less than thirty seconds, to let in the giddy air of their threesome and of the story of French youth known as the New Wave (see fig. 47 in ch. 3).

Five years earlier, in *Breathless*, young people were already fooling around with France's great paintings. In Patricia's bedroom, in which Michel Poiccard is ensconced for about a third of the film, the question arises of a museum being offered to life and love. The room is, indeed, Patricia's "living museum," housing several Picassos, a Klee above the phone, a Matisse of a child wearing an old-man mask, one of Degas' dancers, a small Miro, and a recent acquisition, the portrait of a young woman by Auguste Renoir. Life has stolen these works, first in that they are only reproductions—postcards, posters, pages torn from art books, all pulled out of the museum in the most vulgar and commonplace manner, to serve as decorations in the room of an American student in Paris—and second in that they are alive, chanting the words and gestures of love, juxtaposed to the two lovers' existence. Patricia keeps referring to them—"Have you seen my new poster?" "Do you like this poster?" "Do you find her prettier than I am?"—while Michel makes fun of them, opting for actual flesh over the colors and lines of the paintings. In the central dialogue of this scene, both glib and boorish, Patricia is hanging her new Renoir and says, "Not bad." "Yes, very good," Michel answers while caressing her buttocks. "Do you like this poster?" "Not bad . . ." "He was a great painter, Renoir!" "I said not bad!" he shouts back emphatically, looking straight at the Renoir with his cigarette hanging from his mouth, like a potential buyer in a gallery assessing its value. Art thus invites itself into the lovers' conversation, while their life creeps into the works, like in role-playing, thanks to a few close-up inserts, as if the images of the paintings could only find their true meaning when confronted with life. Godard imposes the true context for these images: Paris, 1959, a furnished room in a small hotel where a couple of idle young people transform a freewheeling pictorial and libertine discourse into a love scene between the sheets. And this very sequence is also French history, given that de Gaulle and Eisenhower, through the magic of montage, soon make a cameo appearance in Patricia and Michel Poiccard's Paris. Cinema appears here as the evil object that contaminates art and topples it headlong into history. Renoir, Matisse, and Picasso leave their frames for Patricia's room, where they take over the life of a young woman of 1959, while maintaining their aura as major works of art, since it is these painters, these paintings, these references that, literally, animate the characters' lives. If Godard's cinema immediately declares its wariness of the official locations where art is transmitted, and of cultivation in general, it remains nonetheless fascinated by the work of art itself. Only it chooses to wrench the work of art away from cultural

65 ▶
Breathless
(JEAN-LUC GODARD, 1960). A SUBJECTIVE VIEW OF ART THAT TAKES IT OUT OF THE MUSEUM AND THRUSTS IT INTO ITS TIMES— AMIDST BODIES AND FACES (JEAN SEBERG AND JEAN-PAUL BELMONDO), GAZES AND SENTIMENTS.

heritage and graft it onto life, grant it an existence in the world—to enter it, in a sometimes sensational way, into history (fig. 65).

In his 1963 film *Les Carabiniers* Godard pushed his critique of the museum a step further, through a strange game of cards played by the four protagonists of the film: on the one hand, Ulysse and Michel-Ange (Ulysses and Michelangelo), soldiers on leave from a brutal, unjust, and pointless war; on the other hand, Venus and Aphrodite, the women (mother and daughter) who are waiting for them to return home and share their loot, which takes the form of a mysterious suitcase that allegedly contains "all the treasures of the world." The process of unpacking the suitcase, to the sounds of sacred organ music and martial drumbeats, reveals heaps of postcards from all over the world, grouped thematically, into "monuments," "natural wonders," "works of art," and so forth. Here again, the reproduction prevails over the original, and the miniature has symbolically displaced the unique artistic aura. It "begins with the monuments" (the pyramids, Karnak, the Parthenon, the Coliseum, Angkor Wat, etc.); then come the "cars," the "naked girls," and the artistic masterpieces, more or less always the same. Returning from their tour of duty, the soldiers ransacked, respectfully, the local masterpieces—a little earlier in the film, Michelangelo even saluted a Rembrandt self-portrait ("a soldier salutes an artist") pinned to the wall of a house he coveted before proceeding to humiliate a woman and simulate her rape—and brought them back home. For Godard this is precisely how museums are filled, by the capture and pillage of images from elsewhere (fig. 66).

The farcical tone notwithstanding, this mockery is not without historical force in French culture, where the national museum was largely fed by state plunder. It evokes Bonaparte's repatriation, for his own greater glory, of masterpieces from Italy and Flanders, and later from Germany and Spain, by his armies deployed across Europe, and his parading them triumphantly through Paris at the *fête des Arts*, on the ninth and nineteenth Thermidor, year VI (July 27–28, 1798). In his denunciation of the predatory fraud of the museum the filmmaker echoes the diatribe of Quatremère de Quincy, who, in his *Lettres à Miranda*, attacked Bonaparte's Louvre and the practice of transferring works of art from their cultural and political contexts.[9] From the perspective of this royalist aesthete, the museum disfigured the image of art and extinguished its aesthetic quality: it displaced the artwork, sequestered and appropriated it. In the name of a new France, become the only true land of the arts by virtue of the freedom it had conquered and imposed on Europe by force of arms, Bonaparte and his museum, the very foundations of French heritage policy,

66 ▶
Les Carabiniers
(JEAN-LUC GODARD, 1963). TRAFFICKING IN ART AND *ART VIVANT*: THE SOLDIERS SHARE THEIR LOOT PILLAGED FROM WRETCHED MUSEUMS.

gave these images a national significance and confined them to a space for their protection, worship, and presentation. The museum transformed the conquered, repatriated, and domesticated images into ultimate masterpieces. Yet, Quatremère vehemently objected, it mummified them, depriving them of their living substance by depriving them of their vital context, notably that of eternal Rome. Art is alive and visible only in its context, Jean-Luc Godard also insisted in *Les Carabiniers* by mocking these predators and rapists who unpack their loot triumphantly, like hucksters peddling their junk.

This image of the "theft museum," of the "rape museum," resurfaces regularly in Godard's films, which revel in an acerbic critique of the art market: in *Nouvelle Vague*, where masterpieces are sold illicitly on the street between two limousines, or, in one of his very late films, *Eloge de l'amour*, in which museum curators are ridiculed with the line, "Come on, we all know what they're like, the Louvre curator doesn't just want to protect the Winged Victory, he wants to be the author of the protection himself, on an equal footing with Phidias himself."[10] Later in the same film the same sentiment is reiterated: "My dear, thieves will be thieves, national museums notwithstanding." The Louvre's curator fancies himself the artist: such an imposture is blatant theft, the theft of the aura of the work. For the artwork can only remain alive outside the museum, when infinitely reproduced, through the love affairs and exchanges between the characters, escaping all predatory, academic, or pedagogical control, as though it were disseminated in history by life and sentiment. In other words, Godard reverses the theory of the aura of the work of art as developed in 1933 by Walter Benjamin—in "The Work of Art in the Age of its Technical Reproducibility," which is based on the irreducible singularity of all works of art—and conversely echoes Malraux's praise of the virtues of the photographic reproducibility of images. In the filmmaker's view, restoring the work's aura through its physical presence in a museum is a fraud, since its aura has in fact been stolen by the museum, which does not return it to the visitor's gaze but rather neutralizes and sequesters it—puts it to death. The classical museum, in Godard's films, amounts to a vast abduction of art. This destabilization of the museum is designed to at once undermine, mourn, and reveal. This leads logically to Godard's *Histoire(s) du cinéma*—which can be read and seen as a definitive destruction of the institutional museum and its ideal reconstitution, following Malraux's principle of the museum without walls—and, later, to *Voyage(s) en utopie*, the 2006 exhibit at the Centre Georges Pompidou in Paris, where the filmmaker literally exploded from within the museum mission of a major French art institution. The constant montage of films and paintings restores dignity, fecundity, and infinite interpretative malleability to the art exhibit. It is this very flight out and away from the traditional museum and into the museum without walls that the film itself constitutes that gives Godard's images the power to make history.

After seeing *Pierrot le fou* in 1965, Louis Aragon famously hailed Godard with a question that expressed the extent of his admiration: "Jean-Luc Godard, what is art?" In the eyes of the writer Godard was the new Delacroix, the one person who could answer the impossible question, since he managed, through film, to repaint the world, to apply a coat of paint—blood red, chiffon red, revolution red, epic red—to history: "Pierrot is, thus, like Delacroix's Sardanapalus, a film in color.... It is not just that it is well photographed, that the colors are beautiful. It is well photographed, and the colors are very beautiful. But it is something else. The colors are those of the world as it is. Better even: Godard is not content with the world as it is, and makes it over in his own way. He likes gaping wounds and the bright color of blood. In *Pierrot le Fou* red sings like an obsession."[11]

The obsession is with history. To thrust painting into the century means, for instance, to suddenly shoot Van Gogh's *Café at Night* in full frame and color cinemascope. To paint the world over also means filming a dialogue between Jean-Paul Belmondo and Anna Karina that cuts back and forth between a Pierrot by Picasso and a female portrait by Renoir rather than the faces of the actors. Just like the Anna Karina character in this film, who (for good reason) is called Marianne Renoir, and who does not resemble a Picasso portrait by chance—"Jacqueline in profile," according to Aragon—and who, thus named and referenced, can better and more wildly traverse France, flaunting her fate-line as well as her thigh line. In the end it is in a Picasso blue that Ferdinand blows himself up in a ribbon of azure dynamite—just like that, at once a profoundly desperate and casually flippant gesture. More to the point, it is an act taken under the auspices of pictorial elegance, a vital and fatal elegance that is the hallmark of its time, but nonetheless "impersonating" beforehand the Vietnam War through mime and pop art *happening*. Aragon ended his long panegyric in a similar confusion between art images and present history: "I wanted to talk about art. And all I have talked about is life," he wrote, slamming the door in the face of those curmudgeons who accused Godard of "excessive romanticism,"[12] when the filmmaker was only making excessive use of time, as a canvas on which to spread the sharp colors of his pictorial experience of history (fig. 67). The filmmaker would return to this, in

La Chinoise and *Weekend*, the apex of his "red period"—this time in a pictorial rather than a political sense. *Weekend* is the work of a painter who violently throws color on his celluloid world, the moral of which is told by a painter-actor, Daniel Pommereulle, who invites himself into the film as a mad and radical hitchhiker: "I am proclaiming the end of the grammatical age and the beginning of the flamboyant."

Godard used another means of infusing art images into history through film, thus reviving and fertilizing history with images: he "directed" paintings by assigning them bodies. This was the core of his project in *Passion*, made in 1981, in which the agonies of creation are embodied in eight *tableaux vivants*, including Rembrandt's *Night Watch*, El Greco's *Raising of Lazarus*, Rubens's *Assumption of the Virgin Mary*, as well as several masterpieces by Goya, Ingres, and Delacroix. In each Godard makes art subordinate to history in that it is made palpable, alive, literal, acted, represented in the flesh in the most faithful way, with the artworks punctuating the film as a fiction parallel to that of the social drama: a tyrannical boss harasses his female workers, and one in particular, a political leader and a Catholic, whom he manages to lay off. Inversely, history is condemned to being a Promethean struggle against matter, the sensuousness of paintings turned into shapes, dates, and events. This is what *Passion* is all about: constant shifts between art and history. What matters in the film is not the paintings but paintings being made, and unmade, and made over again, and the same goes for history: a plant, a strike, a boss, the union's defeat, a female worker who leaves under police escort. Through the filmmaker Jerzy, who directs and films within the film, Godard reinvents famous canvases, explores them, deconstructs them, pushes them to the limit, combines them, and explodes them—what Jacques Aumont has called the "cinematization"[13] of art, the becoming-cinema of all art. Godard goes further, however, since he works on the historical material in the same way, taking it, mixing it, alternating between hope and despair, collective enthusiasms, and individual defeats. At the crossroads of art and history, the bodies in these tableaux vivants and those at the factory all participate in the same vast embodiment of images, sensations, and ideas.

In the introduction to the script for *Passion*[14] Godard explains that this projection of art, even ancient art, into contemporary history—which then reformulates it—was made possible by a montage of reproductions, photographs, and quotes:

67 ▶
Pierrot le fou
(JEAN-LUC GODARD, 1965). IMAGES IN LIFE, BOOKS, AND ARMS, OR THE LIVING MUSEUM OF THE CENTURY, BY JEAN-LUC GODARD.

One could say that there is, on the one hand, the real world of work and, on the other, the spectacle of the recreation of paintings. That is ice and fire. But everything is burning with a passion that excites the mind like a volcano on the verge of eruption. In fact, the idea is to have the scenes of the super-production of paintings serve as so many purely emotional close-ups within the scenes of real action.... Not a historical scene in the style of Cecil B. DeMille, but a painting by Delacroix, full of cries, tears, the clanking of armor, and the pounding of horses, which culminates with two women, at the bottom right corner, their backs bending under the shock, a movement which is echoed in the stillness of a woman worker, frozen in weariness and fear, slumped in a café after the policemen have arrived. (490, 493–94)

The painting thus seeps into the real, like art into history. The canvas is the emotional close-up shot that brings life into the cold factory and breathes life into the female workers, just like images are the living clarification of a present history that is both complex and in need of interpretation: its hermeneutics not so much learned as lived (fig. 68).

From Langlois to Godard: A Historical Passage Through Images

Godard's conception of art in history—working through comparisons, parallels, projections, reproductions, inventions, embodiments, cinematizations, and, in any case, as the escape of images from the museum—was fueled by two avowed influences: his experience of Henri Langlois' museum of cinema, and the careful and passionate reading of André Malraux's *Museum Without Walls* and *The Voices of Silence*.[15]

Jean-Luc Godard was "trained" by Henri Langlois and his cinematheque, which he frequented from 1948, at age eighteen, along with all his confederates of the New Wave generation. As Godard himself has often said, his cinephilia and his cinema were both born at the cinematheque: "as filmmakers and creators, we, of the New Wave generation, were born (very late actually, at age twenty or twenty five) in a museum, the Museum of Cinema run by Henri Langlois. Delacroix was not born at the Louvre, Gide was not born on rue Sébastien-Bottin. We, however, we were born in a museum."[16] The iconoclastic filmmaker who took art out of the museum to innervate his films and irritate the world was thus apparently himself spawned in a museum. The paradox, however, is in fact not one at all, since the museum of cinema designed by Henri Langlois was the exact opposite of a museum in the classic sense, an anti-Louvre, so to speak, closer to Patricia's room in *Breathless*, to *Pierrot le fou*'s world-red, and even to *Passion*'s tableaux vivants than to the great gallery at the Louvre. Indeed, the Langlois museum did not contain much beyond a few fetish objects, cameras, posters, costumes given by admirers, and a beautiful collection of objects and artifacts that preceded and accompanied the birth of the medium of cinema (Will Day's collection, acquired thanks to Malraux)—treasured as so many artifacts that the guru inventoried, loved, commented upon, and combined, building ingenious parallels and elaborating brilliant reinterpretations of the history of cinema, a history of cinema that was three centuries old and borrowed heavily from art, including cave paintings. The museum contained, above all, films, since Langlois screened films often, before he acquired the space or the will, in the very early 1970s, to turn his museum into a site that could be visited by common folk (fig. 69). Yet even before it became open for guided tours, the French cinematheque was called the "museum of cinema" at the explicit request of Langlois, the "dragon who guarded its treasures."[17] Indeed, the Langlois screening room borrowed from the museum the idea of a living experience of art history. The cinematheque was "programmed" to bring together, contrast, and compare widely different films, in the same way that a museum visit, if it were living, would offer a parallel and simultaneous vision of masterpieces from distinct periods, schools, and countries. Screening as an act of creation: the logic and will of the programmer, passing from museum to projection room, imposed themselves as essential figures of the culture of the twentieth century.

The logic affirmed by Henri Langlois was first and foremost archival—"save everything": films, archival material (manuscripts, printed materials, storyboards, costumes, drawings), machines, technical objects, even if this was done in a rather odd and idiosyncratic way. Langlois was a strange curator and had always considered himself mostly an amateur, in the noble sense of the word, a cinephile (including the pathological and maniacal aspects suggested by the expression), and a lone knight fighting against the world, including the government (the Langlois scandal of February-March 1968 is a perfect illustration, including its subsequent mythologization). The site he designed was closer to a cabinet of curiosities than a respectable museum. Yet the whole thing was inspired by a vision, that which leads from "conserving" to "presenting."[18] Adopting a perspective allows for the *presenting* of films and objects from among those that are being simply *conserved*. It was in the screening room that Langlois demonstrated his museological conception of the history of cinema. His "save everything" philosophy followed from an idiosyncratic view of "what needs to be shown," and hence programmed.[19]

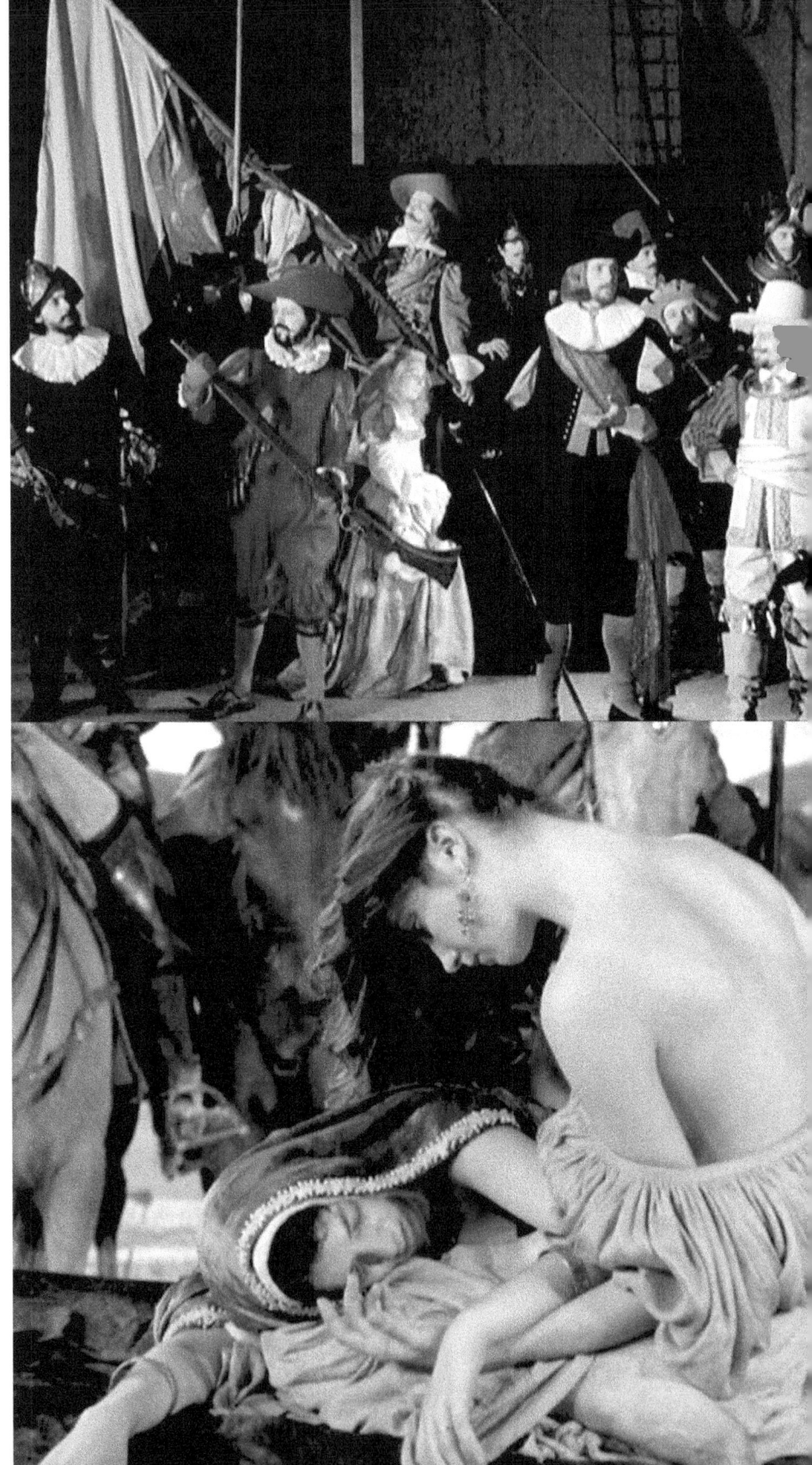

68 ▶
Passion
(JEAN-LUC GODARD, 1982). WHEN THE PAINTINGS OF REMBRANDT, DELACROIX, INGRES, AND GOYA COME TO LIFE, HISTORY, AGAIN, FINDS EMBODIMENT.

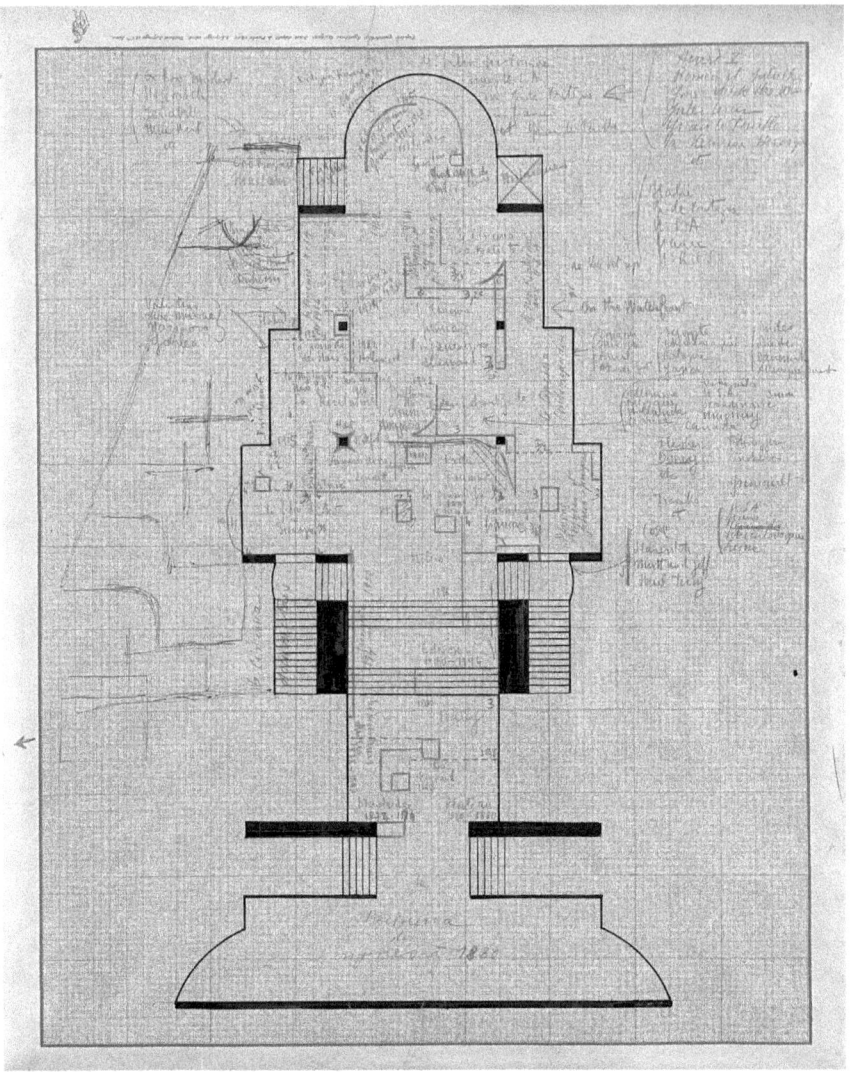

69 ▶
Museum of Cinema project (1972).
PLAN DRAWN BY HENRI LANGLOIS FOR HIS MUSEUM AT THE FRENCH CINÉMATHÈQUE.
(PHOTO COURTESY BIFI)

The accumulation thus only makes sense through a deliberate theory and organization of oblivion and selection, which Godard summed up in a definitive and provocative assertion: "Films should be burned, as I told Langlois, but beware of the inner flame. Art is like fire: it rises from what it consumes."[20] The material conservation of films does not suffice, for there is another form of conservation, which Langlois called "spiritual"[21]—a process that involves tracing the poetic and aesthetic echoes between works, which requires confrontation, juxtaposition, and montage, and makes possible the programming and museum-like exhibition of films. In Langlois' view the museum and the screening room (which he conceived as absolutely inextricable) established a pantheon of films, representing a narrative of cinema's forms. By drawing comparisons and putting forward an interpretation of the history of cinema, they initiated an entire generation of spectators and visitors into cinephilia.

Indeed, the cinematheque represents the moment, in the history of cinema, when the viewing of older films led to the creation of new ones. The New Wave learned cinema through the films that were programmed by Langlois, which in turn gave rise to cinema. In this way, seeing the films of Griffith, Lubitsch, Keaton, Murnau, Lang, and Hawks, together with Hollywood B-movies, for which they had a soft spot, and feeling a sense of kinship with masters like Renoir, Rossellini, Becker, and Ophuls gave rise to Godard's films, as well as to those of Truffaut, Chabrol, Rohmer, and Rivette. Langlois' visionary character and the way he presented his films at the French cinematheque, together constitute an oeuvre, which in turn produced new films, since modern cinema, after all, was conceived at the cinematheque. Revealing the history of cinema through parallels drawn between classic silent films and surrealist avant-gardes, film noir and neorealism, turn-of-the-century serials and Hollywood B-movies, the great burlesque films and American comedies—all this contributed to the rebirth of cinema. This was a perspective that was creative of forms and that became as a result itself part of the history of cinema. This "cinematheque-museum," as Dominique Païni has written, was first and foremost a training ground for the gaze, a university for taste and discrimination. From its very beginning, however, in 1936, this was no classical museum of fine taste nor an inventory of collections nor even a catalogue of films. Its mission consisted in offering a narrative of the history of cinema, which time and changes in taste were free to rewrite. Langlois' cinematheque-museum embodied the "shift from the early phase of accumulation and cataloguing to that of confrontation and evaluation."[22] It embodied that moment when cinema was recognized as an art; it was a museum of the cinematographic art, charged with all the provocation that such a claim contained in a cultural and intellectual context in which cinema remained generally and massively underestimated.

Godard has repeatedly pointed out how much he owes to such a conception of the cinematographic art. His sense of montage and collage, his love of citation, his impulse to bring together shots and tableaux, to combine various cinema genres and make them his own—all this was Langlois' influence, which is palpable throughout many of Godard's films. Indeed, Langlois was to remain his "method": Godard favored selecting sequences and shots, freeze-frames, and repetitions, over the classic narrative forms of conventional cinema history. Just like Langlois, who wanted to "hang" film sequences in his museum[23]—his museum of cinema project included the idea that about thirty film sequences would be shown, in situ, and seen in the course of a visit, a project he had to renounce for technical reasons—Godard pursued, in many of his films, this idea of a confrontation between various shots through montage. He proceeded on the hypothesis that his films would be the result of programming, organizing fragments and references, and combining them with a reflection on the century's history. This is what drives *Histoire(s) du cinéma*, the most direct extension of Langlois' teachings. In it Godard immerses art in the century's history and completes the shift of the Langlois museum from art museum to historical museum: he takes the spectator through a cinematographic itinerary that, building on his cinephilia and a body of films worthy of the son of the cinema he had never ceased to be, reformulates a visual history of the twentieth century. It is both a history in images (the visual world of the twentieth century, in which cinema played a structuring role, alongside painting), and a methodological proposition (a visual form of history). Seeing *Histoire(s) du cinéma* as part of the Langlois lineage is both to understand cinema as part and parcel of the century's visual culture—indeed, its embodiment—and to be exposed to another way of making history, a way that shapes the forms of the narrative, the writing, and the researching and representation of the world. Hence, the ideas of montage, flashback, close-up, freeze-frame—to name but a few of the Godardian cinematographic forms—belong not only to film but to the mental universe of the people of his century. How could historians do without these, then, when they undertake to rethink their methods, their writing, and their relationship to the past?

From *The Voices of Silence* to *Histoire(s) du cinéma*, or, The Fraternity of Metaphors

If Jean-Luc Godard entered the sacred order of cinephilia at Langlois' cinematheque in 1948, it was in 1951 that he read Malraux's *The Voices of Silence*—thus completing the pair of nearly simultaneous influences that shaped his conception of cinema. This large tome, with its many black-and-white illustrations, was published by Gallimard in its Galerie de la Pléiade collection. The twenty-one-year-old Godard derived such pleasure from reading it that Malraux immediately assumed a place in his pantheon of references and most-quoted authors, both in his critical pieces in *Cahiers du cinéma* and in his early films. It was not until 1966, and the ban on Rivette's *Suzanne Simonin, la religieuse de Diderot*, that Godard broke with de Gaulle's "minister of Kultur."[24] But until that moment Malraux remained, in Godard's view, "the most fascinating character in modern French literature," and his writings on art attested to his "adventurous spirit," which was capable of "bringing statues to life" and "resuscitating History."[25] What did Godard make of such a thick picture book? Dominique Païni, in an article published in *Art Press*,[26] linked the maturation process that led to *Histoire(s) du cinéma*—Godard's declaration of faith—to *The Voices of Silence* and pointed out their common ambition, almost fifty years apart: to achieve the ideal museum, which must segregate the work from the "profane" world and juxtapose it with opposite, rival, and distinct works. This museum, for both Malraux and Godard, entailed confrontation more than conservation, but also a conversation between metaphors and metamorphoses. Confronting and comparing excerpts of films, shots, and scenes, Godard had elaborated a series of hypotheses about the history of art and the history of the century fused together, in the same way as Malraux, in his *Museum Without Walls*, used photography to compare works and submit them to his own demonstration. The two projects were also similarly driven by the same mad passion: Malraux, without any scholarly legitimacy, handled more than seven thousand years of images, driven by the conviction that parallels would reveal the meaning of the history of art. Godard edited hundreds of sequence shots, clips, photographs, and texts into six hours of video. Malraux used photography, and Godard used video—the very tools that are said to have destroyed the aura of the work of art—in order, on the contrary, to reclaim meaning (and hence another kind of aura) through comparison.

The two "artists," thus, brought art out of the traditional museum, and the young filmmaker was surely not indifferent to the harsh critique of the museum that opened Malraux's book, in which the writer described the heritage institution as a mutilation, offering his own museum of the real instead: a museum without walls, in printed form, a museum of photographic reproductions which the author contrasted with one another, commented upon, and connected through citation. Such praise for the photographic reproduction of artworks (accessibility, equality, showcasing of neglected arts and civilizations, freedom of comparison), and of the use of fragments and elements, had a major impact on Godard. Art history thus turned into "the history of what can be photographed,"[27] and the museum without walls resurrected, via the book of reproductions (like films that contain video clips), the dead art contained in traditional museums. Art thus finds new life in the museum without walls, through the photographic compilation of artworks, from Mesopotamia to modern art, and their now authorized confrontation with one another, through the art of making connections between elements. Thus, the museum without walls assembled works of art, in the interest of clarity of thought, through the principles of fraternity, sorority, or equality, without concern for time period, school, or any other category of art history. Once made possible, this new mode of compilation, these new comparisons, engendered a brand-new history of art—a history in which, in Malraux's view, form became style and, according to Godard, the century was embodied in a "thinking form."[28] For both men the museum without walls constituted a metamorphosis in progress that reorganized itself as history.

Godard did not stop, in 1951, at the first section—"Museum Without Walls"—of Malraux's *Voices of Silence*. He also read the following sections and, most notably, "The Metamorphoses of Apollo," which presents the idea that when art is broken, regressed, damaged, imperfect, mutilated, it is at its most beautiful, its most moving, its most "in-its-times"—an idea that found a direct echo in Godard's praise for the historical recontextualization of all works of art, as opposed to their conservation and restoration. Malraux wrote, "Seldom is a Gothic head more beautiful than when broken."[29] And Godard took up in his films the idea that time and history should be visible in the work itself, inscribed in it like an imprint, in order to have perfect art and imperfect beauty. Authenticity and the emotion one feels when confronted with a work of art are traces of history revealing the truth of the artist who created it. Then came Part III—"The Creative Process"—on the recombination of art, where Malraux brings together, through the interplay of reproductions and commentary, works of art from different countries, periods, and levels (folk art as well as fine art), viewed in different ways (focusing on both specific elements and sweeping syntheses). The encounter between vastly different things, the intermingling of art, becomes a form of "artistic creation" in itself. And the virtue of dissimilarity makes this process of mingling even more frenetic, more satisfying, and more creative. Godard shared Malraux's faith in the power of the revelation-confrontation, which would later inform many of the minister's cultural decisions—faith in the confrontation with the work of art as the very essence of emotion and culture for all. The more sudden the confrontation, the more powerful the impact of the artwork. With Malraux such a faith in the innate and revelatory confrontation between the people and the masterpiece led to the opening of cultural centers (*maisons de la culture*) throughout France, which were designed "to structure the encounter between man and art."[30] In Godard it led to the poor and ignorant soldier in *Les Carabiniers* recognizing Rembrandt as a true comrade-in-arms, when confronted with the artist's most famous self-portrait (fig. 70), as well as to the female workers in *Passion*, who naturally reenact the masterpieces of classical art as tableaux vivants. Thus, the two theoreticians of art injected images into the history of their times: the people, the spectators, were directly confronted with the works, and from such a confrontation, devoid of any other cultural mediation, an opening onto beauty, and hence culture, could arise. Both shared a profound, populist, and prophetic belief in a form of conversion to art, a vision of the work of art as a road to Damascus. Both—the former in his texts, the latter in his films—sought tirelessly to dramatize the encounter with art, "the sense of creation that the work with which we are confronted imposes on us,"[31] as Malraux formulated it. Only this emotion was capable of seizing "us," opening "us" to art, and cultivating "us." The image as a modern form of trial by ordeal: Malraux and Godard agreed on this sort of artistic theory of love at first sight.

The last section of *The Voices of Silence* was explicitly quoted by Godard in *Histoire(s) du cinéma*: indeed, the title of the fourth chapter of Malraux's book became that of the fifth episode (3a) of Godard's series: "Aftermath of the Absolute." This episode deals with modern art as the transformation of the world into painting, which directly echoes Aragon's interpretation of Godard's films at the time of *Pierrot le fou*. Being in the world is thus seen as the sometimes-vulgar fate of modern art. Godard bore this principle both as his mission and as his cross before turning it into his manifesto. Cinema projects art into history: such is its historical destiny, so to speak. It transforms the classical museum into an anthropological museum—a museum of man—which was also Malraux's ultimate goal.[32] Godard had prophesied this historical role: "In my view, grand history is the history of cinema. It is grander than the others because it is projected. The other histories can only be scaled down. Cinema is necessary to unearth the truth of history. Only cinema, through recounting its own (hi)stories, recounts History. For cinema is the fraternity of metaphors."[33]

Godard built a work of art from the legacy of Malraux's museum as an imaginary form. His work is a montage, at once phantasmal and concrete, in the way Malraux used to say: "We cannot feel but through comparisons."[34]

Godard is the direct heir of this comparative thinking about art, as he demonstrated, once again, in his film on MOMA, *The Old Place*, which the New York institution commissioned him to make in 1998. In this film-essay, which is close, both in form and in content, to *Histoire(s) du cinéma*, the filmmaker pays homage to the conception of art and of the museum developed by Iris Barry, the American first lady of cinema who, influenced by Langlois and his ideas, founded the MOMA film department in 1934. The film offers, again, a reorganization of history through collage and montage of clips, shots, images, and quotes, with commentary in Godard's voice and that of his partner, Anne-Marie Miéville. As part of the great 1938 exhibition at the Jeu de Paume museum in Paris, Barry treated visitors to her "Brief History of American Cinema," which was designed as a confrontation between various fetish objects and a montage of "fragments" extracted from twenty-three films, which were shown both separately at various points of the visit and together in a final one-hour session. The exhibition catalogue points out that visitors could compare film clips—from *The Execution of Mary, Queen of Scots* (1894), *The Kiss* (1896), *In the Rapid-Transit Tunnel* (1903), Griffith's *The New York Hat* (1912), Ince's *The Fugitive* (1914), Chaplin's *The Immigrant* (1917), Stroheim's *Greed* (1923), Keaton's *The General* (1927), Disney's *The Skeleton Dance* (1929), and others—with objects, sets, and costumes used on the very same films, in an eminently modern conception of the museum exhibition of cinema, which is reminiscent of Godard's "contextualization." It was an exhibit that featured excerpts of films: in short, both Langlois' museum and Godard's *Histoire(s)* rolled into one.

Iris Barry's 1938 exhibit ended with a motto: "the world in which one enjoys such spectacles cannot be an entirely unhappy one, and the art that makes them possible cannot be deemed a negligible one."[35] Godard's film on MOMA, sixty years later, opened with an "exercise in artistic thinking," which was formulated as follows:

> The idea is to create connections. Just as stars are drawn closer to one another, even as they move further away from one another, held together by physical laws, to form a constellation, certain thoughts are drawn closer together and form one or several images. Thus, in order to understand what is going on between the stars, between the images, one must first examine simple connections. Everything is, thus, far away. But at the same time, in fact, close. And no doubt between the infinitely small and the infinitely large, we will manage to find a middle ground. . . . Artistic thinking begins with the invention of a possible world, or of a fragment of a possible world, and confronts it, through experience, work, painting, writing, filming, with the outside world. This endless dialogue between imagination and work enables the formation of an ever more acute representation of what is commonly called reality.[36]

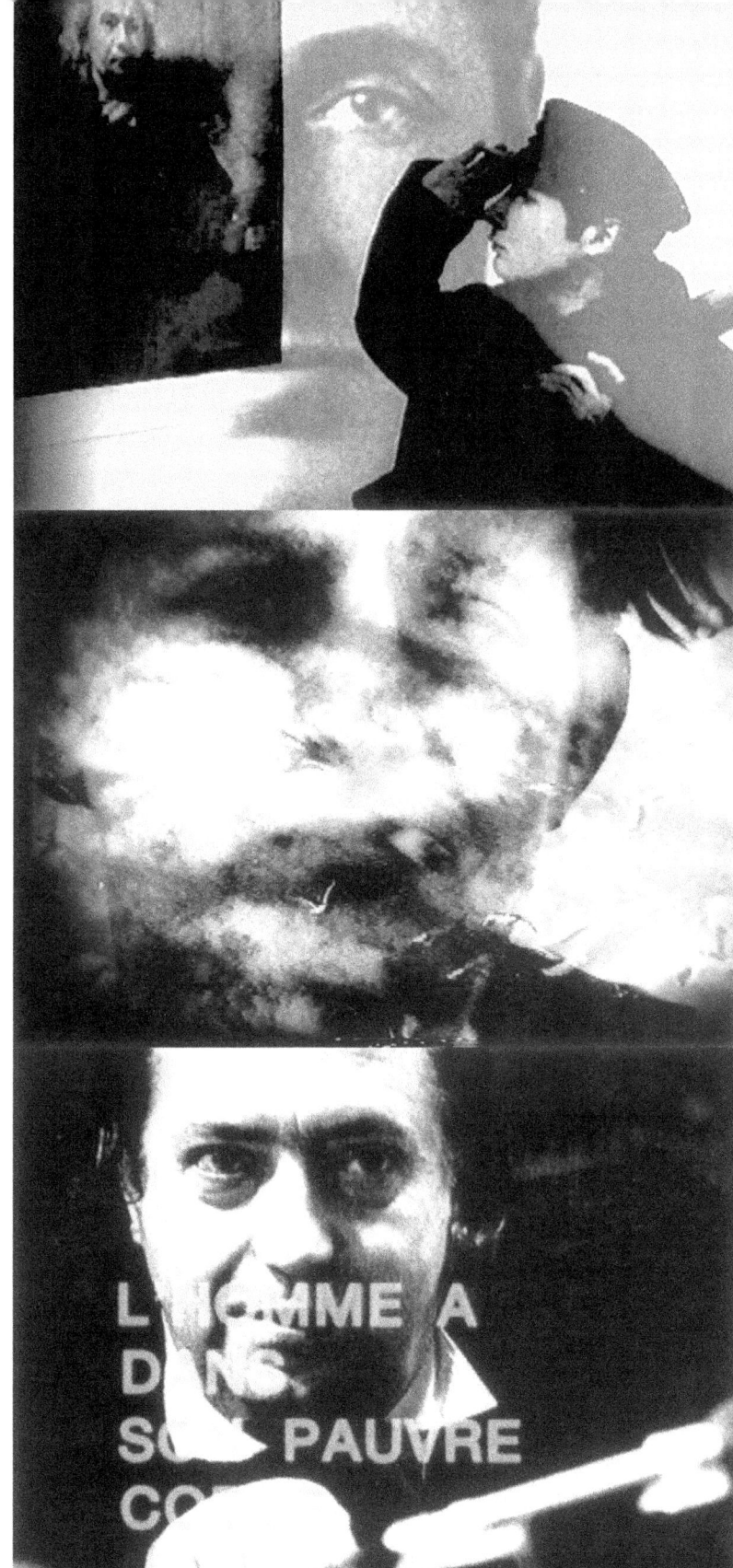

70–72 ▶
Histoire(s) du cinéma
(JEAN-LUC GODARD, 1988–98). REMBRANDT, MALRAUX, AND LANGLOIS, THE BROTHERHOOD OF THE EXHIBITORS OF IMAGES.

At that moment, while Godard's text, which sounds like a paragraph from *The Voices of Silence*, is being spoken and heard, the film offers a visual illustration of such a convergence of images, which is specific to Godard's ideal museum: two female tennis players, a ritual salute, images of work, a Virgin Mary, a movie theater, Lascaux together with Picasso, a *pietà*, Adam and Eve, and, in conclusion, Pialat's Van Gogh, exclaiming: "Hey! There's what's-his-name!"

This key passage from *The Old Place*, which offers rare insight into Godard's conceptual thought, was echoed a year later in *Eloge de l'amour*, by another defense and illustration of connection: "Here's what's-his-face. We tend to forget that the ancients worked only through links. This is the fundamental question. It is from Delacroix or Matisse that we will have the answer."[37] The answer to the imposture and posture of the traditional museum lies in this conception of the link, borrowed from Malraux's museum without walls. *The Voices of Silence* and the cinematheque made such a deep impression on Godard that any semblance of interval that intercedes in his work between film images, between photograms and paintings, between shots and the world immediately becomes a comparative space. Godard evinced an obsession with comparison whose every virtue he thoroughly explored and by every possible means:

> Films have ceased, in my opinion, to be "seen," since "seeing" for me always involves the "possibility of comparison." Not comparison between two things, nor between an image and how one remembers it. Rather, comparison between two images and, as we see them, to spot a number of links. If one says that Eisenstein, in such and such film, picks up parallel editing, which was theoretically first developed by Griffith, then Griffith should be screened on the left, with Eisenstein next to it. Then we could see, as in court, if something is true or false. And we could argue. Granted, two theaters right next to each other might be hard to find. But today, video provides a solution. Films can be transferred onto video and compared.[38]

Malraux's museum without walls, Langlois' cinematheque, and Godard's cinema are all ideal places where artworks regain their aura through the incessant interplay of comparison. Malraux (fig. 71), Langlois (fig. 72), and Godard are the theoreticians and practitioners of what may be called a *museum-montage*. The first made a book out of it, the second a museum of cinema, and the third a series of eight digital films. *Histoire(s) du cinéma* doubtless made the greatest strides down this Malrauxian and Langloisian path of the history of art.

The Historiographical Virtue of *Histoire(s) du cinéma*

This opus, begun in 1988 and completed in 1998, with a running time of almost six hours, evinces unrivaled ambition and incomparable form, making it one of the ultimate achievements of the cinema of our times. If the twentieth century can be said to have begun, artistically speaking, in a creative zone inaugurated by the first screening of the Lumière brothers' cinematography and reached its peak with the consecration of Picasso's *Demoiselles d'Avignon*, then the *Histoire(s) du cinéma* can be said to constitute its closure—both the final destination of the Lumière brothers' train and the aesthetic manifesto of an art of montage, of fragments and shards, which was inaugurated by cubism. Those who have not seen *Histoire(s) du cinéma* have missed the century's end. It is as though the film endeavored to be all of cinema, all at once, in eight episodes: "1a. All the Histories"; "1b. A Single (Hi)story"; "2a. Only Cinema"; "2b. Fatal Beauty"; "3a. Aftermath of the Absolute"; "3b. A New Wave"; "4a. The Control of the Universe"; and "4b. The Signs Among Us."

Godard was already entertaining such a project in the late 1970s, when he held a conference at Montreal's Conservatoire d'art cinématographique in the fall of 1978, following on one by Henri Langlois, who had just died. In his *Introduction à une véritable histoire du cinéma*, which unfolded over the course of seven trips to Canada, the filmmaker was already remaking the history of his art, drawing on and comparing clips from his own films and from films by directors he admired, from Lang to Hitchcock, from Minnelli to Nicholas Ray, from Preminger to Mizoguchi, from Ford to Rossellini, from Tod Browning to Eisenstein, from Fuller to Scorsese. He presented his project thus:

> I would like to recount the history of cinema, not just chronologically but also archaeologically and biologically. In trying to show how movements have arisen, just as in painting, we can narrate a history—how perspective was developed, when oils were invented, etc. In cinema, also, it did not all happen at once. It happened through men and women who were themselves part of a community, who have a history of their own, and who at a given moment in time expressed themselves and impressed that expression, or expressed their impression, in a certain way. There must be multiple geological layers, cultural landslides, and to do this well, you need resources for vision and analysis, not necessarily very powerful ones, but ones well adapted to the task. All this, the geology and geography of society and its history, all this is contained in the history of cinema, and yet it remains invisible.[39]

In 1978, however, the "resources for vision" and the "resources for analysis" quickly ran out, just like the money from the Montreal Conservatoire, which had pledged to invest ten thousand dollars per session but could only come up with seven. A decade later, withdrawn in his Swiss laboratory, in Rolle, Godard found the technical resources of digital video to realize his project.

What comes out of these eight films is a way of narrating cinema through shards of memory, through, that is, fragments of the history of an art that, for Godard, is both intimate and universal: film sequences, gestures, bodies, words, movements, as so many fetishes that inform this visual remembrance—both sacred and gnostic, both individual and shared—of the universe. This theory of the revelatory shard is rather well suited to the cinematographic form of perception of the world in the twentieth century, this cult of the revealing moment that reflects memories of the images of history, this phenomenology of the significant detail where, suddenly, everything makes sense thanks to the universal connections established by cinema and its multiple vision. These are the shards that Jean-Luc Godard used and combined to compose his *Histoire(s) du cinéma*: those that made sense to him, once given form, will make sense to all, and these intimate experiences that communicate, thanks to cinema, will constitute the common basis for what may be called a simultaneously intimate and collective history.

The ultimate achievement of this theory of the revelatory shard—as so many fragmented emblems of history—was developed by Godard in his analysis of Alfred Hitchcock's mise-en-scène (fig. 73), in episode 4a of *Histoire(s) du cinéma*, entitled "The Control of the Universe." He speaks in a voice that appears to have spanned the entire century:

> All you remember is a handbag, a bus, a glass of milk, the blades of a windmill, a hairbrush, a row of bottles, a pair of glasses, a sheet of music, a bunch of keys—because with these, through these, Hitchcock succeeds at what eluded Alexander, Caesar, and Napoleon: seizing control of the universe. Ten thousand people might never forget Cezanne's apple, but a billion spectators will remember the cigarette lighter in *Strangers on a Train*. If Hitchcock can be seen as the only *poète maudit* to have experienced public success, it is because he was the greatest creator of forms of the twentieth century, and because it is forms that tell us what is going on deep down. And what is art if not what transforms forms into style, and what is style but man himself? It is thus a blonde who is not wearing a bra, tailed by a detective who is scared of heights, who will provide us with proof that all this is just cinema, i.e. the infancy of art.[40]

These four minutes dedicated to Hitchcock seem to sum up, condense, and carry out the work and formal thinking developed by the young critics of the New Wave—between 1949 (when *Rope* was released in Paris) and 1966 (when François Truffaut's book on and with Hitchcock was published), this bit of film meticulously, explosively, and creatively juxtaposes Hitchcock's images and statements, excerpts of his films and critical assessments, as told by Godard. The images and the words, turned fetishes, are intoned as a vision of history, restoring to the eye and ear the role that Alfred Hitchcock played for the young Turks: "the greatest creator of forms of the century," that is, "the infancy of their art," as well as the richest source of cult and fetishistic detail in the contemporary world. History here takes the form of a mosaic, bringing together around a common meaning all the emotions and memories born of these emblems, which Godard's film and voice-over enumerate.

To these shards of film, the chosen moments that he draws from his memories and his cinephilic visions, the filmmaker adds shards of life: of his own, through his continuous presence onscreen, as an artist working at the editing table, reading, selecting documents; through his voice, whispering somberly from beyond the grave or proclaiming like an oracle (figs. 74, 75); as well as of twentieth-century lives, through dozens of photographs, archival images, excerpts of speeches, and documents that form a collective visual memory of our times, drawn mostly from newsreels to which Gaumont, a coproducer of the films, granted the filmmaker access. Godard's prophecy is thus an intimate epic, the confession of a child of the century who was also a child of cinema, and whom all human beings could nonetheless recognize as their alter ego. Conversely, Godard identifies with all, especially with those who have suffered in this century of extremes from history's violence and cruelty (figs. 76–78). It is a kind of prosopopoeia: I, cinema, am talking. Or rather: I, Jean-Luc Godard, cinema embodied, narrate the indeterminate (hi)stories of my century. As Jacques Aumont says in his interpretative essay on *Histoire(s) du cinéma*, Godard is "the keeper of the museum of the real" that is cinema, from which he draws, conserves, and re-presents all the details he deems relevant.[41] Godard has never made any secret of his personification of the intertwined history of cinema and of the century, as he explained in *Libération*, in April 2002:

> I must admit that I do feel a bit like the sales rep for images on earth. . . . In the 1950s and 1960s, we were in touch with those who had founded cinema. We were raised to hope that everything could be seen and known, because cinema was still

73–75 ▶
Histoire(s) du cinéma (JEAN-LUC GODARD, 1988–98). HITCHCOCK, GODARD (CHILD), AND GODARD (GROWN): MELANCHOLY OF THE MASTERS OF IMAGES.

76–78 ▶
Histoire(s) du cinéma
(JEAN-LUC GODARD, 1988–98). FROM HITLER TO FRANCO, VIA MABUSE: AFFILIATION BETWEEN THE MANIPULATORS OF IMAGES.

within man's grasp. Experiencing half of an art form's entire lifetime gives you incredible insight, it's as if Matisse and Picasso had been around when perspective was invented. The secret has been lost, but memory persists. We need witnesses, even if it has a slight "last of the Mohicans" feel to it, or Don Quixote. Such melancholia is deadening, but also rejuvenating. And this is why my own story intersects with those of many others, of all others, their silences, their passions. . . . In the twentieth century, cinema has been the art that allowed souls—as they were called in Russian novels—to intimately experience their (hi)stories within History. Such a fusion, such a perfect fit, such a desire for fiction and history together will never be seen again. Only cinema was able to hold together this "I" and this "us." From this standpoint, both a clip of footage of the Nuremberg trials and a Hitchcock shot express what we were. Both are cinema.[42]

Godard explicitly expresses the same idea in an episode of his *Histoire(s) du cinéma*: "cinema was the only way to go, to narrate, to realize, myself, that I have a history."[43] This is also what makes *Histoire(s) du cinéma* often feel like a confrontation with images returned from the dead, often sound like a tale told from beyond the grave, as though one were attending the great awakening of the dead on the battlefield of cinema, as at the end of Gance's *J'accuse*, where scores of Great War veterans come back to life. Godard has entered an unmistakably melancholy phase of his existence, and his conception of history bears traces of it. "Death happens," he has also said, "and suddenly one is in mourning. I don't know why exactly, but I did the opposite. I was in mourning first, but death did not come. I was in mourning for myself, my one and only companion, and I could sense that the soul had tripped over the body and forgotten to take it along when it left."[44] This Cassandra—as he nicknames himself, describing himself as "like a legend" in *The Old Place*, while he calls his partner Anne-Marie Miéville "Miss Clio"—is an aging, fragile, often intemperate, lyrical, and sometimes cranky form of romantic melancholia.

If the man is melancholy, his conception of history tragic, and his mission quasi-messianic, Godard did find in digital video the tool of a historian. He managed to use to the fullest all the resources of his video lab: clips, images, photograms, words, photographs, footage, everything that produces fetishes and that neither Malraux nor Langlois could tap into in their day. Most of these fragments are edited using the technical resources of video art: freeze-frame, movement breakdown, superimpositions, collage, special effects, insertion of titles and phrases, constant interweaving of black, white, color, paintings, photographs, texts, and films. Godard uses his "right of citation" to summon up together all these visual fragments, drawn from his own collection of videotapes and from documents supplied by Gaumont, refilming paintings, inserting slogans and catchphrases, recording his commentary, a conversation with the critic Serge Daney, filming a few actors reading classic literature (Juliette Binoche, Julie Delpy, Denis Lavant, and Alain Cuny), and editing the whole with his customary virtuosity. Yet by developing a comparative tool (video), he also developed a device for museum exhibition, since Godard freely plunders images and paintings from the traditional museum and "exhibits" them in film. *Histoire(s) du cinéma* appears to come out of a lab, a crypt, or a workshop, from where the artist, sorcerer's apprentice, and high priest invented a form.

That form, made up of these shards, of these sounds and voices, edited into choppy and antithetical movements, shedding a light of gloom and doom, which is supposed to echo that of origins, is essentially lyrical: it is the epic of all films and all peoples, constituted from fragments and details of each. What we are dealing with here is a cinematographic form of autobiography of all, in which a man, looking for his own reason in his (hi)story, ends up shedding light on the reasons of history. Through such a "montage-museum" Godard has fashioned a historian's logic through film: in *his* museum he is a historian. This is why he has left the traditional museum: the comparative powers of montage have turned his museum without walls into a workshop as much as a laboratory of history.

Can *Histoire(s)* Redeem History?

Is Godard's ideal museum not also an impossible dream, then, characterized by a seemingly intractable contradiction between the despised traditional museum as a space for the exhibition and preservation of art, the museum as the imaginary world of montage—a utopia if ever there was one—and the museum as history incarnate, with the added dimension that all may enter, all may speak, and thus the risk that no one would fully recognize themselves in this cacophony of voices and fragments of bodies? Godard is, of course, always happy to unsettle spectators, as the oracular discourse he himself delivers in the final episode makes clear: "This is what I like in cinema in general, the saturation of magnificent signs bathing in the light of their absence of explanation."[45] Yet is the thesis that sums up these *Histoire(s)*, as Jacques Rancière points out[46], not first and foremost a confession of powerlessness: the history of cinema as a rendezvous with history that was missed—a failure that Godard tries to remedy with his *Histoire(s)*? Didn't cinema, or rather the filmmakers bogged down in the cinema system, more often than not neglect History, with a capital *H*, in favor of the stories offered by scriptwriters and the literary tradition of plots and characters?

Indeed, this idea of betrayal-abdication is the thesis with which Godard begins *Histoire(s) du cinéma*, whose first episode focuses on the collective guilt of cinema at times of rising danger—Nazism, war, occupation, collaboration, and the Final Solution. Episode 1b, "A Single History," in particular, is haunted by the guilt of cinema's major figures, these "great directors who were incapable of thwarting the thirst for vengeance and violence that they had staged over and over again,"[47] and who are made responsible—through Godard's montage, now become ruthlessly accusatory, just as it can be incredibly redemptive at other times—for the catastrophe of Stalin and Hitler. The illustrated succession of the Hollywood, socialist-realist, fascist, and national-socialist periods is indeed very damning: cinema is depicted as enslaved to industry, instrumentalized by propaganda, and, in the end, turned into a vector of death. Godard's thesis, Rancière writes, "counterposes two types of (hi)stories: the stories of the film industry illustrated with images with an eye to cashing in on the collective imaginary, and the virtual history told by these same images. The style of montage Godard develops for *Histoire(s) du cinéma* is designed to show the history announced by a century of films, but whose power slipped through the fingers of their filmmakers, who subjected the 'life' of images to the immanent 'death' of the text."[48] Godard thus bears the weight of cinema's guilt—a cinema that failed to save the century from the extremism that led it to its demise, a cinema that even hastened this demise, as though blind to history. But Godard also plays the redeemer: he attempts, with *Histoire(s) du cinéma*, to retrospectively salvage the century through cinema. Indeed, using fragments of films made by other filmmakers—the films that ignored History—he remakes and reedits the films they failed to make. *Histoire(s) du cinéma* becomes a redemptive project: from these guilty images (guilty of neglecting history, of blinding the people to it, and of leading to disaster), Godard makes innocent ones. All of a sudden—through montage, juxtaposition, poetics, lyrical fragments, connections, and parallels—these images become capable of saving the world, become icons of history. In Godard's view, for instance, it is Italian and American postwar cinema that alleviated the century's guilt for producing totalitarian ideology.

This is what Philippe Sollers meant when, discussing *Histoire(s) du cinema*, he quite rightly invoked "the Last Judgment for films": "Saint Godard's pronouncement is clear: from the very start, it has to do with the realm of the dead, and the theme of apocalypse haunts the entire series. Godard is there, sitting behind his mic, or at his typewriter, or else standing, like a conductor of ghosts, and he revives these thousands of shadows that were projected onto screens; he judges them and saves them. This is the Last Judgment for films, determining their guilt or innocence in relation to the history of the century."[49]

History is thus the moment of truth for cinema, and Godard organizes this trail so as to save the films of his cinephilic pantheon, and hence save himself, in the twilight of his life. And this explains why one of the essential texts for grasping Godard's project over the past two decades is the last of Walter Benjamin's writings, the famous "On the Concept of History," which he wrote in the spring of 1940 and which constitutes an approach to the question of the redemption of the past. Taking inspiration from a painting by Paul Klee, *Angelus Novus*, which he owned and cherished, Benjamin defines "the Angel of History," the metaphor most often quoted by Godard. The messianic task of redeeming the past, which Godard takes on in *Histoire(s) du cinéma*, was formulated by Benjamin and passed on, handed off, to the filmmaker. "There is a mysterious tryst between previous generations and the one to which we belong ourselves," Alain Bergala wrote, as a kind of Benjaminian epigraph to Godard's work. "We were expected on earth. For we are heir, like each of the human crews that has preceded us, to a portion of the messianic power. The past is calling for us to exercise it, has a right over it. There is no evading its summons."[50] At the end of episode 1b, accepting this legacy and these redemptive questions, Godard has a Klee angel blinking alternately with his own self-portrait as shown in *Soigne ta droite*, coming out of a plane with a book, *The Idiot*, in his hand—Klee's angel and Godard the idiot, blinking back and forth, like an homage and a recognition in aesthetic-poetic rhyme. The filmmaker makes this clear in the ultimate episode, when he tries to directly define his own conception of history: "What is history, deep down? Very deep down, with Malraux, Péguy, Braudel. . . . Ah, history is a somber faithfulness to fallen things. I warned you, Clio, a witness is always a martyr."[51] This is why in Godard's work cinema takes on a sacred value, which alone can give him this messianic role: to redeem history as the film passes over the editing table of the celluloid prophet. "Cinema," he says, "is neither an art nor a technique; it is a mystery."[52] Cinema, according to Godard's logic as explained by Rancière, is seen as a mystical art precisely because it is capable of redeeming history: "It is the light that inscribes the movement, the spiritual energy of the real

79 ▶
Pierrot le fou
(JEAN-LUC GODARD, 1965). THE GAME OF LOVE BRINGS ART BACK TO LIFE.

which reveals the real energy of the spirit, the sacred cause that redeems history's sins."[53]

This idea of redemption through cinema has had two major moments, according to Godard, who made it the focus of his *Histoire(s) du cinéma*. Two cinema moments transformed its entire history: the newsreels that were shot at the opening of the death camps and then neorealism. Cinema betrayed, failed, in not filming the horror. It should have been there at Auschwitz because it was in its essence to be there, *hic et nunc*. It was its duty. Yet it was not there. Only the documentaries shot in the winter and spring of 1945 could make up for its absence: "even completely scratched up, a simple 35 mm rectangle can single handedly redeem all of the real."[54] The newsreel footage of those who survived mass death redeemed even Hollywood, that modern Babylon: "And if George Stevens had not been the first to use 16mm color film at Auschwitz and Ravensbrück, Elizabeth Taylor's bliss would probably never have found a place in the sun."[55] George Stevens the Auschwitz cameraman thus raises George Stevens the Hollywood director of *A Place in the Sun* (starring Elizabeth Taylor) to historical glory. And then neorealism and "the great Italian cinema" redeemed all compromises with the studio industry, both in Hollywood and in Europe: by going out onto the streets at last, by filming life where it was lived, this cinema not only reconnected with the Enlightened art's true origins but also constituted a kind of resurrection of images. Here

Godard is at his most lyrical. His epic then takes on the redemptive power of faith: yes, neorealism redeemed all of cinema by realizing its mission at long last, that is, to film history in the making, and subjected its characters, its plots, its little stories (*histoires*) to the big one, history (*Histoire*). It is in this way that a world so devoid of history, the world that was bitterly denounced in *Le Petit soldat*, can suddenly turn into its opposite: when cinema succeeds, sometimes, in turning its (hi)stories into History.

Godard's demonstration reactivates the historical power of cinema through a constant process of making connections: in *Histoire(s) du cinéma* any image may be brought together with another and thus be either condemned or saved. He turns all images into images of something else, which is capable of revealing their truth. This is the historiographic virtue of montage, since what makes history, definitively, is the connections drawn between images:

> This is what bringing two images together makes you see: the young woman who smiles in a Soviet film is not exactly the same as the young woman who smiles in a Nazi film. Yet the Tramp in *Modern Times* is exactly the same, at the beginning, as Ford's workman filmed by Taylor. To make history is to spend hours looking at these images and then, suddenly, to bring them together, to trigger a spark.... Experienced in this way, cinema then becomes a metaphor for the world. It remains an archetype, involving all at once an aesthetic, a technique, and an ethics.[56]

The greater the leap between the two realities brought together through images, the stronger the sense of historicity. As Godard has often pointed out, images are not strong because they are brutal or fantastic but rather because the association of ideas they conjure up is a valid leap: "for the stereo system also works for history."[57] The pulsation of images offered over the six hours of *Histoire(s) du cinéma* represents the apex of Godard's montage, in which the maniacal juxtaposition of these visual citations, in multiple and baroque ways, clearly constitutes the motor of history for the filmmaker. "To place two images side by side is called Creation, Miss Mary," says the Maestro in *Je vous salue Marie*. Gilles Deleuze has said of Godard's connective art: "What counts is the mad, captive energy, ready to explode. When two images are brought together there is a detonation, a combustion, a dissipation of the two condensed energies. It burns quickly and subsides, but even as it does so, it illuminates."[58] Like sparks of cinema to guide our historical investigations and redeem the century.

6

DEMODERN AESTHETICS ▶
FILMING THE END OF COMMUNISM

◀ 80
French poster for *Khrustalyov, My Car!*
(ALEXEI GUERMAN, 1998). (PHOTO COURTESY BIFI)

HISTORIANS AND OBSERVERS agree that the Soviet Empire collapsed with astonishing speed. "The Roman and Ottoman empires took more than two centuries to fall apart, the Soviet empire less than two years. The event was sudden and unforeseeable," wrote Jacques Rupnik at the very beginning of his book *The Other Europe: The Rise and Fall of Communism in East-Central Europe*.[1] This remains one of the major historical mysteries of our times. The concept of a "revolution in reverse" has been floated by some, especially in France, where the Soviet collapse coincided with the celebration of another revolution, the bicentennial of the 1789 French Revolution.[2] Others have compared the phenomenon to the revolutions that spread throughout Europe in 1848. Yet the "revolutionary" comparison is unconvincing, since no democratic people's republic got rid of communism following the classic paradigm of revolution, however "de-revolutionized": that is, the advent of a new society in and through violence. The fall of communism was not accompanied by historical romanticism, even if it did at times trigger hope and excitement. And no blood was shed either. A historical epoch, deemed out of date and out of service, surrendered without a fight and was retired, tossed into the dustbin of historical systems, the scrapheap of *anciens régimes*, without significant protest or resistance. Nostalgia would come later, to be sure, but neither glory nor ardor, monstrosity nor madness, accompanied the downfall. There was not even sadness—a system had imploded, collapsed from within, and nobody noticed until the loss could be objectively established. The only thing that appeared in the moment was a devastated landscape, a vacuum where shortly before there had been glimmering buildings; well-equipped armies; fabulous productivity and social welfare statistics; indomitable athletic, cultural, and scientific pride; and well-ordered and well-dressed, if not exactly fashionable, populations.

A Demodern Collapse

This devastation of the communist world, this ruination of objects and beings, this disintegration of minds and bodies, manifested itself in film, both before and after the collapse of the Soviet Empire. A cinematographic form of history was able to convey a sense of the agony of the communist system, both when its body was still moving and after it had ceased to do so, whereas television images—when they were not downright manipulative, as in 1989 in Timisoara, Romania—were often content to show falsely romantic crowds gathered around palaces and walls, on boulevards and squares, and may even have contributed to the impression of a dynamic of successive, and almost embedded, "de-revolutions."[3] If anything, however, there was a conspicuous absence of dynamism, as if suddenly the center had disappeared, and death had seized the former system, left behind by history, like old and forgotten furniture, in its entirety. Indeed, disintegration was a central trope, together with a related series of images and metaphors (the corpse, the ruin, the return to a primitive wilderness, the disaster, the apocalypse), and emerging from communism consisted, for the most part, in a brutal shift toward nothingness, transition to a vacuum. These were the prevailing images of dereliction, of what Rupnik termed "catastroika"[4]—Gorbachev's famous perestroika gone tragically awry. This cinematographic form of history is, thus, essentially characterized by its shapelessness.

What do we see in films as the iron mantle of communism is collapsing? What does the iron mantle even look like when it is no longer in use and has been left rusting on the backstage of history? Several synthetic propositions of historical-aesthetic theory have been advanced. First, the *purgatory theory* holds that forty years of communist rule in Central and Eastern Europe represent a long parenthetical transition to Westernized images, which take a roughly similar form, today, whether they are produced in Hollywood or Moscow, Paris or Warsaw, Taiwan or Budapest. Second, the *theory of nostalgic return* holds that what now remains to be seen, in the wake of communism, is the precommunist state, a return to primitive images, to the original Russian condition. Third, the *liquidation theory* proposes that there is nothing to see. The images—and the studios that were used to produce them—have been swept away by the tsunami triggered by communism's collapse. According to this theory, all the images produced in Eastern Europe, like all the film shoots that take place there, are a sham, at least in terms of their being local productions, since they are almost always produced by Western companies. And finally, the *broken refrigerator theory* suggests that the entire system has shut down—because it was too old, no spare parts were to be found, the operating manual was lost—and everything left inside became rotten. Images were and are produced, but they mostly just depict the process of putrefaction at work on the former order of things. This chapter will take up these various theories to determine the unifying concept of a cinematographic form of history capable of recording the collapse of communism, which may be characterized as the juxtaposition of "demodern aesthetic forms."

"One day we will realize that our triumphs in reinforced concrete are now nothing more than the excrement of civilization," wrote Leonid Abalkine, a

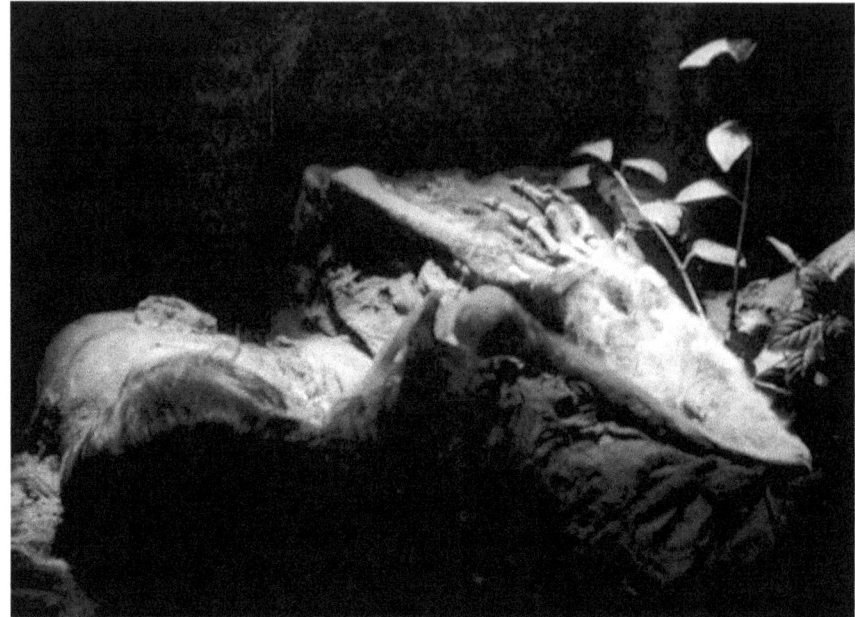

81 ▶
Stalker
(ANDREI TARKOVSKY, 1979). A PUTREFACTION OF AESTHETIC DECOMPOSITION GNAWS AT THE WORLD AND BRINGS IT BACK TO ITS PRIMAL ORIGINS.

former Soviet academic, in February 1989.[5] It is no longer just the refrigerator that has broken down here; it is the raw material of modernity that constituted the Soviet system that is succumbing to rot: the reinforced concrete, the urban development, the radiant city, the planned towns in the countryside, the well-ordered buildings and avenues, the modern housing for all. The images that are projected onto this modern pride of another era are images of ultimate disintegration: of "excrement," says Abalkine, as well as of filth, mold, putrefaction, ruin, dilapidation, and morbidity (fig. 81). The concept of "demodernization" has been used, especially among economists, sociologists, and historians, to describe this phenomenon. In 1992 François Fejtö quoted a Romanian dissident who, in describing his country under Ceausescu's dictatorship, spoke of "economic demodernization" to evoke conditions in which electricity and heating-oil consumption had reached an all-time low while local oil was exported abroad and spectacular plans were daily affirmed about the future industrial progress of the People's Republic.[6]

As early as 1990, in his major work on the German army during the Second World War, *Hitler's Army: Soldiers, Nazis, and War in the Third Reich*, the Israeli historian Omer Bartov used the concept of demodernization to describe the conditions under which German troops fought on the eastern front in 1942.[7] Demodernization here refers to the deterioration of material conditions on the front and the return to more archaic forms of combat and daily life. At the beginning of the war, at the height of its success, the Wehrmacht had waged war based on an innovative and efficient use of modern equipment. However, from the winter of 1942 onward, in the Soviet Union, the majority of German units found themselves forced to continue the fight under the most precarious conditions. Equipment quickly became obsolete and ammunition scarce, while they confronted a better-armed enemy. For lack of tanks Hitler's soldiers had to dig holes to protect themselves and fall back on a basic form of trench warfare, as though slipping back in time to an earlier world war. This demodernization led to despair and a "brutalization" of behavior, resulting in the appearance of a new heroism: German soldiers became more ferocious, more fanatical.

It is in this sense that some historians of the Great War use the term *demodernization*, notably Frédéric Rousseau in an article published in 2000, in which he explains that between 1914 and 1918 men had to renounce most of the attributes of early-twentieth-century Western life, abandoning not only modern comforts and hygiene but also their relationship to food, intimacy, modesty, and death: "To live for months on end in holes dug in the ground or in makeshift log and thatch cabins constituted a demodernization of normal living conditions."[8] In each of these cases it was as though the process of civilization had been reversed at a given historical moment: technical and industrial modernity remained present, affirmed, referenced, but history mounted an attack from the rear, and men experienced, during a time that was both exceptional and yet quotidian, a regression in their conception and practice of modern life.

The sociologist and philosopher Alain Touraine has conceptualized the "modern" usage of *demodernization* to designate the "fundamentalist" movements that demand from their populations an intentional regression, on the scale of modernity, in their behaviors, mores, culture, and economic activity. In the first chapter of his 1997 book, *Pourrons-nous vivre ensemble? Egaux et Différents (Can We Live Together? Equality and Difference)*, Touraine proposes that demodernization "can result only in the fusion of a communitarian ideology and a modernizing project controlled by an authoritarian power" in the name of religion, the nation, and tradition.[9] A modernized world of technology and markets is thus detached from an archaic world of culture and customs, with the latter, officially and publically at least, ruling the former. The severing of ties that used to bind individual freedom and collective efficiency is what Touraine labels demodernization: the concept of modernization is abandoned yet without renouncing the modern world. The Islamic republics and kingdoms, as well as the various fundamentalist Christian communities, especially in the United States, are given as cautionary examples of this demodernization.

Moving away from the economic, technical, military, and sociological domains, to arrive at a cinematographic form of history, entails a shift from demodernization—a technical social scientific term—to the "demodern," a notion with more aesthetic and literary resonance, since it was as "moderns" that most of the artists and intellectuals, from the middle of the nineteenth century onward, from Baudelaire to Barthes and Godard, have defined themselves—or rather, according to the paradox identified by Antoine Compagnon, as "antimoderns": "the antimoderns, as opposed to the traditionalists, are in fact the modern ones, the true moderns—not fooled by modernity, but wise to it. The hypothesis might sound strange: exploring the antimodernity of the antimoderns will reveal their real and enduring modernity."[10]

Four important films that have marked the history of Eastern European cinema have expressed this demodern pathology and appear to offer a diagnosis of the collapse of communism. Andrei Tarkovsky made *Stalker* in 1979, Emir Kusturica *Underground* in 1995, Alexei Guerman *Khrustalyov, My Car!* three years later, and Aleksandr Sokurov *Russian Ark* in 2002. All are about a world that is collapsing, dragging down with it the most modern symbols and figures of the regime, which has sometimes itself already been reduced to ruin. None announce the imminent arrival of a new world or a new man.

In 1979, while Tarkovsky was shooting and then editing *Stalker*, the Soviet army was venturing onto Afghan territory, and in the eyes of some this unruly hornet's nest marked the beginning of the end. But the system was still in place—seemingly solid, restrictive, intrusive, and depressing—as the filmmaker himself complained in June 1983, in a letter to the president of Goskino, the Soviet organization in charge of producing and supervising films in the USSR:

> I have devoted all my strength, all my know-how, and all my abilities, to Soviet cinema. Over the course of my twenty-year long career in this country, I have not received a single award or prize, and I have not been invited to take part in one Soviet festival! Doesn't this reveal your true attitude toward my long and, I can assure you, difficult labors? . . . When I was hospitalized for a heart attack, nobody came to see me. Only once did a strange individual come, and that was to determine whether I was really ill. As if I had the plague. When I was still convalescing, I asked the film-

makers' union for a prescription for a cure at a sanatorium specializing in cardiovascular diseases. I was turned down.... If there had been a good reason for it, I would have been starved to death, together with my family, a long time ago.[11]

Communism had fully collapsed by the time Kusturica began to make *Underground*, which received the Palme d'Or at the 1995 Cannes Film Festival and triggered passionate debates—accused of being pro-Serb, which it, indeed, is. But the film focuses mostly on the Eastern European system, which it describes through a revealing metaphor: a basement in which the illusion of an autarkic, productivist, heroic, and democratic world prevailed for forty years. "My theory about communism," the director has explained, "is that everything was a sham, a fiction, a hoax. Fundamentally, communism was a system that never evolved. And people bought into the fiction as if it were reality. In these cases, there is no choice, you are headed for disaster, for catastrophe. As George Orwell said, political language is designed to make lies sound truthful. This is why one can also say that, in terms of cinema, the best part of communism was its mistakes. And Yugoslav communism made quite a few!"[12]

Khrustalyov, My Car! was shot between 1995 and 1997 by the great St. Petersburg-based director Alexei Guerman. It is a bitter and gloomy satire on Stalin's last days, when everything was still frozen. The director introduced fire, burning cinders, and chaos into this ice-cold universe, showing how the sclerotic system had, in fact, never really worked. The film is ruthless. It makes painfully clear that communism, besides the petrification it had imposed for decades, constitutes a legacy that continues to corrupt everything a full ten years after its collapse. A kind of "political Chernobyl,"[13] as Guerman described communism and its aftermath in 1999, has effected a "long term contamination of Russian art," which he lamented: "Our art has become freer. Indeed, it has! But has it become better? No, it has not! There has been no new Rublev, even though all the necessary conditions were present. We were granted freedom, and what has happened? What has kept us from pulling ourselves up, from speaking up? We probably wasted too much energy at some point to obtain the right to tell small truths, and cannot see big ones now. But time will put everything back where it belongs: the present will fade, while art—if art there is—will remain."[14]

A profound sadness haunts these filmmakers and their films, and it might well be precisely this that has turned these modern Russian (and Serbian) artists into demoderns. Aleksandr Sokurov is probably the most melancholy filmmaker there is. When he shot *Russian Ark* in December 2001, Vladimir

Putin had been president of the Russian Federation for two years and had pulled off, or so it seemed, the transition from the former Soviet Empire, which had spawned him, to the new regime, which he now represented, both in his vitality and his undemocratic foibles. But Sokurov had little interest in the present, steeped as he was in the past. In a memorable single take of nearly ninety minutes he presents a visit to the Hermitage Museum in St. Petersburg and fragments of a very ancient history, dating back to before the communist era, featuring a czar dining with his family and a Russian minister chatting with a French diplomat in a tailcoat. And what if this was what the end of communism was all about? He declares, through frail, flickering, and hazy images, that the system that had supposedly brought everyone together around a modern ideal had been to no avail; that it could be forgotten at a moment's notice, with a few images conjuring up the Russian past; but also that the present failed to connect up with the past, that the sutures could not hold; and that images are floating in an elusive space-time continuum. Both in his interviews and his films, Sokurov confesses that he feels as though he has experienced death and has woken up from a long eighty-year coma. Communism, which literally fails to make an impression on film in Sokurov's work, is this spectral zone in which everything gets lost, got lost, never to be seen again.

Andrei Tarkovsky's *Stalker*: Communism Put to the Test of the Zone

The first to tread into this zone of specters was Andrei Tarkovsky, who made it the subject of his fifth film, *Stalker*. Tarkovsky was a nineteenth-century artist stranded in contemporary cinema. Not that he denied the possibilities of cinematic art—quite the opposite, his world is made of visions that are beyond the capacity of literary narrative—but he strove to defect from Soviet cinema, that art form born of the pioneering spirit of the 1920s and then petrified under Stalin. Tarkovsky, who steered clear of the socialist realism advocated by Andrei Zhdanov, did not participate in the experimental myth either, and he rejected both Bolshevik avant-garde culture and its sclerotic Stalinist variant. Indeed, the filmmaker reached further back, appearing to film upstream of all notions of "Soviet" art and to have fled the twentieth century altogether to reconnect with the Russian cultural past. He laid claim, sometimes with considerable arrogance, to this "Russian path." This is quite clear in his 1966 masterpiece, *Andrei Rublev*. In *Stalker* he took on other risks: he plunged the vestiges of Soviet civilization into the mystical Russian waters of yesteryear, waters capable of instantly transforming, altering, damaging, and ruining these remnants. In this film, with its strange temporality, the artist is projected into a future time—that of postcommunism, which is imagined as not long after 1979—in order to recall Russian spiritual and visual culture, the icon culture, which he manages to bring to life on film in all its intensity. What bothered the bureaucrats of Soviet cinema so much was not the frontal attacks on the regime, nor the occasional political allusion, so much as this "elsewhere," this place beyond or before communist culture.

Stalker, which Tarkovsky shot in 1979, as he was turning fifty, was a film beset by every manner of difficulty. Yet it was also the film that first earned him international renown. Following up on *Solaris* (1972), his third film, Tarkovsky again sought refuge in science fiction, at least in a semblance of science fiction that enabled him to escape from overly zealous bureaucratic censors. It purported yet again to be an adaptation of a short story by the Strugatsky brothers—"Roadside Picnic," published in 1972—about the discovery of a mysterious "wish room," which is supposed to fulfill the desires of all those who enter. As early as January 26, 1973, Tarkovsky wrote in his journal: "I have just read the Strugatsky brother's fantastical short story. It would make for a great screenplay."[15] In 1976 the filmmaker adapted the story for the screen with the help of the authors themselves: a stalker (hunter) leads two characters, a writer and a scholar, through a mysterious zone to the room. The film was to be shot in the Tajikistan desert and then in an abandoned power station near Tallin, the capital of Estonia. Shooting began in 1977, but the rushes revealed serious technical glitches resulting from the mishandling of a new type of Western film by Soviet labs. The Goskino suspended shooting. Frustrated by the delays, and very upset by the suspension and the constant humiliations to which he was subjected by Soviet bureaucrats, Tarkovsky suffered a heart attack in April 1978. It was not until the following year that the film could be shot and final edits made. It was well received on its Moscow release, but the USSR refused to designate it the official selection for the Venice Film Festival in September 1979. *Stalker* was then sold to a Dutch distributor, who released it in Amsterdam in the spring of 1980 and presented it at the Rotterdam Festival. This automatically disqualified it for the Cannes competition in May 1980, despite an official request from the French festival, where it was, in the end, screened as a "surprise film" with a minimum of promotion, which by no means displeased the Soviet authorities.

What did they fear from *Stalker*? François Forestier, a critic for the French weekly *Express*, probably put it best: "God is alive and well, and living in Moscow. He appears in *Stalker* with a certain haughty magnificence; he lurks in the tall grass and the wastelands, slips past the armed guards, and fills the wide-open spaces of eternal, dialectical, and materialist Russia. Tarkovsky, who directed this sumptuous metaphysical saga, may claim, to calm things down, that 'there is no organ designed to feel God'; however, the latter haunts this film, which was paradoxically presented at Cannes under the banner of Uncle Joe."[16] Soviet cinema authorities preferred films that glorified eternal Russia and sent to Cannes lyrical works on nature's grandeur and epics on human nature by Bondarchuk, as well as Konchalovsky's *Siberiade*. They did not appreciate having these values subjected to Tarkovsky's mystical gaze, for his gaze subjects everyone and everything—characters, space, time, objects, civilization, wilderness—to the test of revelation through dereliction. Those who best endure devastation and deprivation, who accept the loss of everything and embrace their frailty, are the ones who trigger beauty in the shot. The others are condemned to spinelessness and moral decay.

This can be seen as the test of the demodern, which the filmmaker applies to everything that could be seen as representing the Union of Soviet Socialist Republics at its best, or at least its most modern: science and nuclear power, which were, of course, state secrets. On the face of it *Stalker* need not refer to Soviet Russia to work and make sense as a film. It is enough for it to play on other values and other anxieties: fear of the world coming to an end, fear of a third world war, and the promise of divine intervention. Yet in the eyes of the Goskino authorities in 1980, there was no doubt that *Stalker* was about the present-day Soviet Union, which figures not so much as the zone at the heart of the film as that which surrounds it and forbids access to it, that which tries to penetrate it in order to contain and destroy it. Tarkovsky had already sent Soviet officialdom into a panic with *Solaris*, in which another mythical symbol of Soviet modernity—the exploration and conquest of space—was put to a similar test of degradation through mysticism. In that film, adapted from a novel by Stanislaw Lem, a cosmonaut named Gibarian is driven to suicide by the blind audacity of Soviet science, which strives to explore every nook and cranny of the universe and rule over it all. From then on, doubt and worry worm their way into scientific certainty. The planet that another cosmonaut, Kris Kelvin, is sent to explore has the power to bring to life forms emanating from the memories of those who come near it. The film is then no longer driven by the progress of scientific exploration but rather by the mystical doubts and hesitations of a disturbed mind, and even the erotic visions dwelling in the memory of a man who is awestruck by infinite space, suddenly bursting onto the screen in this science-fiction film that proves to be above all introspective.

Soviet science, put to the test of the demodern, is represented in *Stalker* by the central figure of the "professor," one of the two men the stalker is leading through the zone. The character, a physicist, is the very embodiment of Soviet modernist thinking: a materialist, he represents reason against the amoral defeatism of the writer and the wounded and visceral spirituality of the stalker himself. He confuses scientific research with the search for truth. He sticks to facts, and his credo is the experimental method. He is the one who, materially speaking, provides the team with a modicum of modernity and defines its purpose: to explain a phenomenon that appears to be beyond understanding. Jacques Gerstenkorn and Sylvie Strudel, in what remains the most in-depth study on the film to date, compare him to the inspector in Fellini's *Intervista*, who has been called "to investigate a miracle." A scholar—this is how he describes himself to the writer—who has done his homework well—he knows the story of the zone and the stalker's biography—he observes everything, interrogates, takes notes, demands clarification. This modern *homo sovieticus* even declares that he is "hoping to obtain the Nobel Prize" for his prospective discovery, since the mystery of the zone has become a subject of deep interest for the international community of scholars—a card at the beginning of the film mentions the questions raised by "Professor Wolles," a Nobel laureate in physics. But in fact, the scientist harbors another, secret, ambition that the spectator only finds out about at the end: to blow up the heart of the zone, the "wish room," with a twenty-kiloton bomb concealed in his coat and thus to put an end to the mystery. Today this would figure as a terrorist act. But at the end of the 1970s a peculiar kind of arms race was still on, which, above all, offered assurances based on science and in the name of a balance of terror: the destructive capacity deployed by the scholar is of equal strength to the force of the spiritual faith held by the stalker. But the professor is in the wrong, and Tarkovsky's film is bent on sending him a blunt message: true knowledge could not care less about his kind of knowledge. Humbled, yet sincerely moved by the stalker's despair, which is revealed in a long monologue delivered on the threshold of the wish room, the physicist renounces his earlier ambition. He leaves ruefully in the end, having lost his way in his scientific quest, with the demodern trap of doubt, which has been instilled by the film, in mind: "But so, I don't understand at all. What was the purpose of coming here?"

Yet in *Stalker* the principal trial of the demodern is applied to space, to the specific space called "the zone." A few words, like decoys, are offered early on to provide some explanation of the place: "What was this zone, then? A fallen meteor? A visit by cosmic beings? Whatever it was, in our country there occurred the miracle to beat all miracles: the zone. Troops were sent. They never returned. The zone was cordoned off by the police. That was just as well. . . . Actually, I'm not really sure." This zone, as we are subsequently shown—with its unsettling topography, its carcasses of a devoured world, its rusted hulks at the bottom of streams, its dilapidated and overgrown houses, its wilderness, its underground tunnels, its sewers and basements that look like the bowels of an old factory or power station, and its ubiquitous water—is the antimatter of the Soviet Empire. It is a place endowed with a peculiar acid that strips the symbols of communist society of their prestige, leaving only scraps of debris in their place.

Once one is in the zone, all measurements of time and space lose their value, and geometry no longer applies—triangle ABC, to quote a cynical comment by the writer, has no chance of corresponding to triangle A'B'C', nor any other triangle for that matter. The straight line seems to be the longest distance between two points, and one has to move along sideways, knowing that retracing one's steps is impossible, following a piece of fabric tied around a bolt and thrown forward. Covering a few yards can take several hours—having to pass through tunnels, under waterfalls, across rivers, and through bogs, more than would seem possible. It is just as well, then, that everything can speed up in this world devoid of markers and rules. Hiking manuals, topographic maps, and statistical forecasts are of no use and might as well be tossed aside in this universe that only a crank, a visionary, a sorry wretch, a "blessed soul," a traditional Russian *iurodivi*—that is, the stalker himself—can understand and "feel." It is he, in the end, who creates the zone: whereas nothing in its physical appearance distinguishes it from any other abandoned corner of the decrepit Russian countryside, with its abandoned old factories and run-down houses, he transforms it through his visits and his instinct, his faith in its power and beauty, into a receptacle of the sacred. The spatial progress is a spiritual initiation, and he follows a quasi-religious ritual rather than a rational progression. It is as if Tarkovsky was intent on constantly maintaining and reaffirming the ambiguity of the vague geographical notion of the zone, at once an area governed by industrial and commercial urban rationality—an escheated land through which visitors are condemned to roam blindly and into which only a handful of misfits ever set foot—and the basis of a possible, and often heightened, spirituality—a space of "sacred enclosure." This indeterminate character, in *Stalker*, is precisely the way of the demodern (fig. 82).

This may be why its access routes are so well guarded. For, on the face of it, nothing should need protection in this zone, nothing precious at least, and

82 ▶
Stalker
(ANDREI TARKOVSKY, 1979). A DAMAGED AND SUNKEN SPACE, THE ENTRAILS OF A DISCARDED SOVIET FACTORY, ABANDONED TO NATURE AND FLOODING WATER.

83 ▶
Stalker
(ANDREI TARKOVSKY, 1979). A FORBIDDEN AND PROTECTED AREA, GIRDED BY BARBED WIRE, OVER WHICH SOLDIERS STAND GUARD.

the danger it poses is only relative, unless it is a foreboding—but we should not attribute such powers of divination to Tarkovsky—of nuclear disaster, such as was indeed to happen at Chernobyl in 1986, the very year of the filmmaker's death, and which also, in a paranoid parallel, led the army to protect a devastated and dangerous zone. Law surrounds this zone of nonlaw, girded by gates, barbed wire, patrolling soldiers, tension and identification checks, watchtowers and traps. To penetrate the zone, one must first elude its guards, which itself involves a game of hide and seek between the intruders and the forces of law and order, which scan the darkness with floodlights. For forty-five minutes the three men Tarkovsky follows in *Stalker* are put to this test, filmed at night in a black-and-white world permeated with mist and strewn with obstacles. This strikes the opening note of the film, resonant of fear and disgust, detritus and grime—the shameful and risky crossing of a lethal wasteland. Through abandoned warehouses, dried up waterways, on foot and then by Jeep, clandestinely making headway along railroad tracks on an old handcar, our "heroes" manage to make their way into the zone (fig. 83). Their sooty progress toward a border that has to be crossed at all costs, whatever the dangers, calls to mind other flights, like those of refugees into the free zone in France during the occupation, or into the West, on the other side of the wall, during the cold war. It was no doubt this sense of imprisonment that caused Soviet authorities to object, since the passage into the zone is as much an escape into the open air as a spiritual initiation. For the stalker the passage is also his way of fleeing from the prison in which he had been held for so long by the system: indeed, he says he has just finished serving five years, and he still bears marks of incarceration, such as his deep cough and the scars of torture. He is a weak and pathetic being, with irradiated flesh—his daughter is a mutant—a convict escaped from some godforsaken gulag.

Everything in *Stalker* appears meaningful—yet another trap laid by Tarkovsky, who reveled in leading souls and reason astray—but the meaning that is most drawn to the elements described above is the exploration of a desolate, pre- or postapocalyptic, hypermilitarized and paranoid world, a postindustrial wasteland on the verge of environmental catastrophe, a besieged concentration camp universe whose modernity is in tatters. It, thus, roughly prefigures the state of the Soviet Empire as it would later appear when it abruptly disintegrated, between 1989 and 1991, ten years after the film was shot. Tarkovsky pushed a world that still "held together" over the edge into apocalyptic turmoil and visualized the impact a decade in advance of reality: the camera lingers softly over the traces of an empire in its watery grave, like the relics of a lost civilization, a junkyard of the Soviet age: Soviet coins, pistols marked "made in Czechoslovakia," Kalashnikov rifles, clock mechanisms, springs, pages of a "revolutionary" calendar, chipped plates, syringes, neon tubes, scraps of barbed wire, and moss-covered tanks. Other fragments of a defeated modernity emerge: bent lampposts, broken girders, ruined bunkers, and the mangled carcasses of trucks. The dysfunction figures as essentially aquatic, as if all these emblems of the communist regime's power and coercive force had been consigned through water and by water to their primal uselessness. The zone's ambient humidity (cesspit, pond, lake, stream, waterfall, drips) degrades the modern and reclaims it as demodern (fig. 84).

The other form of disintegration in *Stalker* is that of time, as if the time of the film itself and the historical time of the Soviet Empire had both dissolved in the film. Tarkovsky prefers long takes, and single shots of more than five minutes are not uncommon in his films, since pacing is a key element for a filmmaker who calls himself "a sculptor of time."[17] *Stalker* thus obeys its own temporality, which is not to be measured in minutes and hours, in this two-hour-and-forty-one-minute film, but in shots: 142 blocks of time in all, sculpted individually and together by the creator.[18] For the Russian director the cinematographic form is first and foremost this time sculpture. It enables him to blur the chronological framework of man, and more specifically of modern man, whose time is so precious that it is organized into tight schedules in which every minute is accounted for. *Stalker*'s time is devoid of markers, following an achronology that alone can allow the characters to "take their time" and hence to waste it. The waste is essential, the equivalent in temporal terms of penetrating the zone in spatial terms. In fact, the zone offers several chronologies at once. The "after" appears to reign, with relics of a disfigured and fallen time strewn about, but the zone can also suddenly take charge of the "before," which is even the objective of the quest. To find the wish room, to enter it, consists in inhabiting a preexisting time, before the realization of one's desires. Having faith in something brings one back to the before, the time of hope, of a possible happening. Each of the film's shots is caught in this return to origin, a cinematographic approach to time that is akin to prayer in the liturgical order, since each prayer is turned toward a genesis that is faith. To believe in something is to believe in creation. Tarkovsky borrows this movement of faith from religious temporality, a movement that brings each thing back to its origin. As he is sculpting time, he is performing an act of faith.

84 ▶
Stalker
(ANDREI TARKOVSKY, 1979). TRACES OF THE SOVIET EMPIRE IN ITS WATERY GRAVE, LIKE THE RELICS OF A LOST CIVILIZATION: A CLOCK MECHANISM, THE GRIP OF AN AUTOMATIC PISTOL, THE SHOCK ABSORBER OF A TANK— THE JUNKYARD OF A DEFEATED, RUSTING, WORN-OUT, AND BROKEN MODERNITY.

The stalker, on the one hand, is precisely such a being from the before: his speech can only be conjugated in the future tense. The writer and the physicist, on the other hand, are characters from the after: "We have lived," they say repeatedly, as they traverse the time of disenchantment and disillusionment. The temporal progress of *Stalker* consists in gathering these characters together, an imperfect meeting, which leads to failure but is to be read as a regression, an antievolution, a countermodernity: the time of the after tends to recur as that of the before, the irretrievably lost ideal of the world's infancy. The zone is thus a "temporal space," a space of ritualized progression, which is at once a leap from place to place and a return in time. The final failure, the refusal to enter the wish room, suggests the writer's and the scholar's incapacity to come to terms with the before time. They are unable to believe in ignorance, to forget the knowledge and experience that weigh on the modern world; they guess its age and turn it into an afterworld (fig. 85).

This conception of time in *Stalker* is a cinematographic war machine let loose in Soviet history, for the 142 shots and blocks of time of Tarkovsky's film are a countermanifesto against the 3,225 shots and temporal fragments in Eisenstein's *October*, the other maestro of Russian cinema. They are a world apart, both aesthetically and ideologically. Both Tarkovsky and Eisenstein sculpted time—the former with large shears, working and shaping broad swathes of supple and contemplative time, the latter with a chisel, hewing edited fragments into an edgy and significant structure. Against Eisenstein's intellectual, fragmentary, and discursive conception of montage looms Tarkovsky's emotional, flowing, narrative vision of poetic montage. "Eisenstein's scientific montage was replaced by Tarkovsky's poetic montage," as Jacques Gerstenkorn and Sylvie Strudel put it.[19] For Tarkovsky it was a way to oppose the modern, as he called for in his numerous writings on montage—the demodern form of slow temporal disintegration.

The filmmaker was also keen to manifest this scale of values through a very personal use of color in the film. Three registers are deployed: sepia, black-and-white, and color. Their use is simultaneously simple—black-and-white for the world around the zone, color inside the zone itself, and sepia for dreams—and highly spiritual, placing the spectator in front of a mystical spectrum. The black and white, which itself results from a decolorization of the color print, acts as a signifier of the deterioration of the spiritual state of Soviet society. All the shots in the "gulag," from which the runaways manage to escape, are in this monochrome, as well as most of the figures of empire—

85 ▶
Stalker
(ANDREI TARKOVSKY, 1979). THE SCHOLAR, THE WRITER, AND THE STALKER: THREE WAYS OF COMMUNING WITH THE ZONE. "WHEN MAN THINKS OF HIS PAST, HE BECOMES BETTER," SAYS THE STALKER AT THE THRESHOLD OF THE WISH ROOM.

soldiers, arms, buildings, locomotives, railings—and the bar where the three adventurers have arranged to meet, and where they return in the end, after their failed quest. Representing "a theological treatment of the print,"[20] color manifests the presence of the sacred: it takes hold of the zone's lush green wilderness, of the stalker's appearance (his blue jacket), of the shimmering depths of the waters in which a Christlike fish swims, as well as of the gold that shines for a while inside the wish room, as the quest nears its end. Colors attach themselves to the hypersensitivity to the sacred manifested by Tarkovsky's heroes. Indeed, the filmmaker made no secret of his ambition to film the world as a series of icons in motion, by immersing himself in the artistic tradition of the Russian church.

Consigning the modern to black-and-white and filming the demodern in color, Tarkovsky has seemingly reversed the traditional references, leaving the exegetes to grapple with the proper interpretation of his film. The few occasions where he did comment on his film, it was for his own benefit, in his essay *Sealed Time* (published posthumously) and in his diaries, which remained unpublished for some time. In the former he wrote sarcastically:

> I have often been asked what the zone stood for, what it symbolized, and people came up with the most unbelievable interpretations. This kind of question fills me with rage and despair. The zone doesn't symbolize anything, nor for that matter does anything else in my films. The zone is the zone. The zone is life. And any man who crosses it either breaks or survives. It all depends on the sense he has of his own dignity, and of his ability to distinguish what is essential from what isn't.[21]

This assertion, however, did not deter him from venturing, in a diary entry dated December 23, 1978, a more precise interpretation:

> In this film, I try to explode the relationship to the present, and turn toward the past, where our society has made so many mistakes that it is forced today to live in a kind of fog. The film deals with the existence of God within man, and about the loss of spirituality through the acquisition of false knowledge. To enter the zone is to unlearn the world and to become capable of sculpting one's being in order to see God, which happens suddenly. I am afraid of the future: of the Chinese, of natural disasters, of apocalyptic upheavals. My God gives me strength and faith for the future![22]

This way of dissolving the Soviet present (in sepia, water, the divine, catastrophe) and striving to unlearn the knowledge taught by the system as a synonym for progress is very precisely for Tarkovsky a way of demodernizing the world in order to attain and cherish mystical power.

Such a power comes from the past—"When man thinks of his past, he becomes better," says the stalker at the threshold of the wish room—but is available mainly to the weakest. This is what the final shot of the film makes clear, by lingering, in color, on Ouistiti, the stalker's daughter, who is paralyzed and dumb, a mutant undergoing a process of genetic regression toward some kind of primal state, who displays all the signs of the highest spirituality, using her parapsychological powers to move glasses through the sheer force of her gaze. This final image of a suffering yet possessed child functions as a distorted, reversed, and ironic allusion to the tradition of Soviet cinema, which generally concludes its futuristic explorations on the faces of stout and radiant children, the embodiments of a triumphant materialism and an assured modernity. Tarkovsky thus offers regeneration to fragile beings, the only ones truly touched by God's grace. The only characters he trusts are those whose senses are alert, who have opted for belief, instinct, and faith over reason. The spiritual dimension of Tarkovsky's world is encompassed in that choice. All his films, his countersystem, aim to give primacy to the last ones: the child, the madman, and the witch are the first to drink from the waters of rejuvenation. Calls for regeneration ring too familiar to miss the founding paradox of Tarkovsky's world. The new man served as the model for Soviet society, which produced athletes to worship and Stakhanovs to emulate.[23] With Tarkovsky the *homo novus sovieticus* has given way to the wounds of the weak; the bodies that were muscled up in the name of communism have been eclipsed by a book of icons from which *iurodivi* figures issue forth in blue and gold.

Indeed, this contrast was long the hallmark of the filmmaker's impertinence. At the beginning of the credits of his Soviet films the official emblem of Soviet cinema would appear: a socialist-realist couple, moving forward, spurred on by the hammer and sickle of inexhaustible modernization (see fig. 94). Then followed the film, which offered, in strong contrast, a spectacle of destitution: the stalker with a vermin stain on his head, the child with a monkey name, and so forth. This ritual contrast, characteristic of Tarkovsky' first five films, *Stalker* included, expresses the chasm between the one kind of regeneration and the other. Rather than the affirmed modernity of a fit body, Tarkovsky prefers the uncertainty of sickly and wounded bodies, which chasten the arrogance of the future. Christ, as the stalker reminds us, was pain and suffering before he was a hero.

Alexei Guerman's *Khrustalyov, My Car!* Communism at the Bottom of History's Closet

Yuri Klensky is chief of medicine and a neurologist at a Moscow hospital, as well as a Red Army general. He divides his time between his hospital, his teeming household, and his mistresses. A good-natured giant, an alcoholic, and a quintessential Slav, he is idolized both by his family and his colleagues. At the beginning of 1953, the so-called Doctors' Plot, organized by Beria, was designed to purge the remaining party officials around Stalin. Klensky was forced to flee, and he disappeared while a lookalike took his place in Soviet society. Klensky was subsequently arrested, sent to the gulag, and tortured. But soon thereafter, as Stalin lay dying, the doctor was freed by Beria and called to the deathbed, where he witnessed the master of the Kremlin's final agony. Ten years later, he has become the leader of a gang of traffickers and is seen on board a train crossing Russia.

Summed up thus, *Khrustalyov, My Car!* sounds like a simple enough film. And, indeed, it is if one does not insist on trying to read history behind the film, directed by Alexei Guerman, who himself has said, "Russian history cannot be understood intellectually, it cannot be measured with a ruler."[24] Yet at the Cannes Film Festival, where it was screened in 1998, and later at the New York Film Festival, in September of the same year, the film was received with skepticism, simply because the spectators tried to see in it a step-by-step, day-by-day account of a moment of Russian history in 1953: the death of Stalin, preceded by the Doctors' Plot, in which a group of doctors were the victims of an anti-Semitic purge. However, this history is, precisely, not narrated. It is seen, and it is felt, but it can only be understood as a series of bifurcations, gestures, rituals, visions, strange locations, and unfamiliar atmospheres. The story is offered, in its cinematographic form, as one of disorientation and chaos: a story of the defeat of bodies, of the disjunction between fact and explanation (with sequences made of fragments that remain open to conflicting interpretations and to the least-reasonable impressions). History as a laboratory, history in shambles—both experimental forms are interwoven into a shifting, touching, multidimensional fabric. And the impression remains, ten years later, that this work—which does not fall easily into any category— aesthetic, historical, sociological, or fantastic—combines them all in a living nightmare in black-and-white. Indeed, it could find no clear place within the representational forms of history or cinematic genres existing at the time. But now, Alexei Guerman's film imposes itself as one of the most ambitious attempts to reincarnate a moment of communist history—that of the reign of terror, as seen from the standpoint of its final collapse.

Viewers of *Khrustalyov* feel as though they are being subjected to a chaotic trial, which can only be described using a metaphor of natural disaster—a hurricane, a flood. This film belongs to that family of cinematographic objects that defies categorization according to taste. It is a kind of "carnivalesque accounting of the Soviet era," as Jacques Mandelbaum described it in the French daily *Le Monde*.[25] Its construction seems to obey no rule except that of attaining the limits of understanding and pushing them. It is one of the most striking representations of a world gripped by the paranoid gap between reality and its appearance, the perfect definition of the system of terror put in place by Stalin. "It was an immense empire of lies," Guerman himself said. "Everything was concealed, disguised. And a terrible fear kept people quiet, especially about the existence of camps and the millions of dead. The people were broken. And, on the other hand, there was a desire to believe mixed with the fear. The victory over Nazi Germany contributed to the rise of this mixture of faith and dread. Propaganda was colossal. When we were little, we were asked at school: 'Who do you like best, your mother or comrade Stalin?' And one was of course expected to answer Stalin."[26] Through an aesthetic of accumulation and derailment, through a systematic overcrowding of shots, through energy and constant aesthetic inventiveness, Guerman manages to recreate this paranoid world, commingling fear and joy, which, while inextricably joined together, are constantly escalating and outbidding each other. This cinematographic form can be seen as a way for the filmmaker to exorcize history as much as to show it. This is why *Khrustalyov, My Car!* is the "ultimate Russian film" on Stalinism,[27] the one that displays a maximum of historical effect and intelligence since it takes care not to take refuge in denunciation or hide behind moral platitudes: the film pushes its aesthetic of chaos to an extreme in order to represent a time that is otherwise generally described as being in a state of paralysis. It is, thus, the *bardak*, the mess, which, as a kind of poetic trance, best represents history, for the aim is rather to evoke its mental effervescence, its imaginary epic, than to provide a meticulous chronicle. In this respect *Khrustalyov, My Car!* operates very much in the vein of Fellini. It is to Stalinism what *Amarcord* was to fascism: less a documentary or commentary than an extravagant and outraged excrescence.

The film ruthlessly leads its characters, and its spectators, astray, into a maze of visions, a labyrinth of objects, a hovel of bodies. Yet the film also takes into account its own title and, as literally as possible, straightforwardly depicts the comical scene in which Beria, right after the death of his master Stalin, calls for his driver, Khrustalyov, and his car, as if to say: "Run for your life!" or "Devil take the hindmost!" Indeed, this is what the expression "Khrustalyov, my car!" has come to mean in the language and mythology of Russian society. But Guerman shot this mythical scene as a mad vision, in the manner of a paranoid chapter in Dostoyevsky, a vision that contaminates, upstream and down, all of the film's shots. Guerman has worked his story as a form of cataclysm introduced into history, somewhere between Noah's Ark, in which everyone is crammed to escape the Flood; the Last Judgment, at which all creatures meet their fate in a state of abject terror; the Last Supper, where everyone dances on the volcano of impending death; and the terrifying charge of the Horsemen of the Apocalypse. The film rises to the challenge of a history that has always been a source of fascination for the West, even while it remained impervious to logical explanation. "In my opinion, all these European leftist intellectuals never understood anything about what was happening on our side."[28] This is how Guerman himself viewed the good conscience of pro-Soviet France. For the main culprit here is not so much the historical Stalin—depicted in the film as a grotesque and petulant cadaver, whose agony is punctuated by an ultimate fart—as the eternal Russian despot, represented in the film by the striking though more banal character of Klensky, a likable domestic tyrant and pathological embodiment of the father of the family, just as the other was the father of the people. This vision of history spreads like a disease, originating in terror and despotism, and contaminates the entire Russian body. Such a critical philosophy of history appears to illustrate the nation's suffering, as well as constitute its essential fate; indeed, it suggests that in the final reckoning there are no innocent victims. A man, indeed a supreme icon, might have been at the center of everything, but everyone participated, however blinded and manipulated they might have been, in the will to believe and the feelings of fear, and even in the denunciations and the regime of coercion.

If *Khrustalyov, My Car!* remains an enigma, Alexei Guerman himself might have a lot to do with it, since he continues to be a mysterious filmmaker. A jovial, cheerful, and good-natured fellow, he is also prone to sudden disappearances, refusing for days on end all attempts at communication, becoming autistic, melancholy, temperamental, and antisocial. He is, himself, an elusive character. His uncommon career has made him a man of few films—five in almost thirty-five years: *The Seventh Companion*, in 1967, never released in Western Europe; *Trial of the Road*, in 1972, a demystifying war chronicle set in 1942 German-occupied northwest Russia, in which all heroism, all official optimism, and any idea of a light at the end of the tunnel are crushed and in which a ferocious sense of humor and a strong sense of the grotesque are already palpable; *Twenty Days Without War*, in 1976, in which a war correspondent, again set in that period, spends his leave of absence in Tashkent, far from the conflict, as well as from Russian society—a film in which he developed his method, his technique, and his poetics: to follow, camera in hand, with the chaos of history raging, a character who wreaks havoc and then suddenly sows harmony and smoothness; and, *My Friend Ivan Lapshin*, in 1982, which follows a Russian administrator, head of criminal investigations in a remote small town during the 1930s, and in which Guerman yet again radicalizes his filmmaking, which now consists of fragments torn out of the memories of characters and the troubles of history, with shadowy corners and sudden illuminations, irreparable lapses and sensual explosions. In the end all that matters to the director is history, his own mixed with that of the USSR. He does not tackle it through reconstruction of a finished product—that is established, recognized, classified—but rather through an ocean of passing sensations, of consumed visions, of contradictory truths, of dreams floating just beneath the surface—the whole resting on the balance between visual innovation and aesthetic restraint. Largely shot in black-and-white, the images do not appear saturated or erratic but rather feel controlled and guided by the filmmaker's precision and his direction of actors.

The Goskino and Soviet censors did not appreciate this conception of history, and Guerman's films were all banned, released in second-tier Soviet cinemas three to five years after they were shot. In the West, Guerman and his cinema received belated recognition in the mid-1980s, when his films were finally screened (in 1986 in France). The director became a symbol of dissidence and resistance to the Goskino, and then of *perestroika*, when he was appointed administrator of Lenfilm, the large Soviet studio in Leningrad. Guerman has thus always been presented as the advocate of a new direction in practice. *My Friend Ivan Lapshin* was authorized in 1985. The film heralded the arrival of glasnost, the opening up of possibilities, and of ruptures. "I was pulled out of the mire, cleaned up, and sent out into the world to tell of all the wonderful changes," says Guerman ironically about the fraud of perestroika in cinema.[29] Together with Tenguiz Aboutadze's allegorical film on post-Stalin guilt, *Repentance* (1984), and Nikita Mikhalkov's *Burnt by the Sun 2* (2010), on the 1936 purges, *Khrustalyov, My Car!* represents a cinematographic return to the Soviet past, and more specifically, to Stalin's terror.

A symbol and a public figure as much as a filmmaker, Guerman shepherded *Khrustalyov, My Car!* through a very long process (fifteen years of maturation and hurdles overcome, almost three and a half years in production), as the dream of achieving at long last a reconciliation between the misfortunes of a people and the intimate experiences of his own childhood. His film bears "the unbearable pain of being Russian." Guerman pays tribute to the collective self-mutilation that made "films from here so frightening"; he depicts fate as a cannibalistic monster devouring countless body parts worthy of a Bruegel painting; and he anchors his cinema in a style that never allows an escape from this pain: "I always wanted the shooting of my film to take place here, in Russia, despite more comfortable conditions the French co-production would have allowed. I also refused to use French film—it embellishes everything. Our reality must be filmed with our film!" he said, to illustrate the "tragic darkness" he so wanted to capture.[30] The solemn weight of collective history (Guerman compared his film to the launching of an "enormous aircraft carrier") accounts in large part for the lengthy development and production process of the film. The shooting of such a work could not possibly go well and had to take forever. It was preprogrammed, so to speak, in its internal script, that Russian history is the history of a people that is, perpetually, not doing well.

But this panoramic film is also a kind of epic and chaotic vision of the director's intimate world. The personal memories are themselves the site of a passage that took time, as though it had been necessary to slowly and patiently wait for the graft to take between what belongs to all (the end of Stalinism) and what comes from one (a childhood under Stalin). The filmmaker himself said it very well:

> An artist uses his life half of his life. I was keen to tell the story of my generation, of that time and those events that I witnessed, as a little boy, so that the image and the materiality of that time would remain. . . . This gave rise to a film whose script is more than half my truth. To shoot it, I had to try to love its characters. But how? By imagining that they were my family. My father, a rather well known writer, was never a general, but he met Stalin twice, he had lunch with him. I thus belonged to a kind of social elite, not the upper crust, but still, an elite. But as the character of the son demonstrates, I was merciless with myself. Half the story is thus real. The other half is built around a possible course of events: What would have happened for these characters if, rather than escaping misfortune, they had found themselves at its very center?[31]

Thus, pushing this hybrid of collective destiny and personal memory to its most tragic and moving, Alexei Guerman shot a film that at one and the same time opens and closes the exorcism of Stalin, which gives meaning to his own life by confronting the history of a people with his own haunting memories: "for me, and I mean this without vanity, this film strikes a kind of final note in my life."[32]

What does the film show? The life, in 1953, of an odious and magnificent giant in the midst of a slum he calls his hospital, a tangle of bodies and objects he calls his family, and a web of complications that constitutes his love life (figs. 86, 87). In each case it is as if there were just too many things to show. These heaps constantly recur in the peculiar modality of the performance, of the eternally recurring acting out. This accumulation reveals the truth of a collective story and a life, for it forces everyone to search, to decipher within an ever more complex materiality of existence. It is as though cinema had managed to be where, precisely, no camera has ever been able to capture the density of problems that combine and clash, when history generates them in abundance. The characters in *Khrustalyov, My Car!* are in the same bind as the entire country: everyone is caught inside a labyrinth that brings them back to the enigma of their lives trapped within Stalinism. This cinema has the audacity to declare that it is intent on making sense of this enigma and on taking a stand squarely at the ineffable core of history, with its enormous, wounded, and monstrous bodies, its nervous breakdowns, its meanderings, and its radical ellipses. "We got lost," says Guerman today,[33] privately convinced that nobody ever managed to find their way again. Yet there is a cinematographic means of getting one's bearings: it entails getting even more lost, being torn away from history by the ebbs and flows of consciousnesses and lives.

Seeing *Khrustalyov, My Car!* is to experience this compelling sense of being lost, if we may say that the spectator's disorientation could rise to the level of madness of an entire people and its history. The film's form, which is so invasive, and sometimes even embarrassing, follows the path of a subjective camera rambling among crowds, gleaning and stealing gestures, phrases, memories, sometimes like a raptor swooping down on its prey, sometimes like a caress tracing the curves of a body. This highly personal style, this cinema, which manages to maintain the confusion—in the strong sense of the term—while distinguishing every detail, was Guerman's invention:

> Directing films is both a stance and a state of mind. For others, who know perfectly well how to shoot a scene and show it, it is a profession. But I am a cinema

86–87 ▶
Khrustalyov, My Car! (ALEXEI GUERMAN, 1998). AN OGRE LOST IN THE USSR OF A DYING STALIN. "WE ARE LOST IN HISTORY," CONFIDES ALEXEI GUERMAN.

dilettante. I know practically nothing about my craft. I made it up as I went. I try to penetrate each shot, to fill it with my existence. Otherwise I am unable to make films, I am simply not interested. This is why I renounced editing, why I do without shots and reverse shots, why I always find it more interesting to film sequence-shots, even though it is rather taxing and requires a lot of rehearsing. For I always try to shoot from the perspective of my character, to film what he sees. The camera must react and reveal what he feels, and not directly show events and situations.[34]

To film history, for Guerman, consists first and foremost in formally recording all the contradictory feelings that an entire people and he himself as a child, together, have experienced in the face of this history—not to offer a reconstruction of history but sensitive representations of it, linked inextricably in a tangle of visions: "to try and revive life so that the people of that time find their place in it again."[35]

The beauty of this work resides in this mad ambition to make various memories of the last moments of Stalinism overlap, but not completely, so that each exceeds and overflows the others. This sensory recollection of facts leads to an extraordinary moment of cinema, three quarters into the film, when Stalin dies "for real / for fake," snatched from a subjective vision of history. It summons up the impossible memory of a cinema that, at the time, had abdicated its responsibilities and devoted itself to the glorification of the "Gelovanian" body double of the dictator,[36] and that, thus, suddenly found itself imageless and obliged, in a way, to retrospectively invent a possible representation of history. Klensky is thus called before a Stalin in agony, bloated with secretions and medicines, and can do nothing but clinically confirm the death under way, which is convulsing the dying man in final malodorous jolts. But this prognosis is itself frightening, for even though he might be powerless to prevent certain death, he might still be held responsible for it. Both a spectator and an actor in the despot's final agony, Klensky expresses compassion, secretly sarcastic yet terrified. This is a banal death, pitiful in its trite self-evidence, as well of course as a metaphor for the great Soviet body, paralyzed and decomposing. And it is, furthermore, the guilty memory of the survivors, whose fear is echoed in the terror triggered by some of the images in *Khrustalyov, My Car!*: the rape of the general, the stench of Stalin in agony, the medical experiments conducted on mutants at the hospital. Having to endure such images represents the test of truth of a political system. The film also offers happy recollections of the tragedy, which constitute the most unexpected and probably the most accurate representations of Stalinist terror: "The entire history was full of blood and horror, but it also involved something deeply attractive to human beings, and I wanted the film to also capture the intense appeal of the totalitarian regime."37

To close the film, Guerman opted, daringly, for an incongruous and brilliant image: a hysterically laughing man trying to balance a half-filled glass of water on his head—cinema's ultimate challenge to Stalin. But this challenge is more than just another bit of tragic antics about the communism of the time. It is also a retort addressed to Stalin's regime, for which a curious cinematographic form, at once monstrous and virtuosic, is substituted—a strict reproduction of the fear and faith of the time, filmed as a paranoid and jubilant maelstrom. This formal gamble rests on the idea that a film can exorcise a period by bleeding it clean of its fears, its beliefs, and its laughter, too, which are all washed our way in a form deemed to be cathartic. It is this very form that can be identified in this film as an example of the demodern aesthetic. In Guerman's film the demodern is convoluted and preposterous, dreamlike and cruel, mesmerizing and spastic. It partakes of the traditional *rapture*: a fit of emotion, which may lead to supreme joy or to extreme terror, overdosing on its own excess. Through its demodern form, *Khrustalyov, My Car!* gives Stalin, a flatulent balloon, the same treatment to which Syberberg had subjected the Führer marionette in his masterpiece, *Hitler: A Film from Germany*. In a 1978 essay on Syberberg, Serge Daney spoke of the special status of a film that transforms history into an extraterritorial space where the filmmaker assumes state power to call Hitler before a "cinematographic court."38 This is what Guerman proposes, in the end, when he takes on the challenge of using his opponent's weapons against him: to judge him and annihilate him. Thanks to this filmmaker, the "demodern trial" of Stalin's very bloody communism was held.

Aleksandr Sokurov's *Russian Ark*: Communism Sapped by Nostalgia

Three years after *Khrustalyov, My Car!* and Stalin's pathetic agony, the Cannes Film Festival was paid a visit by yet another phantom of the Union of Soviet Socialist Republics—Lenin, in Aleksandr Sokurov's *Taurus*. In that film the founder of Soviet communism agonizes for an hour and a half, in a Chekhovian *dacha* painted blue, sometime between the end of 1921 and early 1924. His gray and puffy face, eaten away by the signs of imminent demise and deformed by mad fits of anger, shows signs of life only when seized by bitterness or by dreams of childhood and grandeur. The "Taurus" of the title refers as much to the animal that is sacrificed to ensure the survival of a regime as to the Minotaur, both monster and victim, powerful yet solitary, cut off from the world and in the end crushed by history. At the end of 1921 Lenin was ill, suffering a second stroke on December 16, while Stalin was rising inexorably to power. No sooner had the civil war ended, the NEP been launched, and the Union of Soviet Socialist Republics officially created, than the first censorship body was established. As the country of communism was passing from one regime to another, Lenin was trying to recover from his stroke, far from Moscow.

Sokurov's film, although based on a narrative of Lenin's illness and death that is well-documented by archival sources, does not reconstruct the historical figure's final agony as a chronicle but as a series of successive visions, some of which involve the historical character (played by an extraordinary actor, Leonid Mozgovoy) and others that more closely resemble the inventions of an artist. A strong sense of anxiety oozes from the images, in which Lenin, an irritable old man, swings from regret to remorse, from bitterness to feelings of power and glory, and from memories to strange ritual ceremonies. It is a tragic dirge, a lament, combining softness and fury, constantly veiled in the astonishing sfumato typical of Sokurov's photography—pictorial, hazy, obscure, crepuscular.

This plunge into the intimate sphere of a defeated "hero" is punctuated by a series of microevents: a doctor, who diagnoses "sensory motor aphasia"; then Lenin's wife, Krupskaya, who watches over him and tries to tempt him to go on a picnic that threatens to turn into a drama; and the decadent choreography of guards and servants, probably informers, who listlessly take care of his body, bathe and wash him against his will, and dress him in a straitjacket after one of his fits of madness, during which the decrepit titan, infirm and without posterity, broke several precious objects. Halfway between *King Lear* and *Exit the King*, the despot is beyond pathetic, often helpless, reigning over the chaos of a typical Russian patrician household. He is "the cherry orchard on the cake,"[39] quipped Jean-Pierre Léonardini, in *L'Humanité*, when he described this funereal essay on a figure whose political conviction withers as the film progresses, a scathing critique of a regime that appears to be in the process of dissolving. The key moment, however, is Stalin's visit to the senile wreck, with thunder rolling in the distance. It provides the stage for a rather grandiose face-to-face confrontation, full of grunts, gasps, and wails, all memory of which quickly escapes the old man, who cannot even remember the name of the functionary who has just, on behalf of the Communist Party, presented him with a cane featuring a swan's-beak handle. When the father of the

October Revolution finds himself alone, on his last leg, it is only to embrace death, which visits him in a ray of sunshine that breaks through the clouds. The one-two punch of Russian cinema, Guerman and Sokurov successively killed off Stalin and Lenin in the same moving, if worm-eaten, burst of history, flatulent in the case of the Uncle Joe, on a more dusky note for his mentor. The disintegrating body is the organic metaphor for a system, communism, trapped in demodern artistic visions.

Born in 1951 in Siberia, Aleksandr Sokurov made thirty-five films in fewer than thirty years. His intense activity stands in sharp contrast to the slow pace, which was both intrinsic and imposed, of Tarkovsky and Guerman, the younger director's proclaimed masters and alter egos. Characterized by a charismatic aura, an assertive mysticism, a rabid nationalism, and a ruthlessly singular universe, Sokurov's cinema harkens back to painting and poetry rather than the academicism of cinematic art. It could nonetheless be seen as "modern" in its avant-gardism, since, as opposed to Tarkovsky and even Guerman, the only cinematographic reference he acknowledges—besides Bresson—is a mannerism inspired by the 1920s, the era of Soviet experimental films by Eisenstein, Kulechov, Kozintsev, and Dovjenko:

> Russia is the birthplace of cinematographic aesthetics. If France developed its technique, and America its commercial side, it is Russia that enabled individual creation to blossom in the 1920s. Yet these years had been dangerously forgotten. Soviet cinema, from the 1930s onward, felt it had to go the way of these other countries: commercial sentimentalism, narration, representation. The aesthetic principle was entirely discarded. The impressions I remember most vividly are all connected to Eisenstein's *Strike* and Kozintsev and Trauberg's *The New Babylon*. There is a link between the 1920s and what I am trying to do. Our cinema was for a long time in a paradoxical position, where politics overrode aesthetic questions, much to the detriment of Soviet culture. The right to aesthetics must be vindicated anew. We must now repair things by drawing inspiration from the 1920s.[40]

On the one hand, Sokurov draws on the primitive Soviet aesthetic (Eisenstein's art of montage and the fragment) as a possible model—which is probably the main reason why the filmmaker remained a member of the Communist Party from his youth until the end of the 1980s. On the other hand, he advocates a form of radical aestheticism, free of any political or entertainment, or even narrative, imperative. Thus, he is both "modern" in certain of his references and avant-garde experimentations, and "demodern" in his brand of aestheticism removed from the present, advocating for an art out of any historical or commercial context. In fact, Sokurov's art is as much sacrificial as it is redemptive: it aims to hasten disaster so as to reconnect, through his aesthete's vision, with a form of innocent primitivism, of funereal renewal. This apocalyptic approach engenders a struggle to save Russia's soul—a struggle that involves certain mystico-religious trends in contemporary Russian society but that infuriates the more rationalist advocates of perestroika. This conception of art and the role it confers on the artist are reminiscent of Tarkovsky's sacramental vision of cinema and also explains why Sokurov is generally considered the natural heir of the creator of *Stalker*.

Sokurov thus combines in his films, and especially in his "fictions," both a profound mysticism and an impulse for experimentation. This gives an idea of how difficult it is for the spectator to know how to react to the visions unfolding in *Whispering Pages* (1994), *The Days of Eclipse* (1988), *The Lonely Voice of Man* (1987), *Save and Protect* (1989), *Mother and Son* (1998), *Father and Son* (2003), or even in the "historical" trilogy consisting of *Molokh* (1999, on Hitler), *Taurus* (2001, on Lenin), and *The Sun* (2005, on Hirohito). Jostled by a camera wandering vertiginously among collapsing sets, confused by abrupt changes in focal lengths, the use of colored filters, and the constant recourse to flattened images as surfaces to project onto and to "paint," the spectator is both lost in and hypnotized by the screen, which is to be approached visually, like a painting. The spectator is also caught in the filmmaker's persuasive power, however, under a spell that works as a kind of conditioning in mystical and funereal atmospheres. Sokurov looks to the "eternal" Russian soul and toward death as an initiation into mystery and an eminently desirable redemption. He laments the present and aspires to a restoration, whether nationalistic or ideological, of former times. This requires no explanation. His films are about radical sensations, in which resides their entire strength: the senses take charge, through a radically novel aesthetic experience that is both experimental and disconcerting, and bear the profound meaning of a reactionary vision of history. As the Russian critic Mikhail Yampolsky has put it, "Sokurov is an avant-garde director with a moral streak, combining a radical aesthetic with a traditional philosophy of life."[41]

This shock, both visual and ideological, is also experienced in Sokurov's "documentaries," which constitute fully half of his oeuvre. Because they relentlessly renewed and commented on the work of the director of *Russian Ark*, these "documented films," which combine archival footage, testimonies, poetic visions and interpretations, and sometimes reenactments, can legitimately be considered "essays." Ever since his first feature film, *The Lonely*

Voice of Man, which he directed in 1978 as his graduate thesis at VGIK (the Moscow cinematography university), Sokurov has recorded in his documentaries some of the most startling, the most bizarre, and sometimes the most disturbing images. Each time, he set up a device that had more to do with painting, reading, or even art installation than with cinema, and he seized upon bodies, landscapes, fragments of sets, and colors with his camera, producing images that he then edited into historical (collages of footage), intimate (as in diaries), or musical (as in scores) versions. These essays often present portraits of writers (Dostoyevsky, Solzhenitsyn, the Japanese writer Shimao), filmmakers (Tarkovsky, Kozintsev), singers (Chaliapin), historical figures (Stalin, Hitler, Landsbergis, Yeltsin), and anonymous figures caught in daily life situations (a peasant woman, bored sailors) or in extraordinary situations (soldiers on the Afghan front). These documentaries, whatever their subjects, are haunted by the threat of imminent disappearance. They are thus fragments of pure melancholy, and death hovers over each shot, moving furtively from a chant to a burst of laughter, from a photo to a narrative. Experimental to the point of radical decomposition—plodding and obscure, followed suddenly by speed, light, and incarnation—these films wield a hypnotic power. They could almost be seen as a continuum, one after the next, in a sleep state, by turns profound, light, disturbed, silent, peaceful, and anxious, for what they have to say is conveyed through sensation rather than knowledge, through a soul transfer rather than an information transfer. They are literally melancholy intonations, which Sokurov himself has often called "elegies" and that he hears as "Europe's funeral chants."[42]

As the filmmaker describes them, "these elegies convey my romantic idea that cinema is another life. Cinema no longer as a means of communication, but rather as a life that is other."[43] This journey through the century also offers "another history"—of which *Russian Ark*, one of Sokurov's last films, is a perfect illustration—based on two governing principles of construction and signification: lament and restoration. In an essay on Sokurov, Giorgio Agamben has pointed out that lament is the very content of this peculiar kind of cinema.[44] Elegy indeed contains, in its primary definition, this idea of lament. In ancient Greece *elegos* designated a "funeral lament" expressed in poetic form and conveying a political message: the exhortation to commit one's life to defending the Greek polis. The elegy is thus poised at the delicate yet fusional nodal point of political commitment and poetic lament. It is in relation to this specific meaning that the director's work must be seen. But what do they lament, asks Agamben? The Soviet Union, ancient Russia, Europe, sure, but what else? "Sokurov's lament has one central object: power, or more precisely the void at its center, the inexorable return of which occurred, in the USSR, in 1989, simultaneously the year of the first elegy and of the disintegration of communism."[45] This is a lament for the end of communism, which is by no means a regret but rather a way of staring obstinately into the void that has formed with its collapse, the void that is imprinted, in Sokurov's films, on the motionless and often silent faces of the *nomenklatura*, including Yeltsin himself (in *Soviet Elegy*), who is caught with a dazed look on his face as he watches television in a room bathed in aquarium light: a surface for lament that prefigures the pallid and contorted portrait of Lenin in *Taurus*. The lament is counterbalanced by a second principle, which, on the contrary, constructs the image, fills it with sensations and visions and tracks signs of the ancient and the primitive on the surface of the present. This is, in Sokurov, the very image of restoration, a restoration that is simultaneously aesthetic, pictorial (in the sense of a painting that has been cleaned and has become visible again), and historical (political). Sokurov's cinema seeks to revive, in lively tableaux, Russia's various epochs. He is undeniably nostalgic for a time when "the idea of Russia coincided with the idea of the beautiful."[46] This is a precommunist, or rather pre-Stalin, conception of the country's restoration, a Sokurovian transcription of the demodern aesthetic.

To lament and to restore: this is the double action at work—rhetorically, pictorially, and historically—in *Russian Ark*, which was screened at the Cannes Film Festival in 2002. "I open my eyes, and I see nothing. I remember only a great misfortune, everyone trying to escape. Impossible to remember." This is the voice-over whispered feebly against a black screen, as if from beyond the grave, which opens the film, as though the filmmaker was waking from a coma that lasted several days, months, or even years. The voice is soon carried away by the image, the beginning of a single dynamic shot of eighty-seven minutes and twelve seconds, an immense visual recitation in which Sokurov will comment, or rather lament, for an hour and a half. The form of *Russian Ark* is not entirely contained in this technical feat, yet it follows from it, as does an aspect of the cinema of the maker of *Mother and Son*, that which aspires to experimental virtuosity. The German director of photography Tilman Büttner, a Steadicam specialist, filmed this unique sequence shot, the longest in the history of cinema, carrying 77 pounds of equipment on his shoulders and back, at the Hermitage Museum, which had been specially reserved for the shoot, on December 23, 2001. Sokurov, based on three dress rehearsals, directed and coordinated the movement of 860 extras, all dressed and made-up on location, through the thirty-six rooms successively visited by the Sony HDW-F900 digital camera. Following three false starts, the fourth attempt was a success: the take began at 1:50 p.m., with the full knowledge that two hours later night would fall on the world's northernmost metropolis. Two hundred lights had been placed along a meticulously planned route. The take ended at 3:18, after nearly a mile of continuous movement, recorded on a portable hard drive system whose storage capacity was up to one hundred minutes of images, unheard of with classic 35-mm film.[47]

In this highly charged place for Russian history—the Winter Palace and Hermitage Museum, built by Peter the Great, turned into a museum by Catherine II, inhabited by czars, haunted by the court, assaulted by the October revolutionaries, plundered and burned in 1917, and then restored as one of the world's major art museums—Sokurov's choice of a single continuous shot takes on a clear historical significance: his cinematographic form of history is this continuum of periods, this seamless ribbon restoring moments of Russian and Soviet history in as many paintings as are visited with a striking sense of proximity. It is, according to the filmmaker, "a pure moment of cinematographic drive,"[48] and that drive is a dynamic remembrance of history. This form may also be seen as a nostalgic daydream through the meanderings of Russian time and space or as an experiment carried out by a nineteenth-century mad scientist, a kind of Jules Verne of Russian history, inventing a form of endoscopy to probe the veins and arteries of a country, all the way into the heart and brain, exploring a culture's fantasies, desires, pains, and fears. Sokurov stares into the face of history and never blinks: he develops a cinematographic form that allows him to no longer sleep in history's bed, eyes wide open toward the past.

This film-long sequence shot begins with the preparations for a ball: men in uniform and women in finery enter a palace sometime in the early twentieth century. The excitement is palpable. It is winter, snowing slightly, and cold. The voice-over wonders aloud: "Am I invisible, then? They take no notice of me. What is this spectacle? Let's hope it is not a tragedy." The voice has found its image, as Sokurov himself made clear in an interview: "Whereas the image is my legs, the sound is my soul."[49] Yet soon after they have entered this palace, which is also a museum, the voice and the moving images encounter an alter ego, a man in black, old and disheveled, who strikes up a conversation with the camera and the voice and who will serve as our tour guide. We learn that this man is a foreigner, a European, a marquis, a diplomat, living sometime after the reign of Catherine II, speaks Russian, and is very familiar with court rituals, as well as many of the old paintings hanging on the walls. We imagine a Marquis de Custine, constantly ironic, nostalgic, temperamental but also a seducer, who appreciates female beauty as well as the arts, and finally a traditionalist and reactionary, using and abusing the phrase "times have changed for the worse" with disarming ease. The voice-over, the image, and the man in black appear to get along rather well, and as they begin their visit, it becomes a conversation with the past and not only a reflection of the past, which takes place within the site of heritage conservation, par excellence: the museum. Sokurov's cinema is a machine for conversing about history and conserving time: "For me, history is a unified temporal space. I live in these periods, and none has ever ceased to exist. A historical period cannot entirely disappear."[50]

As the film proceeds through the palace-museum's rooms and galleries, this restoration becomes visible. First, there is Catherine II attending a rehearsal for a ballet she has composed and directed. The marquis comments: "Russia is like a theater, a theater of joy and grief." The czarina is seen again, later, in the company of children learning to curtsy, then rushing across a snow-covered alley, leaning on a servant, in urgent need to relieve herself. Soon, the Hermitage Museum galleries appear in succession; only now the contemporary galleries are peopled with global tourists wandering about haughtily, stopping in front of masterpieces they no longer even try to understand. The marquis does not miss the opportunity to reproach a young man, who is frightened off by this black phantom talking to him about the Gospels in front of a seventeenth-century religious painting depicting the apostles Peter and Paul. This is followed by several encounters in the large painting galleries: with Van Dyck (*Madonna of the Partridges*), Rubens (*Bacchus*), and Rembrandt (*The Prodigal Son*), as well as with two old scholars, "smelling of formaldehyde," whom the filmmaker appears to know quite well. He introduces them to the man in black, along with two strange women on whom the marquis appears quite keen. Indeed, he becomes so excited by the two that the museum guards are obliged to intervene, politely but firmly requesting that he keep his distance. The first one is blind and offers commentary on the paintings, based on what she feels through her "fingers that see everything"—on their colors, their history, and their forms. The second one dances as she talks in front of the canvasses, as if she were a ballerina inspired by the great masters. We later learn these are angels. In the meantime the marquis has been through the great sculpture gallery and rhapsodized in front of Canova's *Three Graces*. Only art can save Western man, "make up for" the erring ways of his chaotic history. This is the meaning Sokurov gives to these museum sequences that restore paintings through vision and speech, a pictorial Second Coming that is revealed through the title's metaphor: the Russian ark is nothing other than the Hermitage Museum, as the Noah's Ark of an entire civilization.

It is on the great white stair, where a young couple is in the midst of a violent argument, that the voice-over and the marquis exchange a few words on the meaning of revolution and its destructive force. A contemporary of the Terror, the latter recalls the "havoc wreaked by the Convention," while the filmmaker talks about the "great fire" that followed the storming of the Winter Palace, which marked the beginning of communist rule: "Our Convention lasted eighty years; it was terrible." The man in black inquires: "Under what regime did you live? A Republic?" "I don't know what kind of regime it was," answers the voice-over wearily, to which the monarchist replies: "I do not believe Republicanism to be a good regime." At this point the lament almost appears to center on a void: a long, nonexistent, yet terrible regime, made all the more terrible for the fact that this communist rule escapes description, cannot be named, since it has disappeared suddenly into the nether world of history, as though blown out from within; hence it is impossible to restore—either visually or through memory—an eighty-year void. Two scenes, however, do allow Sokurov to restore just a bit of Soviet communism, through two nightmares happened upon by chance, behind a furtively opened door. First, the man in black enters a darkened room against voice-over warnings: "not that door, not that door!" It leads to the storerooms and the sculpture restoration workshops, yet it is cold; it is even snowing, and there is a tired old bearded man hammering nails into coffins. Terrified, he pushes the marquis away, screaming and gesticulating threateningly: "corpses and coffins only!" The voice-over then offers a whispered explanation: this is the war against Germany, and the besieged city lost a million souls. He then comments: "In Russia, they say freedom is priceless." Another episode, possibly even more frightful, takes place a short time later: sometime in the late 1940s, three men—the museum's directors—are standing around the czars' throne. They notice that the fabric is frayed and the gilding chipped, that the object is falling apart. However, the money and even the will to restore it are lacking. They seem terrified, guarded, as they whisper about "wiretapping" and "impending disasters." Thus, the czars' throne is left unrestored, while Sokurov, in a few words whispered by pallid faces, restores Stalin's terror.

"The czars may have been despots, but they loved beauty and opulence. How beautiful this is!" the marquis exclaims in front of one of the first imperial restorations offered in *Russian Ark*—the reception thrown by Nicholas I for the son of the Iranian shah, which seals, before the entire court gathered for the occasion at the Winter Palace, an alliance that was to make up for the massacre of the Russian embassy in Persia. This outburst encapsulates the film's ideology, both aesthetic and conservative, and ruthlessly so: the czars, in a pearly and ceremonial ambience, represent an ultimate form of Russian beauty, a remote, lost, almost hieratic, beauty but a beauty in which Sokurov's profound nostalgia is invested. The pomp and circumstance of the court's rituals, governed by an almost choreographic sense of etiquette—the imperial poses of austere paternal majesty, the glimmering crinoline and sparkling military uniforms, the light trot of crowned children, blood princes and princesses, the luxuriousness of the porcelain sets and silverware—the grandeur of it all is meticulously and obsessively restored in the film. The marquis thus sees with Sokurov's camera and comments in his own voice on several imperial tableaux: Peter the Great running after a general with a whip in his hand, as a strange persecution ritual; the Persian reception; a more intimate dinner scene, featuring Nicholas II in the company of his wife and children, as he has just scolded Princess Anastasia; and finally, as the high point of this spectacle of czarist grandeur, the last ball to be held at the Winter Palace, in December 1913, with its three thousand guests (figs. 88–90). Moving freely from mazurka dancers to orchestra, from gossiping old duchesses to blushing young ladies, from provincial aristocrats to cadets of the imperial army, Sokurov reaches the pinnacle of his restorative power, which is immediately followed by the final lament, which is both visual and dynamic: the guests descending the great stairs as they depart the ball—having had their fill of beauty, opulence, and dancing—toward a future that we know to be tragic. The ultimate conversation between the voice-over and the marquis articulates this requiem for history:

> VO. I am sad.
> MARQUIS. Let's go!
> VO. Where to?
> MARQUIS. Straight ahead.
> VO. What's there?
> MARQUIS. I don't know, but let's go!
> VO. Goodbye, Europe! It's over. I grew up here, but today, strangely, I no longer recognize the house. It is as though everything were adrift. All of Russia is proceeding to the exit, its own exit from history.

88–90 ▶
Russian Ark
(ALEKSANDR SOKUROV, 2002). A WORLD FOREVER GONE THAT THE ENERGETIC FILM, SHOT IN A SINGLE TAKE, ATTEMPTS TO BRING BACK TO THE SURFACE OF THE SCREEN.

At last, the impressive gallery of portraits ends—after a final slow-motion sequence that seems to numb Sokurov's entire take, this hour and a half of pure historical continuity—at a concealed door. The camera exits through it and sails off on the Neva, the great gray river, as though it were the mythological Styx in Hades, an immense ocean of frozen time giving off clouds of white smoke. "We are condemned to sail for eternity." The ultimate lament seems dedicated to the convicts of communism to come, of this system that has engulfed the flower of Russia in death, frozen its soul, and yet has so completely collapsed, neither keeping its "promise" to last for eternity nor finding a visual incarnation worthy of the absolute beauty to which Sokurov assigns historical representations. "Only communism could fall into and through nothingness," comments the filmmaker.[51] If the czars' empire translates endlessly into visual aesthetics, communism appears, on the contrary, as an utter visual lack. It is nothing but the primal fade-in, from which the filmmaker's voice emerges as though from an eighty-year coma, and the final fade-out where the last ball of the empire dissolves into a final funeral dirge. Between necessary lament and impossible restoration, Sokurov's communism is a pure collapse of cinema, a rushing into the abyss.

Emir Kusturica's *Underground*: Into the Bowels of Communism

In May and June 1995 intense polemics surrounded the presentation of Emir Kusturica's *Underground* at the Cannes Film Festival, not to mention its ultimate crowning with a highly controversial Palme d'Or. Several intellectuals who had not seen the film denounced it vehemently as pro-Serbian propaganda, while the war was still raging in the former Yugoslvia.[52] Beyond the terms of this debate, however, the film must be recognized as a powerful vision of communism and its collapse, in the form of an allegorical and historical fable. Indeed, this demystifying carnival is a major political film on the Stalinization of Eastern Europe (with Tito's regime in Yugoslavia as principal exemplar), a zany and tragic celebration, as well as a burlesque reflection on the combined powers of cinema, illusion, lies, and electricity—what Milan Kundera has called "communist kitsch,"[53] interpreted as both the appearance and essence, profoundly intertwined, of the system that collapsed at the end of the 1980s. The locus of the demodern in Tarkovsky's film was the zone, in Guerman's the clutter, and in Sokurov's the ark. In Kusturica's work this role is played by the basement. In each of these films, though in very different ways for each of these master directors, style consistently and successfully seeks to effect the same disintegration of the values and symbols of the communist regime. Tarkovsky leads communism astray by rambling in the zone; Guerman exorcises it through chaos; Sokurov dissolves it into the space-time continuum; and Kusturica implodes it in his basement by inflating balloons that serve as illusory fetishes.

His hair stands straight up on his head, his face abruptly freezes into a grin, and, like a cartoon character, smoke comes out of his ears. The man is literally jolted by an electrical shock, which he sinks his teeth into, gives himself over to, body and soul. On several occasions Blacky, one of the two heroes in *Underground*, receives just such a jolt of electricity, causing him to jerk about like a grotesque and burlesque puppet suddenly turned electric eel—as if, at regular intervals, Kusturica's movie needed to "recharge" by plugging into certain sources. Blacky the electrician is one of them. Wedding parties, of which there are three in the film, are another, purveying other regenerative fluids—wine, laughter, tears, and music. Each time these figures occur—never spontaneously, since they are expected—the film appears to refuel and start anew, as though these resupplies gave *Underground* the possibility of remaining generous throughout and conferred on the story and the images their own passionate power. For Emil Kusturica offers a lot in this film, a lot of himself and a lot of what his life, his history, his country, have gone through. All these threads, knotted together by the filmmaker's demiurgic power, form a highly heterogeneous and unnerving substance, a kind of magma.

Indeed, how are we to sum up the film's plot, spanning fifty years of Yugoslavian history? First movement: April 1941. German bombs are falling on Belgrade, punctuating as much as interrupting the alcohol- and music-saturated ceremony, organized by Blacky's friend Marko, in honor of Blacky's induction into the Communist Party. In the name of communism Marko and Blacky start a lucrative business, trafficking and dealing in all sorts of things, especially arms, often working out of the former's basement. Meanwhile, out of a rather childish form of sentimentalism, both men fall in love with the same woman, Natalija, who regularly fraternizes with Nazi occupiers. It is in the name of this sentimental rivalry that the two friends—boozers, crafty and carefree oafs, who are not, however, without a certain panache—become resistance fighters and partisans, even heroes, since they kill several Germans right in the middle of Belgrade's theater.

Second movement: 1961. Under Tito's regime Marko, a close associate of the great man (whom he kisses several times in various photomontages engineered by Kusturica), has become the poet laureate, author of the founding narrative of the regime's mythical origins (the partisans' fight against the Nazis), and protector of the arts in the country of official culture for all (fig. 91). At home, in his basement, which has become a full-fledged underground world, he keeps Blacky (who in the eyes of the communist world above has died heroically) and his many grotesque, degenerate, crippled, lecherous creatures under the false impression that the war of liberation is still raging, that Marshal Tito is the only hero capable of bringing it to a successful end, and that in the meantime they must continue manufacturing arms and rifles (through the sale of which Marko and Natalija make a fortune, as true party apparatchiks), to the sounds of gypsy music in a shady and archaic world (fig. 92). This historical manipulation is engineered by Marko from above, communicating with the basement through a trapdoor: he plays sirens, recordings of bombings, German songs, and the myth takes hold. But after overly indulging during a wedding party held in the basement, one of the local creatures, a wily young monkey, blows everything up by sneaking her way into a tank that goes haywire and begins firing real rockets. The people of the bowels come out into the open and discover the fraud of their fictitious world, frozen into a junk shop of an eternal communism of people's liberation—a world that collapses for good with Tito's death, on May 4, 1980, and at his successive funerals in each of the republics that make up the Yugoslav confederation. The body of the great man is scattered, the system blows up, and "Yugoslavism" is consigned to the cemetery of untenable ideas become objects of nostalgia.

Third and final movement, which is less relevant here, since it does not deal with the metaphor of communism as an artificial land but rather its historical consequences: 1991, and the war between Serbs and Croats. The spectator meanders among armed militias (all corrupt and cruel), summary executions and scorched earth tactics, suicides and the violent deaths of the film's protagonists, one and all pathetic victims of the tragedy of history. The former Yugoslavia is torn to pieces; the UN is as powerless as it is corrupt; Blacky has become the harebrained head of a Serbian militia; Marko deals arms to both sides; Natalija has become a bitter and greedy old woman; and a shady middle-man, played by Kusturica himself, deals drugs and trades in automatic weapons. It is the end of a country, assassinated by a history whose allegories and warnings it failed to grasp, turning a blind eye to the repeated tragedies and the noble causes that served to mask them.

In the course of this living and macabre panorama, full of despair and humanism, all registers are mobilized—from farce to tragedy, from bombastic theater and intimate drama to epic and socialist realism—just as no genre is

91 ▶
Underground
(EMIR KUSTURICA, 1995). THE POET-COMRADE IS IN CHARGE OF OFFICIAL CULTURE IN THE COUNTRY OF TRIUMPHANT TITOISM. KUSTURICA'S PHOTOMONTAGES BRING MARKO, THE FICTIONAL CHARACTER, TOGETHER WITH TITO, THE ACTUAL COMMUNIST LEADER, IN DELIBERATELY KITSCH IMAGES.

92 ▶
Underground
(EMIR KUSTURICA, 1995). ABOVE, MARKO'S APARTMENT, WHERE HE ARTIFICIALLY PERPETUATES (HERE, THROUGH AN AIR-RAID SIREN) "WAR COMMUNISM." BELOW, THE CELLAR IN WHICH THIS FORM OF COMMUNISM HAS BEEN FROZEN AND IS STILL PRACTICED, TWENTY YEARS LATER (MANUFACTURING ARMS FOR THE PARTISANS).

left out—war movie, documentary, burlesque comedy, musical, and film-within-a-film. The film changes pace and style, quickly and constantly. "All the armies have passed through my land,"[54] wrote Kusturica, and the filmmaker took snippets of life and death from each, which form the underground foundations of his war film, organized and divided into three "wars." The various moods that carry this film-organism from one jolt to the next, one attack to the next, one crisis to the next quickly blur into one another. All characters are there, registering their presence on the screen, but they may just as well disappear for a twenty-year hiatus, fragment into pieces—like Tito's body in May 1980, carried by special mortuary trains through all the regions of Yugoslavia—or die and be born again.

The film's heterogeneity figures as a vital force, as a fertile and varied soil. The film's composition feeds off of the generalized decomposition. Everything is haunted by its opposite, and all the inhabitants of this chaotic world are endowed with a capacity for metamorphosis that is synonymous with survival. This heterogeneity, this sense that "anything can happen," transforms the film into a historical continuum in which life circulates between the various floors, the various levels, the various periods, reinvigorating a mechanism that appeared mortally wounded. In this regard *Underground* adopts the frenzied and open-ended structure of a cartoon, drawn out over nearly three hours. Yet, paradoxically, heterogeneity also acts as a force of unmasking, a force of truth, and hence a force of demystification/demythification, which makes this a political film, the most evocative and sophisticated of the films about the Stalinization of Europe. This truth is both political and cinematographic. Or rather, it is political because it is cinematographic, since it is located in the work of the film itself. Kusturica reveals everything, from the epic conditions of the shooting and the many crises that erupted (the filming was drawn out over more than a year, marked by many dramas, discoveries, and accidents that are made visible in the chaotic structure of the film) to the techniques behind his special effects (for example, the wire that enables the bride to fly through the air) and even the reasons for these effects (when characters are "embedded" in archival footage, the bits of films that are not made for them and publicly reject them). Kusturica goes so far as to take his spectators on a tour of his own set, behind the scenes, to see his Moritone and his special-effects table. The operation of political unveiling is always paired with a revelation of the intimacy of cinema. Everything is offered at once, and the spectator sometimes even intrudes into the film, like Blacky on the filming of his own story, an untimely guest, curious and destructive of a cinema story that meets a country's history (fig. 93).

The subject of *Underground* is history framed by the narrative markers of a fairy tale ("Once upon a time there was a land . . ." is the preface to the film), history told in terms of a mythical cycle of war as eternal renewal (as seen in the series of despairing titles of the three parts: I: War, II: Cold War, III: War) or, more precisely, the cycle proper to communist frost and thaw. The only cooling that occurs here, however, is in the country's history. And whether its history is hot (war or thaw) or cold (the other war or Stalin's freeze), it

93 ▶
Underground
(EMIR KUSTURICA, 1995). THE UNDERGROUND WORLD (A VIEW OF THE SETS): INSIDE COMMUNISM'S BASEMENT. (PHOTO © PETER MOUNTAIN; COLL. *CAHIERS DU CINÉMA*)

continues always to produce mythical traces of its existence. In Kusturica's film history is not a chronicle but a cataclysm, an epic of mythological proportions, which perversely follows the paths of official history. Resistance to the Nazi occupier, the war of the partisans and its compendium of heroic anecdotes, the country's modernization as expressed in speeches, doublespeak, sparkling new factories, symmetrical housing blocks, culture for all, and sport as a ritual of national glorification, in the end, Yugoslavia itself—these are all just so many myths on which the Tito regime fed, which it sutured together into a seamless ribbon for "writing history." Kusturica's force and governing principle is to take this history literally, with its canonical moments and conventional imagery, to take it and to overexpose it, to subject it to his bursts of energy. The homogeneous history then implodes into disjointed but revealing pieces, following Barthes' law of the "mythification of myth": "the best weapon against myth is perhaps to mythify it in its turn, and to produce an *artificial myth*: and this reconstituted myth will in fact be a mythology. Since myth robs language of something, why not rob myth?"[55] So how is the communist myth to be "robbed"? By making it artificial, that is, by openly manipulating it, ridiculing it as a caricature of itself, inflating it with symbols and conceits. This is *Underground*'s idea: to turn the communist myth into a metaphor (that of the basement, which artificially prolonged the life of war and resistance communism) and the regime's language into films that cross paths and, through a process of contamination, are pitched against one another. The metaphor overexposes the myth as a laboratory experiment (the basement is nothing but the revealing cave of a mad and megalomaniacal scientist), and the interweaving of films explodes the homogeneity of the political language.

Similar in this respect to Chaplin's *The Great Dictator*, *Underground* dives into the manipulation of history, but it does so by going down to the basement, the metaphor for communism and its illusions. How is a world of lies made to look like reality, like a reality that is more beautiful still than reality itself? Thus, in the basement turned into history's underground, the film masterfully exposes the massive fraud that was communism, with its myths, its sacrifices, both necessary and heroic, and its illusions erected as dogma. It mounts a challenge to the communist Years of Lead on the terrain of cinematographic form, as though Kusturica had managed to undo the collectivity celebrated by Tito's regime through his own form of conviviality, a countercollective expressed in fairs, music, and strange rituals, in a basement that serves as his crucible of history. The carnival here signifies to a frozen and teetering society that it is, indeed, going to die at any moment from a kind of overdose of laughter, song, dance, and words.

Two worlds coexist in the film, displayed in a double spatial metaphor, especially in the central part of the film. The first, the outside world, is all orderly rituals and official ceremonies. It celebrates the heroes of anti-Nazi resistance and of Tito's communism, whose champion is Marko, a man of power and a poet, the regime's organizer and bard, the one who provides it with both its faith in progress and modernity, as well as a lyrical doublespeak. This artificial world is illustrated by two communist imageries: first, the unveiling ceremony for the statue of Blacky, "hero of the Resistance," mythified by socialist realist style and honored in a puffy speech overladen with stylistic figures:

> Comrades, I have the great honor of inaugurating the statue of our national hero, Peter Popara-Blacky. He is a symbol of our fight against fascism; his personality and his achievements shall remain forever with us—his friends, his comrades in arms, his fellows. I take this opportunity to recite a few lines from my latest collection of poems on the war of national liberation: "Why does the wind always blow/When our dear and gentle ones are commemorated?/Why does the wind beat against/Our brothers' windows and doors?/Is it only the wind blowing/Or is the sky crying with us?

As for the sanctimonious film shot by an official filmmaker on the life stories of Marko, Natalija, and Blacky (a story that adheres to the codes of the founding narrative of the antifascist struggle), it is cheerfully entitled *Spring Is Coming on Its White Horse* and also conforms to a socialist realist aesthetic.

The second metaphorical locus is the basement, the underground, an allegorical figure right out of Mitteleuropa, where Blacky, his cohort, and close friends—manipulated by Marko—have taken refuge. Convinced that the "war of liberation" is still going on, they participate in the resistance effort by manufacturing arms, and by subterraneously, surreptitiously recreating an autarkic and rebellious microcommunity. This is a historical place of reference, a world of its own that mimics a form of "war communism" that was the bedrock of Soviet identity until 1921 and that mythically inspired all the postwar people's democracies. It is a world focused on the coming liberation, on arms manufacturing, and on the collectivization of production and of ideas, with its share of deprivation, conditioning, propaganda, lack of connection with the real world, and lack of autonomous life. This world was held together by a sense of sacrifice and the collective glorification of myths, heroes, and ceremonies: for example, Tito's watch, a reinvigorating fetish that Blacky holds tight to his heart while bursting into tears; or the chants that rise from the communist bowels of the earth, enthusiastically intoned by the people: "You, Comrade Tito, you, the people's hope, you are the darling of both the old and the young/You, Comrade Tito, our spring flower, Serbia will never forget you/A violet has bloomed on the pillow where Comrade Tito's head is resting." The double metaphor is thus clear: this is about Eastern Europe, cut off from the rest of the world for decades, ideologically and economically exploited by the USSR, and where the only news that circulated came from the state-controlled media, which would turn anecdotes into propaganda and rehearse ad nauseam the same glorious founding narrative of the regime. In this film Marko and Natalija are in charge of the outside communist business, while a deceived, deluded, and manipulated Blacky runs the world of communist galley slaves down in the basement.

Kusturica has explained that the conceit was inspired by a play by Dusan Kovasevic: "the basement in *Underground* came from Kovasevic's brilliant idea, where people are manipulated and live in a basement. It is a film about manipulation, about the way a few individuals, the *nomenklatura* in a communist regime, can maintain most of the others in their power. In Tito's time, people were kept in a kind of metaphorical basement, cut off from others and under the impression that they were living the happiest days of their lives."[56] These "happiest days"—artificially produced and reproduced in countless statues, films, poems, fetish objects, values, narratives, and myths—were manufactured by political spectacle and by a whole aesthetic system that was as shallow as it was gleaming. As I have noted, Kundera referred to this aesthetic system as communist kitsch. For him this was not just bad taste but an entire mode of political behavior specific to communist dictatorships: communist man's need for kitsch "is the need to gaze into the mirror of the beautifying lie and to be moved to tears of gratification at one's own reflection." This artificial identification is supported by rituals and official ceremonies, themselves conducted to prevent the emergence of kitsch's enemy: "the questioning man."[57]

Manipulation, revealed for what it is, thus plays a key role in the film, which constantly intertwines three other films within the epic narrative, all of which constitute bits and pieces of the Yugoslav myth: first, newsreels from 1941 (when the Germans entered Zagreb, Slovenia, and Belgrade) to 1980 (Tito's death and funerals), which are visibly appropriated by *Underground*'s characters (especially footage from the 1960s, showing the great rituals of Tito's regime, pompous reenactments of the origins of communism); then, the socialist-realist film glorifying resistance fighters, shot at the same time as Kusturica's film, which tells the story of the same three protagonists, in a mythical vein and ham-acting style; and finally, the great spectacle of war (blaring sirens, bombings, sacrifice, heroism, and *Lili Marlene* as the simultaneously heartrending and ambiguous anthem), which further entrenches the underground world in its basement isolation and its archaic certainties. *Underground* glues back together, in an exultant collage, the pieces of these "ideal" films that never existed outside the imagination. These films, all colorful, grimacing, and hyperkitsch, are devoured by the historical metaphor of the basement constructed by Kusturica, a metaphor whose most interesting incarnation is as a chimera, a mutant hybrid, a monstrous organism that eats up myths and processes them into a giant artifice: communism itself. Communism is here seen as a concept that is produced and undone by history, revived by melancholy and nostalgia, an early symptom of the "open fracture of the soul" from which all of Kusturica's characters suffer.[58]

The filmmaker is thus not content with creating a metaphoric space of communism or with exposing its mythical and artificial mechanisms. By blowing it up from within, he invents a cinematographic form that actually captures the collapse of a system. As Jacques Amalric, himself a fine connoisseur of the communist system, wrote:

> Kusturica throws in our faces a masterful autopsy of what used to be called in doublespeak "existing socialism," while also throwing that vision into the fire. The most efficient and the crudest—in both senses of the term—manipulation ever achieved by this historical form of socialism was to persuade, by any means necessary, tens of millions of people that the struggle against Nazism and fascism was perpetual. The conceit of the basement, where one of the film's protagonists is locked up and engages for years in pathetic military preparations to the sounds of vengeful slogans broadcast by a pathetic video-acoustic contraption, while the usurpers parade around on the surface above, will become canonical—especially since all it takes, in the end, is a chimpanzee to expose the hoax and destroy everything. Sorry for those who would still have it that the cold war was actively won, whereas the socialist system simply imploded.[59]

The basement world is the one in which communism did not evolve but rather regressed to its own primitive form, war communism. From the outset it is a "demodernization" of the socialist system, conveyed through a series of symbols: the army of communist pride, represented in the tunnel by an old rusted tank flaunting its red star and by the uniforms adorning, more often than not, animals or deformed bodies; industrial productivity, another obvious symbol of socialist modernity, represented in the basement by a makeshift assembly line that only produces antiquated rifles; modern urbanism, which has degenerated into a series of model-size buildings made out of matches, built by a halfwit; and electricity, a supreme marker of modernity brought to the people by socialism, that flows from a dynamo driven by a cohort of breathless characters who take turns pedaling a series of old bicycles. The only thing that really works in the bowels of communism is the circulation and elimination of excrement, through a rather primitive but efficient system of chamber pots and canvas shit-cabins. The world below makes, of course, for a sharp contrast with the socialist proposition above, that is dealt with by the official propaganda film, in which rifles always work, factories yield maximum outputs, streets are perfectly symmetrical, armies parade in lockstep, and heroes are all endowed with chiseled bodies and superb mustaches—a well-ordered world that progressively unravels nonetheless. *Underground* effects a delirious transfer of modern socialism into demodern communism before exploding it all in an excess of vitality.

This part of the film culminates with the two worlds communicating and converging through resemblance, in a common demodern aesthetic. The wedding ceremony in the basement prefaces and punctuates their reunion by implosion, as all of Kusturica's mad machines begin to move to the sound of gipsy music—a veritable ship of fools taking charge of communism's relics and passing in the process from life to death. The monkey gets behind the wheel of the partisans' old tank and starts firing rockets right and left. The match buildings catch fire, and the primitive communist people rush out into the open on wheeled beds turned troop transports—a strange spinning top, on which are hooked musicians twirling at full speed, setting the tempo. With people pouring out through sewers, the basement explodes, and soon after, up on the surface, the embodiment of socialism himself is dying: Tito's body, as seen in archival footage, is carried from town to town to the sound of music that recalls the founding of the regime, *Lili Marlene,* and the German occupation. "Communism was an immense basement," a doctor concludes a little while later, when treating men at his lunatic asylum who claim to have spent the nearly forty years of Tito's rule in a basement.

If both the soul and history are clearly laid bare, fractured open, by *Underground*'s powerful metaphor, it is because Kusturica has painstakingly wrapped the film's melancholy in flesh and blood, embodied its history. It is as if communism was exposing its bowels, in that basement we visit and get lost in—and in which spectators and protagonists alike are "digested" by the acids produced by the film's phenomenal energy. Europe is similarly riddled with landmines, through and through, crisscrossed by underground tunnels where all manner of trafficking has proliferated, where everything is recycled, including excrements and organic matter. In the end the metaphor only works because of the bodies that inhabit it, a halfway house of haggard, pathetic, and burlesque faces. To restore communism's history so as to film it—to drive it out of the basement—consisted in recreating the former bodies, the bodies of the "before" of the country's history, and mixing them with more recent ones, of the "after history." Hence the constant and bizarre impression that haunts the spectator of *Underground* of being confronted with the primitive and the degenerate, the birth and death of bodies, without any sense of maturity outside of artifice and disguise. The heroes are young, then old, passing abruptly from voracious pleasure-seeking to suicidal death wish, from virility and femininity to the degenerate state of the old Ceausescu couple (Marko/Natalija), and, when they are seen in middle-age, their faces are made-up like those of vaudeville actors, their gestures are mechanical and puppetlike, and they cry crocodile tears, in a kind of daze, like in fairy tales or never-ending dreams. This highly particular temporality of bodies is one of *Underground*'s mysteries—since the same ones are charged with both telling and bearing fifty years of history—and ultimately one of the mechanisms that holds the film together.

With Kusturica exuberance and carnival always take over tragedy, transcribing it into their own style. This burlesque trafficking, this dealing in joy, reveals how the filmmaker was able to tell the history of communism in his country—by sending shockwaves through the screen, ripping it apart, and filming the impact—all the way to the final implosion of the system, and the victory of the primitive over knowledge, unreason over reason, wild music over propaganda verse, frenzy over apparent order, unbridled conviviality over rigid dogma, regression over glorious progress, and the demodern over the modern.

A Few Images for "Those Who Are Lost"

This trajectory of four films raises the question of the cinematographic form proper to the end of communism. From *Stalker* to *Underground*, via *Khrustalyov, My Car!* and *Russian Ark*, Russian cinema has depicted catastrophe and collapse. Why was it incapable of representing the transitional years of 1985 to 1989, called perestroika and glasnost? It was as if, between Tarkovsky's prophetic vision of a world coming to an end, being engulfed in *Stalker*'s zone, and the three successive films, nothing could be recorded of the regime's attempts to reform communism from within. These attempts failed, of course, and the system was not reformed—it collapsed. Yet what about glasnost cinema? It must be said that no unknown or forgotten aesthetic continent was discovered at that precise moment, and the few filmmakers who did appear then—Vassili Pitchul, Pavel Lounguine, Vitali Kanevski—all simply fell into line. Eastern European cinema remained overwhelmingly dominated by Guerman, Sokurov, and the Hungarian director Bela Tarr—filmmakers who emerged before perestroika and the end of communism and who were not especially linked to that period, even if they may have benefited from the "thaw" that cinema experienced in the second half of the 1980s.

Thus, if perestroika opened up possibilities and lifted taboos, it was not "the miracle that mechanically engenders masterpieces," as Guerman put it.[60] Russia, and the part of Europe long known as "Eastern," might well have formed a region of the world that was too heterogeneous, too immense, and all the more scattered for having been held together by and based on violence for so long, to offer its artists anything other than the isolation of the *maudit*. This historical and aesthetic fate allowed singular worlds to flourish against the system but was not conducive to the development of a full-fledged cinema movement, school, or tradition. Soviet cinema had norms imposed on it for too long—from the 1920s avant-garde to socialist realism under Stalin, and even under Khrushchev's thaw in the 1960s—to readily embrace any "collective" endeavors. If artists had always defined themselves in relation to state power, it was consistently according to the "official"/"*maudit*" divide and not a less-troubled form of collaboration that, as in France for instance, has long enabled public subsidy of "social films" that are made wholly independently but that nonetheless give a sense of the social and political state of an ongoing historical moment—films that I designate here as a cinematographic form of history. Soviet society, especially during perestroika, did not receive what Serge Daney, in a special issue of *Cahiers du cinema* made in the USSR in 1990, called "cinematic justice."[61] What it did receive was mostly images of the past, of Soviet cinema and its "golden ages," if often viewed through a very critical lens, but few if any images reflecting the uncertain, and even elusive, present, before the final collapse. The filmmakers of the late 1980s who would or could confront the present were few and far between, even though they seem to have had a strange and variable experience of the ongoing reform.

While Mikhail Gorbachev, who became general secretary of the Soviet Communist Party in March 1985, implemented a range of symbolic reforms, and even organized the first free multicandidate elections in March 1989—followed by the fall of the Berlin wall in November 1989, which he officially approved—perestroika had great difficulties making inroads into the world of cinema. It did, however, have some impact. A few unauthorized movies did come out in theaters, such as Guerman's *My Friend Ivan Lapshin* and Kira Muratova's *The Asthenic Syndrome*, while in May 1986 the Fifth Congress of Soviet Filmmakers broke from tradition and elected Elem Klimov, a symbol of renewal, as its director, just as the reformist Kamchalov was taking over from the conservative Yermach at the head of Goskino, the state cinema organ. Tarkovsky, who died in exile in Paris in 1986, was officially rehabilitated the following year, and in April 1989, by decree, the studios were given full autonomy—a first step toward a production system independent from the state. Yet the reform of cinema from within did not lead to any representative body of work, even though in May 1987 Tengiz Abuladze's anti-Stalinist film *Repentance* fetched three awards at Cannes and *Robinzoniada* won the Camera d'Or—prompting several Western critics to proclaim that that year's festival was "bathed in the colors of glasnost."[62] Only one film truly harnessed the winds of change: Vassili Pitchul's *Little Vera*, which was a full-blown hit at the Soviet box office when it was released in September 1988. One out of five Soviets went to see it, but this success was due more to a fashion frenzy than to any sense, on the part of the public, of seeing itself convincingly represented onscreen. Indeed, *Little Vera* is particularly rich in sordid details and dwells on the dark side of life, in a kind of voyeuristic exhibitionism. This suggests a paradox of sorts: in the country of actually existing communism the most sinister thing, the most dilapidated, was precisely the social world, the common life, a material disaster that translates aesthetically as a defeat of representation. "Materialism as a system gave rise to the most pathetically ugly and poor material culture of the century," as Serge Daney put it.[63] And it is impossible to represent, outside of heavy allegory, the official imagery of the regime or the autistic ramblings of alienated artists. "We are lost," as Alexei Guerman would say.[64]

It was only the collapse of the system itself—and hence the apocalyptic form that enabled its recording, in Guerman, Sokurov, and Kusturica's films—that could at last "visually translate" communism, which had been so impossible to represent in its attempts at internal reform. Slavoj Žižek has suggested that he found it disturbing to be confronted with films that deliberately choose "the spectacle of mythical excess" and thus pitch "aesthetics against ideology, form against history."[65] It is this apocalyptic temptation that marks all four films presented here as illustrations of the various ways in which the

94 ▶
Stalker
(ANDREI TARKOVSKY, 1979). SOVIET CINEMA'S OFFICIAL LOGO. THIS ENTHUSIASTIC MOVEMENT TOWARD MODERNITY IS OFTEN CONTRADICTED BY THE FILMS THAT FOLLOW THIS COMPULSORY BEGINNING.

end of communism was filmed. *Stalker* and *Khrustalyov, My Car!* and, even more so, *Russian Ark*—with its technological feat, an eighty-seven-minute sequence shot—privilege form over history, an overinvested, almost oversized, form that can be connected to the assertive aestheticism of the Russian and Eastern European tradition of cinema. Žižek fears such a form will blind spectators to history. I would rather see it as a revelation of history, made even more manifest through the virtuoso and grandiloquent turn it takes: to record the collapse of communism not as a document but as a "fabricated" and ironic allegory of history, an aesthetic form of the demodern.

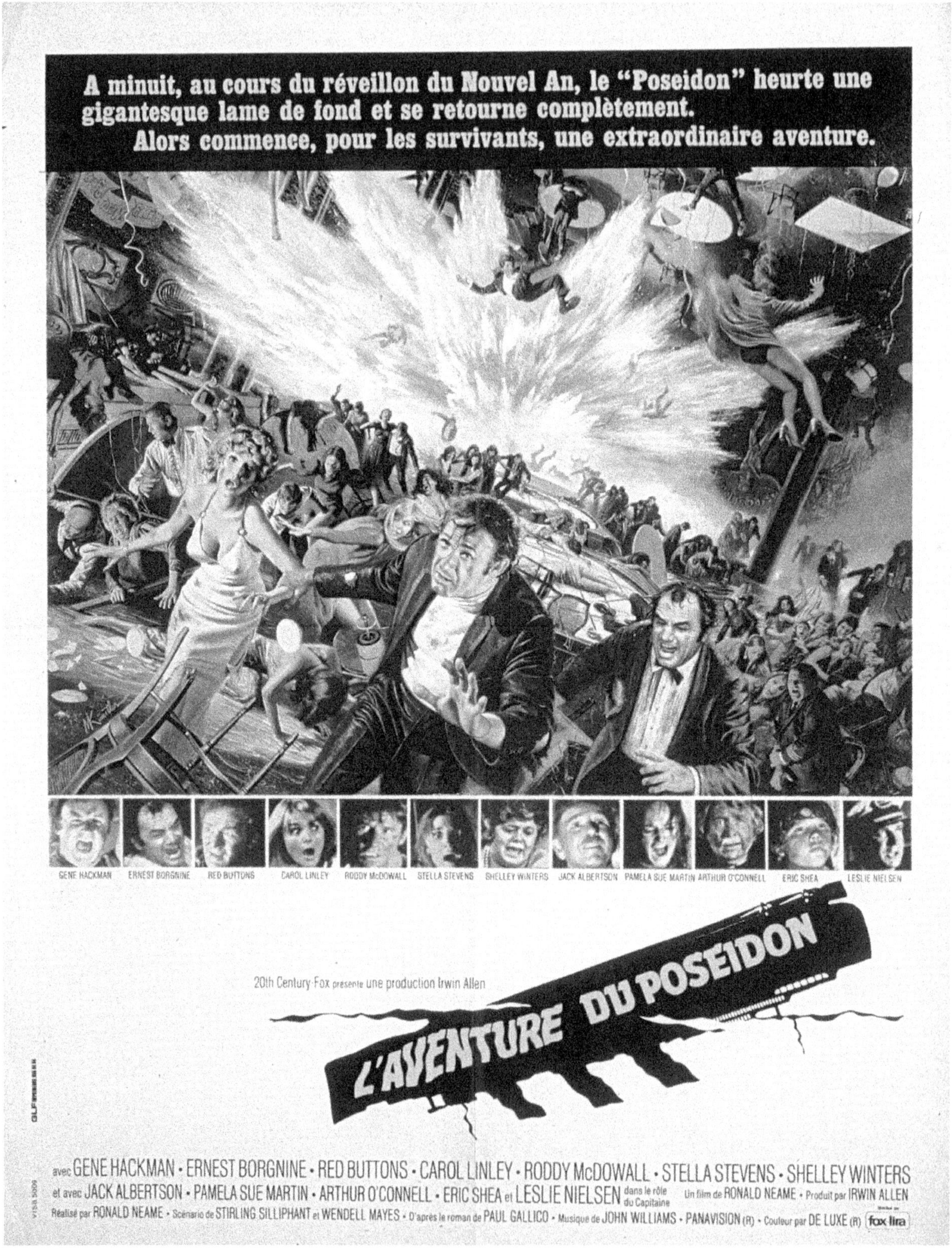
A minuit, au cours du réveillon du Nouvel An, le "Poseidon" heurte une gigantesque lame de fond et se retourne complètement.
Alors commence, pour les survivants, une extraordinaire aventure.
GENE HACKMAN
ERNEST BORGNINE
RED BUTTONS
CAROL LINLEY
RODDY McDOWALL
STELLA STEVENS
SHELLEY WINTERS
JACK ALBERTSON
PAMELA SUE MARTIN
ARTHUR O'CONNELL
ERIC SHEA
LESLIE NIELSEN
20th Century-Fox présente une production Irwin Allen
L'AVENTURE DU POSEIDON
avec GENE HACKMAN · ERNEST BORGNINE · RED BUTTONS · CAROL LINLEY · RODDY McDOWALL · STELLA STEVENS · SHELLEY WINTERS
et avec JACK ALBERTSON · PAMELA SUE MARTIN · ARTHUR O'CONNELL · ERIC SHEA et LESLIE NIELSEN dans le rôle du Capitaine
Un film de RONALD NEAME · Produit par IRWIN ALLEN
Réalisé par RONALD NEAME · Scénario de STIRLING SILLIPHANT et WENDELL MAYES · D'après le roman de PAUL GALLICO · Musique de JOHN WILLIAMS · PANAVISION (R) · Couleur par DE LUXE (R)
fox lira

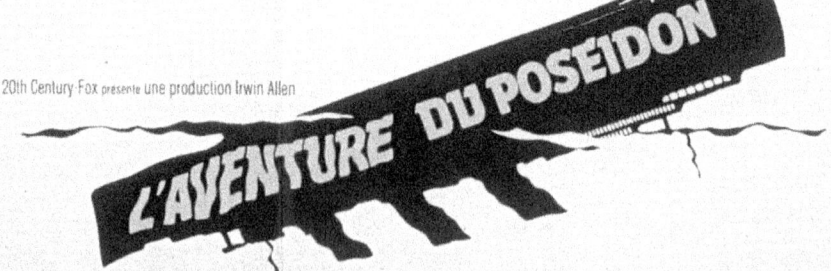

7
AMERICA UNRAVELED ▶
MASTER FICTIONS IN CONTEMPORARY HOLLYWOOD CINEMA

◀ 95
French poster for *The Poseidon Adventure*
(RONALD NEAME, 1972). (PHOTO COURTESY BIFI)

▶ IT HAS ALWAYS BEEN notoriously difficult to separate out aesthetics, economics, and politics, especially in the case of American cinema. Everything makes sense when the three are brought together: a type of production entails a certain style, which reveals a particular historical moment. This configuration is precisely what I have called a cinematographic form of history. In the case of contemporary America and its dominant cinema, it appears that this form has to be aesthetically poor to be financially powerful and politically revealing. The current industrial productions generate shallow images, a cinema that is disconnected from reality, deprived of the epic quality of myth, and devoid of any original substance. Such a cinema refers only to itself and to the desires attributed to its spectators, even if these are counted in the tens of millions; it is a fundamentally closed system. In this sense the industrial aesthetic of contemporary Hollywood is intrinsically political, since it aims to maintain the economic and cultural dominance of the United States over the world.

Revealing Resurgences: Under the Whip of Catwoman

There is very little of everyday America, of its life and work, in major contemporary Hollywood films. It has been displaced by an abstract and fantastical representation of America, which is easily exported to the rest of the world, supported by a few plotlines (superheroes saving the planet, expected clichés, conventional locations, A-list actors), combined with techniques for the artificial reproduction of the world and "special effects" that are as stunning and spectacular as they are, in the end, meaningless. America as it presents itself here is smooth, polished, powerful, and stereotypical: families for whom unity is the primary value; perils as sure to arise as they are to be ultimately overcome; imposing landscapes and majestic cities; sensual women in narrowly delimited roles; territories that are cleansed of their social, racial, and economic detritus; carefully allocated minorities; and omnipresent violence channeled as a release mechanism, an exorcism, a catharsis of the modern world. Hollywood inexorably relegates to the invisible margin all particularity and diversity, all dysfunction and protest, as well as any politically incorrect discourse: cinema America appears to be a compromise according to the rules of good intentions and consensual values. This cinema is "global" rather than anchored in the complex and contradictory reality of any actual place.

This is not news, of course, since the "dream factory" has always favored appeals to the "general public" over attempts to capture a troubling reality.

Yet this golden rule appears to have become more rigidly cast than ever before. This is Hollywood's "Silver Age," following on one of its golden ages, the 1970s, marked by the exceptional creativity and renewal of young auteurs (Scorsese, Coppola, De Palma, Cimino, among others) operating within a studio system that was uncharacteristically open to taking risks. This was a period of filmmaking, dubbed by the critics as "New Hollywood,"[1] which focused its cameras on a marginal and rebellious America—in all its violence and license, its energy and failures—a country at once alive and wounded, explored at its limits and in its most radical experiments. The break with this period was essentially economic, triggered by a double phenomenon: the spectacular failure of one of New Hollywood's flagship productions—Michael Cimino's *Heaven's Gate*, in 1980—and the commercial success of the first blockbusters: the big-budget productions that spawn sequels, prequels, and remakes. Steven Spielberg's *Jaws* (1975), George Lucas's *Star Wars* (1977), and another Spielberg film, *Raiders of the Lost Ark* (1981), imposed not only new rules of the game for the economics of cinema but for aesthetics as well, which were to be strictly obeyed by films aspiring to commercial success: ceaselessly changing special effects and recording techniques; stock characters, sets, and situations; and the establishment of an ironic distance in relation to heroes and graphic violence.

This cinema, thus, must be approached without illusions as to artistic merit, yet it calls for close examination, or rather oblique examination, against the grain and in its interstices, however narrow, and especially through the genres it deploys and exploits: fantasy, horror, disaster, gothic, teen comedies, and so forth. Then and only then can one not despair of Hollywood. It is, indeed, in these genre films—or at least those that manage to refrain somewhat from the frenzied commercial exploitation of the teenage market—that all the weird and wild elements revealed in the New Hollywood cinema of the 1960s and 1970s resurface. These films will serve here as my *corpus princeps*—the films made by a generation of filmmakers who first appeared in the 1980s making films that belonged to then neglected genres in Hollywood but that were soon annexed to the standardized cinema: Tim Burton, Robert Zemeckis, James Cameron, David Lynch, Joe Dante, John Landis, Sam Raimi, Ethan and Joel Coen, Renny Harlin, John McTiernan, Rob Reiner, Harold Ramis, Bobby and Peter Farrelly, Oliver Stone, Darren Aronofsky, John Carpenter, and Jonathan Demme. To the age-old question of the mediocrity of their films and their audiences—"You churn out films for Coke-guzzling teenagers"— these new American filmmakers seem to have found a response. They are members of a new generation, albeit somewhat older than their audiences, for whom this void has been an inspiration, in the way a black hole sucks in anything that comes its way, both the most inane conventions and the most radical inventions. In this way Hollywood films cannot be so easily dismissed as elements of a mass culture, interesting only as illustrations of the broad sociological trends in contemporary America. It is paradoxically within this machine full of dangling wires and short-circuits that the sources of a new avant-garde, a *New Experimentalism*,[2] can be found.

Examining these films is also a way of talking differently about Hollywood cinema and America—neither as pundit (lauding the French cultural exception and heaping scorn on commercial, spectacular, and inane cinema) nor as booster (celebrating technology and marketing techniques) nor even as cinephile (adopting the discourse of auteur legitimacy, whereby at the margins of the American system a few auteurs, independent artists, and piratical geniuses, manage to survive, while the rest is nothing but a standardized cinema of genres, producers, actors, and subjects that are all entirely worthless). The aim here is to take Hollywood cinema for what it is—the visual development, in cinematographic form and with the support of considerable technical and financial resources, of a series of "master fictions" that reveal, through identification or rejection, certain values, beliefs, and fears. Contemporary American cinema no longer obeys a single "revealing precipitate," as it did in the 1960s and 1970s, according to Jean-Baptiste Thoret's analysis of that second golden age through its primal trauma: the short twenty-six-second film shot by Abraham Zapruder of John Fitzgerald Kennedy's assassination, on November 22, 1963, which recorded live the Dallas killer's gunshot entering the president's brain:

> In the history of American cinema, Zapruder's film—and the debates to which it gave rise—figures both as a matrix (aesthetic and thematic) and a configuration: a precipitate of tropes and patterns that, in a central or peripheral way, explicitly or implicitly, infuse Brian De Palma's cinema—from *Greetings*, in 1968, onward—as well as a whole spectrum of critical cinema of the time, from experimental films to conspiracy cinema in the 1970s, Andy Warhol's series, and the most violent productions and horror movies, which it unquestionably inspired. Many Hollywood productions also offered fascinating fictional treatments of these few seconds that broke the century, and America itself, in two.[3]

Such is the compelling theory developed in Thoret's book *26 secondes, l'Amérique éclaboussée: l'assassinat de JFK et le cinéma américain*. Indeed, if one were to isolate a revealing cinematographic form, the Dallas tragedy recorded by Zapruder unquestionably launched an era of cinema characterized by violence and conspiracy, the main obsessions of the New Hollywood directors, who gave them center stage. Kennedy's assassination called into question, and led to a systematic critique of, America's dominant values. Thus, on November 22, 1963, America entered what Marc Chénetier, in an essay on post-1960s American fiction, called, borrowing from Nathalie Sarraute, "the age of suspicion."[4]

Over the past twenty years the "revealing precipitate" has given way to a number of "master fictions"—an expression coined by the anthropologist Clifford Geertz and appropriated by American historians of representation, notably Lynn Hunt, Natalie Zemon Davis, and Simon Schama, to designate the narratives that both structure and reveal the beliefs, commitments, rejections, and values of a given community.[5] These fictions, according to Geertz's analysis of primitive societies in Java, both describe a real event and enable this description to accede to the level of the imaginary. Through this concomitant double anchoring, both "real" and "mythic," the development of these fictions in movies has enabled American society to represent itself at a turning point in its history. Here these "master" fictions also take on a particular force in the sadomasochistic sense of the term: these are realist and mythic narratives that hurt America; that is, they constrain, assault, hit, and insult it. In short, they subject it to a sadomasochistic trial, which is obviously desired and desirable, adorned as it is in the most seductive attire.

The quintessential embodiment of this concept in contemporary American cinema is Catwoman, as she (re)appears in Tim Burton's 1992 *Batman Returns*. Catwoman is a submissive and bitter secretary who returns from the dead (her boss pushes her from the top of a tower, but she picks herself up from her fall, as though wrenched back from the dead by the cats who scratched and bit her) as a pussycat dressed in a shiny, black PVC bodysuit, intent on lashing back at the men who have humiliated her, cracking her whip and terrorizing the male race (fig. 96). As played by Michelle Pfeiffer, Catwoman is an openly sadistic female figure, a dominatrix who governs America's men, turns them into her slaves, brings them to heel, castrates them with her perfectly calibrated whiplashes. During nights of feline, sensual, and sadistic folly, she engages in constant combat against, and sometimes crushes, the most aggressive symbols of American virility, whether they be superheroes like Batman, sexual maniacs like the Penguin—an amphibious monster, part-man, part-penguin—or young macho-men who randomly cross her path.

96 ▶
Batman Returns (TIM BURTON, 1992). CATWOMAN, THE LEATHER-CLAD AND WHIP-CRACKING DOMINATRIX WHO INFLICTS PAIN ON AMERICA.

Catwoman is the female character that has triggered the most commentary in the American press, particularly around her two characteristic aspects, sado-masochism and feminism. Some have taken offense at the presence of such a character in a "kids'" movie—a woman covered from head to toe in skintight leather, striking lascivious poses, and taking an openly perverse pleasure in cracking her whip. Michelle Pfeiffer, indeed, embraced a kind of dominatrix feminism, which runs directly counter to the standard Hollywood depictions of submission:

> She is a feminist and a sadist, but she does not target men only. Everyone gets their fair share of whipping. Even in the television series, which I devoured as a child, Catwoman broke quite a few social and gender taboos, and titillated America's sexual imagination. I was eight years old then, and little girls were raised to be cute and polite, not to become physical and aggressive characters, who take such pleasure in being evil. Here is a woman who dresses as a black cat, and you are never quite sure whether she is seductive or malevolent. This ambiguity fascinates me.[6]

The ambiguity between seduction and evil characterizes rather well the master fiction of contemporary American cinema as a whole: indeed, it aims to seduce audiences while terrifying them, to appeal to them while assaulting them, in short, to give them a good whipping, submitting them to the dreaded trial of yearned-for suffering.

The first of these narratives analyzed in this chapter, the disaster, whose resurgence is manifest in the apocalyptic narrative as a contemporary tale of violence, best fulfills this longing for terror. The disaster film is conjugated all at once as a religious, scientific, and political narrative of America. Apocalypse is, as René Girard has pointed out, a "revelation." Through the flourishing genre of the disaster movie, America's haunting desire for violence is revealed onscreen. On the other end of the spectrum, though just as revealing, is the flurry of what American critics have called "very bad films" and "trash comedies," or what will be referred to here as "bad-taste films," that is, ironic and parodic departures from American values (family, religion, hygiene, the normative body, handicap accessibility, tolerance of racial difference, and obesity), through the celebration of explicitly vulgar countervalues: obscenity, scatology, sex, luxury, ugliness, deformity, showing-off, and so forth. The Farrelly brothers (*There's Something About Mary*) are currently the zany and bawdy masters of this special kind of disreputable comedy, which serves as an outlet for an uptight America, muzzled by political correctness. Finally, the principal master fiction to reveal a cinematographic form, dealing precisely with the crisis of the visual that saps contemporary Hollywood, follows the craggy path of a return to a more primitive form of cinema, whether gothic or peopled with the living dead, where heroes lose their technoid prestige; where bodies shift from light to darkness; where public spaces turn into dens, caves, labyrinths, margins; where monsters and killers are spawned; and where corpses, ghosts, and the living dead reemerge. It is Tim Burton's cinema that, today, develops this master fiction most lavishly. In this world the emperor has no clothes; America is pried open, unraveled, and subjected to the destructive desire of these films. Because the time of their filming is also that of the history they reveal, because they develop a cinematographic form that itself produces history, these fictions often convey a better sense of the state of America at a given moment than any clinical diagnosis.

End-of-the-World Films

Tomorrow, the world comes to an end. Only cinema still buys into this idea. Even if some still play the role of prophet of doom, they belong to the astrological-media fringe, and their credibility is near zero—perhaps because their rhetoric is not powerful enough to conjure up visual representations of what they are announcing. Such evocative power, realistic enough to persuade yet playful enough to keep the dream or nightmare at bay, only cinema can wield today, with its technological and digital animation tools and special effects for recreating and destroying the world. If cinema today forms a world of its own, it is first and foremost thanks to the spectacular aura with which it alone is endowed and to which crowds from all over the globe are drawn. Millenarian hopes and fears, turned into an end-of-the-world spectacle that is both terrifying and captivating, like a (de)construction game taken to its ultimate limits, has conquered theaters worldwide. Examples abound, and there is no question that most of the recent successes at the global (and thus American) box office are films in which the historical present is subjected to the rise of the very old menace, updated with a few contemporary technical touches, of planetary Armageddon: aliens invading as a symbol of the apocalypse (*Independence Day, Mars Attacks!, War of the Worlds*); cataclysm on a planetary scale (*Armageddon, Deep Impact, The Day After Tomorrow*); monsters produced by the hubris of Western civilization returning to devastate their creators (*Godzilla, The Lost World: Jurassic Park, King Kong*); the destructive fury of a digital world gone mad (*The Matrix* and its sequels). It is not only James Cameron, the filmmaker most representative of our age, who is obsessed with visions of the world coming to an end, whether in the present, as in *Terminator*, *Aliens*, *The Abyss*, and *Avatar*, or in the past, as in *Titanic*. These films represent many of the principal popular hits of the past few decades. This phenomenon begs investigation: why and how did it arise?

The end of the world is, of course, nothing new in cinema. Leaving aside the great biblical tales of silent days—which would bring down the walls of Sodom and Gomorrah, destroy the Temple, punish Babylon, and thus mime, for a mesmerized audience, a cardboard apocalypse—four periods and four genres of the end-of-the-world film can be isolated prior to the recent revival. Just after the nuclear detonations at Hiroshima and Nagasaki, Japanese and American teams filmed the impact of the bomb on the two cities, the surrounding countryside, and the inhabitants. The most terrifying images—shot, for the most part, by Japanese cameraman Akira Iwasaki—record, in a kind of documentary daze, the impact of the apocalyptic *pikadon* directly on the burnt and molten bodies, the enduring or emerging traces, the eyes that have seen the invisible. The American teams, which arrived a bit later, focused on the material destruction and the ongoing radiation effects. The status of these images—which the U.S. military kept secret until 1965, and then partially released and edited into a three-hour-long film, *Effects of the Atom Bomb*—is revealing as to their cinematographic role. The filming was an act of recording and testimony, with various purposes (scientific, military, historical, etc.), which sought to preserve the memory of the event as much as to measure the effects of the first atomic bombing. These images are the archive of the unprecedented in the contemporary world. They record a destruction nobody could predict and show for real, in cinematographic testimonial time, a historical time that was suddenly projected forward to its radical and terrifying aftermath.

During the 1950s, fantasy films—American and Japanese, for the most part—proliferated and formed what might be described as *crisis fictions*. As fiction these films obey certain rules, even if they push them to their limit: monsters, aliens, archetypal good guys and bad guys, coherent and recognizable narrative structures. As crises they are symptomatic of their times, though usually in a playful way: the red scares that punctuated the cold war, the Soviet nuclear tests, the Korean War, the Cuban Missile Crisis. Or, as in the *Godzilla* series (begun in 1955 by Inoshiro Honda, the creator of this very successful monster that inspired many remakes), the effects of the nuclear bombings and the sacrifice of tradition—the fantastical mark of the trauma of war, which had remained taboo, in Japanese society of the 1950s. The first category of films, American B-movies, offers an apocalyptic and futuristic bestiary of stunning diversity: *Return of the Ape Man* (Phil Rosen, 1944), *The Magnetic Monster* (Curt Siodmak, 1953), *The Beast from 20,000 Fathoms* (Eugène Lourié, 1953), *Them!* (Gordon Douglas, 1954), *It Came from Beneath the Sea* (Robert Gordon, 1955), and *Tarantula* (Jack Arnold, 1955) all feature the return or emergence of a monster born of humanity's hubristic experiments (often at the atomic level). *War of the Worlds* (Byron Haskin, 1953), *Day the World Ended* (Roger Corman, 1955), and *This Island Earth* (Joseph Newman, 1955) depict aliens coldly intent, in Soviet fashion, on cleansing the planet of humans, especially Americans. Nathan Juran's *20 Million Miles to Earth* (1957) combines both strains: its destructive monster, brought back to Earth from Venus by a team of American officers, makes every effort to exterminate any humans who come near, a forerunner of *Alien*. Godzilla, for his part, is a giant lizard from the depths of the ocean, called forth by nuclear radiation. In the Japanese films in which he appears through ingenious yet clunky animation techniques, the monster is himself a kind of nuclear explosion: he spews a beam that destroys all matter, incinerates entire buildings, and disintegrates humans. Yet in the end Godzilla is vanquished, in a victory that figuratively avenges the Japanese military failure. Indeed, Godzilla is destroyed in the ocean by a mad scientist who dies with him in an underwater explosion, thus paying cinematographic tribute to the kamikaze.

These monsters, emerging from water, desert, and ice to invade the civilized city, these extraterrestrial beings, climbing out of their saucers to do combat with the U.S. Army and its nuclear arsenal—all these figures of the cinematographic space-time continuum also exist in contemporary historical time, so much so that it is possible to say that the historical (mostly cold war) crises only updated a kind of cinema that is otherwise timeless (these monsters are not new, nor are their corresponding heroes and narrative structures). Moreover, the impact of these films derives from very recent historical events, which are projected onto fantasy fiction. B-movies for the most part, however, these films do not possess a level of realism sufficient to the violence they describe, which is essentially that of a dream or a nightmare. Spectators cannot believe in the reality of an extraterrestrial being whose fictional status is betrayed by every seam on its costume, of a monster whose claim to realism is belied by each glitch in the clunky animation techniques. But spectators may well believe in the reality of the Soviet threat and the actuality of an impending nuclear apocalypse. In these films it is thus historical time, present in everyone's mind, that allows us to see what cinematographic time conveys, through its conventional sets, and what lurks behind its stock heroes and characters.

From the mid-1960s onward, end-of-the-world films dealt with disasters under the pressure of, on the one hand, an ideology (now more on the left than on the right) that took a critical view of the arms race and, on the other hand, experiments in modern cinema with editing and live footage. In 1964 Stanley Kubrick's *Dr. Strangelove* inaugurated this cinematographic period in a satirical farce about American nuclear paranoia that does a ridiculous dance around the mushroom cloud of nuclear explosion—the darkest and most sarcastic vision ever produced of the end of the world. Peter Watkins also worked on this kind of paranoia, in *The War Game* (1965), picturing the effects of a nuclear bombing as the transformation of the British political system into a military dictatorship. The realist quality of the visual effects is that of "cinema direct," in 1960s militant style, as Watkins films live reportage of a "reconstruction" of the explosion, the destruction and the police and military law-and-order operations on a panic-stricken population gone mad. These films may be defined as disaster films: films of "after the bomb," after historical events, after both Auschwitz and Hiroshima, but in which these disasters are projected into a near future (the time frame of these films is the present, or the immediate future, in quasi-documentary style) of Western society. It is the time that follows the end-of-the-world fiction. The hyperrealist quality of the visual effects concerns this posterity. The "during-the-bombing" moment, for the most part, still escapes visual representation and is only made present through its effects. It is in the "after-the-bombing" time frame that the narrative and temporal construction of the disaster occurs. The disaster itself is only seen through both the "after" and the "before," combined together through editing techniques that are specific to cinema and in which the before is mirrored in the after, and vice versa.

As early as 1959, Alain Resnais' *Hiroshima mon amour*, and then in 1962 Chris Marker's *La Jetée*, had offered this kind of fiction of cinematographic and historical time knotted together by a fear of the apocalypse. What can be seen in the protagonists' eyes (the Japanese man in *Hiroshima mon amour*, and the woman, shaved bald after the war, or the woman in *La Jetée*, whose gaze suddenly freezes in terror at what she sees and we cannot) is disaster, but this can only be understood via a visual and mental projection into the future time of after the event. It is through such a projection in time that we understand that the woman's eyes in *La Jetée* reflect the hero's death and that the lines in *Hiroshima mon amour*—"you are killing me, you are doing me good"—are a way of atoning for or curing through love the two originary disasters at the foundation of the modern world, an essentially melancholy and historical civilization "after" extermination and bombing. Cinematographic time, through editing and live footage, manages to render, in either the form of an essay or a militant act, the rupture at the heart of contemporary history, which is profoundly traumatized, however subconsciously, by its origins.

The year 1972 marked the beginning of the modern era in disaster films and cinematographic apocalypse, with the considerable success of *The Poseidon Adventure*, giving a badly needed boost to a movie industry in critical condition and revealing audience desire for crisis cinema. A wave of disaster films ensued, piling up fires, shipwrecks, crashes, earthquakes, eruptions, and pandemics of all kinds. The narrative architecture of these feature films, as well as their spectacular rendering, enhanced by advances in special effects and reconstructions, highlighted the public demand for apocalyptic fiction, as well as the collective desire for its resolution. American disaster films are direct master fictions of crisis, taking over, in a different genre, from the fantasy films of the 1950s: master fictions for thinking crisis.

How did cinema produce specific images—dealing with serious political issues, at precise historical moments—designed to support, as a kind of symbolic prosthesis, the collective sensibility, either by dramatizing prevailing preoccupations or, on the contrary, by making light of the conjuncture? When a civilizational order begins to give, to crack, threatening collapse, disaster movies surface as a revelatory sign, among others, of the ambient anxiety. These productions generally feature some sort of cataclysm that brutally befalls the community, disrupting its harmonious existence. A tragedy is offered up as a fear object, which allows the audience to localize, to circumscribe, and to focus their anxiety, which is in fact linked to a real state of distress, to some actual traumatic crisis. It is a strange form of catharsis, which grants, through the phobic enjoyment of apocalypse, an intense and perverse satisfaction. At a time when American society was experiencing tensions in three of its traditional pillars—the army, defeated in Vietnam; the presidency, discredited by the Watergate scandal; and the dollar, destabilized by the oil crisis—spectators flocked to disaster fictions, which mimed and metaphorized this social bankruptcy, while also offering a narrative in which the sense of responsibility, guilt, and fear, while certainly present, is nonetheless redeemed by the sacrificial deaths of droves of extras and a few heroes, and in the end sublimated by the final victory of the forces of good, which always prevail. The cinematographic time continuum here is that of myth, which offers an allegorical reading of the crisis affecting the historical present, while warding off current fears through the eternal return of the structural and archetypal conventions of mythical narratives.

The same kind of apocalypse is deployed, with a certain gratification, in current cinema. Today's end-of-the-world movies offer a kind of synthesis of their predecessors, through the four periods of cinema history outlined above. In the first place they are often remakes or reprises of earlier films. Most of the fantasy and disaster movies of the 1950s–1970s period have become, over the course of repeated viewings, classics of American cinephilia. This is probably one of the keys to understanding what can be called the crisis of onscreen violence in contemporary Hollywood films. As this cinephilic recycling would suggest, Hollywood has nothing new to offer. Mimicry, imitation, and citation constitute the theoretical mode—at once cognitive, narrative, and fetishistic—of the present times. Within this immense circle, graphic violence has lost some of its original edge. As Walter Benjamin said about the image in the age of its mechanical reproducibility, what it lost as soon as it entered that new era was its aura, the emotional and affective power of the unique. Similarly, images can be said to have lost some of the force of their violence through a process of reproduction, which has now become almost immediate and infinite, by the proliferation of contemporary visual modes. Representations of violence tend to increase because of this process of imitation: images are reproduced, constantly ratcheting up the level of violence, since the violence of the original representation quickly loses much of its force. Like overused words, overprojected images, however charged, become meaningless. This is television's big problem, for instance: its words and images quickly wear out.

Over the past twenty years many American directors, often nourished by a certain kind of cinephilia, have shown interest in updating the apocalyptic myth: Tim Burton, in *Mars Attacks!*; Joe Dante, in *Matinee* and *Gremlins*; Steven Spielberg in *Jurassic Park* and *War of the Worlds*; Roland Emmerich in *Godzilla* and *Independence Day*; James Cameron in *Piranha*, *The Abyss*, and *Titanic*. All these films have appropriated the world of exterminating monsters, colonizing extraterrestrial beings, famous shipwrecks, and spectacular disasters from older films, and they have done so within a genre that is now particularly active and innovative: science fiction action films. These contemporary films develop a rich, complex, and subtle interplay between cinematographic and historical time. The only historical element that seems to have vanished from these films—or that is only residually present as a historical wink—is precisely the one that (in *Dr. Strangelove* or in other global nuclear threat films) used to give these American epics a contemporary feel: the cold war and the nuclear arms race with the Soviet Union. These films offer a radically different kind of encounter between cinematographic time and the historical time of myths, cycles, or chronicles of events. Indeed, disaster films can now play on several conceptions of historical time in order to conjure up the end of the world in the here and now, offering a reality in images of widely anticipated future ecological disaster.

The most striking characteristic of this cinema is the appropriation, in its representation of disaster, of the raw time of the primary document. The chronicling of destruction is made hyperrealistic by the power of new technologies to reconstruct and deconstruct. It has, so to speak, become possible, thanks to special effects, to film the end of the world. The filming of apocalyptic scenes is meticulously choreographed by a ballet of digital effects, virtualized by postproduction techniques that add essential realistic touches, and managed by a production system that deploys technology and human power on a quasi-military scale and level of efficiency. In 1945 Iwasaki recorded, with a single camera, the end-of-the-world set that was Hiroshima after the bomb. Today, to obtain such a result, a whole raft of special effects and a vast production system are required—the entire power of cinema is invested in the violent destruction of a set. This gives it a realistic power. The collapse of New York in *Independence Day*, *Armageddon*, *Godzilla*, and *War of the Worlds* is unquestionably spectacular. But the spectacle is that of documentary illusion, in the mode of historical time, as if the aliens and monsters of 1950s cinema, quintessentially fictional figures, could, through special effects, come to life in a realistic world. The challenge looms as a test and a trial for contemporary American cinema: can it recreate the apocalypse? And, like the circus acts of yesteryear, it is this test that draws crowds into darkened halls. But we all know that fiction and illusion, here, are as excessive as the project itself is unreasonable. For these films seem to have incorporated within them the punishment for the hubris of attaining in representation the power of a creative and destructive God.

In this sense these fictions belong to a cyclical temporality of primal origins. It is, after all, the origin of the world that is represented here, in the heralding of its destruction—what can be built can be destroyed. Not only does cinema offer itself as a set, but it incorporates the core fiction of this apocalyptic return of (and to) origins: punishment for the world's hubristic attempts to escape the eternal cycle. This is a return to the very foundations of American civilization: a literal reading of the Bible, political Puritanism, which, in these films, smites American society for its technological, sexual, and moral transgression, for its sinful pride. The world has lost touch with its origins, and disaster strikes in order to recall civilization to a greater sense of humility before God, nature, and man. All recent disaster films—including *Armageddon*, *Deep Impact*, and Roland Emmerich's *The Day After Tomorrow* (2004), in which havoc is often wreaked on a global scale—share this feature: a society that has pursued technological progress too far is brutally brought back to its beginnings through a disaster, which acts as a purge and a cyclical return to core values (heroism, sacrifice, love, respect for hard work, and social harmony). The cinematographic time itself plays on this register of historical cycle, not only through ubiquitous images of circles, certain camera movements, sets, and editing but also through the use of heroes directly inspired by the early years of the American nation. Halfway between founding fathers and Puritan ministers, these heroes are charged with saving the earth (America) from destruction (they inevitably succeed) but also with leading it to a new respect for its forgotten origins (an arduous task, and it remains uncertain whether they manage it).

The most interesting disaster film of the late twentieth century, James Cameron's worldwide box-office hit, *Titanic*, plays constantly on this peculiar relationship between cinematographic and historical time. The film gave rise to almost messianic expectations: to see, in the most famous shipwreck in history, both a human disaster (the end of the world in flesh and blood) and a mechanized disaster (a technical calamity). Yet it is not the world of today that sinks to the bottom of the ocean but the former one: the European nineteenth century. The fictional power of the film consists in proclaiming that this disaster was nonetheless creative. For what is at stake in this shipwreck is the palingenetic cycle of rebirth from destruction. The New World is born from this sacrificial disaster: Rose, the central female character, is reborn American from the sacrifice of her American lover, himself steeped in everything that was modern in the Old World (painting) and the New (democratic aspirations). Cameron stages here modernity's infatuation with its apocalyptic origins: it is today's technology that enables the film to become a fiction, summoning up Rose's narrative, as a survivor turned embodiment of the century (her photos capture this role: they designate her as cinema's contemporary, as a modern representation, the technical feat of aviation, and feminism as a form of political emancipation). What the public wants is as much this narrative construction (the long sentimental flashback) as the recreation of the primal disaster of the modern world. *Titanic* offers a vision of the end of the world that is also a vision of its origins.

To the temporality of the documentary chronicle and the cyclical temporality of the return to origins, a third narrative and visual modality is sometimes substituted, that of mythical time: the past, with its titanic and biblical monsters, symbols of the scourges that befell modern Babylon; the future, with its extraterrestrial creatures, shattering the earth with demonic superiority, or else invading and colonizing it. In classical myth the shift from oral narrative to visual representation prompted the use of masks as symbolic mediators. In disaster films such a function is performed by special effects, which indeed serve to animate monsters. Special effects—because they give a realistic aspect to the extraordinary, to the apocalypse—enable the catharsis to operate and effect a fusion of cinematographic time and the specific mode of historical time that is myth. Thus, when cinema encounters and recounts mythical history through special effects, the spectator is made to feel the reality of his awe (faced with Godzilla, or *Independence Day*'s Martians, to the three-foot organic machine in *War of the Worlds*), while simultaneously naming it as extraordinary fiction. The special effects produce the sensation of "what if it happened for real?" and hence the question "what would I do?" But it enables this to happen through the cinematographic guarantee it provides that "it is all an illusion" in the end. The spectator thus sees his or her life and death inscribed in the film, through the verisimilitude of fiction, while remaining at a playful distance. And today, at this level of spectacle, only cinema can achieve this. To visualize disaster—this is a challenge that only cinema is in a position to meet. It feeds messianic expectations and anxieties, which are no longer real and have become pure fads—like an end-of-the-world game on a vast scale. This master fiction builds on maximum identification on the part of the spectator and, at the same time, on the thrill such identification provides. The destruction of New York City, taken as the emblem of the modern city, is a giant construction/deconstruction video game. It used to be the discovery of relics of the megalopolis that signaled the end of the world (*Planet of the Apes* and *Escape from New York* contain the paradigmatic images); now, this trial entails the actual destruction of the modern city.

This cinema surely fails to inspire the kind of true terror and awe that the Japanese cameraman Iwasaki, in Hiroshima, and the French directors Resnais and Marker, reflecting on the effects of the bomb, were able to convey, through the simplicity of raw footage and the complexity of modern cinema. And this filmmaking has become, for the most part, virtual. Godzilla has never set foot in New York, nor even has a scale-model of him rampaged through a miniature city. This was the animation technique used in the Japanese films of the 1950s. Its inadequacy blunted the violence of the images, but at least something was recorded in the world, even if only a doll-sized world, a puppet world, an animated world. Now, actors stare at nothing and scream their terror into a void: the monster will be generated later using a graphics tablet and computer-generated animation. This virtual reality certainly makes possible a more "realistic" feel (actors' screams, explosions, cities ablaze) and the seamless insertion of the monster into the film, but it defeats all representation of the film "for real." This phenomenon is akin to, and further reinforces, the process of image reproducibility. Proliferating reproducibility and technical virtuality have both contributed to an increase of violence in images, while denying the violence of the image.

The opening credits of *Armageddon*, an archetype of the American apocalypse blockbuster, offers a model for this kind of disaster cinema turned playful virtual spectacle. The sequence is unquestionably violent, inflicting the maximum violence possible on our civilization: its utter destruction. It is also about visual spectacle—cinema in its drive to offer a visual narrative of the ultimate disaster. In eleven minutes, not one minute more, the world falls apart, a level of destruction that is truly frightening if one *really* looks at it: tens of thousands killed, New York City half destroyed by a meteor shower, the most advanced technology in ruins (the Atlantis shuttle), and the end of the world announced for eighteen days hence. The images are replete with violence of all kinds. Yet the effect has already worn thin: next time films of this kind will have to annihilate the planet in half the time, with twice as many explosions, and ten times as many casualties. And not only because this long credit sequence features a whole range of ironic and distancing elements (characters, references, humorous anecdotes), which serve to keep the reality of violence at bay, to contain and disperse it, and ultimately to make the film watchable. The film's impact is also consistently blunted by the culture, history, aesthetics, and multiple mediations with which it must contend. Society has become increasingly secularized, and the dread inspired by an avenging God has largely receded; society has become virtualized, and the concrete fear of disaster or nuclear conflict has become a simulation game in which the spectacular has replaced the real; society has become regulated, and the vectors of violence at the global scale (war, the nuclear arms race, ecological disaster, natural cataclysm) are now better controlled and contained by mechanisms of global governance and environmental norms. Films are forced to take these historical developments into account, even while brutalizing them with an extreme violence enabled by the capacity for digitally synthesized realism and the expectations of an audience in search of strong emotions. This end-of-the-world cinema is, indeed, secular, virtual, and normalized: God no longer hovers over its images; the shooting no longer constitutes its ultimate test, and its conventions are ubiquitous. The end of the world has become a pure cinematographic code, detached from any historical reality, as if cinema decided it could do without history, master it and replace it as it pleased.

But cinema should beware of history's revenge—not only is the world now threatened by a multitude of small-scale apocalypses, as a result of the proliferation of mininuclear powers, but its final destruction has become a realistic hypothesis in the eyes of many scientists, alarmed by the global overdevelopment that continues on, despite all warnings, plundering both human and natural resources. Furthermore, history, which appeared so remote from cinema's concerns, or at least so cut off from its challenges and technical capabilities, seems to have suddenly resumed its hold over it, and in the most violent way, precisely through disaster. Indeed, the Al-Qaeda terrorists who conceived and carried to their apocalyptic end the attacks of September 11, 2001, on the World Trade Center seem to have been inspired by disaster films; and the images, broadcast on endless loop, of the planes crashing and the towers collapsing look as though they could have been staged, or more precisely arranged, by one of the orchestrators of Hollywood mass destruction—even to such a degree that America appeared to have been trapped in one of its master fictions that openly and massively mesmerize the public. This surely accounts, at least in part, for the profound symbolic impact that the images of September 11 had on the American, and the Western, and even the global, imagination. Even though not a single corpse, of the three thousand mourned by New Yorkers on that day, was shown, these images struck everyone as a colossal crime because they had already been seen in fictions, incorporated as technically plausible in cinema, playfully modeled in video games and on hard drives, and were suddenly resurfacing through history's *veduta*—with a force that all of *Armageddon*'s meteors could never rival.

"Very Bad Films": Inside the Laboratory of Bad-Taste Films

The origin of cinematic spectacle is the morgue. In the late nineteenth century crowds would come to attend "cadaver scenes." They came to look into the faces of death, to observe the traces of violence, to see the imprint left by life on these bodies. Macabre displays were even specially provided for the reconstruction of recent "cases"—crimes, accidents, mysteries—reenacted by the very protagonists themselves, though now as corpses.[7] This morbid curiosity attests to an early desire for cinema, a curiosity moved, as is cinema, by a passion for spectacles that mimic, for real, banal bodily impulses. The spectacle of death was not the only one to be subsequently appropriated by onscreen bodies. Spectacles of love, fear, laughter, and movement were quickly added to the list to such an extent, in fact, that sex films, monster films, bodybuilding films, sports films, and burlesque films became the first true cinema genres. The simple spectacle of bodily impulses, shown frontally and directly, was enough to fill the screen and the theater with the many enthusiasts of the morgue, circus, freak show, stadium, brothel, and gym.

Cinema and those who nurture it have worked tirelessly ever since at not so much eradicating but rather channeling these vulgar body impulses. The history of cinema is one of gradual and steady cultural ennoblement of primitive bodily impulses—not by denying them, since they were the very energy and origins of cinema, but by organizing them and assigning them a recognizable field: films designated "peculiar." Hence pornography, nudist films, documentary films, sports films, B-movies, and the like were charged with channeling bodily impulses, while the majority of films idealized and beautified onscreen bodies. These urges were sublimated by the cinematographic art in its most godlike aspect: the filmmaker's style, perspective, and mise-en-scène. The primal bodily impulses—of death, sex, fright, combat, and laughter—were thus still acceptable onscreen but only when properly presented: either as belonging to a particular genre or as part of a filmmaker's vision. Monsters, corpses, and sex were acceptable but only as incorporated into specified genres or else stylized by Bunuel, Fellini, Hitchcock, and Bergman. Cinephilia, more than anything, was particularly keen on reconnecting with these bodily impulses that had been banned from mainstream cinema, hence its passion for all genres of excess and for films that present the vulgar surplus of bodies.

Where are they to be found today, these bodily impulses that give cinema its original power and provide it with a source of perpetual renewal? They are still there, in the margins of cinema. There remains a prolific industry of horror and pornographic films, for the big screen as well as, increasingly, video and the Internet—the bulimic belly of private consumption of primal instincts. Filmmakers, for their part, have appropriated these banal impulses to an even greater extent, so much so that we no longer speak of filmmakers smuggling mise-en-scène into genre films but rather, and more straightforwardly, of genres that adapt to auteurs—a sign of the definitive victory of the auteur model. The recognition of cinema as an art, the intense praise of mise-en-scène and style, triumphed with the obliteration of the classic distinctions between genres, and especially of the tight separation between high cinema and genre film, between mainstream and marginal, between good taste and bad. From then on, all bodily impulses, however primal, were liable to stray into any film, provided they obeyed the auteur's direction.

There is another "type" of film that also plays on the power of primal bodily impulses and which, from this standpoint, proves to be a fascinating laboratory, if viewed seriously, that is, considered literally, forgetting any value judgment on its degree of "auteurism" as well as any consideration for the hierarchies that serve to legitimize and delegitimize genres. Since the early 1990s, it has yielded films such as *Death Becomes Her* (Robert Zemeckis), *Groundhog Day* (Harold Ramis), *The Long Kiss Goodnight* (Renny Harlin), and *Very Bad Things* (Peter Berg), but the most famous examples are to be found with the vulgar and trashy series *American Pie*, the grotesque horror film parody series *Scary Movie*, and the cult classics by brothers Peter and Bobby Farrelly (*There's Something About Mary*; *Me, Myself, and Irene*; and *Shallow Hal*). All these films have one point in common, perhaps only one: they all violently satirize the American way of life, and they satirize it through bodies (their regression, explosion, multiplication, metamorphosis, decomposition, and capitulation). In their subject, as well as their object, they may be called bad-taste films, or "very bad films" (VBFs), in the coded language of American teenagers.[8] Ugliness, obscenity, vulgarity, scatology, morbidity, the pathetic, and the grotesque constitute their backdrop, in front of which bodies convulse like shabby puppets mimicking and mocking the obsessions of upright, proper, and self-righteous America. These bad-taste films have replaced the auteurist and cinephilic consciousness of prestige films with an iconoclastic use of signs of the present times, to the exclusion of all other temporal references, feverishly satirizing our world through overdoses of today, excesses of the current moment. These films are undoubtedly regressive but through an excess of contemporary bodies and norms, not through an explicit return to the primitive. In the cycle of cinematographic time they attain the highest bodily impulses through degeneracy and regression rather than melancholic flashbacks that consciously drive filmmakers to recover a more primitive age. These humorous, trivial, scatological, morbid, and obscene films may be said to be wholly postcinematic, while most directors in the world yearn, for their part, to reconnect with the precinema, even if it entails entirely recreating it, with all the necessary means.

The movement from genre films to auteur films to bad-taste films marks more than just a change in attitudes. The power of this last category, indeed its defining feature, consists in negating the axiomatic rules that govern the other two, even if their aim remains the same: to depict primal bodily impulses onscreen. For bad taste rejects genre as well as mise-en-scène. While all spectators know what to expect when they go to a genre film, which openly trades in certain kinds of bodies, bad-taste films strive to take their audience by surprise. They proceed stealthily, embarrass or amuse in unexpected ways, and "deceive," sometimes as a way to tap into mainstream audiences. See, for example, the poster for the biggest hit of the bad-taste films, the Farrelly brothers' *There's Something About Mary*: it works only insofar as it conceals the film's bodily deviance. Who would suspect *There's Something About Mary* of offering a form of radical sexual regression, when the poster simply features the former model Cameron Diaz as a sweet magazine cover girl? The same applies for the poster of Peter Berg's *Very Bad Things* (1998), also starring Cameron Diaz, which is another illustration of the "trash comedy" genre. That poster tells an even bolder lie: it features the actress as a fresh-faced young bride, while the still shot in fact captures her at the very moment when, in the film, she is shouting extremely vulgar insults to her "girlfriends," after which she proceeds to wipe the sweat from her underarms with the proverbial bridal bouquet and smash a man's face in with a lamppost. Meanwhile, the five other pleasant faces displayed on the poster are taken from one of the most horrific scenes in the film, in which these five white guys are pressing a door shut on a dying black man whom they have murdered. Thus misrepresented in the posters as to their nature and intention, these films escape genre categorization in order to position themselves elsewhere. They look their spectators in the eyes, in the present, and—through effects of surprise, enjoyment, and shock—take apart their daily lives: social behaviors, normative rituals, television framing and popular press narratives. These films, put before their audiences in this manner, cause everything that these audiences bring with them—their daily lives, their fictional world, their common imagination—to implode, through the use of the grotesque, the morbid, and the obscene. These bad-taste films, deploying the element of surprise, thrive on the lived experience of their spectators and riff on it constantly. And it is this immediacy and this game that they both enjoy.

The most famous gag in *There's Something About Mary* serves as an emblematic illustration of this kind of enjoyment of the present: a man looking for his own sperm, a situation that perfectly conveys the orgasmic, regressive, and deeply disturbing character of this Farrelly brothers' comedy. The character, played by Ben Stiller, has just been masturbating in the bathroom, his eyes fixed on the page of a girlie magazine he has hastily torn out, and then crumples up as his arduous labor is coming to an end. But where has the issue of his pleasure gone? He checks every corner of the bathroom, pats himself down—nothing on his clothes, nothing on his hands. He checks the wall opposite, and even the ceiling. Nothing. The doorbell rings: the girl of his dreams, Mary, has arrived to pick him up for dinner. He opens the door. "What's that on your ear? It looks like a gob of . . . hair gel. Great! I ran out." She scoops up the sticky secretion with a brisk swipe of the hand and just as swiftly rubs it into her hair. And voila! Cameron Diaz with the most radical hairdo of the day—a sperm-styled pompadour, a degenerate Tin Tin (fig. 97).

Of what use would mise-en-scène be here? This kind of film can only disdain it as useless, as an excess of artiness, aesthetics, and culture. The efficacy of the bad-taste film lies elsewhere: in the direct connection between the bodies onscreen and the spectators in the theater, which lies at the core of this cinema, and in relation to which the overly visible mediation offered by an auteur's style can only seem frivolous and unbearable. Of course, in some sense these bad-taste films are auteur works. Harold Ramis, Peter Berg, and the Farrelly brothers all make films from scripts they write themselves, in which a very special world is conjured up through narratives about the fortunes and misfortunes of these bodily impulses. Yet mise-en-scène is in their view a game to be strictly proscribed—indeed, it is the taboo of their ignoble art. These films obey the dictates of the spectator's gaze, not the filmmaker's, and they do not seek to convey a formal organization of time and space. Indeed, the main idea is precisely to disorganize everything, to implode everything, and to show as directly as possible bodies that are alive, bounding, and rebounding. To assess these films on the basis of a single criterion of mise-en-scène is, thus, a sure way to miss their point entirely. For their reference is not cinema, its stories and bodies, but "people's lives"—that is, television and tabloids. These films read like revisited reality shows: *Big Brother* reworked by an excess of bodily instincts. Not necessarily intellectualized, better written, better acted, or better shot but rather dismembered, taken to pieces, undone, and decomposed by the force of the grotesque and the literal presence of bodies.

97 ▶
There's Something About Mary
(BOBBY AND PETER FARRELLY, 1998). WHERE HAS THE ISSUE OF HIS PLEASURE GONE? IT IS HANGING FROM THE EAR OF THE ABSENT-MINDED GUY (BEN STILLER) AND SERVES AS HAIR GEL TO STYLE THE HAIR OF THE INNOCENT GAL (CAMERON DIAZ).

Peter and Bobby Farrelly invented the bad-taste genre with *There's Something About Mary*. Just as eighteenth-century French boudoirs always featured "books for one-handed reading,"⁹ the Farrelly brothers—in a style that is both glib and deviant, both connoisseur and voyeur—appear to have made a "one-handed" film, staking out for itself a special place within American cinema and, indeed, a place in the sun, since *There's Something About Mary* was one of the biggest surprise worldwide box-office hits of the past few years. It is as if exposing to the full light of day everything that the American cinema industry is supposed to have purged itself of—sex, decay, bodily secretions of all kinds, sadism toward the weak and handicapped, political incorrectness (fig. 98), social satire, and provocative and iconoclastic positions—had enabled the collective release of an audience corseted in the fictional and formal rules of polite cinema. The Farrelly brothers' film became the vehicle for a carnivalesque eruption from spectators who have come together in a darkened room to foment a plot against the conventional film fare they are normally served, which is polished, ordered, and kept on a close leash. Thus, the film does not belong to anyone in contemporary American cinema: it is the product principally of its audience's release, if also a bit of the perverse imagination of its creators.

What it features is generalized regression. The Farrelly brothers have produced a film that, to draw bold comparisons, would rank with such major comedies about regressing to childhood as Howard Hawks's *Monkey Business*, Jerry Lewis's *The Nutty Professor*, and Blake Edwards's *S.O.B. There's Something About Mary* also qualifies as the vulgar consummation of the openly grotesque and flatulent *Jack*, which Francis Ford Coppola failed to pull off in 1995. The Farrelly brothers have succeeded, where the older filmmaker failed, in that they saw their conceit through to the end, both narratively and aesthetically, formally and subversively. The story of *There's Something About Mary* is that of a return to childhood, or at least to awkward adolescence, as well as a return to a just as awkward era. Indeed, the Farrelly brothers film the 1970s as the "adolescence" of the present and, conversely, '70s teenagers as "primitive" versions of the degenerate heroes they become fifteen years later. High school campuses—the colors, mannerisms, arguments, clothing styles, hairstyles, faces, braces, seduction, and appropriation rituals—appear as the prehistoric cave of American society, a cave in which males are constantly strutting and parading about, engaging in multiple combat to seduce the principal female. They are so agitated that they hurt themselves, abuse themselves, mutilate themselves, and put their poor unfinished bodies through

98 ▶
There's Something About Mary
(BOBBY AND PETER FARRELLY, 1998). THE FARRELLY BROTHERS EXPLODE THE SIGNS OF AMERICAN NORMALITY BY OVEREXPOSING THEM: HERE, SOCIAL HARMONY PUSHED TO A BURLESQUE CARICATURE.

exquisite forms of torture. The two filmmakers torment these bodies with a sadistic virtuosity matched only by the level of uncontrollable laughter with which the spectator is seized as he or she is made to witness the incredible series of misfortunes that befall the characters. Their laughter is a kind of Bakhtinian "anxious laughter,"[10] which is pushed even further: an anguished hilarity. It is triggered by Ben Stiller's penis painfully stuck in his fly, by the corpse that, according to a burlesque and morbid logic, occupies the "death seat" in the car, by the dog that greedily French kisses women and ends up in a full-body cast following a fit of drug-induced madness and autodefenestration. The film, thus, confronts each spectator with the grotesque trial of his or her own laughter—primal regression, a barbaric frenzy.

If the primal is what stands at the beginning of this burlesque evolutionary chain of males and females, its end point is no less trying (even if it is always depicted in the style of an amusing test): degeneration. Each character is indeed endowed in the film with its own degenerate mask, which gradually imprints on the face as the film unfolds. *There's Something About Mary* imposes its narrative as a sometimes incoherent, broken, elliptical, and dilapidated story of recovery. Indeed, the film comes to an end as everyone finds his or her revealing mask, which shows onscreen the promised degeneration. Tracking the geographical movement of the film—from the primal scene of America (WASP New England) to Florida, the ideal location for a sunny, residential decomposition—the characters carry on their bodies marks of their gradual decay. Woogie, the psychotic suitor, scratches his face more and more frenetically and yet continues to deny the obvious—his face is a bubonic and purulent eruption—until he finally squeezes out everything that has been growing on it to declare his love to Mary. He speaks of love and literally empties the abscess of pus. As for Matt Dillon, he revels in playing the Hollywood romantic lead gone awry—the vain beefcake trying to maintain his sexy looks, the flirtatious cad with a lewd smile on his face, the young athlete developing a bit of a beer belly, the ideal son-in-law turned perfect loser, flaunting a trim mustache that betrays simultaneously both his instinct to please and his utter spinelessness. And even Cameron Diaz, the perky young blond everyone wants, reveals the mark of degeneration on her body. Her body is indeed split in two: it represents the contemporary model ideal, of course, the international star of the day, but her face as well as her looks also seem to take on the most grotesque expressions and positions. A magnificent conceptual object, this body carries in its Barbie-Doll perfection and magazine cover-girl face, the countersign of its own decadence: most of the time, it walks precariously balanced on slender legs, at the edge of the precipice, when, with lightning speed, while uttering the crudest expressions and onomatopoeia, the whole face appears to fold up along the line of its immense mouth—an exposed scar, a gaping sex, a grotesque crack, which collapses Cameron Diaz into an obscene Muppet Show marionette.

To say that the Farrelly brothers feel perfectly at ease among this motley crew of primal beings and grotesque masks is a euphemism. They sketch out a portrait of forbidden and taboo America, a land that is decomposing through laughter, a society stripped of its values and bodily standards, in a direct line with what Frank Tashlin had attempted in his day, building on Jane Mansfield's explosive looks and Jerry Lewis's apelike expressions. Only the Farrelly brothers also put classic cinema (and mise-en-scène) through the same test of corrosive laughter. And this time it does not emerge unscathed, thus setting them apart from their glorious elders. Howard Hawks, Frank Tashlin, and Blake Edwards were still operating within the world of cinema; they were stylish enough to preserve its movement, perspectives, lines, and compositions, even if they roughed up their actors and story lines a bit. They were even "great" directors, orchestrating mise-en-scène with eyes wide open. The Farrellys have shut their eyes and adopted their characters' perspectives—not out of condescension but out of a kind of immediate identification, out of a schoolboy understanding for the people they film, the actors who play them, and the spectators who watch them (the end credits take the form of a home movie). They thus present each and every spectator with a strange and hilarious cinematic object, the first smash hit of the trash comedy genre.

At around the same moment a film that may be seen as the culmination of the genre was released, though to a much more limited audience: Peter Berg's *Very Bad Things*, released in 1998, is a genuinely brilliant film, which is haunted not by style but by bodies. What appears, at first, to be a light and bawdy comedy about two groups of friends—one male, the other female, celebrating a bachelor and bachelorette party, respectively—quickly and steadily degenerates into a spectacle of corpses. Through the glazed eyes of death the film sees only its own decomposition, spectators their own enjoyment in the face of the other's death, and their own fright when suddenly confronted with their own. This constant visual exposure makes the film and the spectator increasingly nervous and culminates in the final fit of madness, which is both destructive and hilarious. *Very Bad Things* is founded on the logic, the pleasure, and the industry of killing games. What happens if, through a deregulation of the senses and of the rules, dead bodies keep piling up and, perversely, each of these bodies insists on imprinting itself on the film for as long as possible? What quickly happens, when confronted with such morbid impulses, is that the film goes mad and implodes all aesthetic rules and all social conventions that might have kept it under control. In the name of this uncontrollable logic the characters end up killing each other off, cutting each other to pieces, and recomposing according to the funeral rites and impulses specific to each civilization (the Christian and Jewish traditions regarding the burial and handling of mortal remains are constantly contrasted). The cadaveric form takes over in the end: the minds, which only think in terms of extermination and elimination (how the industrial method used in the Nazi final solution reoriented a film that started as a prankster comedy toward death), as well as the mise-en-scène, which literally disintegrates, degenerates, and putrefies into a frenetic rhythm that bangs corpses together in a pathetic macabre dance.

The film's last shots reveal that the negative impulses at work in bad-taste fictions have slowly but surely contaminated everything, corrupted all. All have contributed their share—one has lost a leg, another his mind, and yet another his life. There is no room left in this mad world for the normality that was present in such excess at the film's beginning, indeed with cloying self-righteousness and common vulgarity. It is at that moment, when the cadaveric form has taken over everything, that Cameron Diaz goes mad. A disjointed puppet, an enormous howling mouth, she strolls about within her own insanity through an America that no longer recognizes her. The pretty doll, presented as perverse from the outset, has transformed into a primal object. Her body escapes her, and she is going to smash it against the screen, this poor little thing that bespeaks the poor state of the world—that is, the fact that in the master fictions of bad taste we work hard at losing cinema in order to lose ourselves.

Tim Burton, America's Primitive

In this survey of the master fictions of Hollywood cinema and what they reveal about contemporary America, one filmmaker stands out, one who has already been mentioned several times, since he straddles them all: Tim Burton, director of *Edward Scissorhands*, the first two Batman films, *Ed Wood*, the disaster film parody *Mars Attacks!*, the gothic *Sleepy Hollow*, and the Roald Dahl adaptation *Charlie and the Chocolate Factory*. At fifty years old he is probably the American director of the post–New Hollywood period who is most famous around the globe and the most appreciated among cinephiles: an auteur who, whatever genre he happens to be revisiting, always walks the narrow path between the expectations of the Hollywood studios with whom he insists on working and his own visions and obsessions, born of his singular and irreducible universe. It is a world whose principal obsessions are worth noting in that they represent, to a considerable extent, the master fictions of contemporary America.

Burton often takes the traditional access route to the primitive world: the fairy tale. Indeed, the tale, that childhood disease of narrative, haunts his fictional world. *Edward Scissorhands*, like many films of the creator of *Frankenweenie* and *Big Fish*, obeys the narrative conventions and manners of the ghost story. When Edward, an unfinished being whose hands have been replaced by knives and scissors, is found and adopted by a middle-class family who lives in a pretty yellow house, Burton's film turns into a modern tale that grafts the disquieting gothic world onto the "American way of life." The film then provides an opportunity to raise an essential question: how does a body that has been scarred by traces of death, that has been literally reconstituted from parts of dead bodies, recount its very contemporary story? Answer: not in a strict past, as would a literal adaptation of the Frankenstein myth, but through the contamination of the present by the past, of the seemly (Peggy, the woman who adopts Edward, is a cosmetics sales representative) by the unseemly, of the clean by the filthy. For this body bears several morbid traces, as well as a sickly form of narrative: the ancient tale revisited through the violence of contemporary society.

In this sense young American directors rely more on the narrative elasticity of the fairy tale—its fragments, its glitter, its loops, and its shortcuts—than on the narrative line of the classic tale, to capture an audience they know to be more sensitive to the mood swings and zigzags of video games than to the accumulation of knowledge of the written culture and novels of the Anglo-American tradition. As Tim Burton himself lucidly explained:

> America does not have a great sense of culture, of history. The way I grew up was quite close to that of my hero, Edward Scissorhands. It was very shallow, without much emotion, or much passion, and almost entirely devoid of significant events, or words to talk about them. I thus developed other means to express what could not be expressed, such as fairy tales, comic books, and animated films. These are strange forces that attempt to represent the abstractions of life. Often they are rather violent, or at least they do not follow from the logic of things that are taught at school. Thus, if you ask an adult what a fairy tale is, he will say it is a story for children. But if you have him read the tale, if you draw its characters for him, he will be horrified by its content and visuals. In addition, the fairy tale is not a story, but a mental representation in which teenagers project themselves in order to experience something else. . . . What I like in tales, is something very simple, direct and emotional, which also works on the scale of reality and daily life.[11]

Edward Scissorhands, Burton's creature, is that simple and emotional being out of a fairy tale that "fictionalizes" by grafting itself onto the real scale of 1990s small-town America. As a result, Tim Burton films the reassuring world of normality, as well as its margin, which is haunted by death and the proliferation of scars (fig. 99). This film illustrates a return of the real of urban fear (both political and racial) via the fairy tale. Since the beginning of the 1980s several indications and several features have pointed to this kind of resurgence: Ridley Scott's *Legend*, Rob Reiner's *Princess Bride*, Wes Craven's *The People Under the Stairs*, Sam Raimi's *Conan* and *Evil Dead* series, and more recently the global hits *Harry Potter* and *Lord of the Rings*. The fairy-tale revival was first effected through a radical change of scenery, through a fascination for the exotic: following the Dungeons-and-Dragons fad, the stories as well as the characters were plunged into a playful elsewhere. The project was ambitious, for it borrowed from the fairy tale's primitivism, uprooted it

99 ▶
Edward Scissorhands
(TIM BURTON, 1990).
EDWARD'S FACE AND
HIS SCISSOR-HANDS
HIGHLIGHT THE
PRIMITIVISM OF A
CHARACTER THAT THE
AMERICAN MIDDLE
CLASS NONETHELESS
TRIES TO DOMESTICATE.

from the cheap world of Disneyland fairies and Cinderellas, and reinvigorated the fantasy film as a fundamentally disquieting rite of passage, dealing with evil, demonic, monstrous forces, as much as with enchantment, in the hero's pursuit of an ideal of the good and the beautiful. But this genre nonetheless held the primitive legend at bay, as an indirect reference: Scott's *Legend*, for instance, fails because it essentially seeks to recreate the fairy tale as outside time and as unreal. However, this resurgence remains a considerable force. For the first time the American quest for identity through adventure was invested somewhere other than on the frontier, whether it be the frontier of the western, the child's world (Disneyland), or science fiction projecting the horizon of the American West onto the conquest of space. The quest for primitive legend led instead to the invention of an alternative history, which is particularly disquieting for America, revisiting as it does European textual and spatial forms: the fairy tale, most often in its English or German variants, in this case the Grimm brothers, shrouded in mystery and terror.

Burton makes rather different use of the fantasy tale. This very American primitive time and space, this narrative of the other, in what is essentially the Gothic tradition, becomes grafted directly onto the contemporary town in

Burton's films, like the fairy-tale castle in *Edward Scissorhands*, which looms over the small town of Tupperware. Rather than through recreation, it is through a process of juxtaposition and then contamination, that is, through a fundamentally sickly process, that Burton's "suburban tale" proceeds. This process of contamination presents several characteristics that are unusual in American cinema, starting with a new architectural setting. At the intersection of the very ancient and contemporary techniques, the film's space is in itself an object to be filmed, or rather refilmed. The architecture is relentlessly metaphorical: fixed or movable partitions, holes, chasms, interior shafts, secret passages, inherited from the architectural style of the fairy tale; all this creates a parallel place, a countersite, incorporated within the classic American space, an eloquent architecture, in that the setting makes sense through the bodies to which it refers. Hence its decisive logic, which allows the fantasy tale to meet the suburban tale, is itself an analogy, of the possibility of combining two dissimilar and heterogeneous objects.

This analogical spirit leads Peggy to Edward, a sutured, scarred, and incomplete antihero: here stands the (futile) conviction that modern cosmetics will give the ancient monster a rosy complexion and conceal all his scars in America's present. Carrying the cult of the healthy and hygienic body to an extreme, Peggy is confronted with the depths of fantasy, in its comical, pathetic, as well as horrifying aspects. It is the analogical extension of the real world's logic that leads into fantasy. The fairy tale takes charge of the immediate story of suburban anxiety, for its images and characters carry to an extreme the inclusions and exclusions of a real town: the white community, which quickly made Edward its mascot, ends up in an all-out manhunt to lynch him. The alien teenager, clad entirely in black, made up entirely of stitched-together body parts, is hounded back to his primitive castle. The suburban tale denies the innocence of the Disneyland fantasy by grafting the primitive tradition, with all its violence and terrifying sickly bodies, onto the primitivism of the contemporary suburb's social relations. This meeting of two monsters, the fantastical and the suburban, is key. Just as in the 1940s Tex Avery invented a new form of animation that infused the children's tale with political anxiety (in his famous Hitler-Wolf), so Burton has found a new way of telling his very old tales by building on today's fear and violence.

Tim Burton's special ability to beget monsters, his teratological gift for bringing the creatures of childhood fairy tales into the world, ends up giving rise to a world that is profoundly undone, haunted and corroded by the rot and affect that corrupts all characters. If the child-monster "grows" so well in *Batman Returns* (1992), as it does in *Edward Scissorhands*, it is because the soil is just right, degenerate enough, a rich blend of end-of-the-world and end-of-cinema. Gotham City, Batman's town, suggests a between-two-worlds landscape, poised somewhere between dusk and dark, which calls forth the strangest creatures, sheltering in the marginal spaces of caves, sewers, rooftops, and so forth. All these beings carry cinema within them, developed by cinephilia and in Burton's childhood dreams, and are doomed to suspicion and exclusion, the product of a degenerate vision and shunned by normality. Burton's work thus seeks to explore these interstices, these archaic forms: he opens up onto a world of disappearances, of partition, where "it smells of death,"[12] where prey lurks and wildcats prowl—in short, everything that children are forbidden to see. *Batman Returns*, thus, is the children's movie to keep away from children: a world in which the logic is puerile, the thought melancholic, the flesh putrefying, and the impulses morbid.

Indeed, Burton does his thing with dead bodies. The four main figures in *Batman Returns*—Batman, Penguin, Catwoman, and Max Shreck—all return from the dead, and they do not forget what the experience was like. The trauma, the ordeal of the end, opens the first episode: a child, the future Batman, is witness to his parents' assassination. A similar journey opens the second installment: *Batman Returns* starts with a birth that is, at the same time, a path toward the abyss. Penguin, the child rejected by his parents because of his monstrous physical appearance, floats along sewer streams aboard a straw cradle. It is not so much Moses that Burton is invoking here as Greek mythology: the descent into the netherworld, on the putrid and frigid waters of the river Styx, on board Charon's boat. This superb credit sequence bears an icy mark that will imprint the entire film with the sign of death. This mark can be seen in every face, every metamorphosis, and every pathological mutation. Batman has never been so melancholy, a sad ghost lending his increasingly split body—half weakling, half mighty knight—to this story of phantoms. In this way Max Shreck, wearing Christopher Walken's diabolical and terrifying visage, is, above all, a direct descendant (both physiologically and cinephilically) of his quasi-namesake Max Schreck, the actor who played Murnau's Nosferatu, the bat-man who rises from his coffin.

Selina's mutation into Catwoman represents the crowning moment of this suicidal logic of a return to a life of scars and memories of death. Selina falls headfirst backwards, and the camera goes with her: Max has just pushed her off the twentieth floor of Shreck Tower. Smashed on the ground, in the snow, Selena has died, when a pack of cats pays a visit to her corpse. One penetrates her mouth with its paw and tongue, others sniff her and mew over her, and yet another devours her finger and sucks her blood. At this point her eyes suddenly open, seeing from the other side. Michelle Pfeiffer, finally confronted with her true role, gets up, but she will maintain the death-pale complexion of a corpse. Back at home she ransacks everything, spray-painting her overly pretty clothes black, as well as her doll house. Selina, still a corpse, is looking for a second skin that would put some life back into her. She tears her model secretary outfits and pounces on an imitation leather trench coat: here is the "creator" at work. Burton offers his version of the recycling fad: a piece of imitation leather and a few stitches to make a cat skin, a thimble and a few needles for claws. Filmed in this way, the fashion lesson turned physiological molting does not just reveal a new character. When Catwoman picks herself back up, mewing, in her tight black sheath, the wall behind her reads "Hell Here" in pink neon letters—her very first claw marks. Burton films her resurrection as a descent into hell, punctuated by a fall, a rape, an awakening, and a fit of destructive rage. It is this ordeal, this suicidal destiny, that enables the characters to put on their real skin and take on their true destiny, which gives *Batman Returns* its illuminated feel. Gotham City is a town from beyond death, where people throw parties, decorate Christmas trees, and create superheroes, a town with the sole objective of forgetting that each one is a ghost, whose only joy is to put makeup on corpses. Each ghost carries his or her death with aplomb, and the film functions only by taking charge of this amusing mourning suit, which also serves as a mournful party jacket.

Returning from the dead, all the figures in *Batman Returns* carry a heavy burden—a skin that has been marked by the fires of hell, of course, a shell and makeup that both conceal and reveal deformities, as well as a past, a history. Each creature carries a little piece of history, a bit of landscape, in that brain-dead city without a past that Gotham claims to be. The land these creatures return from is not just peopled with the cinephilic figures Burton invokes to provide a past for his own film. More to the point, these beasts are steeped in a profoundly European culture. Europe is the real land from which these ghosts, now monstrous in the eyes of American city dwellers, are "returning." In the margins of Gotham City, stories, bodies, terrors passed on from the old house, from forgotten lands, are still prowling: first, Dickens and his Mister Pickwick, that Mister Penguin reprises; then the Transylvanian vampire whose thirst for blood runs through Max Shreck's veins; and the medieval witch and her cats, reincarnated as Catwoman; and finally, the very "English Gothic" mansion and butler that serve Batman so well. This is not even to mention the wandering gypsies of the world of nineteenth-century novels, which Burton remodels as street clowns and acrobats who exert a carnivalesque terror over the city. The film ends with a death shriek, with the piercing voice of punk singer Siouxie howling *Face to Face*: an uncompromising ending, not very grateful to the system that enabled it. "Don't pretend this is a happy ending," says Catwoman to noble Batman, who wanted to save her from an ultimate and fatal showdown with the vampire Max Shreck. No happy ending: Catwoman demands one last confrontation with death, just like the Penguin and Max Shreck, who all lose their living-dead lives and return to their original corpse state. Then everything collapses into a deliriously destructive ending: Tim Burton takes a sledgehammer to the beautiful sets that were built for him, kills off his creatures, and leaves Batman all alone, to return to his melancholia.

In the spring of 1998 Tim Burton adapted *The Legend of Sleepy Hollow*, or *The Headless Horseman*, a short story by Washington Irving. The film enabled him to fully explore the gothic form and establish himself as its champion for an entire generation of young spectators, thus marking a genuine revival in contemporary America. The filmmaker delved into the world of Washington Irving and into that particular text, which was published as part of *The Sketchbook of Geoffrey Crayon*, in 1819. It belonged to a genre that was then in fashion, albeit more so in Europe than America: the gothic novel, *noir* or horror literature, typical of the wave that began in 1764 with Horace Walpole's *The Castle of Otranto*, which was quickly followed by several classics of the genre, poetry of the tombstone and the living dead: Ann Radcliffe's *The Italian, or the Confessional of the Black Penitents* (1797), Matthew G. Lewis's *The Monk* (1797), Hoffman's *The Devil's Elixir* (1816), Mary Shelley's *Frankenstein* (1816), and Charles Robert Maturin's *Melmoth the Wanderer* (1820). This literature was born of an abrupt rupture in taste, which signaled the shift from the Enlightenment to romanticism. During the fifty years following the publication of *The Castle of Otranto*, about three hundred novels and literary works were produced in the genre, involving nearly one hundred authors, major and minor, for the most part in England, Germany, and France. Many of them borrowed from the world of Walpole, that terrifying Strawberry Hill aristocrat, who composed his atmospheres as a "visual drama" (Eluard), carrying to its dark incandescence that point when reason loses control, "under the effect of the most profound emotion of the soul" (Breton). Visits to the ruins of abbeys and castles; hallucinatory passages through dark woods; disquieting visions of fragments of rock, trees, and caves; recurring figures of witches, bloodthirsty lords, cruel mothers, and ogres, of pale heroines and the rational libertines who set off in search of them; narrative tropes of confinement, separation, quest, impossible family gatherings, amorous encounters, and the sorcerer's apprentice; and, above all, the obsessive presence, like a leitmotif, of ghosts and specters returning unappeased from the dead. "Once across the bridge, the phantoms come to greet us." This phrase has served as an initiation into the world of gothic ever since it was inscribed as an intertitle in Murnau's *Nosferatu*.

That long dark narrative, which spread across a Europe convulsed by revolution, war, and unprecedented social, political, and economic upheaval, projected the civilized world toward a fictional destiny incarnated in frightening details: landscapes, ruins, figures, apparitions, each in turn telling of this trauma and expressing the nightmare that served as the fictional vehicle for civilizational crisis. "The Gothic novel," as the Marquis de Sade wrote at the time, "was the indispensable fruit of the revolutionary tremors that were felt throughout Europe: black is pathognomonic of the great trouble that has seized us."[13] It was as though it had become necessary to fight off the fear with the most eccentric and somber fictions, with the establishment of a metaphysics of nightmare, with its cohort of tyrants, lords, old barons from England or Hessen, bloody *sans-culottes*, all somehow accomplices to the terror regime, living in their dilapidated fortresses and prisons, and working in cahoots with older forces of evil—demons, fairies, creatures of the haunted mythology of darkness—to frighten the new heroes of the times, all those young and handsome romantics, and prevent them from making their way into the scientific, hygienic, rational, and democratically minded future. The European novel thus buried itself in ruins and interred narrative under a tombstone. The violent story of the fight between the forces of light and darkness would conjure up and manipulate specters, often with mechanical virtuosity, in an era where technical inventions were accumulating at an accelerating rate and civilization was reaching the apex of its artisanal savoir-faire. It was, in the end, the human body itself that turned into a spectral machine—the biological and vitalist experimentation on the human being, both dead and alive, both the corpse and the animal, in order to reshape it through perverse crossbreeding and quixotic technical operations. The dark mood was inspired by the resulting anxiety, as a consequence of gestures and impulses gone wild. There is no getting away with attacking the human body or the body politic.

Tim Burton belongs to this historical and visual gothic tradition, this "ideal and modern nightmare" (Baudelaire) that widely reshaped the Western imagination two centuries ago. His world is heir to Walpole's literary legacy, albeit via Edgar Allan Poe and the American macabre, while his visual and musical inspirations are multifarious: horror films, comic strips and ghoulish cartoons, the "Goth" punk bands of his youth, and above all, ever since childhood, a way of conceiving of civilization via its darkest, most secret, and solitary margins. Tim Burton had not read the classic gothic novels—neither Walpole, nor Irving, nor Baculard d'Arnaud—and he probably knew of Poe's world through its later film adaptations rather than its original written form, yet his culture remains profoundly gothic. This gothic form is now familiar in the media and has been bastardized by the recent and massive American "Goth" revival, which started in the late 1970s and which he experienced personally as a rebellious form of belief, of imagination, of looks. His famous "raven's nest" hair, evocative of rock singers such as Nick Cave, Adam Ant, and Siouxie, figures as the contemporary signature of this profoundly gothic presence and faith.

Burton is not only a gothic artist who is unaware that he is one. Not only do his films, ever since the beginning, feature conspicuous signs of this lineage—frightful details (masks, living dead, caves and castles, nightmares and ghosts), archetypal figures (Vincent, Frankenweenie, Edward, Catwoman, Bela Lugosi, and the Headless Horseman, among numerous others), *machines célibataires*, and aesthetic ruins. Like surrealism in its time (Eluard, Breton, and Artaud were the vehicles for a major gothico-romantic revival), Tim Burton and his powerful imaginary world may be said to reinvent the gothic. *Sleepy Hollow*, in this regard, is not a simple illustration of the Goth culture and its revival among American teenagers but a reimagining and reincarnation of the style, starting with the way the narrative and landscapes of the film reveal the hero's angst and the social upheaval that then seized a society haunted by the biblical Puritanism of its founders. *Sleepy Hollow* is nothing but an immense external projection of the affliction that dwelled within Ichabod Crane, the film's hero (played by Johnny Depp), a modern investigator guided by his highly developed faculty of reason, in love with an innocent young virgin, and confronted with the archaic and moralistic world of elders, both in New York and in the town of Sleepy Hollow. This stormy interior landscape takes a visual form that is at once gloomy, ruined, and sublimated. More than a trendy invocation of a dark and romantic mood, the gothic form is here a truly intimate aesthetic, a nightmare that gives expression to the artist's soul. Moreover, Tim Burton's gothic aesthetic is characterized by a dynamic that is specific to heterogeneity and movement. *Sleepy Hollow* is a film that assimilates everything.

It is made from the intersection of references and adaptations, of imitations, cross-references, parodies, and superabundant accumulations of genres and archetypes. Tim Burton's gothic style works as an archaeology of his own knowledge and his entire existence. The film thus successfully overcomes the limitations in which his poetry might have remained imprisoned, trapped in the simple illustration of a trendy genre, in other words petrified. This fluidity among styles, references, genres, and figures constitutes Burton's own gothic aesthetic, against the classic puritanical culture and the standardized mise-en-scène characteristic of recent Hollywood mass-market productions, including those that revisit underground genres. *Sleepy Hollow* is a major film, one in which the spectator's interpretative activity is constantly alert, as if on its guard, as measured in terms of playful and erudite intensity as much as fright. It is also a profoundly gothic film, in that its component parts, depending on their combination with or isolation from one another, change meaning and shape, following the appropriations, successive or simultaneous, that are made of them. This constant circumvolution and playfulness gives it a simultaneously subversive and rallying power.

For all these reasons *Sleepy Hollow* quickly became seen as and proclaimed one of the fullest symbols of Goth culture in the Western world. Ichabod Crane and his terrifying visions became a legitimate heir to the Burtonian heroes of the filmmaker's gothic youth, such as Vincent, Edward, Jack Skillington, and Catwoman. The gothic remains one of the only youth cults that can boast a literary and artistic tradition that is entirely its own. It has survived the traps of consumerism and mass culture that threaten youth cultures more and more aggressively and has been transformed, for Tim Burton's heroes as well as for the filmmaker himself, into a viable lifestyle and aesthetic, a legitimate cultural and social identity, even while remaining marginal and rebellious.[14] Burton the Goth did not simply tolerate social diversity and deviance; he celebrated them, sublimating an increasingly dull, homogeneous, and commercial world through his praise of the esoteric and the exceptional and his celebration of dark beauty and carnivalesque laughter, which are capable of turning situations upside down. The gothic form for Burton is an aesthetic as well as a political and moral manifesto—a dark and humorous satire thrown at an academic, consumerist, desensitized, and Puritanical culture.

Tim Burton also enjoys interspersing doses of both humor and horror throughout *Sleepy Hollow*. It never becomes satire—the point is not to mock tales of horror and Ichabod Crane's frightened reactions—but rather a way of mixing laughter and horror together, which is precisely what is achieved through the filmmaker's development of a gothico-grotesque atmosphere, which is not unlike a Bruegel painting, Hieronymus Bosch's intricate details, or Van Gogh's mad fits. To laugh, then, when Burton, Johnny Depp, and their crew give their own interpretation of Ichabod Crane's relationship with his superiors, who despise and censure him, and of the links between the man of science and the headless horseman who relentlessly pursues him, is to laugh at a representation of Tim Burton vs. Hollywood, the filmmaker being tortured by Jon Peters, his producer at Warner Bros., during the filming of the two *Batmans*.[15] In this light *Sleepy Hollow* presents an opportunity for the filmmaker to exact his sarcastic revenge. As for horror, Tim Burton chose to concentrate it in the representation of the severed head, a haunting fear that runs through the ages from the terrified hypnosis of the Greeks confronted with the Gorgon's face, an image that is here made even more savage by the wailing brass of Danny Elfman's musical score and the syncopated rhythm of the shots depicting the frenzied galloping of the ghost rider. Two dozen decapitations punctuate the film, lacerating it to the core. Each one is different in style, whether accomplished with axe or sword. The filmmaker becomes not just the executioner but also the illustrator of the death sentence—both director of the execution and observer of the victims' expressions, frozen by the blade; both anatomist, like his character Ichabod Crane, and preacher of a frenetic and terrible *danse macabre*; both narrator of Dantean stories, replete with living dead, and knight of the Apocalypse, lopping off heads on the fly. Reviving the tradition of decollation narratives—a genre that flourished in the late eighteenth century, a period preoccupied with the victims' suffering, which carefully inventoried the expressions of stupor, surprise, pain, and pleasure that flashed across their faces—Tim Burton made his film as bloodcurdling as possible. *Sleepy Hollow*'s horror is as sharp as a freshly honed blade (fig. 100).

Whereas America is always expected to produce an image of what is to come, of tomorrow, "scenes of future life," representations of a rationalized, hygienized, and cybernetic body, Tim Burton offers instead a spectacle of bleak, wounded, primitive, stitched-up, gothic, and bloody bodies—bodies that have experienced death. His world rests on an old tradition, long integrated into the world of fantasy, which has prevailed through the long lineage of Frankensteinian monsters and living dead. Frankenstein's monster, in a way, is to American film fiction what *L'Arroseur arrosé* is to the French scenes filmed by the Lumière brothers: the bodily accident that gives rise to the story. Tim Burton's cinema strives explicitly to rekindle the spectator's desire to be

100 ▶
Sleepy Hollow
(TIM BURTON, 1999).
THE FILM'S GOTHIC
WORLD CAN BE SEEN AS
A SYNCRETIC VISION OF
AWE-INSPIRING IMAGES:
GRISLY SETTINGS, A
MACABRE ATMOSPHERE,
A HORROR FILM, MORBID
EFFECTS, CHIAROSCURO
LIGHTING, THE LIVING
DEAD, CONTEMPORARY
"GOTH" CULTURE,
GHOSTS RETURNING
FROM THE PAST, AND
SO FORTH. EACH TIME,
THE CHARACTERS ARE
CONFRONTED WITH
THE PRESENCE OF
DEATH, AND TERROR IS
EXPRESSED IN THEIR
MESMERIZED AND
FRIGHTENED GAZE.

swept away, to be enchanted by fear, which was the role of popular ghost stories in earlier times. Here the primitive deeply impresses itself on the film and conjures up the darkest master fiction ever to have surfaced in America.

If this cinema is bound to be less human, it perhaps redeems itself by becoming more political. This experience of the primitive does, indeed, present powerful political stakes for an America in a constant state of fear of social upheaval. This cinema—which operates first through decomposition, excision, and destruction, and then through suturing back together stories, images, and bodies—is a subversive Trojan Horse sent by Burton into the heart of the teenage spirit. What is being cut up and recomposed is the social fabric itself, which all these scissors and sewing needles have turned into a highly unstable substance. On the one hand, this cinema feeds on signs of stability, for everything is born, underground, out of quiet harmony: New York at its most normal in Sam Raimi's *Spiderman*, the pleasant suburbs at the beginning of Burton's *Beetlejuice* and *Edward Scissorhands*, Joe Dante's cute Gizmo in *Gremlins*, the house-next-door at the start of Wes Craven's *The People Under the Stairs*, and the glittering Broadway musical in Robert Zemeckis's *Death Becomes Her*. All this is to better steer things off their peaceful course, to better disrupt the harmony. It quickly becomes apparent that the sense of order and color of Burton's small towns only serves to give rise to the black monster, the resurrected corpse that comes to inject new life into them, bring them to climax through terror, just as Wes Craven's house strives to hide the disturbance and the horror under the stairs and within the walls; and the gremlins, the exact mirror image of the little girl's teddy bears (though related to them through a corrupted lineage), strive to achieve social evil by systematically inverting all taboos and misreading the user's manual for every object they get their hands on. They locate monstrosity precisely in the objects that America would claim as its own, introducing insecurity and danger precisely where adult society tries to eliminate them. They do away with harmony by ingesting, digesting, and vomiting it up, as so many evil and burlesque practices. Thus are delineated both an attitude in relation to the rest of the world that is common to all the antiheroes of these filmmakers—a bulimia of signs, which they take great pleasure in devouring—and a position: they all come between objects that communicate (television, cinema, bodies), intercepting their expressions and manifestations, in order to film their own grotesque and horrific countershot. Television, like cinema, is sucked dry from within and charged with unexpected missions: to campaign in support of the abominable Joker and then in support of the degenerate demagogue the Penguin, for instance, in the two *Batmans*, or to allow the gremlins to get together and sing, or rather howl, Walt Disney songs. Conversely, just as they capture the natural emissions of communications machines, jam them and misappropriate them, these characters form relays with those who should communicate only through conventional and polite codes (the idiom of what has come in America to be called the politically correct). They are the vectors, through successive mutations, of miscegenation between different ethnic groups and minorities; they carry to an extreme handicaps and physical defects, open up routes between childhood and death, the clean and the unclean, hygiene and decay, and between the living and the dead.

By interfering with the natural signs of harmony and combining bits of bodies and cultures deemed incompatible, by engineering heterogeneity and mutation, these films end up offering a deeply subversive political parable: what they "disappear," and this time with no hope of return, is the very form of the American dream of a unitary society. The master fiction in these primitive films is that of a mingling of moods, bodies, and images, which the America of hierarchical values and principles tries its best to avert. The joyously violent philosophy at work in these subversive films is captured in the highly carnivalesque phrase—as the Penguin says to Catwoman in *Batman Returns*, explicitly citing the destructive slogan made famous during the Watts race riots of 1965—"Burn, baby, burn."

American Cinema Put to the Test of 9/11

New York City, September 11, 2001, 8:46 a.m.: CNN cameras, quickly relayed by other TV channels worldwide, are fixed on the World Trade Center. The northern tower is ablaze—a Boeing 767 has just crashed into it. Ten minutes later, another plane hits the south tower: "visual evidence carried live of an inconceivable attack."[16] At 10:05 the first tower collapses in a cloud of dust, followed soon after by its twin. At 10:28 this symbol of American power is no more. These images of apocalypse caught up with America, since they felt oddly familiar: disaster films had, in a way, already shown us many of them, often some even more spectacular still. And yet, not quite. If the images had already been filmed, they remained fiction. Now, all of a sudden, as if the off-screen subconscious of America and its mythology were coming to life, they became real. It had already been filmed, yet it had remained inconceivable. Only the repeated broadcast of the same shots of the two towers on fire, of their subsequent dramatic collapse, and then of images of the source of the end of a world (the isolation of a plane-dot in the sky hurtling toward the immense wall of glass and colliding in a fiery blaze) enabled the rest of the world to grasp the reality of this representation of the impossible. In this interplay between representation and history no dead bodies were seen, only a few living ones jumping from the blazing towers, while the dust that covered everything, transforming those frantically fleeing the scene into gray ghosts, figured as the only "organic" trace of mass death.

In what would seem to be the encounter par excellence between a Hollywood master fiction and American history, any resemblance to existing reality was purely coincidental. It was as if the accumulation of special effects had somehow neutralized the real and made fiction extraordinary, literally unbelievable. "It's like in the movies," as some stunned TV viewers said. "Reality Worse Than Fiction," read newspaper headlines the next day. But the shock effect of these images of New York on September 11, 2001, was neither an extension of film nor a trespass on its effects. Film had failed to pave the way. Quite the opposite, if we were stunned speechless, if the constant warnings (from TV commentators) not to confuse reality and fiction were pointless, it was because the movies had shown radically different images from those seen on TV that day. It would, indeed, be possible to assemble bits of Hollywood films of the past fifteen years—John Carpenter's *Escape from New York*, John McTiernan's *Die Hard* and *Die Hard: With a Vengeance*, James Cameron's *True Lies*—and come up with a story line that combined Islamist terrorists, the hijacking of planes, a crash into the World Trade Center, and a series of explosions, massive destruction, and casualties in the thousands. Yet the story would also necessarily entail a certain kind of ending: the American hero, revealed to himself by the disaster, reconnects with the "true values" of the frontier pioneers or founding fathers in order to punish the guilty—Bush and his crusade against the "axis of evil" perhaps (at least, in his dreams). No, the shock effect was not so much linked to any scenario, however striking, as to a form of representation. It was, first and foremost, a matter of images, of a kind of sudden visualization of the unheard of. Recent films had attempted such visions of the apocalypse: in the mid-1990s New York City had been devastated several times. The eleven-minute-long credit sequence at the beginning of *Armageddon*, for example, even if it features a meteor shower rather than suicide planes, is probably the closest to what was experienced in New York on September 11, 2001. And yet these film images express the exact opposite of what was seen on September 11: they show the technological challenge of destruction, successfully met through special effects, not the "live" assassination of a symbol of American power, reduced to a plaintive victim. In short, death is absent from these films, even if shots of dead bodies abound, whereas in the footage of September 11, death was pervasive, even without seeing a single corpse.

American cinema takes its capacity for spectacle to an extreme but at the same time maintains a pleasant distance from death. The images of September 11, however, were perceived and experienced without detachment, without an aesthetic sense of any kind, either fictional or playful. The script was the same, the level and type of destruction was comparable, and yet the nature of the visual representation was radically different. What were we shown? Still shots, from afar, of the twin towers, and the delicate and difficult mapping of the second plane's route before it crashed into the tower; then a few shaky images of the skyscrapers' collapse, recorded with a small camera by a cameraman running away from the blast; the smoke, which hid as much as it revealed, and the all-pervasive dust—a sad, wounded, bitter spectacle of gray desolation in ashes. And then, the deafening silence of a clear sky. In short, many elements that a pre–September 11 American film would have rejected out of hand in favor of a close monitoring of the unfolding disaster that makes the most of all the steel and glass explosions, that focuses on a few model destinies with which spectators can identify, and that is steeped in an obligatory heroism, allowing for the saving of a few children, as well as, above all, the face of empire. The images of September 11 constitute the archive of contemporary disaster precisely because they avoid all the effects deployed in cinema. They are neither its continuation nor its supersession, even less its culmination; rather, they constitute its most scathing critique.

If these poor images make sense, it is first and foremost because they seize the reality of an act, as a recorded document can constitute evidence of murder. This is exactly what the writer Russel Banks expressed in his private diary: "We react first to the fact that the building was shot, as though it were a living being, and not just a symbol of American power and optimism. The World Trade Center is the center of world trade, it is the United States, it is us. And under our very eyes, in broad daylight, through these images, this footage, it was attacked, shot dead, exactly like the solitary assassin, shooting from a window on the top story of a building in Dallas, shot a bullet through the throat and neck of John F. Kennedy."[17]

The collapse of the WTC is indeed a mirror image of the Dallas assassination and, in this capacity, appears as the end of a cinematographic form that was born in 1963 with Zapruder's footage. It feels as though we are back in a moment when history and fiction cannot be told apart, at the theoretical point where the one enables the other to be articulated. It is a never-ending movement through which each jumpstarts the other, as though, on September 11, cinema had been present in anticipation, with its fictional weapons and special-effects techniques, and yet only history could add that frisson of truth. History offered "another fiction," a fiction that went beyond fiction.

It was not, then, cinema that foreshadowed history—rather, it was history that critiqued cinema in allowing itself to outstrip it. Now, has the latter responded to the critique, has it caught up with history again? In other words, is there a post–September 11 cinema, as there was a post–Kennedy assassination cinema? It may be argued that any such "updating" was immediately ruled out by the American system of images, which in the hours following the attacks refused to show the dead bodies of the victims, the truth of death in action—thus, failing to begin the symbolic and psychological grieving process that has always taken place, individually, domestically, collectively, in the presence of mortal remains. This is what Jean-Luc Godard argued, for instance, in an interview he gave on this very question:

> Once past the stupefaction induced by the spectacle of the destruction of the father's house, we saw the same thing over and over again. Or rather, we saw nothing. Images in a loop, always the same, with commentary stuttered by an army of anchormen. To see is not so much an issue of the place that one films, but rather of knowing what one wants to film. Everything that could have been shocking, disturbing, or upsetting, was systematically cleaned up. Not a single body, no trace of violence, of fire, or of blood, just the greatness of the towers in ruins. Everything that was below or above fiction did not find a place. People took the event as yet another story, however unimaginable—but this is the characteristic of so-called American films to be unbelievable. And everything that might have gone against that grain, actual dead bodies, more profound and more painful things than the simple "axis of evil," was sidelined by the system. That United States citizens cannot stand seeing their own dead is one thing, but that they remodel the images of it is quite another, and rather unsettling. They are into purified propaganda. In the end, we can't show anything anymore. What then rules as the only and unchallenged master of it all is commentary on the event, turned into a universal visual stereotype.[18]

Unsurprisingly, Hollywood cinema responded by trying to turn the September 11 attacks into fiction: in *Flight 93* (2005) Peter Greengrass tried to establish the course of, and recreate the last moments aboard, the fourth plane hijacked by the terrorists, which crashed on its way to Washington, D.C.; and in *World Trade Center* (2006) Oliver Stone recreated in a naive and demagogical way the heroic, yet also very human, efforts of two Port Authority Police Department employees, Will Jimeno and John McLoughlin, in the middle of the WTC rubble on the morning of the attacks. Oliver Stone has said that he drew inspiration from two exemplary real life narratives.[19] Yet everything in his film feels fake: a faux pas, wrong turn, artifice—which, in dealing with such a subject, is unforgivable, even unwatchable. *World Trade Center* constantly adopts a kind of distance from its subject, that of the reconstruction, in which every shot becomes a wink, every uniform a morbid fetish, every broken and saved life a personal and national destiny, and even sometimes a mystical one, as in the ridiculous scenes featuring miraculous and salvific apparitions (Christ himself stretching out his hand to one of the victims who survives the tower's collapse, as well as nineteen other blessed ones). September 11 here is pure fiction, tailored to an already existing genre even when posing as truthful testimony and, to be sure, anything but a cinematographic form of history revealing America's transformations (fig. 101).

Oliver Stone's film was previewed in September 2006 at the Deauville American Film Festival, which organized a retrospective entitled "America, Five Years Later." In the dozen films that were screened—aside from two television "mockumentaries," one recreating, minute by minute, in real time, the Boeing 93 flight that crashed in Pennsylvania (Brian Lapping, Bruce Goodison, and Phil Craig's *The Flight That Fought Back*), and the other focusing on what happened in the two towers over the course of the 104 minutes that elapsed between the first terrorist plane crash and the collapse of the second building, based on a hundred testimonies and the September 11 Commission report (Richard Dale's *9/11: The Twin Towers*)—the trace of profound historical trauma left by the attacks was palpable, not so much in the ultimately reassuring presence of firemen, policemen, and other rescue workers but in the very absence of father figures, who were literally evacuated, swept aside, dismissed and returned to mainstream American cinema, which still features suburban American daily life, devoid of superheroes and wonder women. This failure of the father figure, which is featured, in one way or another (escape, repeated absence, muteness, illness, weakness, failure, cowardice, perversion, powerlessness), in two-thirds of the films screened, is so widespread it betrays a profound and quasi-clinical distress, a pathogenic neurosis: the men have failed to protect America from danger, and the women are left alone to cope, to live, survive, raise children, and take responsibility for their own desire and longing for independence.

101 ▶
World Trade Center (OLIVER STONE, 2006). THE FILM RECONSTRUCTS THE VIOLENCE PERPETRATED AGAINST AMERICA, A COUNTRY THAT ENJOYS INFLICTING PAIN ON ITSELF AND PRACTICES A KIND OF CATHARSIS THROUGH AN EXCESS OF PAIN: AN IMPERIAL IDENTITY FOUNDED ON THE RUIN.

In the end the only film to date that attempts to open its own form up to post-9/11 America is Steven Spielberg's *War of the Worlds*, which was shot in 2004. With regard to mise-en-scène the film is rather disappointing in that it trades exclusively in spectacle. Spielberg has always striven to be of his times as much as to mark his times, and this is why *War of the Worlds* is the most important Hollywood film of the early twenty-first century: it is the only one that has moved to the other side of history, post-9/11, and even post–Iraq War. *War of the Worlds* shows America at war but as though it had already lost. The country is destroyed at heart, and the most powerful nation in the world cannot provide heroes capable of saving itself. After focusing for fifteen minutes on the daily life of a fragment of a family—a father, a crane operator played by Tom Cruise; a teenage son; and a younger daughter (it is a motherless, not a fatherless, film, Spielberg's only concession, if not to the fundamental values of America, at least to box-office values, Cruise being a commercial guarantee)—in a cookie-cutter suburb of a big city, the sky clouds over, the power goes out, and the telephones go dead; violent lightning strikes, and an immense sprawling mechanical monster suddenly materializes from underground. It destroys everything in its path with its disintegrating laser beams. The film begins as a classic end-of-the-world movie, not unlike Roland Emmerich's *Independence Day*, released nine years earlier: urban apocalypse in half an hour.

It is then that Spielberg sidetracks the end-of-the-world narrative and veers into a new, post-9/11, one. First he proffers a direct citation: the head of the family, still dazed after escaping the monster and making it safely back home to his fragile shelter, bears only one trace of his recent narrow escape—the dust that covers him from head to toe. When he sees himself in the mirror, it is a World Trade Center survivor he sees. He immediately wipes off the reference, as if it would have been disrespectful to the 9/11 victims if he had left it any longer (fig. 102). But from that moment on, as if contaminated by the painful memory of the attacks, Spielberg's film tells only of America's defeat: it is filled with scenes of exodus, of frantic flight on the roads, and of civil war—Americans fighting over the few cars that still run, over food, over news—as well as of a powerless army, broken by superior extraterrestrial force, and of private, militarized, and authoritarian militias taking over the task of maintaining law and order and providing security. America is almost instantaneously turned into a desperate and fascistic empire. And what's more—unlike in *Independence Day* and *Armageddon*—there is no hero to save it, since Tom Cruise is content with playing the model father, at the head of a family already torn apart. He manages to keep it alive, and even reconstitute it anew,

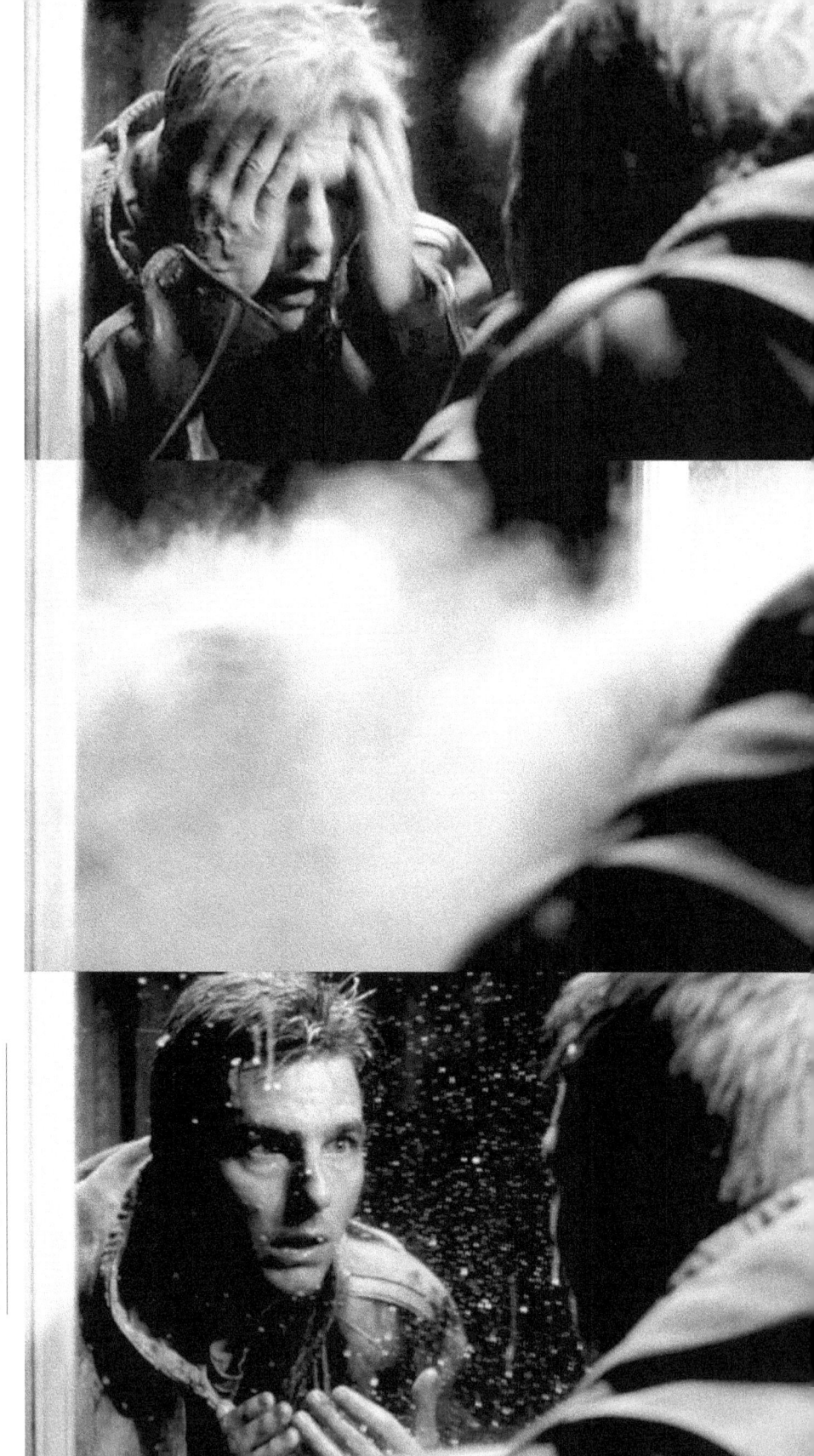

102 ▶ *War of the Worlds* (STEVEN SPIELBERG, 2005). TOM CRUISE, SURVIVOR OF DISASTER, BEARS THE TRACE OF THE ONGOING DESTRUCTION OF AMERICA: THE GRAY DUST OF THE END OF THE WORLD, THE DUST PRODUCED BY THE COLLAPSE OF THE TOWERS ON SEPTEMBER 11.

103 ▶
War of the Worlds
(STEVEN SPIELBERG, 2005). THE CHILD IS BLINDFOLDED SO THAT SHE CANNOT SEE HOW HORRIBLE THE WORLD HAS BECOME.

but this is achieved only through an open renunciation of all civic and national responsibility. His war is strictly private, and in his eyes the worst disaster would be the breakup of his family.

Devastated landscapes, a river overflowing with corpses, an exodus of population, urban riots, bombings—the terrain is America itself, and the exterminating monsters offer no justification, nor do they engage in any form of negotiation. Despite the conventional happy ending, we know America has lost, has become a kind of Iraq occupied by foreign troops that enjoy overwhelming technical supremacy. If the film begins with a direct reference to 9/11, it ends on an even more powerful image: so that his daughter is not forced to see how horrible the world has become, the father has no choice but to blindfold her (fig. 103). The gray dust is the shroud surrounding an America that has been struck to the core, and the blindfold is the emblem of its incapacity to recover. *War of the Worlds* is Spielberg's anticipatory narrative of the avoidable defeat of the American empire. It is the first defeatist film in a cinema that is overly accustomed to triumph. It marks the revenge of history and the worst of its master fictions: the end of empire. It is, for contemporary America, a tomb: "Calm block here fallen from a dark disaster."[20]

CONCLUSION ▶
ALL HISTORIES ARE POSSIBLE

THE RELATIONSHIP OF cinema to history follows three essential vectors. First, there is the quasi-heuristic ability of cinema to become "reconstruction," in the past as well as the present, by restoring history's reflexive depth, offering history a kind of second chance, that of replaying itself onscreen using the means of the cinematic arts: sets, immersion in original documents, the bringing to life of bodies and characters of another age. Former times are thus revived in the time of cinema through the genre of the "historical film." Here cinema acquires the power of being the marker of historical time, of plunging back into the past through reconstruction, even while revealing the contradictions, tensions, and debates of its own times.

Second, there is the quasi-mechanical ability of cinema to "embalm the real," that is, to preserve, probably better than any other art form, what I would call an archival reality or a documentary reality of history. Cinema renders the experience of a visual confrontation with what has been, in telling detail, the history of the century. It appears to snatch fragments of history from the periods through which it operates. It makes history as a matter of course. I am alluding here to moments in films where crowd scenes, faces, gestures, lines of dialogue, singular fragments, take hold as fetishes that organize vision and then a visual remembrance of history. The twentieth century could then be encompassed in a Bogart expression (fig. 104), a Renoir flash of desire, a Malick landscape, a McCarey witticism, a slamming door in Hawks, a moment of waiting in Antonioni, a face in Godard (fig. 105), a slip of the tongue in Truffaut, a dream in Tarkovsky, the return of a zombie in Burton—the theory of the special fragment that illustrates the century's worldview; the cult of the revealing moment in which memories of the images that have made history resurface; the phenomenology of the significant detail; the religion of the "I remember," in which, all of a sudden, everything makes sense through the historical connections established by the cinematic arts.

Finally, cinema is endowed with the quasi-conceptual ability to offer itself as history. It becomes an ideal tool to elaborate an interpretation of history. Montage is an exemplary case in point, as a cinematographic form that brings together, in a flash, images of cinema and images of the century. Cinema single-handedly carries out what Walter Benjamin defined as the essence of the

104 ▶
Humphrey Bogart in *The Big Sleep*
(HOWARD HAWKS, 1946). EVERY GESTURE, POSE, ATTITUDE, AND OBJECT IS MANIFEST ON BODIES AND FACES AS A FETISH OF AMERICAN HISTORY.

historical: "what has been comes together in a flash with the now to form a constellation."[1] Or even what Claude Lévi-Strauss said about the intellectual and aesthetic operation of montage: "With such a cut-and-paste technique, the work proceeds from a double articulation . . . for the units of the first articulation are already works that are then combined and organized into a work of a higher order."[2]

In Godard, especially in his *Histoire(s) du cinéma*, the poetic form consists precisely in this world-making capacity, achieved out of fragments of film edited together with shards of history's archives and memories, this "constellation of sparks." What has been retained from the memory of cinema and the memory of history is not an additional, and cumulative, memory; it itself constitutes a history, thanks to the connections established by montage, which constantly reopens interpretations of history and transforms it into a constellation of facts that have at last found their images.

The cinematographic forms of history that I have attempted to home in on in the various chapters of this book are located at the crossroads of these three filmic dimensions—reconstruction, archive, and interpretative tool—bequeathed to the historian by cinema, bits snatched from history by an art that is at once intimate and universal. Each of these cases (the return of the fact of extermination in fictional images, the effects of New Wave style, images of demodern dilapidation in Eastern European cinema, and images of masochistic self-punishment in American cinema) highlights the extent to which cinema seems to have become, especially in the second half of the twentieth century, the art of history par excellence, the modern form of historical representation. And, in the same way, the individual filmmakers who are taken up in this book—Sacha Guitry, Peter Watkins, Jean-Luc Godard—have all imparted a form that establishes an intrinsic link between cinema and history, making us see, through their mise-en-scène and montage, that the century could make itself visible, principally and essentially, only through the eventful, stylized, and edited-together images of cinema.

If, indeed, the twentieth century is embodied in these cinematographic forms, however minor or marginal, this book is intended not only as a narrative of the art of cinema as a historical form but also as a cinematographic repository of the bodies and gestures, the habits and presence of creatures of our time. Indeed, our relationships to the most common things bear the indelible mark of the experience of cinema, while also constituting a perceptible trace of the presence of history. Cinema operates on a register of the possible that is so vast as to allow for excess, passion, lyricism, violence, and

105 ▶
Breathless
(JEAN-LUC GODARD, 1960). JEAN-PAUL BELMONDO REPRISES BOGART'S GESTURES AND POSES FOURTEEN YEARS LATER: MANNERS ENTER INTO HISTORY THROUGH THE NEW WAVE.

grand spectacle. Nevertheless, one of the most moving of these possibilities remains withdrawal: the dimness of the world, the contemplation of a landscape, the underplaying of actors, the tedium, a way of capturing better than any other art the warp and woof of the everyday and the minor resources of the trivial. As Chris Marker aptly puts it in *Le Dépays*: "after having made all possible voyages around the world, I am only interested in the banal."[3]

There resides, in this special capacity of cinema, a movement that can alter anyone's vision of history and way of narrating it, what Natalie Zemon Davis perceives in all films as a phenomenally powerful historical narrative. This capacity—which is at once heroic, bloody, passionate, tragic, and epic, *as well as* trivial, banal, weak, and lifeless—constitutes cinema as a gaze and narrative of the century and thus as a privileged form of history. It is also, as the historian Arlette Farge points out, a form of legitimization of the self in the world: it suddenly becomes legitimate to go get a bottle of milk, smoke a cigarette, admire a landscape, because cinema has shown it as an aesthetic and historical act. Thanks to cinema, twentieth-century—and now twenty-first-century—human beings identify with an entire history, from coexistence with the great events of the world all the way to a resolve to perform naturally the most commonplace gestures and habits. The time of the banal, in film, is just as powerful as that of the exception. In this resides a profound sense of history and the possibility for each individual to recreate his or her identity within infra-ordinary history. It is an ethics, even a source of pride: thanks to film, all have a history, and all histories are possible.

Is cinema endowed with a historiographic capacity of its own? Is it able to produce history as a function of its very form? My case rests, and the present book is entered into evidence: the cinematographic form is historical and the filmmaker a privileged historian. In return the historian, called on and stimulated by the challenge, presents history through fragments of films. This is only to acknowledge a certain definition of film, which also stands as its manifesto: cinema—all cinema—is historical through and through. The being-history of cinema inheres in its very nature, as this book has tried to show, at once archive, object, and actor of history. This definition presents itself as the key to viewing and understanding films: they reveal history to us precisely where nobody had sought it before. Cinema projects art into history; and therein lies, in some sense, its "historical" destiny.

The present book is intended to affirm the arrival of what might be called the *age of history in film*. History is the interpretative key for cinema, one that presents itself in the very moment that some consider marks their common end. The revelation of grace and incarnation was the basis of André Bazin's reading of cinema in the immediate postwar period; the style of mise-en-scène was the cornerstone of the young Turks' cinephilic vision of cinema ten years later, a style that they proceeded to develop in their own New Wave films of the early 1960s; the following decade made politics the key concept for revealing and demystifying cinema—the entire grammar of film could be interpreted through a political prism; the final decades of the century proceeded to explore cinema as a world in itself, what might be called the "visual" world of the image, in all its possible states (from television to video, and then digital) and in all its new geographical extensions. Today it is cinema as history that imposes itself as the form for viewing and re-viewing films. Each period has given rise to its cinematographic fetish, its tool for representing the world: the revealing veil, in the postwar period; the camera as pen in the 1960s; the cine-tract ten years later; then the *tout-écran*; and, the DV camera at the turn of the century. Another one is now available to us: the movement of form that leads from the camera as pen to the camera as history.

Notes

Introduction: The Cinematographic Forms of History

1. See Gilles Deleuze, "Preface to the American Edition of *The Time-Image*," in *Two Regimes of Madness: Texts and Interviews, 1975–1995*, edited by David Lapoujade (Cambridge, MA: MIT Press, 2006).
2. François Truffaut, quoted in Antoine de Baecque and Serge Toubiana, *Truffaut: A Biography* (New York: Knopf, 1999), 27.
3. Quoted in the preface to Jean Starobinski, *L'invention de la liberté* (Geneva: Skira, 1964).
4. Jean Starobinski, *L'invention de la liberté, 1700–1789; suivi de 1789, les emblèmes de la raison* (Paris: Gallimard, 2006), 7.
5. Jean-Paul Sartre, *The Words* (New York: Vintage Books, 1981), 118–19.
6. Marc Ferro, *Cinema and History* (Detroit: Wayne State University Press, 1988), 29. Originally published as "Le film, une contre-analyse de la société?" *Annales ESC* 1 (1973): 109–24.
7. Serge Daney, *Persévérance* (Paris: POL, 1994), 158–59.
8. Dudley Andrew, "The 'Three Ages' of Cinema Studies and the Age to Come," *PMLA* 115, no. 3 (May 2000): 341–51.
9. Deleuze, *Two Regimes of Madness*, 284.
10. Arlette Farge, "Écriture historique, écriture cinématographique," in *De l'histoire au cinéma*, edited by Antoine de Baecque and Christian Delage (Brussels: Éditions Complexes, 1998), 111–25.
11. Jacques Revel, "Un exercice de désorientation: *Blow up*," in *De l'histoire au cinéma*, edited by Antoine de Baecque and Christian Delage (Brussels: Éditions Complexes, 1998), 99–110.
12. See Natalie Zemon Davis, *Slaves on Screen: Film and Historical Vision* (Cambridge, MA: Harvard University Press, 2002), esp. chap. 1, "Film as Historical Narrative."
13. Arlette Farge, "Le cinéma est la langue maternelle du XXe siècle," in "Le siècle du cinéma," special issue, *Cahiers du cinéma*, Nov. 2000.

14 Deleuze, *Two Regimes of Madness*, 215.
15 Jean-Louis Comolli and Jacques Rancière (eds.), "Le miroir à deux faces," *Arrêt sur histoire* (Paris: Centre Georges-Pompidou, 1997), 13.
16 Walter Benjamin, *Selected Writings*, vol. 4 (Cambridge, MA: Harvard University Press, 2005), 256.
17 Ibid., 396.
18 Marc Bloch, *Les Caractères originaux de l'histoire rurale française* (Paris: Les Belles Lettres, 1931), 14.
19 Siegfried Kracauer, *History: The Last Things Before the Last* (New York: Oxford University Press, 1969), 53.
20 Ibid., 57–58.
21 Siegfried Kracauer, "Photography," in *The Mass Ornament* (Cambridge, MA: Harvard University Press, 1995), 50.
22 Louis Delluc, *Écrits cinématographiques*, vol. 2, pt. 1, *Cinéma et Cie* (Paris: Cinémathèque française, 1986), 123.
23 Jacques Rancière, "L'historicité du cinéma," in *De l'histoire au cinéma*, edited by A. de Baecque and C. Delage (Brussels: Éditions Complexes, 1998), 45.
24 Jacques Aumont, *Amnésies. Fictions du cinema d'après Jean-Luc Godard* (Paris: POL, 1999), 114.
25 Quoted in Christian Delage, *Chaplin, la grande histoire* (Paris: Jean-Michel Place, 1998), 7.
26 Deleuze, *Two Regimes of Madness*, 353.
27 Jacques Rancière, "Les mots de l'histoire du cinéma," *Cahiers du cinéma*, Oct. 1995, 48–54.
28 Alain Badiou, "Cinema as a Democratic Emblem," *Parrhesia*, no. 6 (2009): 3.
29 Quoted in Louis Guilloux, *Absent de Paris* (Paris: Gallimard, 1951), 182–83.

1. Foreclosed Forms: How Images of Mass Death Reemerged in Modern Cinema

1 Alain Bergala, *"Monika" de Ingmar Bergman* (Crisnée, Belgium: Yellow Now, 2003), 14.
2 Jean-Luc Godard, *Arts*, July 30, 1958.
3 Ingmar Bergman, *Images: My Life in Film* (New York: Arcade, 1994), 295–96.
4 See Antoine de Baecque and Serge Toubiana, *Truffaut: A Biography* (New York: Knopf, 1999), 27.
5 This list of newsreels is taken from the book that has become the reference work on the subject: Sylvie Lindeperg, *Clio de 5 à 7: Les actualités filmées de la Libération* (Paris: CNRS, 2000), 156–71.
6 Annette Wieviorka, quoted in ibid, 168.
7 Ibid., 164.

8. Alain Resnais, "Les photos jaunies ne m'émeuvent pas," an interview with Antoine de Baecque and Claire Vassé, in "Le siècle du cinéma," special issue, *Cahiers du cinéma*, Nov. 2000, 70–75.
9. Jean Galtier-Boissière, *Journal, 1940–1950* (Paris: Quai Voltaire, 1992), 440.
10. Jorge Semprun, *Literature or Life* (New York: Viking, 1997), 110.
11. See Joshua Hirsch, *Afterimage: Film, Trauma, and the Holocaust* (Philadelphia: Temple University Press, 2003).
12. Quoted in Lindeperg, *Clio de 5 à 7*, 178–80.
13. See Georges Didi-Huberman, *Images in Spite of All: Four Photographs from Auschwitz* (Chicago: University of Chicago Press, 2008).
14. Quoted in Christian Delage, "Nuremberg, le premier procès filmé," *L'Histoire*, no. 303 (Nov. 2005).
15. Quoted in Lindeperg, *Clio de 5 à 7*, 239.
16. Christian Delage, *La Vérité par l'image, de Nuremberg au procès Milosevic* (Paris: Denoël, 2006).
17. Joseph Kessel, "Le procès de Nuremberg," *France soir*, Dec. 3, 1945.
18. Jacques Aumont, *Du visage au cinéma* (Paris: Etoile, 1992).
19. Serge Daney, *Persévérance* (Paris: POL, 1994); and most notably the article entitled "Le travelling de Kapo," *Trafic*, no. 4 (1992).
20. On foreclosure, a key concept for Lacan, and its definitions see Jean Laplanche and Jean-Baptiste Pontalis, *The Language of Psychoanalysis* (London: Hogarth, 1973), 164–65; Jacques Lacan, "On a Question Preliminary to Any Possible Treatment of Psychosis," in *Ecrits* (London: Routledge, 1977); Jean Laplanche, *Hölderlin and the Question of the Father* (Paris: PUF, 1961); Vincent Descombes, *Objects of All Sorts: A Philosophical Grammar* (Oxford: Basil Blackwell, 1986).
21. Jacques Rivette, "De l'abjection," *Cahiers du cinéma*, June 1961.
22. Daney, "Le travelling de Kapo," 17–18.
23. Jacques Rivette, "Sur M. Verdoux et Charles Chaplin," *Cahiers du cinéma*, Aug. 1963.
24. Daney, "Le travelling de Kapo," 22.
25. Resnais, "Les photos jaunies ne m'émeuvent pas."
26. Ibid.
27. See Frank Brady, *Citizen Welles: A Biography of Orson Welles* (New York: Scribner's, 1989), 380.
28. Peter Bogdanovich and Jonathan Rosenbaum, *This Is Orson Welles* (New York: Da Capo Press, 1998), 189.
29. See David Robinson, *Chaplin: His Life and Art* (New York: McGraw-Hill, 1985), 531.
30. Ibid., 542.
31. Kenneth S. Lynn, *Charlie Chaplin and His Times* (New York: Simon and Schuster, 1997), 441.

32 André Bazin, "Monsieur Verdoux ou le martyre de Charlot," *L'Ecran français*, Dec. 30, 1947.

33 In the spring of 1943 Chaplin's ex-mistress, Joan Barry, took him to court for aggravated assault and neglect. The court proceedings, widely covered by the media, explored the filmmaker's sexual life in considerable detail, making him out to be a pervert in the eyes of the public, even though he was acquitted in the end. In December 1944 Barry sued again, this time to obtain recognition that he was the father of her child, even though a semen sample had concluded otherwise. This allowed for yet another media campaign, in which Chaplin became a "lecherous dog," a "foreigner with loose morals," and a "Jewish Blue Beard." A third trial, on appeal, took place in 1945 and led to a new series of sexual slurs and xenophobic and anti-Semitic insults. This time the court found against Chaplin, who was ordered to pay Joan Barry compensation and alimony for a child that was not even his! Even before the McCarthy witch hunts, which forced him into exile in 1952, the filmmaker was thus virulently attacked in the press as "un-American." See David Robinson, *Chaplin*, 520–28.

34 All these comments were made by Samuel Fuller and recorded in the course of his interview with Emil Weiss, who made *Falkenau, the Impossible* in 1988.

35 Jean Narboni and Noël Simsolo, *Il était une fois Samuel Fuller* (Paris: Cahiers du cinéma, 1986), 115.

36 Luc Moullet, "Cheveux d'or sur soupe au lait," review of *Verboten!* by Samuel Fuller, *Cahiers du cinéma*, June 1960.

37 This quote and the previous ones were taken from Lindeperg, *Clio de 5 à 7*, 232.

38 The "McGuffin" is a concept and neologism invented by Hitchcock to designate the "key" to the mystery, the source and resource of suspense.

39 Roberto Rossellini, *Le Cinéma révélé* (Paris: Étoile, 1988), 26–27.

40 Alain Bergala, *"Voyage en Italie" de Roberto Rossellini* (Crisnée, Belgique: Yellow Now, 1990), 50.

41 James Agee, *Sur le cinéma* (Paris: Cahiers du cinéma, 1991), 144.

42 Maurice Blanchot, *The Space of Literature* (Lincoln: University of Nebraska Press, 1982), 261.

43 Roberto Rossellini, *Fragments d'une autobiographie* (Paris: Ramsay, 1987); see especially the chapter entitled "Sur une boîte en argent."

44 Resnais, "Les photos jaunies ne m'émeuvent pas."

45 Narboni and Simsolo, *Il était une fois Samuel Fuller*, 115.

46 De Baecque and Toubiana, *Truffaut*, 162.

47 Ibid.

48 Rivette, "De l'abjection."

49 Claude Lanzmann, *"Shoah": An Oral History of the Holocaust: The Complete Text of the Film* (New York: Pantheon, 1985). Given its historical and cinematographic importance, *Shoah* would require an entire book of its own. It shall be tackled only

briefly here through a revealing account by filmmaker Arnaud Desplechin, according to whom the film had a decisive impact on his decision to become a filmmaker and on his understanding of cinema:

> The history of the New Wave opens with *Night and Fog* and ends with *Shoah*. These two films marked my birth as a spectator, and then my re-birth as a spectator-filmmaker. In hindsight, I don't think there's been a stronger, more innovative film than *Shoah* in the past twenty years. . . . As a student at IDHEC, I was waiting for the film that Daney and Godard had promised, which was to finally give us the key to the confusing world in which we lived. That film finally came; it was *Shoah*. This film contained all the keys, all the problematics I had been waiting for. All one had to do was take them from the film—for instance, the dubious paradox raised by Godard about "filming the executioners" (not filming the victims in a victimizing way). It was Lanzmann who found the cinematographic solution: he offers no face-to-face encounter between victim and executioner, but a "non-encounter"; it had to be filmed as a triangle of victim, henchman, and witness. Only one film had had such a profound international impact, had challenged all nations so radically: Chaplin's *The Great Dictator*. So, yes, Claude Lanzmann played the same role in my life as a spectator as Charles Chaplin for Truffaut, Godard, and the rest of them. . . . As opposed to Godard, I do not believe cinema failed the century. With Lanzmann's film, cinema has had the painful privilege of enabling us to understand the unthinkable. It was not literature, or painting or theatre, or even philosophy. No, it was a film shown in cinemas, first at the Trois Luxembourg theater, then six months later, in 1985, at the Saint-Germain-des-Prés. Cinema proved capable of answering that which was to remain unanswered. (Letter to the author, Feb. 12, 2001)

50 Jean Luc Godard, "Hiroshima, notre amour" roundtable, *Cahiers du cinéma*, July 1959.

51 In an ironic twist of history: when the DVD of *Kapo* by Gillo Pontecorvo was released by Carlotta Films, in the spring of 2006, most of the additional material focused on interpretations of the film by Jacques Rivette and Serge Daney, whether to confirm or contest them.

2. From Versailles to the Silver Screen: Sacha Guitry, Historian of France

1 An article entitled "Versailles tendance Coppola," published in the weekly magazine *Télérama* on June 22, 2005, describes the favorable yet costly conditions imposed on filmmakers by the public entity in charge of managing the Versailles Chateau.

2. From Versailles to the Silver Screen

2. See "Transformer la mémoire en modernité," in *Nouvel observateur*, May 15, 1996, in which Patrice Leconte recounts the difficulties he encountered when shooting at Versailles; "Deux films et l'histoire," in *L'Humanité*, April 25, 1975, in which Bertrand Tavernier rages against Versailles; "Musiciens baroques," in *Libération*, Aug. 6, 1992, in which Alain Corneau discusses the shooting of *Tous les matins du monde* and says he "would prefer the Creuse province to Versailles any day."
3. The website www.vauxlevicomte.fr details the rental conditions for the castle, the gardens, and specific locations.
4. Jean Renoir, *Le Passé vivant* (Paris: Cahiers du cinéma, 1989), 34–35.
5. *Et Versailles vous est conté* (Paris: Raoul Solar, 1954) contains a full transcript of the author's radio broadcasts; see also *Si Versailles m'était conté*, text by Sacha Guitry (Paris: Raoul Solar, 1966).
6. See application file for the temporary funding of feature films, CNC/Crédit national archive, at BiFi, CN 979 B 542.
7. *Le Film français*, Dec. 26, 1954. The usual formula for determining total French sales is to multiply Parisian box-office receipts by five or six.
8. *Combat*, Aug. 9, 1953.
9. Georges Sadoul, *L'Humanité*, Feb. 12, 1954.
10. François Truffaut, preface to *Le Cinéma et moi*, by Sacha Guitry, edited by André Bernard and Claude Gauteur (Paris: Ramsay, 1977).
11. *Le Figaro littéraire*, Jan. 9, 1954.
12. *Bulletin of the Société des amis de Versailles* 1 (1954).
13. The princess of Lamballe was indeed beheaded in September of 1792 but by the knife of a *septembriseur*, not the blade of a guillotine.
14. *Le Figaro littéraire*, Feb. 24, 1954.
15. *Les Lettres françaises*, Feb. 15, 1954.
16. *Journal officiel de la République française*, Jan. 22, 1954.
17. "Letter to M. André Cornu, Secrétaire d'Etat aux Beaux-Arts, on the film by M. Sacha Guitry, 'Si Versailles m'était conté,'" published in Le Figaro, March 17, 1954.
18. *Journal officiel de la République française*, March 26, 1954.
19. Ibid.
20. Sacha Guitry, foreword to *Si Versailles m'était conté*.
21. Luc Moullet, "*Si Versailles m'était conté*," in *Sacha Guitry, cinéaste*, edited by Philippe Arnaud (Locarno: Yellow Now, 1993), 260–63; and Noël Simsolo, "Monstres et monuments," in ibid., 133–67.
22. François Truffaut, *Cahiers du cinéma*, April 1954; see also Jacques Audiberti, in ibid.
23. See Jacques Audiberti, *Cahiers du cinéma*, Feb. 1956.
24. Truffaut, preface to *Le Cinéma et moi*.

25 See, e.g., Raymond Castans, *Sacha Guitry* (Paris: Fallois, 1993), esp. "Occupé, libéré, acclamé," 347–92; and File on the Commission de recherche historique, Meeting of Feb. 7, 1948, BiFi, CRH 50B2.
26 See *Cahiers du cinéma*, Jan. 1954, in which François Truffaut writes: "This is the appeal of *Si Versailles m'était conté*, despite what all the critics say. What was considered central to French 'grandeur' for centuries—the Christian faith and sense of honor, respect for the clergy and the nobility, all foundations of a hierarchical society—has only a secondary role in it . . . That period when the Church refused to bury Adrienne Lecouvreur was more inspiring for artists than ours, in which barrack comedians are welcome at the Vatican. We are now in the days of Republican airs, and the fall of this film was therefore to be expected as part of the problem."
27 François Mars, "Citizen Sacha," *Cahiers du cinéma*, Oct. 1958.
28 See Ernst H. Kantorowicz, *The King's Two Bodies: A Study in Mediaeval Political Theology* (Princeton, NJ: Princeton University Press, 1957).
29 See Norbert Elias, *The Civilizing Process* (Oxford: Blackwell, 1982).

3. "Me? Uh, Nothing!": The French New Wave, Politics, and History

1 Antoine de Baecque and Serge Toubiana, "A Hussar with His Sword Drawn," in *Truffaut* (New York: Alfred A. Knopf, 1999); Claude Chabrol, *Et pourtant je tourne* (Paris: Laffont, 1976).
2 Antoine de Baecque, *Les "Cahiers du cinéma": Histoire d'une revue* (Paris: Etoile, 1991), see "Positif poussé vers la copie zero," 1:141–46.
3 Michel Mardore, "Un cinéma qui n'a rien à dire", *Cinéma 60*, March 1960.
4 Jean-Luc Godard, *Histoire(s) du cinéma* (Paris: Gallimard/Gaumont, 1998), 1:36–37.
5 Luc Moullet, "Sur les brisées de Marlowe," *Cahiers du cinéma*, March 1959; Jean-Luc Godard, "Hiroshima, notre amour" roundtable, *Cahiers du cinéma*, July 1959.
6 See Jacques Laurent, "La critique des catacombes," *Arts*, Feb. 14, 1955.
7 Emmanuelle Loyer, "Engagement/désengagement dans la France de l'après-guerre," in *Les Écrivains face à l'histoire*, edited by Antoine de Baecque (Paris: BPI du Centre Georges-Pompidou, 1998), 75–94.
8 See Bernard Frank, "Grognards et hussards," *Les Temps modernes*, Dec. 1952; and Robert Benayoun, *Positif*, Feb. 1962.
9 Jean-Paul Sartre, *What Is Literature?* (New York: Philosophical Library, 1949), 274.
10 Bernard Frank, "Grognards et hussards."
11 Ibid.
12 Julien Gracq, *La Littérature à l'estomac* (Paris: José Corti, 1950).

13. See Loyer, "Engagement/désengagement dans la France de l'après-guerre."
14. See Roger Nimier, *Le Grand d'Espagne* (Paris: La Table Ronde, 1950); and André Parinaud, *Arts*, June 19, 1952.
15. See Jacques Rivette, "Lettre sur Rossellini," *Cahiers du cinéma*, April 1955; Antoine de Baecque, "Gégauff, le premier des Paul," *Cahiers du cinéma*, Sept. 1997, special issue on Chabrol (repr. in *Feu sur le Quartier Général! Textes, entretiens, récits* [Paris: Cahier du cinéma, 2008]); and Eric Rohmer, "La revanche de l'Occident," *Cahiers du cinéma*, March 1953.
16. See Antoine de Baecque, *La Cinéphilie: Invention d'un regard, histoire d'une culture, 1944–1968* (Paris: Fayard, 2003), 183–86, 33–61.
17. André Bazin, "Comment peut-on être hitchcocko-hawksien?" *Cahiers du cinéma*, Feb. 1955.
18. André Bazin to Georges Sadoul, cited in de Baecque, *La Cinéphilie*, 183–86.
19. François Truffaut, *Arts*, July 9, 1958.
20. Mardore, "Un cinéma qui n'a rien à dire," *Cinéma 60*, March 1960.
21. Marcel Martin, *Cinéma 60*, March 1960; Benayoun, *Positif*, Feb. 1962.
22. Jean-René Huguenin, *Une autre jeunesse* (Paris: Seuil, 1965).
23. Letter dated Sept. 26, 1960, François Truffaut Archives, BiFi, CCH 1960.
24. Michel Audiard, *Arts*, March 23, 1960.
25. Henri Jeanson, *Cinémonde*, June 30, 1959; Jacques Lanzmann, *Arts*, Nov. 14, 1959; Jean Nocher, *France Inter*, Nov. 15, 1959; Jean Aurenche, *Cinéma 60*, March 1960.
26. Benayoun, *Positif*, Feb. 1962.
27. Raymond Borde, *Premier plan*, May 1960.
28. Bernard Chardère, *Premier plan*, no. 9, May 1960; François Nourissier, *Arts*, April 24, 1960.
29. Jean Cau, *L'Express*, Feb. 25, 1960.
30. Jean-Luc Godard, *Cahiers du cinéma*, Dec. 1962.
31. Jean Collet, *Jean-Luc Godard* (Paris: Seghers, 1963).
32. Michel Marie, *Comprendre Godard: Travelling avant sur "À bout de souffle" et "Le Mépris"* (Paris: Armand Collin Cinéma, 2006), 40–41; Hélène Liogier, "La Nouvelle Vague selon Parvulesco," *1895*, no. 40 (June 2003).
33. Robert Benayoun, *Positif*, July 1962.
34. Roger Nimier, *Le Hussard bleu* (Paris: Gallimard, 1950).
35. Ibid.
36. Jean-Luc Godard, *Cahiers du cinéma*, May 1958.
37. Marie, *Comprendre Godard*, 48–49.
38. See ibid.
39. "L'échéance de la loi de développement pose un grave problème à la profession," *Le Film français*, June 28, 1957.
40. Crédit national file, 1958, BiFi, CN14B10.
41. Jacques Flaud, "Jeunesse commune," *Le Film français*, May 14, 1958.

42 Jean-Luc Godard, *Arts*, April 23, 1959.
43 See *Le Monde*, April 2, 1966; and *Nouvel observateur*, April 6, 1966.
44 See *Combat*, Feb. 12, 1968.
45 Jean-Luc Godard, "Pour un cinéma politique," *La Gazette du cinéma*, Sept. 1950.
46 François Truffaut, *Arts*, May 15, 1957.
47 François Truffaut, *Arts*, December 12, 1956.
48 Catherine Rihoit, *Brigitte Bardot, un mythe français* (Paris: Olivier Orban, 1986), 138.
49 Jean-Luc Godard, *Cahiers du cinéma*, July 1957.
50 Godard, *Arts*, April 23, 1959.
51 François Truffaut, *Arts*, April 29, 1959.
52 Raoul Coutard, *Cahiers du cinéma*, Dec. 1962.
53 Laurent Gervereau, "Une guerre pas si invisible, pas si regardée," in *Photographier la guerre d'Algérie*, edited by Laurent Gervereau and Benjamin Stora (Paris: Marval, 2004), 150–59.
54 Quoted in Benjamin Stora, "*Le Petit soldat*: Godard, ou les ambiguïtés d'une guerre," in *Imaginaires de guerre: Les Images dans les guerres d'Algérie et du Viêt Nam* (Paris: La Découverte, 1997).
55 Ibid.
56 For more on *Octobre à Paris*, in addition to the references in the work of Michel Marie and Benjamin Stora, see "Coups d'État," *Les Inrockuptibles*, Oct. 16, 2001; and "*Octobre à Paris*, à saisir," *Libération*, Jan. 14, 2002. *L'Ufoleis* and *Image et son*, no. 160, March 1963, also published a booklet containing the film's script and commentary on the film.
57 Jacques Rozier, interview by the author, March 5, 2006.
58 Noël Favrelière, *Le Désert à l'aube* (Paris: Minuit, 1960).
59 Guy Chalon, *Cinéma 61*, May 1961.
60 Quoted in Marie, *Comprendre Godard*.
61 See Roland Barthes, *Writing Degree Zero* (New York: Hill and Wang, 1977), in which Barthes compares this "zero degree writing" to a sickly "Orphean dream" of "a writer without literature"; "it represents the last episode of a Passion of writing, which recounts stage by stage the disintegration of bourgeois consciousness" (5).
62 Quoted in René Prédal, "Alain Cavalier, filmer des visages," *L'Avant-scène cinéma*, March-April 1995.
63 *Cinéma 61*, Oct. 1961.
64 Stora, *Imaginaires de guerre*.
65 Quoted in Michel Marie, *"Muriel" d'Alain Resnais* (Paris: Atlante, 2005).
66 Jean-Luc Godard, *Introduction à une véritable histoire du cinéma* (Paris: L'Albatros, 1980), 42–43.
67 See Antoine de Baecque, "Sous les pavés de Mai 68," *Libération*, Dec. 9, 2003; Antoine de Baecque, "Le cinéma de Mai 68," in *68, une histoire collective*, edited

by Philippe Artières and M. Zancarini-Fournel (Paris: La Découverte, 2008); Didier Péron, "Garrel, Mai de maître," *Libération*, Oct. 26, 2005; Jean-Michel Frodon, "Garrel: Le choc et la grâce," *Cahiers du cinéma*, Oct. 2005; and Antoine de Baecque, Stéphane Bourquet, and Emmanuel Burdeau, eds., *Cinéma 68* (Paris: Cahiers du cinéma, 2008).

4. Peter Watkins, Live from History: The Films, Style, and Method of Cinema's Special Correspondent

1. Quoted in Lewis Jacobs, *The Documentary Tradition* (New York: Norton, 1979), 5.
2. Especially in France, where this recognition manifested itself through the release of his films on DVD, the rerelease of new prints of *Edvard Munch* and *La Commune* in theaters (in February 2005 and October 2007, respectively), tributes (at the La Rochelle International Film Festival, during June and July 2004), and a series of major articles in *Cahiers du cinéma* (May 2000, Sept. 2004, and Feb. 2005).
3. Peter Watkins, *Media Crisis* (Paris: Homnisphères, 2003). The original English text was never published but is available on the Peter Watkins website: http://pwatkins.mnsi.net/index.htm. Quotes used in this paragraph are taken from the website.
4. See Ian Aitken, *Film and Reform: John Grierson and the Documentary Film Movement* (New York: Routledge, 1990); and Jacobs, *The Documentary Tradition*, 5.
5. *The Diary of an Unknown Soldier, Forgotten Faces, Culloden, The War Game*, set of 2 DVDs, BBC Edition, 2004.
6. On *Culloden* see Étienne Lesourd, "Images of War, War of Images: A Study of Peter Watkins's Film *Culloden*," master's thesis, University of Nancy-II, 2003.
7. On Orson Welles's radio broadcast of *The War of the Worlds* see Youssef Ishaghpour, *Orson Welles*, vol. 1 (Paris: La Différence, 2001).
8. See Catherine Saouter, *Le Documentaire: Contestation et propagande* (Québec: XYZ, 1996).
9. Quoted in Guy Gauthier, *Le Documentaire: Un autre cinéma* (Paris: Nathan, 1995), 59.
10. Quoted in Gilles Marsolais, *L'Aventure du cinéma direct* (Paris: Seghers, 1974), 72.
11. Patrick Barbéris and Dominique Chapuis, *Roman Karmen, une légende rouge* (Paris: Seuil, 2002).
12. Quoted in Marsolais, *L'Aventure du cinéma direct*, 76.
13. Peter Watkins, "Media Crisis—Suggestions for Use and Personal Prologue," http://pwatkins.mnsi.net/part1_home.htm.
14. Marsolais, *L'Aventure du cinéma direct*, 91–94; Marcel Ophuls, *Veillées d'armes: Histoire du journalisme en temps de guerre* (France: s.n., 1994; published as DVD case with a libretto by Arte video, 2005).

15 On Robert Drew and Richard Leacock see Gauthier, *Le Documentaire*; Marsolais, *L'Aventure du cinéma direct*; and Ingo Neubert, *Drew/Leacock, American Documents* (Baltimore: Trier, 1996).
16 See Marsolais, *L'Aventure du cinéma direct*.
17 Vincent Vatrican and Cédric Venail, eds., *Trajets à travers le cinéma de Robert Kramer* (Aix-en-Provence: Maison des images, 2001).
18 See Tony Aldgate, "Grierson et après: Documentaire, cinéma, télévision au Royaume-Uni dans les années 50 et 60," in *L'Âge d'or du documentaire: Europe, années 50–60*, edited by Roger Odin, vol. 2 (Paris: L'Harmattan, 1998), 9–38.
19 Quoted in Aldgate, *L'Âge d'or du documentaire*, 2:28.
20 Watkins, "Media Crisis—Suggestions for Use and Personal Prologue."
21 See "Uncomfortable Truths: The Cinema of Peter Watkins," http://hcl.harvard.edu/hfa/films/2001janfeb/watkins.html.
22 Yvonne Baby, "La jeunesse et les idoles dans la société," *Le Monde*, May 4, 1967.
23 Peter Watkins interview, *Libération*, Feb. 2, 2005.
24 John Cook and Patrick Murphy, *Freethinker: The Life and Work of Peter Watkins* (Manchester: Manchester University Press, 2002).
25 The Young Republicans group rose up against *Punishment Park* and its supporters among leftist students, especially the SDS.
26 Peter Watkins interview, *Cahiers du cinéma*, Feb. 2005.
27 Ibid.
28 Hubert Damisch and Jean-Pierre Rehm, "La feinte du direct," *Cahiers du cinéma*, Feb. 2005.
29 Gauthier, *Le Documentaire*, 184.
30 See Joseph A. Gomez, *Peter Watkins* (Boston: Twayne, 1979), 44.
31 Henry Chapier, "La Bombe," *Combat*, April 7, 1967.
32 Georges Sadoul, "Un documentaire du futur," *Les Lettres françaises*, April 6, 1967.
33 Jacques Isnard, "Un film de réalité-fiction," *Le Monde*, April 7, 1967.
34 Jean de Baroncelli, in his "Le cinéma" column, *Le Monde*, April 7, 1967.
35 Claude-Jean Philippe, *Télérama*, April 23, 1967.
36 Jean-Louis Bory, "En forme de cri," *Nouvel observateur*, April 5, 1967.
37 Ibid.
38 Samuel Lachize, "Quelque chose de pourri au royaume d'Angleterre," *L'Humanité*, June 21, 1967.
39 Claude-Jean Philippe, *Télérama*, April 23, 1967.
40 Ibid.
41 See Jean-Louis Bory, "Horaces et Curiaces de notre temps," *Nouvel observateur*, Nov. 12, 1969.
42 Ignacio Ramonet, "Force de frappe," *Le Monde diplomatique*, April 1978.
43 Watkins interview, *Libération*, Feb. 2, 2005.

44 Philippe Azoury, *Libération*, February 2, 2005.
45 Watkins interview, *Libération*, Feb. 2, 2005. Watkins's comments in the following four paragraphs are also taken from this interview.
46 Peter Watkins, "Role of American MAVM, Hollywood and the Monoform," http://pwatkins.mnsi.net/hollywood.htm.
47 See Peter Watkins, "Public-Alternative Processes and Practices," http://pwatkins.mnsi.net/public.htm; see also Cyril Béghin, "Portrait groupé," *Cahiers du cinéma*, Feb. 2005 (on collective work with amateurs).
48 Peter Watkins, "Conclusion," http://pwatkins.mnsi.net/conclusion.htm.
49 Stéphane Bouquet, "La Commune libre et naïve de Watkins," *Cahiers du cinéma*, May 2000.
50 Patrick Watkins interview, "Chacun devait écrire ses dialogues," *Cahiers du cinéma*, May 2000. All comments from Patrick Watkins in this paragraph are taken from this interview.
51 About this recent and abundant bibliography see Robert Tombs, *La Guerre contre Paris, 1871* (Paris: Aubier, 1997).
52 Watkins, *Media Crisis*, "Postface: La censure n'est plus ce qu'elle était. De La Bombe (1965) à La Commune (1999)," http://homnispheres.info/article.php3?id_article=45.
53 Ibid.
54 Ibid.
55 Watkins interview, *Libération*, Feb. 2, 2005.
56 The project and activities of Rebond pour la Commune are described in an appendix to *Media Crisis*; see also Caroline Lensing-Hebben, Patrick Watkins, and Jean-Pierre Le Nestour, *Rebond pour la Commune* (Montreuil: self-published, 2000). The organization maintains a website: www.rebond.org/rebond.htm.
57 Watkins interview, *Libération*, Feb. 2, 2005.

5. The Theory of Sparks: A History in Images, According to Jean-Luc Godard

1 The phrase "professionals of the profession" was used ironically by Jean-Luc Godard to thank the members of the Cesar Academy who gave him a lifetime achievement honorary award in 1990.
2 Jean-Luc Godard, "À propos de cinéma et d'histoire: Discours de réception du prix Adorno" ("About cinema and history: Adorno Award acceptance speech"), Frankfurt, Sept. 17, 1995, in *Jean-Luc Godard par Jean-Luc Godard*, vol. 2, *1984–1998* (Paris: Cahiers du cinéma, 1998), 401–5 (originally published in *Trafic* 18 [spring 1996]). The quotations that follow are excerpted from this lecture.
3 Jean-Luc Godard, *Histoire(s) du cinéma*, 4 vols. (Paris: Gallimard/Gaumont, 1998), 1:1b (the pages of these volumes are not numbered). This four-volume work was

published in conjunction with the film, and its organization is identical to that of the film: four volumes, each divided into two sections—designated "a" and "b."

4   Godard, "À propos de cinéma et d'histoire." The quotations that follow are excerpted from this lecture.
5   See Alain Bergala, "Une boucle bouclée," a new interview with Jean-Luc Godard, in *Jean-Luc Godard par Jean-Luc Godard*, 2:34.
6   See François Furet, interview with Antoine de Baecque, in "Le siècle du cinéma," special issue, *Cahiers du cinéma*, Nov. 2000. The quotations that follow are excerpted from this interview.
7   Jean-Luc Godard, *Histoire(s) du cinéma*, 2:2a.
8   Barthélémy Amengual, *"Bande à part" de Jean-Luc Godard* (Crisnée, Belgium: Yellow Now, 1993), 14.
9   Quatremère de Quincy, *Lettres à Miranda sur le déplacement des arts de l'Italie* (1796), introduction and annotations by Édouard Pommier (Paris: Macula, 1989).
10 Jean-Luc Godard, *Éloge de l'amour, texte de Jean-Luc Godard* (Paris: POL, 2002).
11 Louis Aragon, "Qu'est-ce que l'art, Jean-Luc Godard?" *Les Lettres françaises*, Sept. 9, 1965.
12 Bernard Dort, "Godard ou le romantique abusif," *Les Temps modernes*, Dec. 1965.
13 Jacques Aumont, *L'Œil interminable: Cinéma et peinture* (Paris: Librairie Séguier, 1989), 224.
14 Jean-Luc Godard, "Passion, introduction à un scénario," in *Jean-Luc Godard par Jean-Luc Godard*, 1:486–97.
15 Godard paid countless tributes to Langlois' museum and to the Malraux of *Museum Without Walls*. The two principal texts are Jean-Luc Godard, "Malraux mauvais Français?" *Cahiers du cinéma*, May 1958; and Jean-Luc Godard, "Grâce à Henri Langlois," *Nouvel observateur*, Jan. 12, 1966.
16 Godard, "À propos de cinéma et d'histoire."
17 This was Jean Cocteau's phrase, taken up in Henri Langlois, *Trois cents ans de cinéma* (Paris: Cahiers du cinéma/Cinémathèque française, 1986), 268.
18 See Dominique Païni, *Conserver, montrer: Où l'on ne craint pas d'édifier un musée pour le cinéma* (Crinée, Belgium: Yellow Now, 1992), 32.
19 Ibid., 32–35.
20 Godard, *Histoire(s) du cinéma*, 2:2b.
21 Païni, *Conserver, montrer*, 34.
22 Ibid., 17.
23 The project to screen films in the museum of cinema exists: a few pages list the film sequences that were to be screened; see Laurent Mannoni, *Histoire de la cinémathèque française* (Paris: Gallimard, 2006), 425.
24 *Le Monde*, April 2, 1966; *Nouvel observateur*, April 6, 1966.
25 Godard, "Malraux mauvais Français?"
26 Dominique Païni, in "Histoire(s) du cinéma," special issue, *Art Press*, Nov. 1998.

27 Ibid.
28 Jean-Luc Godard, *Histoire(s) du cinéma*, 3:3b; Leslie Hill, "A Form That Thinks: Godard, Blanchot, Citation," in *For ever Godard*, edited by Michael Temple, James Williams, and Michael Witt (London: Black Dog, 2004), 396–415.
29 André Malraux, *The Voices of Silence* (Garden City, NY: Doubleday, 1953), 241.
30 André Malraux, "Discours prononcé lors de l'inauguration de la maison de la culture de Bourges" [April 18, 1964], in Philippe Urfalino, *L'Invention de la politique culturelle* (Paris: La Documentation française, 1997).
31 André Malraux, "Discours de clôture du festival de Cannes" [May 1959], in Urfalino, *L'Invention de la politique culturelle*.
32 Godard, *Histoire(s) du cinéma*, 3:3a.
33 Jean-Luc Godard and Youssef Ishaghpour, *Archéologie du cinéma et mémoire du siècle* (Paris: Farrago, 2000), 67–69.
34 André Malraux, *The Psychology of Art* (New York: Pantheon, 1949–50).
35 Iris Barry, *Trois siècles d'art aux États-Unis* (Paris: Édition des musées nationaux, 1938).
36 Jean-Luc Godard and Anne-Marie Miéville, *The Old Place* (Paris: POL, 2000), 97.
37 Godard, *Éloge de l'amour, texte de Jean-Luc Godard*, 44.
38 *Télérama*, May 16, 2001.
39 Jean-Luc Godard, *Introduction à une véritable histoire du cinéma* (Aix-en-Provence: Albatros, 1980), 21–22.
40 Jean-Luc Godard, *Histoire(s) du cinéma*, 4:4a.
41 Jacques Aumont, *Amnésies: Fictions du cinéma d'après Jean-Luc Godard* (Paris: POL, 1999), 31.
42 Jean-Luc Godard, interview with Antoine de Baecque, *Libération*, April 6, 2002.
43 Jean-Luc Godard, *Histoire(s) du cinéma*, 2:2a.
44 Jean-Luc Godard, *JLG/JLG: Phrases* (Paris: POL, 1996), 14.
45 Godard, *Histoire(s) du cinéma*, 4:4b.
46 Jacques Rancière, "A Fable Without a Moral: Godard, Cinema, (Hi)stories," in *Film Fables* (New York: Berg, 2006), 171–87.
47 Godard, *Histoire(s) du cinéma*, 1:1b.
48 Rancière, "A Fable Without a Moral," 171.
49 Philippe Sollers, "Il y a des fantômes plein l'écran . . . ," interview, *Cahiers du cinéma*, May 1997.
50 Alain Bergala, "L'Ange de l'Histoire," in *Nul mieux que Godard* (Paris: Cahiers du cinéma, 1999), 229.
51 Godard, *Histoire(s) du cinéma*, 4:4b.
52 Ibid., 2:2a.
53 Jacques Rancière, "L'historicité du cinéma," in *De l'histoire au cinéma*, edited by Antoine de Baecque and Christian Delage (Paris: Complexe, 1998), 50.
54 Godard, *Histoire(s) du cinéma*, 1:1b.

55 Ibid.
56 Godard, interview with Antoine de Baecque, *Libération*, April 6, 2002.
57 Godard, *JLG/JLG*, 24.
58 Gilles Deleuze, "L'épuisé," preface to *Quad*, by Samuel Beckett (Paris: Minuit, 1992).

6. Demodern Aesthetics: Filming the End of Communism

1 Jacques Rupnik, *The Other Europe: The Rise and Fall of Communism in East-Central Europe* (New York: Pantheon, 1989). The quotation comes from the preface to the revised French edition: Jacques Rupnik, *L'Autre Europe: Crise et fin du communisme* (Paris: Odile Jacob, 1993), 5.
2 René Girault, "The Democratic Revolutions of 1989," in *A History of Democracy in Europe*, edited by Antoine de Baecque (Boulder, CO: Social Science Monographs, 1995), 57–70; see also Ralf Dahrendorf, *Reflections on the Revolution in Europe* (New York: Time Books, 1990).
3 See Dahrendorf, *Reflections on the Revolution in Europe*.
4 Rupnik, *L'Autre Europe*, 387–88.
5 Leonid Abalkine, *Komsomolskaïa Pravda*, Feb. 1989.
6 See François Fejtö (in collaboration with Ewa Kulesza-Mietkowski), *La Fin des démocraties populaires: Les chemins du post-communisme* (Paris: Seuil, 1997), 118.
7 See Omer Bartov, *Hitler's Army: Soldiers, Nazis, and War in the Third Reich* (New York: Oxford University Press, 1992).
8 Frédéric Rousseau, "Vivre et mourir au front: L'Enfer des tranchées," *L'Histoire*, Dec. 2000.
9 See Alain Touraine, *Can We Live Together? Equality and Difference*, translated by David Macey (Stanford: Stanford University Press, 2000), 34; see especially the first chapter, "Demodernization." See also Danielle Gerritsen and Dominique Martin, eds., *Effets et méfaits de la modernisation dans la crise* (Paris: Desclée de Brouwer, 1998).
10 Antoine Compagnon, *Les Antimodernes, de Joseph de Maistre à Roland Barthes* (Paris: Gallimard, 2005), 8.
11 Andrei Tarkovsky, "Lettre au président du Goskino," June 15, 1983, published in *Le Temps scellé: De "L'Enfance d'Ivan" au "Sacrifice"* (Paris: Cahiers du cinéma, 1989), 232–35.
12 Emir Kusturica, "Souvenirs de bord," in Serge Grünberg, *Il était une fois ... "Underground"* (Paris: Cahiers du cinéma, 1995), 11–12.
13 Alexei Guerman, interview, *Télérama*, Jan. 13, 1999.
14 Quoted in Marcel Martin, *Le Cinéma soviétique, de Khrouchtchev à Gorbatchev (1955–1992)* (Lausanne, Switzerland: L'Âge d'homme, 1993), 181.
15 Andrei Tarkovsky, *Journal, 1970–1986* (Paris: Cahiers du cinema, 2004), 66.

16 François Forestier, "Les piétons métaphysiques," *L'Express*, Nov. 13, 1981.
17 Tarkovsky, *Le Temps scellé*, 6.
18 For the sequencing of *Stalker* see Jacques Gerstenkorn and Sylvie Strudel, "*Stalker*, la quête de la foi ou le dernier souffle de l'esprit," *Études cinématographiques*, nos. 135–38 (Paris: Minard, 1983), 75–104.
19 Ibid., 97.
20 Ibid., 95–96; see also Gérard Pangon, "*Stalker*: Un film du doute sous le signe de la trinité," *Études cinématographiques*, nos. 135–38 (Paris: Minard, 1983), 105–12.
21 Tarkovsky, *Le Temps scellé*, 182.
22 Tarkovsky, *Journal*, 186.
23 Lewis H. Siegelbaum, *Stakhanovism and the Politics of Productivity in the USSR, 1935–1961* (Cambridge, UK: Cambridge University Press, 1988).
24 Alexei Guerman, interview, *Cahiers du cinéma*, special issue on the USSR, Jan. 1990.
25 Jacques Mandelbaum, "On a volé la moustache de Staline," *Le Monde*, Jan. 14, 1999.
26 Guerman interview, *Cahiers du cinéma*.
27 The phrase is borrowed from Gérard Lefort, "À fond la caisse," *Libération*, Jan. 13, 1999.
28 Guerman interview, *Cahiers du cinéma*.
29 Ibid.
30 Alexei Guerman, "Le tournage a été un cauchemar, à l'image des maux dont souffre la Russie," interview, *Le Monde*, Jan. 14, 1999.
31 Guerman interview, *Télérama*.
32 Guerman interview, *Cahiers du cinéma*.
33 Guerman interview, *Télérama*.
34 Guerman interview, *Le Monde*.
35 Frédéric Bonnaud, "En attendant Khroustaliov," *Les Inrockuptibles*, Jan. 13, 1999.
36 A reference to Mikheil Gelovani, Stalin's body double in a dozen Soviet films of the early 1950s, and notably in *The Battle for Berlin*, the prototype for the film maintaining the cult of personality.
37 Quoted in Jean Roy, "Guerman, le frémissement de la vie," *L'Humanité*, Jan. 13, 1999.
38 See Serge Daney, *Cahiers du cinéma*, Sept. 1978.
39 Jean-Pierre Léonardini, "Lénine en fauteuil roulant," *L'Humanité,* May 18, 2001.
40 Quoted in Martin, *Le Cinéma soviétique, de Khrouchtchev à Gorbatchev (1955–1992)*, 179.
41 Mikhail B. Yampolsky, "Le retour à l'image," in *Cinéma et perestroika* (Centre culturel du Limousin, Festival international des Francophonies, April 1994), 95–103.

42. Quoted in Hélène Frappat, "Dieu n'a pas besoin de cinéma," *Cahiers du cinéma*, Jan. 2004.
43. Aleksandr Sokurov, "Nostalghia," interview, *Cahiers du cinéma*, Feb. 1998.
44. See Giorgio Agamben, "L'élégie de Sokourov," *Cahiers du cinéma*, Jan. 2004.
45. Ibid.
46. Ibid.
47. See Joël Chapron, "La folle prise du palais d'Hiver par Alexandre Sokourov," *Le Monde*, May 24, 2002.
48. Aleksandr Sokurov, "Un amour triste et contrarié," interview, *Le Figaro*, May 22, 2002.
49. Quoted in Frappat, "Dieu n'a pas besoin de cinéma," 51.
50. Quoted in Jean Roy, "Voyage dans le cinéma et son histoire," *L'Humanité*, May 22, 2002.
51. Quoted in Jean-François Rauger, "Archéologie vivante du passé russe, au temps de la cour des tsars," *Le Monde*, May 24, 2002.
52. Alain Finkielkraut fired the first salvo in "L'imposture Kusturica" (*Le Monde*, June 2, 1995), in which he accused the filmmaker and his film of being openly pro-Serbian—an article, it must be pointed out, the author wrote before actually having seen the film. The polemic took off before the film's theatrical release, with an article by *Le Monde*'s foreign correspondent in Belgrade, Florence Hartmann, entitled "La production d'*Underground* et ses zones d'ombre," on October 26, 1995. This article claimed the film had been largely financed and supported by Milosevic's Serbia. Kusturica replied with an article entitled "Mon imposture," also published on October 26, 1995, in *Le Monde*. The various positions in the debate are clearly outlined in Thierry Gandillot, "L'affaire Kusturica," *Nouvel observateur*, Oct. 31, 1995.
53. Milan Kundera, *The Unbearable Lightness of Being* (New York: Harper, 1984), 249.
54. Grünberg, *Il était une fois... "Underground,"* 11–12.
55. Roland Barthes, *Mythologies* (New York: Noonday Press, 1972), 134.
56. Emir Kusturica, interview, *Libération*, June 2, 2006.
57. Milan Kundera, *The Art of the Novel* (New York: Harper, 1989), 134.
58. Jean-Pierre Léonardini, "Une vitalité phénoménale," *L'Humanité*, Oct. 25, 1995.
59. Jacques Amalric, "La croisade des bedeaux," *Libération*, Oct. 25, 1995.
60. Quoted in Martin, *Le Cinéma soviétique, de Khrouchtchev à Gorbatchev (1955–1992)*, 181.
61. Serge Daney, *Cahiers du cinéma*, special issue on the USSR, Jan. 1990, 10.
62. Ibid., 7.
63. Ibid.
64. See Martin, *Le Cinéma soviétique, de Khrouchtchev à Gorbatchev (1955–1992)*, 181.
65. For Žižek's extended discussion of *Underground* see his *The Plague of Fantasies* (New York: Verso, 1997), 60–64.

7. America Unraveled: Master Fictions in Contemporary Hollywood Cinema

1. The term *New Hollywood* came into use after the publication of Peter Biskin's *Easy Riders, Raging Bulls: How the Sex-Drugs-and-Rock-'n'-Roll Generation Saved Hollywood* (New York: Simon and Schuster, 1999).
2. The term was used in *Cahiers du cinéma* in the early 1990s, in two successive special issues, December 1992 and January 1993, which offered a revealing overview of the innovations and questions of this new American cinema. The idea of a "new experimentalism" was reworked with the release of the *Matrix* trilogy; see Elie During, ed., *Matrix, machine philosophique* (Paris: Ellipses, 2003).
3. Jean-Baptiste Thoret, *26 secondes, l'Amérique éclaboussée: L'assassinat de JFK et le cinéma américain* (Paris: Rouge profond, 2003), 14; Bernard Bénoliel, "L'expérience interdite: A propos de *26 secondes, l'Amérique éclaboussée*," *Cinéma 07* (spring 2004): 113–21.
4. Marc Chénetier, *Au-delà du soupçon: La nouvelle fiction américaine de 1960 à nos jours* (Paris: Seuil, 1989).
5. See Lynn Hunt, *Politics, Culture, and Class in the French Revolution* (Berkeley: University of California Press, 1984), 87.
6. Tim Burton, quoted in Antoine de Baecque, *Tim Burton* (Paris: Cahiers du cinéma, 2005), 79.
7. See Vanessa Schwartz, *Spectacular Realities: Early Mass Culture in Fin-de-siècle Paris* (Berkeley: University of California Press, 1998).
8. Antoine de Baecque, "Dans le laboratoire des films de mauvais goût," *La Revue des deux mondes*, July-August 2002, 122–30.
9. See Jean-Marie Goulemot, *Forbidden Texts: Erotic Literature and Its Readers in Eighteenth-Century France* (Cambridge: Polity Press, 1994).
10. For Mikhail Bakhtin's discussion of laughter see *Rabelais and His World* (Bloomington: Indiana University Press, 1984), esp. chap. 1.
11. *Cahiers du cinéma*, Dec. 1992.
12. Antoine de Baecque, "Au pays des morts-vivants," *Cahiers du cinéma*, June 1992.
13. Donatien Alphonse François, marquis de Sade, "Français, encore un effort si vous voulez être républicains," *La Philosophie dans le boudoir* (Paris, 1795).
14. Gavin Baddeley, *Gothic: La Culture des ténèbres* (Paris: Denoël, 2004), 136.
15. De Baecque, *Tim Burton*, 146.
16. Jean-Baptiste Thoret, "Filmer le 11-Septembre: Le syndrome Zapruder," in *26 secondes, l'Amérique éclaboussée*, 178.
17. Ibid., 179–80.
18. Jean-Luc Godard, interview with Antoine de Baecque, *Libération*, April 6, 2002.
19. *Le Monde*, Sept. 20, 2006.

20 Stéphane Mallarmé, "The Tomb of Edgar Poe," *Selected Poetry and Prose* (New York: New Directions, 1982), 51.

Conclusion: All Histories Are Possible

1 Walter Benjamin, *The Arcades Project* (Cambridge, MA: Harvard University Press, 1999), 462.
2 Claude Lévi-Strauss, *Look, Listen, Read* (New York: Basic Books, 1998), 7.
3 Chris Marker, *Le Dépays* (Paris: Herscher, 1982).

Acknowledgments ▶

I WOULD LIKE to thank those who—through conversation, reading, and comments—have helped nourish this work through the years: François Albéra, Philippe Azoury, Bruno Bayon, Alain Bonfand, Christian-Marc Bosséno, Nicole Brenez, Stanley Cavell, Arlette Farge, Marc Ferro, Thierry Frémaux, Christophe Gauthier, Laurent Gervereau, Noël Herpe, Danièle Hibon, Vincent Huguet, Youssef Ishaghpour, Nicolas Klotz, André S. Labarthe, Antoine Lilti, Emmanuelle Loyer, Laurent Mannoni, Michel Marie, Manoel de Oliveira, Pascal Ory, Dominique Païni, Claudine Paquot, Élisabeth Perceval, Jérôme Prieur, Jacques Rancière, Alain Resnais, Jacques Revel, Olivier Salvatori, Vanessa Schwartz, Olivier Thévenin, Jean-Baptiste Thoret, Myriam Tsikounas, Agnès Varda, Dimitri Vezyroglou, Slavoj Žižek.

Index ▶

Titles of films are in *italic*. **Bold** numbers indicate illustrations. Initial articles in all languages (e.g., The, L', Le) are ignored in sorting titles, and numbers are sorted as spelled out in English. Notes are indicated by *n*.

Abalkine, Leonid, 249
Abouladze, Tenguiz, 271, 301
À bout de souffle. *See Breathless* (Godard, 1960)
The Abyss (Cameron), 313, 317
Actua-Tilt (Herman, 1960), 146
Adieu Philippine (Rozier, 1963), 140, 143–44, **144**, 156
Agamben, Giorgio, 280
Agee, James, 68
Aldrich, Robert, 112
Alfred Hitchcock Presents (TV series), 62
Algérie en flammes (Vautier and Clément, 1957–58), 141
Alien (Scott), 313, 314
L' Allée du roi (Companeez, 1994), 78
Alleg, Hernri, 150
Allégret, Marc, 133
All the Mornings of the World (Corneau), 78
L'ALN au combat (Vautier and Clément, 1963), 141
Alphaville (Godard, 1965), 116

Amalric, Jacques, 297
Les Amants réguliers / Regular Lovers (Garrel, 2005), **154**, 156
Amarcord (Fellini, 1973), 269
American Pie (film series), 324
Anderson, Lindsay, 172
Andersson, Harriet, 35
And God Created Woman (Vadim, 1956), 134, **135–36**, 136
Andrei Rublev (Tarkovsky), 254
Andrew, Dudley, 9
Angelique and the King (Borderie, 1965), 79
Ant, Adam, 340
Antonin de Mun, Count, 85
Antonio, Emile de, 174
Antonioni, Michelangelo, 13, 356
Aragon, Louis, 112, 218, 231
Armageddon, 251, 312, 318, 319, 321–22
Arnold, Jack, 314
Aronofsky, Darren, 307
Aspel, Michael, 168
The Asthenic Syndrome (Muratov), 301

Astruc, Alexandre, 105
Audiard, Michel, 115
Audiberti, Jacques, 89
Aumont, Jacques, 21, 43, 219, 237
Aurel, Jean, 109
Aurenche, Jean, 116
Autant-Lara, Claude, 133, 142
Avatar (Cameron), 313
Avery, Tex, 335
Avoir 20 ans dans les Aurès / To Be Twenty in the Aures (Vautier, 1972), 144
Azoury, Philippe, 190

Badiou, Alain, 28–29
The Baker of Monceau / La Boulangère de Monceau (Rohmer), 138
Band of Outsiders / Bande à Part (Godard, 1964), 23, **102**, **137–38**, 138, 212
Banks, Russel, 347
Bardem, Juan Antonio, 130
Bardot, Brigitte, 134
Barr, Robert, 174
Barry, Iris, 18, 232
Barry, Joan, 366n33
Barthes, Roland, 113, 147, 252, 371n61
Batman Returns (Burton, 1992), 309, **310**, 311, 336–38, 345
The Battle of Algiers (Pontecorvo, 1965), 70
Baudelaire, Charles, 252
Baverstock, Donald, 175
Bazin, André, 53, 62, 67, 111–12, 132, 361
The Beast from 20,000 Fathoms (Lourié, 1953), 314
Beaumarchais (Molinaro, 1996), 78
Beauregard, Georges de, 130
Becker, Jacque, 112, 227
Beetlejuice (Burton, 1988), 344
La Belle vie (Enrico, 1964), 140, 143, 149
Belmondo, Jean-Paul, 218
Belmont, Vera, 78

Benayoun, Robert, 116, 126
Benda, Julien, 110
Benjamin, Walter, 17, 73, 216, 243, 317, 356
Berg, Peter, 324, 325, 326, 331–32
Bergala, Alain, 67, 243
Bergman, Ingmar, **34**, 35, 45, 323
Bergman, Ingrid, 35, 65, **66**, 67, **74**
Beria, Lavrenti Pavlovitch, 268, 270
Bernhardt, Sarah, 97
Bernstein, Sydney, 37, 61
Bertaut, Jules, 85
Bertolucci, Bernardo, **155–56**, 156, 157
Big Fish (Burton), 332
The Big Red One (Fuller, 1980), 56, 58, **59**
The Big Sleep (Hawks, 1946), **357**
Binochet, Juliette, 241
Blain, Gérard, 121
Blanc, Sylvie, 141
Blanchot, Maurice, 68
Bloch, Jean-Richard, 194
Bloch, Marc, 17, 209
Blondin, Antoine, 108
Blow Up (Antonioni, 1967), 13, **14–15**
Blue, James, 173
Boegner, Philippe, 108
Bogart, Humphrey, 355, **357**
Bogdanovich, Peter, 50
Bokanovski, Gilbert, 81
Bondarchuk, Sergi, 256
Bonnefoy, Yves, 3
Les Bonnes femmes / The Good Time Girls (Chabrol, 1960), 136
Boorman, John, 175
Borde, Raymond, 116
Borderie, Bernard, 79
Bory, Jean-Louis, 108, 186, 187
Bosch, Hieronymus, 342
La Boulangère de Monceau / The Baker of Monceau (Rohmer), 138
Bouquet, Michel, 48

Bouquet, Stéphane, 197
Bourges, Yvon, 153
Bourget, Paul, 108
Bourke-White, Margaret, **44**
Bourseiller, Antoine, 144
Bourvil (actor), 37
Bowie, Geoff, 203
Brandon, Marlon, 176, 177
Brasillach, Robert, 111
Braudel, Fernand, 209
Braunberger, Pierre, 130
Breathless (Godard, 1960), **106–107**, 116, 121, 130, 136, 156, 212, 213, **214**, 222, **359**
Bresson, Robert, 130, 278
Brialy, Jean-Claude, 121
Brissac, Duke of, 84
Browning, Ted, 235
Bunuel, Luis, 323
Burnt by the Sun 2 (Mikhalkov, 2010), 271
Burton, Tim, 28, 307, 332–45, 356; *Batman Returns* (1992), 309, **310**, 311, 336–38, 345; *Beetlejuice* (1988), 344; *Edward Scissorhands* (1990), 332–35, **334**, 344; *Mars Attacks!* (1997), 312, 317, 332; *Sleepy Hollow* (1999), 332, 338, 339–42, **343**
Büttner, Tilman, 281

Cailloix, Roger, 108
Cameron, James, 307, 312–13, 317, 319–20, 346
Les Camps de la mort (1945), 43, 44
Camus, Albert, 112
Canudo, Ricciotto, 6
Les Carabiniers / The Carabineers (Godard, 1963), 23, **206**, 215, **216**, 217, 231
Carpenter, John, 307, 346
Carpita, Paul, 146
Castelot, André, 85

Cau, Jean, 117–18
Cavalcanti, Alberto, 171
Cavalier, Alain: *Le Combat dans l'île* (1962), 123–24, 126, 147; *L'Insoumis* (1964), 140, 143, 147–48
Cave, Nick, 340
Cayatte, André, 133
Cayrol, Jean, 48
Cerchio, Fernando, 79
Cerf, Marcel, 198
Ceux de chez nous (Guitry, 1915), 97
Chabrol, Claude, 104, 105, 133, 227; *The Cousins* (1958), 121, 123, **124, 125**, 130, 136
Chaliapin, Fedor Ivanovitch, 280
Chalon, Guy, 146
Chambon, Alexandre, 69
Chaplin, Charles, 72, 366n33, 366n49; *The Great Dictator* (1940), 21–22, **24–25**, 45, 52, 56, 294; *Monsieur Verdoux* (1947), 52–53, **54–55**, 56
Chardère, Bernard, 116
Chardonne, Jacques, 108
Charlie and the Chocolate Factory (Burton), 332
Charlotte et son Jules / Charlotte and Her Boyfriend (Godard, 1958), 132
Charlotte et son steak / Charlotte and Her Steak (Rohmer, 1951), 132
La Chasse au lion à l'arc (Rouch, 1966), 173
Chénetier, Marc, 309
Chiaureli, Mikheil, 5
La Chinoise (Godard, 1967), 219
Christian-Jaque, 79
Chronique d'un été (Rouch and Morin, 1961), 140, 141
Cimino, Michael, 307
Le cinéma au service de l'histoire (Dulac, 1935), 5
Cintra, Luís Miguel, xi

Clément, Pierre, 141
Cléo de 5 à 7 (Varda, 1962), 140, 144–45, **145**
Cloquet, Ghislain, 128
Coen, Ethan and Joel, 307
Collet, Jean, 119, 121, 187
Le Combat dans l'île / Fire and Ice (Cavalier, 1962), 123–24, 126, 140, 147
La Commune (Watkins, 2000), 23, 160, 162, 184, 194, 196–201, **198**
Comolli, Jean-Louis, 17
Companeez, Nina, 78
Conan (film series, Raimi), 333
Contempt / Le Mépris (Godard, 1963), 156
Coppola, Francis Ford, 307, 328
Coppola, Sofia, 78
Cordillot, Michel, 198
Corman, Roger, 314
Corneau, Alain, 78, 368n2
Cornu, André, 83, 87
Count of Bragelonne (Cerchio, 1954), 79
Le Coup du berger / Fool's Mate (Rivette), 132
Courier, Paul-Louis, 88
The Cousins (Chabrol, 1958), 121, 123, **124, 125**, 130, 136
Coutard, Raoul, 139
Craig, Phil, 349
Craven, Wes, 333, 344
Les criminels (newsreel, 1945), 40
Cruise, Tom, 351
Culloden (Watkins, 1964), 165, **166**, 167, 175, 180, 184, 188, 190, 193, 194, 197
Cuny, Alain, 241

Dahl, Roald, 332
Dale, Richard, 349
Dalotel, Alain, 198
Damisch, Hubert, 185
Daney, Serge, 45, 46–47, 50, 70, 241, 276, 300, 301, 367n51

Dansette, Adrien, 85
Dante, Joe, 307, 317, 344
Daquin, Louis, 133
Dauman, Anatole, 47
Davis, Natalie Zemon, 13, 309, 360
Day, Will, 223
The Day After Tomorrow (Emmerich, 2004), 312, 319
The Days of Eclipse (Sokurov, 1988), 279
Day the World Ended (Corman, 1955), 314
Death Becomes Her (Zemeckis), 324, 344
Decoin, Henri, 79
Deep Impact, 312, 319
Delage, Christian, 41, 42
Delannoy, Jean, 79
Deleuze, Gilles, 13, 16, 26, 245
Delluc, Louis, 6, 20
Delon, Alain, 147
Delpy, Julie, 241
Demain l'amour, 140
Demme, Jonathan, 307
Demy, Jacques, 78, 145–46
Déon, Michel, 108
De Palma, Brian, 307
Depp, Johnny, 340, 342
Desplechin, Arnaud, 366n49
Le Destin fabuleux de Désirée Clary (Guitry), 91
Diable boiteux (Guitry, 1948), 94
Dial M for Murder (Hitchcock), 62
The Diary of an Unknown Soldier (Watkins, 1959), 163
Diaz, Cameron, 325, 326, 330
DiCaprio, Leonardo, 79
Didi-Huberman, Georges, 41
Die Hard (McTiernan), 346
Die Hard: With a Vengeance (McTiernan), 346
Dillon, Matt, 330
Dort, Bernard, 113

Dostoyevsky, Fedor, 270, 280
Douchet, Jean, 40, 105, 109
Douglas, Gordon, 314
Douin, Jean-Luc, 142
Dovjenko, Aleksandr, 278
The Dreamers (Bertolucci, 2003), **155–56**, 156, 157
Dreville, Jean, 79
Drew, Robert, 173
Drieu la Rochelle, Pierre, 111
Dr. Strangelove (Kubrick, 1964), 315, 318
Dufour, Jewan, 85
Duhour, Clément, 81, 83
Dulac, Germaine, 5
Durand, Philippe, 142
Duras, Marguerite, 32

The Edge (Kramer, R., 1968), 174
Edwards, Blake, 328, 330
Edward Scissorhands (Burton, 1990), 332–35, **334**, 344
Edwin Munch (Watkins, 1974), 160, **161**, 184, 189–92, **191**, 203
Ed Wood (Burton), 332
Effects of the Atom Bomb (1965), 313
Eisenhower, Dwight D., 37, 39, 42
Eisenstein, Sergei, 8, 9, 235, 264, 278
Eisler, Hans, 49
Eisner, Lotte, 18
Elevator to the Scaffold (Malle, 1957), 130
Elfman, Danny, 342
Elias, Norbert, 101
Eloge de l'amour (Godard, 1999), 217, 234
Emmerich, Roland, 317, 319
Enrico, Robert, 78, 149
Escape from New York (Carpenter), 320, 346
Europa '51 (Rossellini, 1952), **xviii**, 2, **4**, 32, 35, 37, 65, **74**
Evil Dead (film series, Raimi), 333

The Execution of Mary, Queen of Scots (Griffith, 1894), 232

Falkenau, the Impossible (Weiss, 1988), 57, **58**
The Fall of Berlin (Chiaureli, 1949), 5
Fallois, Bernard de, 108
Family Plot (Hitchcock, 1976), 62
Farge, Arlette, 13, 16
Farrelly, Bobby and Peter, 28, 307; *There's Something About Mary* (1998), 28, 311, 324, 325, 326, **327**, 328–30, **329**
Father and Son (Sokurov, 2003), 279
Fellini, Federico, 257, 269, 323
Fernandel (actor), 37
Ferro, Marc, 7–8, 9, 12
Feu follet / The Fire Within (Malle, 1963), 126, **127**, 128
The Field of Red (Watkins, 1958), 163
58 2/B (Chalon, 1957), 146
Finkielkraut, Alain, 379n52
Fire and Ice (Cavalier). *See Le Combat dans l'île / Fire and Ice* (Cavalier, 1962)
The Fire Within / Feu follet (Malle, 1963), 126, **127**, 128
First Love (Kieslowski, 1974), 8
Flaherty, Robert, 18
Flaud, Jacques, 129, 130
Flight 93 (Greengrass, 2005), 348
The Flight that Fought Back (Lapping, Goodison, and Craig), 349
Fool's Mate / Le Coup du berger (Rivette), 132
Force de frappe (Watkins, 1976), 184
Ford, John, 235
Forgotten Faces (Watkins, 1961), 22–23, 160, 163–65, 172, 194
Forstier, François, 255
Fouchet, Max-Pol, 108

Four Bags Full / La traversée de Paris (Autant-Lara), 133
The Four Hundred Blows / Les quatre cents coups (Truffaut, 1959), 131, 156
Fraigneau, André, 108
Franck, Bernard, 109, 110
Franck, Nino, 108
Frankenweenie (Burton), 332
The French Revolution (Enrico and Heffron), 78
Frenzy (Hitchcock, 1972), 62
The Fugitive (Ince, 1914), 232
Fuller, Samuel, 45, 50, 56–60, 61, 62, 68, 72, 112, 235
Funès, Louis de, 37
Furet, François, 210–11

Gabin, Jean, 115
Galtier-Boissière, Jean, 40
Gance, Abel, 9, 112, 240
La Gangrène (Watkins, 1963), 165
Garratier, Jacques, 130
Garrel, Philippe, **154**, 156
Garrel, Thierry, 201, 202
Gatti, Armand, 196
Gaulle, Charles de, 130
Gauthier, Guy, 185
Gauthier, Jean-Marc, 203
Geertz, Clifford, 309
Gégauff, Paul, 111, 123
Gelovani, Mikheil, 378n36
Gémier, Firmin, 194
The General (Keaton, 1927), 232
Gerstenkorn, Jacques, 257, 264
Gervereau, Laurent, 141
Giesey, Ralph, 97
Gimme Shelter (Maysles, 1969), 173
Girard, René, 311
Girl in His Pocket (Kast, 1957), 130
The Gladiators (Watkins, 1969), 177, **181**, 184, 187, 189, **204**

Godard, Jean-Luc, 3, 21, 65, 72, 105, 109, 111, 115, 128, 131, 133, 134, 139, 153, 208–245, 252, 348, 356, 374n1; *Alphaville* (1965), 116; *Band of Outsiders* (1964), 23, **102**, **137–38**, 138, 212; *Breathless* (1960), **106–107**, 116, 121, 130, 136, 156, 212, 213, **214**, 222, **359**; *Les Carabiniers* (1963), 23, **206**, 215, **216**, 217, 231; *Charlotte et son Jules* (1958), 132; *La Chinoise* (1967), 219; *Eloge de l'amour* (1999), 217, 234; *Histoire(s) du cinéma* (1988–1998), 23, 73, 208, 211, 217, 228, 229, 231, 232, **233**, 234, 235–45, **238–39**, 358; *Je vous salue Marie* (1983), 245; *Nouvelle Vague* (1990), 217; *The Old Place* (1968), 231–32, 234, 240; *Passion* (1981), 219, 223, **224–25**; *Le Petit Soldat* (1960), 118–21, **120**, **122**, 140, 142, 143, 148, 150–51, **152**, 245; *Pierrot le fou* (1965), 23, 218, **220–21**, 222–23, 231, **244**; *Soigne ta droite* (1987), 243; *Une femme est une femme* (1961), 136, 138; *Weekend* (1967), 219
Les Godelureaux / The Wise Guys (Chabrol, 1957), 136
Godzilla (Emmerich), 317, 318
Godzilla (film series), 312, 313, 314
Goha (Garratier, 1957), 130
Gold, Jack, 175
Goldenberg, Daniel, 146
Goodison, Bruce, 349
The Good Time Girls / Les Bonnes femmes (Chabrol, 1960), 136
Gorbachev, Mikhail, 249, 300
Gordon, Robert, 314
Gracq, Julien, 110–11
Graham, Dick, 168
La Grande illusion (Renoir, 1937), 6
Grand-rue / Main Street (Bardem, 1956), 130

The Great Dictator (Chaplin, 1940), 21–22, **24–25**, 45, 52, 56, 294
Greed (Stroheim, 1923), 232
Greengrass, Peter, 348
Gremlins (Dante), 317, 344
Grierson, John, 163, 171–72
Griffith, David Wark, 227
Groundhog Day (Ramis), 324
Guerman, Alexei, 27, 278, 287, 288, 300, 301; *Khrustalyov, My Car!* (1998), **246**, 252, 253, 268–76, **274**; *My Friend Ivan Lapshin* (1982), 271, 301; *The Seventh Companion* (1967), 270; *Trial of the Road* (1972), 270–71; *Twenty Days Without War* (1976), 271
Guitry, Sacha, 3, 22, 37, 90–101, 112, 358; *Ceux de chez nous* (1915), 97; *Les Perles de la couronne* (1937), **90**, 91; *Remontons les Champs-Elysées* (1938), 91, **92–93**, 94; *Si Versailles m'était conté* (1954), 80–90, **82**, **91**, 94–101, **98–100**

Handsome Serge (Chabrol, 1957), 130
Harlin, Renny, 307, 324
Harry Potter (film series), 333
Haskin, Byron, 314
Hastier, Louis, 85
Hawks, Howard, 112, 227, 328, 330, 356
Heaven's Gate (Cimino, 1980), 307
Heffron, Richard, 78
Herman, Jean, 146
Hiroshima mon amour (Resnais, 1959), 2, **30**, 32, **33**, 37, 72, 131, 156, 315
Hirsch, Joshua, 40
Histoire(s) du cinéma (Godard, 1988–1998), 23, 73, 208, 211, 217, 228, 229, 231, 232, **233**, 234, 235–45, **238–39**, 358
Hitchcock, Alfred, 37, 45, 50, 61–63, 72, 112, 235, 236–37, 323

Hitler, Adolf, 280
Hitler: A Film from Germany (Syberberg, 1977), 276
Hoffman, E. T. A., 338
Honda, Inoshiro, 313
Hugenin, Jean-René, 117
Hunt, Lynn, 309

Ice (Kramer, R., 1970), 174
The Immigrant (Chaplin, 1917), 232
Independence Day (Emmerich, 1996), 312, 317, 318, 320, 351
In Prison (TV series, 1957), 175
L'Insoumis (Cavalier, 1964), 140, 143, 147–48, 150
Intervista (Fellini, 1986), 257
In the Country (Kramer, R., 1967), 174
In the Rapid-Transit Tunnel (1903), 232
Irving, Washington, 338
Isnard, Jacques, 186
It Came from Beneath the Sea (Gordon, 1955), 314
It's Your Money They're After (TV series), 174
Ivory, James, 78
Iwasaki, Akira, 32, 313, 318, 320

J'accuse (Gance), 240
Jack (Coppola, F., 1995), 328
Jackson, Robert H., 41, 42
Jacob, Max, 28–29
Jaws (Spielberg, 1975), 307
Jeanson, Henri, 116
Jefferson in Paris (Ivory, 1995), 78
Jennings, Humphrey, 163, 171
La Jetée (Marker, 1962), 315
Jet Pilot (Sternberg), 112
Je vous salue Marie (Godard, 1983), 245
Jimeno, Will, 349
Le Joi Mai (Marker, 1962), 140, 149
Jones, Paul, 176

Jouhandeau, Marcel, 108
Journey to Italy (Rossellini, 1953), 65, **66**, 67–68
Judgment at Nurenberg (Kramer), 72
Juran, Nathan, 314
Jurassic Park, 312

Kamchalov, 301
Kanevski, Vitali, 300
Kantorowicz, Ernst, 97
Kapo (Pontecorvo, 1960), 70, **71**, 367n51
Karmen, Roman, 172
Kast, Pierre, 130
Kazantzakis, Nikos, 165
Keaton, Buster, 227
Kennedy, John Fitzgerald, 173, 347
Kessel, Joseph, 43
Khruschev, Nikita, 300
Khrustalyov, My Car! (Guerman, 1998), **246**, 252, 253, 268–76, **274**, 299, 302
The Kids / Les Mistons (Truffaut, 1957), 132
Kieslowski, Krzysztof, 8–9
King Kong, 312
The Kiss (1896), 232
Klee, Paul, 243
Klensky, Yuri, 268, 270
Klimov, Elem, 301
Konchlalovsky, Andrei, 256
Kovasevixc, Dusan, 295
Kozintsev, Grigori, 278, 280
Kracauer, Siegfried, 18–20, 29
Kramer, Robert, 174
Kramer, Stanley, 72
Kubrick, Stanley, 9, 315
Kulechov, Lev Vladimirovich, 278
Kundra, Milan, 287, 296
Kunstler, Charles, 85
Kusturica, Emir, 27, 301; *Underground* (1995), 252, 253, 287–99, **290–91**, **293**

Kyrou, Ado, 146

Lachize, Samuel, 187
Lacretelle, Jacques de, 84
Lady Oscar (Demy, 1978), 78
La Fayette (Dreville, 1961), 79
Landis, John, 307
Landsbergis, Vytautas, 280
Lang, Fritz, 9, 112, 227, 235; *M*, 8
Langlois, Henri, 132, 222–23, **226**, 226–28, 232, 234, 235
Lanzmann, Claude, 72, 366n49
Lanzmann, Jacques, 116
La Patellière, Denys de, 115
Lapping, Brian, 349
La Rochelle, Pierre Drieu, 126, 128
Laudenbach, Laurent, 108
Laurent, Jacques, 108, 111
Lavant, Denis, 241
Leacock, Richard, 173
Leconte, Patrice, 78, 79, 368n2
Legend (Scott), 333, 334
Legrand, Michel, 145–46
Lem, Stanislaw, 256
Lenin, Vladimir, 276–77
Léonardini, Jean-Pierre, 277
Le Pen, Jean-Marie, 104
Let Joy Reign Supreme (Tavernier), 78
Lévi-Strauss, Claude, 358
Lewan, David, 9
Lewis, Jerry, 328, 330
Lewis, Matthew G., 338
L'Herbier, Marcel, 79
Lindeperg, Sylvie, 39, 61
The Little Soldier (Godard, 1960). *See Le Petit Soldat* (Godard, 1960)
Little Vera (Pitchul, 1988), 301
Lods, Jean, 141
London Town (TV series), 174
The Lonely Voice of Man (Sokurov, 1987), 279–80

The Long Kiss Goodnight (Harlin), 324
Look in on Life (TV series), 175
Lord of the Rings (film series), 333
Loridan, Marceline, 141
The Lost World, 312
Lotbiniere, Anthony, 174
Lounguine, Pavel, 300
Lourié, Eugène, 314
Loyer, Emmanuelle, 109, 110–11
Lubitsch, Ernst, 45, 227
Lucas, George, 307
Lumière, Auguste and Louis, 235, 342
Lynch, David, 307

Madame Du Barry (Christian-Jaque, 1954), 79
The Magnetic Monster (Siodmak, 1953), 314
Main Street / Grand-rue (Bardem, 1956), 130
Malle, Louis, 126, **127**, 128, 130
Malraux, André, 108, 128–29, 130–32, 153, 217, 222, 228–31, 234
Mandelbaum, Jacques, 269
A Man Escaped / Un condamné à mort s'est échappé (Bresson, 1956), 130
The Man in the Iron Mask (1978), 79
Mansfield, Jane, 330
The March (Blue, 1963), 173
Marchand, Corinne, 144
Mardore, Michel, 114
Marie, Michel, 142
Marie Antoinette (Copolla, S.), 78
Marie-Antoinette (Delannoy, 1955), 79
Marker, Chris, 149, 315, 320, 360
Marner, Eugene, 173
Marquise (Belmont, 1997), 78
Mars Attacks! (Burton, 1997), 312, 317, 332
La Marseillaise (Renoir), 79
Marsolais, Gilles, 174

Massari, Lea, 147
Matinee (Dante), 317
The Matrix, 312
Maturin, Charles Robert, 338
Matuszewski, Boleslav, 5
Mauriac, Claude, 108
Maysles, Albert and David, 173
McCarey, Leo, 112, 356
McCormack, Stephen, 174
McLoughlin, John, 349
McTierman, John, 307, 346
Me, Myself, and Irene (Farrelly), 324
Melville, Jean-Pierre, 121
Le Mépris / Contempt (Godard, 1963), 156
Michel, Henri, 86
Michelet, Jules, 208, 209
Miéville, Anne-Marie, 232, 240
Mikhalkov, Nikita, 271
Minnelli, Vincente, 112, 235
Les Mistons / The Kids (Truffaut, 1957), 132
Mitchell, Denis, 174–75
Mizoguchi, Kenji, 235
Mnouchkine, Ariane, 78
Molière (Mnouchkine, 1978), 78
Molinaro, Edouard, 78
Molokh (Sokurov, 1999), 279
Mongrédien, Georges, 85
Monika (Bergman, 1952), **34**, 35
Monkey Business (Hawks), 328
Monsieur Verdoux (Chaplin, 1947), 52–53, **54–55**, 56
Morand, Paul, 108
Moreau, Jeanne, 126
Morin, Edgar, 141
Morning in the Streets (TV series, 1959), 175
The Most Dangerous Game (Schoedsack and Pichel), 182
Mother and Son (Sokurov, 1998), 279, 281
Moullet, Luc, 60, 61, 72

Moussinac, Léon, 6
Mozgovoy, Leonid, 277
Muratov, Kira, 301
Muriel (Resnais, 1963), 143, 149–51
Murnau, Friedrich-Wilhelm, 227, 339
My Friend Ivan Lapshin (Guerman, 1982), 271, 301

Nanook (Flaherty), 18
Narboni, Jean, 57
Nazi Concentration Camps (1945), 41, 42, 44, 60
Newman, Joseph, 314
The New York Hat (Griffith, 1912), 232
Night and Fog (Resnais, 1956), 2, **26**, **36**, 37, **38**, 46–50, **47**, **48**, 133
Night in the City (TV series, 1958), 175
Nimier, Roger, 108, 109, 111, 123, 128
9/11: The Twin Towers (Dale), 349
No, or the Vain Glory of Command (Oliveira, 1990), xi–xv, **xiv–xv**
Nosferatu (Murnau), 339
No Sun in Venice (Vadim, 1957), 134
Noucher, Jean, 116
Nourissier, François, 108, 116
Nouvelle Vague (Godard, 1990), 217
The Nutty Profesor (Lewis), 328

L'Objecteur / Tu ne tueras point (Autant-Lara, 1963), 142
October (Eisenstein, 1927), 264
Octobre à Paris (Panijel, 1962), 143
The Old Place (Godard, 1968), 231–32, 234, 240
Oliveira, Manoel de, xi–xv
Les Oliviers de la justice, 140
Ophuls, Max, 227
Orwell, George, 253

A Painful Reminder (1985), 61
Païni, Dominique, 227, 229

Païsa (Rossellini), 18
Palewski, Gaston, 87–88
Panijel, Jacques, 143
Les Parapluies de Cherbourg / The Umbrellas of Cherbourg (Demy, 1964), 140, 145–46, 156
Parfois le dimanche (Kyrou, 1959), 146
Parinaud, André, 109, 111
Paris nous appartient / Paris Belongs to Us (Rivette), 138
Parvulesco, Jean, 121
Passion (Godard, 1981), 219, 223, **224–25**
Pauwels, Louis, 108
The People Under the Stairs (Craven), 333, 344
Les Perles de la couronne (Guitry, 1937), **90**, 91
Peters, Jon, 342
Peter Watkins-Lithuania (Gauthier), 203
Le Petit Soldat (Godard, 1960), 118–21, **120**, **122**, 140, 142, 143, 150–51, **152**, 245
Pfeiffer, Michelle, 309, 311, 337
Philippe, Claude-Jean, 186
Phyllis and Terry (Satrina and Marner, 1964), 173–74
Picasso, Pablo, 235
Pichel, Irving, 182
Pierre de Fleurieu, Countess, 84–85
Pierrot le fou (Godard, 1965), 23, 218, **220–21**, 222–23, 231, **244**
Piranha (Cameron), 317
Pitchul, Vassili, 300, 301
A Place in the Sun (Stevens, 1955), 73, 244
Planet of the Apes, 320
Poe, Edgar Allan, 340
Point of Order (Antonio, 1964), 174
The Poison Affair (Decoin, 1955), 79
Pommereulle, Daniel, 219
Pontecorvo, Gillo, 70, **71**, 367n51
The Poseidon Adventure (1972), **304**, 316

Preminger, Otto, 235
Primary (Leacock and Pennebaker, 1960), 173
Princess Bride (Reiner), 333
Privilege (Watkins, 1967), 176, 177, **178–79**, 184, 187
Proulx, Maurice, 171
Psycho (Hitchcock), 62
Punishment Park (Watkins, 1970), 180, 182–83, 184, 189, 373n25
Putin, Vladimir, 253–54

Les quatre cents coups / The Four Hundred Blows (Truffaut, 1959), 131
Queen's Necklace (l'Herbier, 1945), 79
La Quille (Herman, 1961), 146
Quincy, Quatremère de, 215, 217

Radcliffe, Ann, 338
Raiders of the Lost Ark (Spielberg, 1981), 307
Raimi, Sam, 307, 333, 344
Ramis, Harold, 307, 324, 326
Ramonet, Ignacio, 187
Rancière, Jacques, 20, 28
Ray, Nicholas, 112, 235
Rebatet, Lucien, 104, 111
La Récréation (Carpita, 1959), 146
Regular Lovers / Les Amants réguliers (Garrel, 2005), **154**, 156
Rehm, Jean-Pierre, 185
Reiner, Rob, 307, 333
Reisz, Karel, 172
Remontons les Champs-Elysées (Guitry, 1938), 91, **92–93**, 94
Renoir, Jean, 6, 9, 79, 81, 112, 227, 356
Repentance (Abouladze, 1987), 271, 301
Resnais, Alain, 40, 56, 128, 142, 320; *Hiroshima mon amour* (1959), 2, **30**, 32, **33**, 37, 72, 131, 315; *Muriel* (1963), 143, 149–51; *Night and Fog* (1956), 2, **26, 36**, 37, 46–50, **47, 48,** 72, 133; *Les statues meurent aussi* (1953), 133
Le Retour (Goldenbert, 1960), 146
Return of the Ape Man (Rosen, 1944), 314
Revel, Jacques, 13
Richmond, Kimbald, 57
Ridicule (Leconte), 78, 79
The Rise of Louis XIV (Rossellini, 1966), **80**, 81
Riva, Emmanuelle, 32, 70, **71**
Rivette, Jacques, 35, 40, 46, 69–70, 72, 105, 113, 227, 367n51; *Le Coup du berger* (1956), 132; *Paris nous appartient* (1961), 138; *Suzanne Simonin, la religieuse de Diderot* (1967), 132, 153, 229
Robinson, Edward G., 50, **51**
Robinzoniada (1986), 301
Rohmer, Eric, 105, 108, 109, 111, 132, 138, 227
Rolland, Romain, 194
Ronet, Maurice, 126
Rope (Hitchcock, 1948), 237
Rosen, Phil, 314
Rossellini, Roberto, 45, 50, 72, 112, 227, 235; *Europa '51* (1952), **xviii**, 2, **4**, 32, 35, 37, 65, **74**; *Journey to Italy* (1953), 65, **66**, 67–68; *Païsa*, 18; *The Rise of Louis XIV* (1966), **80**, 81
Rotha, Paul, 171, 174
Rouch, Jean, 141, 173
Rougemont, Denis de, 108
Rougerie, Jacques, 198
Rousseau, Frédéric, 251
Rozier, Jacques, 140, 143–44, **144**
Rue des prairies (La Patellière), 115
Rupnik, Jacques, 248, 249
Rush to Judgment (Antonio, 1964), 174
Russell, Ken, 175
Russian Ark (Sokurov, 2002), 252, 253–54, 276, 280, 281–87, **286**, 299, 302

Sade, Marquis de, 339
Sadoul, Georges, 6–7, 85–86, 112, 114, 186
Sakiet-Sidi-Youssef (Vautier and Clément, 1958), 141
Salesman (Maysles, 1969), 173
Sanders, François, 123
Sanders, George, 65, **66**
Sarraute, Nathalie, 309
Sartre, Jean-Paul, 5, 108, 109, 112
Satrina, Carole Lucia, 173
Save and Protect (Sokurov, 1989), 279
Scary Movie (film series), 324
Schama, Simon, 309
Schneider, Romy, 124
Schoedsack, Ernest B., 182
Schoendoerffer, Pierre, 139
Schreck, Max, 336
Scorsese, Martin, 235, 307
Scott, Ridley, 333
Secteur postal 89 098 (Durand, 1961), 142
Semprun, Jorge, 40
The Seventh Companion (Guerman, 1967), 270
Shallow Hal (Farrelly), 324
Shelley, Mary, 338
Shimao, Toshio, 280
Shoah (Lanzmann), 72, 366n49
Shoot the Piano Player / Tirez sur le pianiste (Truffautk, 1960), 130, 139
Shrimpton, Jean, 176
Siberiade (Konchlalovsky, 1978), 256
Le Signe du lion / The Sign of Leo (Rohmer), 138
Simsolo, Noël, 57
Siodmak, Curt, 314
Siouxie (singer), 338, 340
Sit In (Young, 19634), 173
Si Versailles m'était conté (Guitry, 1954), 3, 22, **76**, 80–90, **82**, **91**, 94, 95, 96–101, **98–100**
The Skeleton Dance (Disney, 1929), 232

Sleepy Hollow (Burton, 1999), 332, 338, 339–42, **343**
S.O.B. (Edwards), 328
Soigne ta droite (Godard, 1987), 243
Sokurov, Aleksandr, 27, 276–87, 300, 301; *Russian Ark* (2002), 252, 253–54, 279, 280, 281–87, **286**; *Taurus* (2001), 276–77
Solaris (Tarkovsky, 1972), 255, 256
Sollers, Philippe, 242–43
Solzhenitsyn, Aleksandr, 280
Sorlin, Pierre, 7, 9
Soviet Elegy (Sokurov, 1990), 281
Spartacus (Kubrick, 1960), **10–11**
Special Enquiry (TV series), 174–75
Spiderman (Raimi), 344
Spielberg, Steven, 307; *War of the Worlds*, 28, 317, 318, 320, 351, **352**, 353, **353**
Stalin, Joseph, 5, 254, 268, 269, 271, 273, 274–76, 277, 280, 300
Stalker (Tarkovsky, 1979), **249**, 252, 254–67, **259–60**, **263**, **265**, 299, **302**
Starobinski, Jean, 3, 5
Star Wars (Lucas, 1977), 307
Les statues meurent aussi / Statues Also Die (Resnais, 1953), 133
Sternberg, Josef von, 112
Stevens, George, 37, 41, 45, 73, 244
Stewart, Alexandra, 126
Stiller, Ben, 326, 329
Stone, Oliver, 307, 349
Stora, Benjamin, 142, 147
The Stranger (Welles, 1946), 50, **51**
Strangers on a Train (Hitchcock), 62, 236
Strike (Eisenstein), 8
Strudel, Sylvie, 257, 264
Strugatsky, Arcadi and Boris, 255
Subor, Michel, 118
The Sun (Sokurov, 2005), 279
Suzanne Simonin, la religieuse de Diderot (Rivette, 1967), 132, 153, 229

Swallow, Norman, 174, 175
Syberberg, Hans-Jürgen, 276

Tanner, Peter, 37, 39, 61, 62
Tapié, Victor, 85
Tarantula (Arnold, 1955), 314
Tarkovsky, Andrei, 27, 278, 280, 287, 301, 356; *Andrei Rublev*, 254; *Solaris* (1972), 255, 256; *Stalker* (1979), **249**, 252, 254–67, **259–60**, **263**, **265**, 299, **302**
Tarr, Bela, 300
Tashlin, Frank, 330
Taurus (Sokurov, 2001), 276–77, 279, 281
Tavernier, Bertrand, 78, 368n2
Taylor, Elizabeth, 73, 244
Tedesco, Jean, 6
Terminator (Cameron), 313
Them! (Douglas, 1954), 314
There's Something About Mary (Farrelly, 1998), 28, 311, 324, 325, 326, **327**, 328–30, **329**
Thiers, Adolphe, 197
The 39 Steps (Hitchcock), 61
This Island Earth (Newman, 1955), 314
Thoret, Jean-Baptiste, 308
Thou Shalt Not Kill (*Tu ne tueras point*) / *L'Objecteur* (Autant-Lara, 1963), 142
Tirez sur le pianiste / *Shoot the Piano Player* (Truffaut, 1960), 130, 139
Titanic (Cameron, 1998), 313, 317, 319–20
Tito, Josip Broz, 287, 288, 289, 292, 294–96
To Be or Not to Be (Lubitsch), 45
To Be Twenty in the Aures / *Avoir 20 ans dans les Aurès* (Vautier, 1972), 144
Tombs, Robert, 198
The Torn Curtain (Hitchcock, 1966), 62
Touraine, Alain, 251
La traversée de Paris / *Four Bags Full* (Autant-Lara), 133

Trial of the Road (Guerman, 1972), 270–71
Trintignant, Jean-Louis, 123–24, 126, 147
True Lies (Cameron), 346
Truffaut, François, 37, 40, 69, 84, 89, 90, 104, 105, 108, 109, 111, 112–13, 115, 133–34, 139, 227, 237, 356, 369n26; *The Four Hundred Blows* (1959), 131, 156; *Les Mistons* (1957), 132; *Shoot the Piano Player* (1960), 130, 139
Truman, Harry, 41
Tu ne tueras point / *L'Objecteur* (Autant-Lara, 1963), 142
Twenty Days Without War (Guerman, 1976), 271
20 Million Miles to Earth (Juran, 1957), 314

The Umbrellas of Cherbourg / *Les Parapluies de Cherbourg* (Demy, 1964), 140, 145–46, 156
Un condamné à mort s'est échappé / *A Man Escaped* (Bresson, 1956), 130
Underground (Kusturica, 1995), 252, 253, 287–99, **290–91**, **293**, 299
Une femme est une femme / *A Woman Is a Woman* (Godard, 1961), 136, 138
Une nation, l'Algérie (Vautier, Lods, and Blanc, 1955), 141
The Universal Clock, or Peter Watkins' Resistance (Bowie), 203

Vadim, Roger, 134, **135–36**, 136
Vallès, Jules, 197
Van Dievoet, Edouard, 85
Van Gogh, Vincent, 218
Varda, Agnès, 144–45, **145**
Varlin, Eugène, 197
Vautier, René, 141, 144
Verboten! (Fuller, 1959), 58, 60

Vertov, Dziga, 172
Very Bad Things (Berg, 1998), 324, 325, 331–32
Vidal-Naquet, Pierre, 210
Vilar, Jean, 112
Villaine, Anne-Marie de, 142
Voronzov (director), 39
Le Voyage (Watkins, 1986), 184

Walken, Christopher, 336
Walpole, Horace, 338, 340
The War Game (Watkins, 1965), **158**, 167–71, **168**, **170**, 184, 185–86, 189, 193, 202, 315
War of the Worlds (Haskin, 1953), 314
War of the Worlds (Spielberg, 2005), 28, 312, 317, 318, 320, 351, **352**, 353, **353**
Watkins, Patrick, 197, 198, 358, 372n2
Watkins, Peter, 3, 22–23, 160–204; *La Commune* (2000), 23, 160, 162, 184, 194, 196–201, **198**; *Culloden* (1964), 165, **166**, 167, 175, 180, 184, 188, 190, 193, 194, 197; *Edwin Munch* (1964), 160, **161**, 184, 189–92, **191**, 203; *Force de frappe* (1976), 184; *Forgotten Faces* (1961), 163–65, 172, 194; *The Gladiators* (1969), 177, **181**, 184, 187, 189, **204**; *Privilege* (1967), 176, 177, **178–79**, 184, 187; *Punishment Park* (1970), 180, 182–83, 184, 189; *Le Voyage* (1986), 184; *The War Game* (1965), **158**, 167–71, **168**, **170**, 184, 185–86, 189, 193, 202, 315; *The Web* (1956), 163
Watt, Harry, 171
The Web (Watkins, 1956), 163
Weekend (Godard, 1967), 219
Weiss, Emil, 57, **58**
Welles, Orson, 50, **51**, 52, 171, 173
Wheldon, Huw, 165, 175
Whispering Pages (Sokurov, 1994), 279
Why We Fight (film series), 45
Wiesel, Elie, 69
Wieviorka, Annette, 39, 40–41
Wilson, Harold, 171
The Wise Guys / Les Godelureaux (Chabrol, 1957), 136
A Woman Is a Woman / Une femme est une femme (Godard, 1961), 136, 138
World in Action (TV series), 175
World Trade Center (Stone, 2006), 349, **350**
Wright, Basil, 171

Yampolsky, Mikhail, 279
Yeltsin, Boris, 280, 281
Yermach, 301
Young, Robert, 173

Zapruder, Abraham, 308, 309, 347
Zemeckis, Robert, 307, 324, 344
Žižek, Slavoj, 8–9, 301, 302

EUROPEAN PERSPECTIVES

A Series in Social Thought and Cultural Criticism

LAWRENCE D. KRITZMAN, EDITOR

European Perspectives presents outstanding books by leading Europeanthinkers. With both classic and contemporary works, the series aims to shape the major intellectual controversies of our day and to facilitate the tasks of historical understanding

Gilles Deleuze	*The Logic of Sense*
Julia Kristeva	*Strangers to Ourselves*
Theodor W. Adorno	*Notes to Literature*, vols. 1 and 2
Richard Wolin, editor	*The Heidegger Controversy*
Antonio Gramsci	*Prison Notebooks*, vols. 1, 2, and 3
Jacques LeGoff	*History and Memory*
Alain Finkielkraut	*Remembering in Vain: The Klaus Barbie Trial and Crimes Against Humanity*
Julia Kristeva	*Nations Without Nationalism*
Pierre Bourdieu	*The Field of Cultural Production*
Pierre Vidal-Naquet	*Assassins of Memory: Essays on the Denial of the Holocaust*
Hugo Ball	*Critique of the German Intelligentsia*
Gilles Deleuze	*Logic and Sense*
Gilles Deleuze and Félix Guattari	*What Is Philosophy?*
Karl Heinz Bohrer	*Suddenness: On the Moment of Aesthetic Appearance*
Julia Kristeva	*Time and Sense: Proust and the Experience of Literature*
Alain Finkielkraut	*The Defeat of the Mind*
Julia Kristeva	*New Maladies of the Soul*
Elisabeth Badinter	*XY: On Masculine Identity*
Karl Löwith	*Martin Heidegger and European Nihilism*
Gilles Deleuze	*Negotiations, 1972–1990*
Pierre Vidal-Naquet	*The Jews: History, Memory, and the Present*
Norbert Elias	*The Germans*
Louis Althusser	*Writings on Psychoanalysis: Freud and Lacan*
Elisabeth Roudinesco	*Jacques Lacan: His Life and Work*
Ross Guberman	*Julia Kristeva Interviews*
Kelly Oliver	*The Portable Kristeva*
Pierre Nora	*Realms of Memory: The Construction of the French Past*
	VOL. 1: *Conflicts and Divisions*
	VOL. 2: *Traditions*
	VOL. 3: *Symbols*
Claudine Fabre-Vassas	*The Singular Beast: Jews, Christians, and the Pig*
Paul Ricoeur	*Critique and Conviction: Conversations with François Azouvi and Marc de Launay*
Theodor W. Adorno	*Critical Models: Interventions and Catchwords*

Alain Corbin	*Village Bells: Sound and Meaning in the Nineteenth-Century French Countryside*
Zygmunt Bauman	*Globalization: The Human Consequences*
Emmanuel Levinas	*Entre Nous: Essays on Thinking-of-the-Other*
Jean-Louis Flandrin and Massimo Montanari	*Food: A Culinary History*
Tahar Ben Jelloun	*French Hospitality: Racism and North African Immigrants*
Emmanuel Levinas	*Alterity and Transcendence*
Sylviane Agacinski	*Parity of the Sexes*
Alain Finkielkraut	*In the Name of Humanity: Reflections on the Twentieth Century*
Julia Kristeva	*The Sense and Non-Sense of Revolt: The Powers and Limits of Psychoanalysis*
Régis Debray	*Transmitting Culture*
Catherine Clément and Julia Kristeva	*The Feminine and the Sacred*
Alain Corbin	*The Life of an Unknown: The Rediscovered World of a Clog Maker in Nineteenth-Century France*
Michel Pastoureau	*The Devil's Cloth: A History of Stripes and Striped Fabric*
Julia Kristeva	*Hannah Arendt*
Carlo Ginzburg	*Wooden Eyes: Nine Reflections on Distance*
Elisabeth Roudinesco	*Why Psychoanalysis?*
Alain Cabantous	*Blasphemy: Impious Speech in the West from the Seventeenth to the Nineteenth Century*
Luce Irigaray	*Between East and West: From Singularity to Community*
Julia Kristeva	*Melanie Klein*
Gilles Deleuze	*Dialogues II*
Julia Kristeva	*Intimate Revolt: The Powers and Limits of Psychoanalysis*, vol. 2
Claudia Benthien	*Skin: On the Cultural Border Between Self and the World*
Sylviane Agacinski	*Time Passing: Modernity and Nostalgia*
Emmanuel Todd	*After the Empire: The Breakdown of the American Order*
Hélène Cixous	*Portrait of Jacques Derrida as a Young Jewish Saint*
Gilles Deleuze	*Difference and Repetition*
Gianni Vattimo	*Nihilism and Emancipation: Ethics, Politics, and Law*
Julia Kristeva	*Colette*
Steve Redhead (Editor)	*The Paul Virilio Reader*
Roland Barthes	*The Neutral: Lecture Course at the Collège de France (1977–1978)*
Gianni Vattimo	*Dialogue with Nietzsche*
Gilles Deleuze	*Nietzsche and Philosophy*
Hélène Cixous	*Dream I Tell You*
Jacques Derrida	*Geneses, Genealogies, Genres, and Genius: The Secrets of the Archive*
Jean Starobinski	*Enchantment: The Seductress in Opera*
Julia Kristeva	*This Incredible Need to Believe*
Marta Segarra, editor	*The Portable Cixous*
François Dosse	*Gilles Deleuze and Félix Guattari: Intersecting Lives*
Julia Kristeva	*Hatred and Forgiveness*

GPSR Authorized Representative: Easy Access System Europe, Mustamäe tee
50, 10621 Tallinn, Estonia, gpsr.requests@easproject.com

www.ingramcontent.com/pod-product-compliance
Lightning Source LLC
Chambersburg PA
CBHW040736300426
44111CB00026B/2968